Business Communication

Business Communication

Strategy and Skill

Mary Munter

Amos Tuck School of Business
Dartmouth College

PRENTICE-HALL, INC., *Englewood Cliffs, New Jersey 07632*

Library of Congress Cataloging-in-Publication Data

MUNTER, MARY.
 Business communication.

 Includes index.
 1. Communication in management.   I. Title.
HF5718.M85 1987   001.51′024658   86−17043
ISBN 0−13−091919−5

*Editorial/production supervision
  and interior design: Joan L. Stone*
Cover design: Wanda Lubelska Design
Manufacturing buyer: Ed O'Dougherty

Excerpt from J.T. Kidder, *The Soul of a New Machine*, reprinted by permission of Little, Brown and Company.
Excerpt from R. Proodian, "How to Make Your Next Speech One to Remember," reprinted by permission of The Wall Street Journal, © Dow Jones-Irwin & Company, Inc. 1984. All rights reserved.

Printed in the United States of America

10 9 8 7 6 5 4 3 2 1

ISBN 0-13-091919-5 01

PRENTICE-HALL INTERNATIONAL (UK) LIMITED, *London*
PRENTICE-HALL OF AUSTRALIA PTY. LIMITED, *Sydney*
PRENTICE-HALL CANADA INC., *Toronto*
PRENTICE-HALL HISPANOAMERICANA, S.A., *Mexico*
PRENTICE-HALL OF INDIA PRIVATE LIMITED, *New Delhi*
PRENTICE-HALL OF JAPAN, INC., *Tokyo*
PRENTICE-HALL OF SOUTHEAST ASIA PTE. LTD., *Singapore*
EDITORA PRENTICE-HALL DO BRASIL, LTDA., *Rio de Janeiro*

for HJM and LM

Contents

2

The Environment:
Business Organizations and Channels   20

3

The Communicator:
Objectives and Credibility   52

4

The Audience:
Motivation   70

5

The Message: Structure   91

6

The Response: Feedback   114

PART II: Writing Skill

7

Introduction to Business Writing   143

8

Business Documents and Paragraphs   182

9

Constructing Businesslike Sentences   209

10

Choosing Words   234

PART III: Speaking Skill

11

Nonverbal Communication   255

12

Structuring a Presentation   288

13

Visual Aids   314

14

Holding Meetings and Answering Questions   346

15

Job-Search Communication   371
by Paul Argenti

PART IV: Appendixes

A

Correct Words   394

B

Grammatical Definitions   413

C

Grammar and Usage   419

D

Punctuation and Mechanics   446

E

Research and Documentation   463

Index   477

Preface

The way people communicate in business—indeed, the business environment itself—is in the midst of great change. This book teaches students how to communicate in that changed business world. Although other business communication textbooks include new chapters tacked on periodically, many of them are merely updated versions of an outmoded vision of business communication.

What is different?

What, then, does this book, unlike others, include?

STRATEGY, RATHER THAN FORMULAS. Successful business people must be able to think for themselves, not follow rote patterns like automatons. Therefore, this textbook teaches students to set a communication strategy (deciding, for example, what tone and structure the occasion warrants) rather than to copy unthinkingly "good news" and "bad news" formulas.

ELEMENTS OF A STRATEGY. To set such a strategy, students must be able to analyze their environment, increase their credibility, motivate their audience, and structure their ideas persuasively. Therefore, this book, unlike others, includes entire chapters on each of those important issues.

ELECTRONIC COMMUNICATION. Certainly some of the biggest changes in the business environment have been the trends and developments in electronic communication. Instead of a stand-alone chapter on the subject, this book integrates electronic communication throughout. For example, computerized research sources are included in the research section, techniques for composing at the word processor in the composition section, and the pitfalls of some computer graphics packages in the visual aids section.

INTERNATIONAL COMMUNICATION. Another big change has been the increase in the international scope of business and in the possibility of communicating with people in different cultures. Again, instead of merely including a chapter on this subject, this book integrates examples throughout—for instance, examples of the cross-cultural implications of tone or of nonverbal communication.

RESPONSE SKILLS. Much communicating in business is, in fact, responding to others. That is why this book includes a chapter covering listening, reading, and feedback skills.

BUSINESS WRITING FORMATS. Some business communication courses emphasize letters, some memos, some reports. This book is designed to be used flexibly, depending on your needs. Instructors can assign any combination of the letter, memo, and report assignments at the end of chapter 7 to have students practice their writing skills.

GOOD WRITING. Many textbooks concentrate overmuch on business writing formats. This book is based on the assumption that correct usage of letter, memo, or report formats, though important, is not sufficient. Business writing must also be well-constructed, emphatic, and clear.

VARIOUS SPEAKING SITUATIONS. Business people do not deliver only formal oral presentations. Therefore, this book includes information not only on oral presentations but also on a variety of other speaking skills—such as team presentations, meetings, and interviews.

EMPLOYMENT SEARCH. Business students need to *think* about their careers before they write or interview for jobs. The last chapter of this book is therefore devoted to career planning, not just résumé, cover-letter, and interview skills.

What is similar in this book?

Although this book differs from its predecessors in some ways, it also retains many of the successful aspects of other books. Specifically, this book includes information on

COMMUNICATION THEORY, applied in a practical, down-to-earth, and nontheoretical way;

BUSINESS WRITING FORMATS, such as letters, memos, and reports;

WRITING SKILLS, with business applications and examples;

COMPOSING SKILLS, to help students avoid wasting time;

SPEAKING SKILLS, preparing and delivering oral presentations, as well as holding meetings and answering questions;

VISUAL AIDS, including content, equipment, and delivery;

EMPLOYMENT COMMUNICATION, including résumés, cover letters, and interviews.

Course design

This textbook can be used in a variety of ways:

FOR A BUSINESS WRITING COURSE, emphasizing the concepts in parts I and II. A letter-writing course would apply these concepts, using the letter-writing exercises at the end of chapter 7; a report-writing course would apply the same concepts, using the report-writing exercises; and so forth.

FOR A BUSINESS SPEAKING COURSE, emphasizing parts I and III. Instructors may elect to concentrate on oral presentations—or on any combination of oral skills, manuscript speeches, impromptu speeches, team presentations, panel discussions, media interviews, meetings, and job-search interviews.

FOR A BUSINESS COMMUNICATION COURSE, covering parts I, II, and III.

More detailed suggestions for course design, including sample course outlines, are included in the instructor's manual.

Acknowledgments

I am indebted to my students—at De Anza Community College, at Stanford University, and at Dartmouth's Amos Tuck School of Business—for all their ideas and suggestions over the years. I am also grateful to the colleagues who commented on, reviewed, and improved this book:

Paul A. Argenti
Amos Tuck School of Business
Dartmouth College

Arthur Bell
University of Southern California

Barbara Bradford
Florida Junior College

Dwight Bullard
Middle Tennessee State
   University

Carter A. Daniel
Rutgers University

Janet Eckhart-Littlejohn
Plaza Business Institute

George N. Freedman
Duchess Community College

Virgil Harder
University of Washington

Margaret Herbert
University of Houston
Downtown Campus

Jo Ann Lee
Pasadena City College

Paul D. McKinnon
Colgate Darden School
University of Virginia

Roni T. Marshak
Seybold Publications

Lorie Mazzaroppi
Fairleigh Dickinson University

Janice Miller
University of Houston
Central Campus

Carolyn Mullens
Cornell University

Lindsay Rahmun
Oregon State University

Irving Schenkler
New York University

Rita Sturm

Ann Wilson
Los Angeles Trade
   and Technical College

JoAnne Yates
Sloan School
Massachusetts Institute of
   Technology

Three colleagues assisted me with the writing: Professor Paul Argenti wrote chapter 15; Dr. Marilyn Wyatt and Dr. Christopher Ames wrote the chapter-end questions.

Finally, although I have already acknowledged his collegial assistance, I would like to thank Paul for his husbandly love and support, seeing me through two birthings—a baby and a book—in the same exhausting year.

Mary Munter

1

Introduction to Communication

Why Is Communication Important?
Why study business communication?

What Is Communication?
Theories of communication • Definition of communication

Why Is Communication Imperfect?
Psychological barriers • Semantic and physical barriers

IF you can't express your good ideas, then you're at the same level as someone who doesn't even have good ideas. Communication is crucial for any kind of success in business—not just getting promoted, but accomplishing results with and through other people, and meeting corporate objectives. In fact, communication may very well be a business person's most important skill.

These assertions are supported by numerous surveys. As long ago as 1964, *Harvard Business Review* readers ranked "ability to communicate" as the top criterion in a study on what helps promotability.[1] A decade later, personnel managers surveyed by the American Assembly of Collegiate Schools of Business also ranked communication number one in importance.[2] A 1980 study identified the competencies considered important for managers; communication was the most frequently cited quality for all four industries surveyed (banking, distribution, hospitals, and manufacturing).[3] And in a more recent study, over 1000 executives rated the business communication course "very important" more often than any other course in the business school curriculum.[4]

Why Is Communication Important?

Why is communication considered so important? At a very basic level, it is vital to any human encounter. Communication allows us to develop a

[1]B. Bowman, "What Helps or Harms Promotability?" *Harvard Business Review*, (January-February 1964), 6–26.

[2]A. Edge and R. Greenwood, "How Managers Rank Knowledge, Skills and Attributes Possessed by Administration Graduates," *AACSB Bulletin*, 11 (October 1974), 30–34.

[3]J. Thomas and P. Sireno, "Assessing Management Competency Needs," *Training and Development Journal*, 34 (September 1980), 47–51.

[4]H. Hildebrandt et al., "An Executive Appraisal of Courses Which Best Prepare One for General Management," *Journal of Business Communication*, 19 (Winter 1980), 47–51.

civilized society and to transmit knowledge from one generation to another. It dramatically distinguishes humans from other forms of life. It allows us to organize and work together in groups. In fact, without communication, there can be no social organization.

Communication, then, is important to human society and to organizations in general. Its importance is even more pronounced for business organizations specifically. If you think about them, these words of communication expert Harold Janis are certainly true: "The world of business is a world of action. Products are designed, made, and sold. People are hired. Services are rendered. Policies are devised and implemented. Jobs are learned and performed. Yet there is no practical way in which any of these events can take place without communication."[5]

Although communication has always been essential for business, it is especially important today—given current business trends. Companies tend to be larger than ever, and more mergers and acquisitions are on the way. Departments within a company may be spread all over the country, or even the world. With larger companies has come an increase in the number of hierarchical levels and the complexity of organizational patterns. At the same time, the more complex the organization, the more specialized the job each person performs within that organization. This trend toward experts, in turn, leads to increased use of specialized language, or jargon, which only experts can understand. Add to all of this the increase in the constituencies—such as community groups, special interest groups, labor, and government—with whom business people must now communicate, along with their traditional audiences, such as clients, subordinates, and superiors. These additional audiences, of course, mean additional communication. Trends in management style—away from the strictly authoritarian and toward the more collaborative—also make communication more important than ever.

And, as if this weren't enough, recent developments in the electronic communication field are changing the ways in which we can communicate. For example, using electronic mail, we can type messages to one another by means of a computer terminal. Teleconferencing allows us to see and speak with a group of people who are not all in the same place. Word processing makes it easier for us to change our writing. In summary, all these trends lead to more need for an opportunity to communicate in business.

Besides being important in today's changing business environment, effective communication will be important for your personal satisfaction and success. Through communication, you will be able to clarify your

---

[5]J. H. Janis, *Writing and Communicating in Business*, 3rd ed. (New York: Macmillan, 1978), p. 1.

concepts and ideas. You will be able to understand, persuade, and work with other people. In many ways, your success will be based on your ability to communicate: sometimes the only proof of your good work will be the written report or the oral presentation culminating a project.

Not only will you find communication important, chances are you will find yourself spending *most* of your time at work communicating: writing, talking with a group, talking to one person, listening, or reading. Many students imagine communication will account for only a small percentage of their work time. Various surveys, however, prove that business people in fact spend from 60 to 90 percent of their time at work communicating.[6] The specific amount of time will vary with your business, your company, and your working style.

Furthermore, the higher you move in your organization, the more communicating you are likely to do. Supervisors must communicate more than technicians, for example, and managers more than supervisors. As management expert Peter Drucker says: "If you work as a soda jerker you will, of course, not need much skill in expressing yourself to be effective. If you work on a machine your ability to express yourself will be of little importance. But as soon as you move one step up from the bottom, your effectiveness depends on your ability to reach others through the spoken or the written word. And the further away your job is from manual work, the larger the organization of which you are an employee, the more important it will be that you know how to convey your thoughts in writing or speaking."[7] One study concludes that first-level supervisors spend 74 percent of their time communicating, second-level managers 81 percent, and third-level managers 87 percent.[8] Another study shows that CEOs spend 78 percent of their time in oral communication alone.[9]

Why study business communication?

"All right!" I imagine you saying. "I grant that communication is important and that I'll be spending a lot of time doing it. But I'm pretty good at communicating. After all, I talk to people, write notes, read books, get

---

[6]See, for example, P. Drucker, *The Practice of Management* (New York: Harper, 1954); H. Mintzberg, *The Nature of Managerial Work* (New York: Harper & Row, Pub., 1973); and L. Sayles, *Managerial Behavior* (New York: McGraw-Hill, 1964).

[7]P. Drucker, "How to Be an Employee," *Fortune*, May 1952, p. 126.

[8]J. Hinrichs, "Communication Activity of Industrial Research Personnel," *Personnel Psychology*, 17 (1964), 199.

[9]Mintzberg, *The Nature of Managerial Work*, pp. 38–39.

along with other people, and make myself understood already. Why should I study communication?"

The apparent simplicity of communication is deceptive. Just because we all communicate every day does not make us good communicators. Just because some aspects of effective communication are based on common sense does not mean common sense alone is enough. Skilled communicators draw on an extensive and complex body of knowledge, including semantics (the study of word choice), linguistics (the study of language), rhetoric (the study of writing and speaking effectively), psychology, sociology, graphic design, and even computer science. You will explore and apply the scholarship and research from all of these fields in your study of communication.

"Why then," you may well ask finally, "study business communication specifically? Communication is communication: I've taken plenty of English courses and communicated in every one of my other courses."

Good communication does, in fact, cross disciplines: correct grammar and audible speaking, for example, are as necessary in a history class as they are in a business communication class. There are, however, at least five ways in which what you will learn in this class differs from what you have learned, or will learn, in your other classes. First, the subject matter is different: here you will get a chance to practice communicating with concepts and techniques from areas such as accounting, finance, and marketing. The forms are also different: you will, for example, practice writing memos, letters, and business reports—not just term papers, exams, and essays. Third, in this class you will have a chance to practice your oral presentation skills, which—according to various studies—you will probably be using extensively in the business world. Fourth, you may learn a slightly different style: in general, business communication is more objective, systematic, and concise than creative or personal communication. Finally, perhaps the most important difference is that—unlike assignments in other courses, which may emphasize the message itself or the personal expression of the writer or speaker—business communication focuses on the response you elicit from your reader or listener. You will learn to persuade people to accomplish your desired results.

What Is Communication?

I have been discussing how important communication will be for your success in business. What, you might ask, does the term *communication* mean? It is certainly hard to define because it has come to mean practically anything.

We may use the word in numerous ways—all of which are limited. Communication, for example, is not merely the process of transmitting information, as in "She's in communication with the head office right now." Neither is it merely the message itself, as in "regarding your communication of July 9." Communication is not a set of techniques: a beautifully structured letter or an impressive speech may still not get your ideas across. Finally, it is not just a sense of rapport, as in "I have no communication with my boss." Communication means all these things and more.

Theories of communication

To come up with a definition, let's look at some of the important theories of communication.

ELECTRONIC THEORY: One very influential theory is called the mathematical or electronic theory of communication.[10] This idea emphasizes the technical problems of transmitting a message from a sender to a receiver. It is based on, and uses the language of, electronics. The message begins with an *information source*, the mind of the sender (writer or speaker), who *encodes* a message into words and sentences. This message is *transmitted* as a signal (marks on paper or sound waves) through a channel, where it may be distorted by *noise* (such as smudged typing or acoustical problems). As a last step, the receiver (listener or reader) *decodes* the message. Here is a simplified illustration of this theory:

Communicator as "sender" ⎯⎯⎯ Message ⎯⎯⎯→ Audience as "receiver"

The electronic theory is helpful because it introduces the ideas of senders and receivers, and of possible interference. It emphasizes one important aspect of communication: accuracy.

Its usefulness is limited, however, because, of course, people are not machines: it may be possible to design a perfectly accurate electronic communication system, but not a human one. Preoccupation with accuracy—the technique for improving our writing or speaking skills—ignores

---

[10]The founding fathers of the mathematical or electronic theory are C. Shannon and W. Weaver. See their *Mathematical Model of Communication* (Urbana: University of Illinois Press, 1949), p. 7. For a concise description of the theory, see F. Bello, "The Information Theory," *Fortune*, December 1953, pp. 136–41, 149–58; reprinted in *Readings in Communications from Fortune*, ed. F. Weeks (New York: Holt, Rinehart & Winston, 1961).

many other important dimensions of the situation in which we communicate. For example, you might express your ideas perfectly accurately, but company policy forbids what you are proposing. Or, you might express an idea very accurately, but other people in the company don't think you have the right to discuss that particular idea. Therefore, in business communication, we need to look at other theories of communication as well.

SOCIAL ENVIRONMENT THEORY: Instead of looking only to the electronic theory, business communicators must also consider the social environment theory of the social and behavioral scientists.[11] We must consider the situation, the social context in which we will work. When we work and communicate together, we all participate in a social situation. Within that situation, we each agree to assume certain roles—such as "compromiser," "initiator," or "encourager"—based on our part in the activity. Further, we each have a certain status prescribed officially, such as our job title. We need to understand the rules, or the "culture," of the environment in order to communicate: both the official rules—such as company policies and practices—and those unwritten rules regarding to whom, how, and when, and for how long it is appropriate for us to communicate within a certain organization. The following figure adds the social environment to the version of electronic theory we just saw.

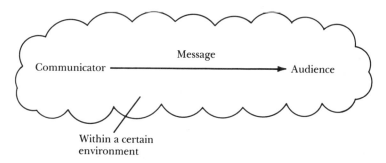

Including the social environment is helpful because it adds the important dimension of the specific social situation. Too often, inexperienced business people neglect to take into account role, status, and rules when they attempt to communicate. A fabulous letter may still fail to achieve its objective if you write to the wrong person at the wrong time. A fabulous presentation may still fail if you are not sensitive to the unwritten rules of the group to whom you are speaking.

[11]For the social environment theory, see J. Ruesch, "Synopsis of the Theory of Human Communication," *Psychiatry*, 16 (August 1953), 215–43.

RHETORICAL THEORY: A third set of theorists add more dimensions to our understanding of the communication process: communication is not linear, but circular; not just sending a message to be received, but producing a response; not static, but dynamic. These qualities of communication are emphasized by rhetorical theory.[12]

Rhetorical theorists provide an important addition to a communication model for business communicators. Many people in business get so caught up in the accuracy of their message and the appropriateness of the situation that they forget the third crucial variable: producing the desired *response* from their audience. The importance of response in business communication is illustrated in the following figure—which incorporates the ideas of accuracy (from the electronic theory) and situation (from the social environment theory) but looks significantly different: this model is circular, not linear.

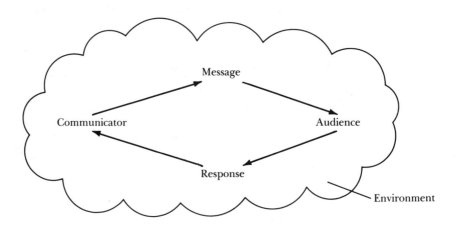

In fact, perhaps the most important difference between business communication and other forms of communication is this circular quality: your business communication effectiveness depends on the result you achieve.

How can you achieve your desired response? That's what the rest of this course will be about. You will learn not only how to be more correct and accurate, and how to be more sensitive to the situation, but also how to identify your audience's needs in order to become what the rhetoricians call "you-centered" instead of "I-centered." In short, you will learn how to be a better communicator.

---

[12]Two well-known rhetoricians, and a representative work of each, are L. Wylie, *Village in the Vaucluse,* 3rd ed. (Cambridge, Mass.: Harvard University Press, 1974); and K. Burke, *A Rhetoric of Motives* (Berkeley: University of California Press, 1969).

Definition of communication

As we have seen, people who communicate in business must incorporate ideas from the electronic, social environment, and rhetorical theories. By incorporating all three theories, then, we come up with a definition of communication:

The process of sharing by which messages produce responses.

Let's look closely at this definition, and examine its implications.

First, note the use of the word **process**. Communication is not merely an end-product, such as a report itself, but an ever-changing flow, such as the process in which you write the report and someone reads it. As communication expert Adnan Almaney notes: "By adopting the process approach, we can perceive [communication] events as dynamic and on-going systems rather than static and stationary."[13] In the process, nothing is static: a communicator's mood, intent, and alertness shift; words and their meanings change for different people in different circumstances; readers and listeners experience mood changes that affect how they interpret what we say or write.

The phrase **of sharing** implies that communication transcends the act of "sending" messages. Consider, for example, a sinking ship transmitting a distress signal too weak to be picked up by any other radio. That message has been sent, but not communicated. Effective communication is not a one-way monologue aimed at a receiver. Rather, it is a two-way dialogue that changes both the sender and the receiver, a sharing. Or, to quote once again from Peter Drucker: "It is the recipient who communicates. The so-called communicator, the person who emits the communication, does not communicate. He utters. Unless there is someone who hears, there is no communication. There is only noise. The communicator speaks or writes or sings—but he does not communicate. Indeed, he cannot communicate. He can only make it possible, or impossible, for a recipient—or rather 'percipient'—to perceive."[14]

The idea of a **message** connotes much more than what is contained in an envelope or shown on a flip chart. The term encompasses ideas, emotions, attitudes, and experiences. First, it includes the message in the communicator's mind—the *information source*, as it's called in the electronic model. Then, there are the two necessarily symbolic methods for transporting those ideas from the communicator's mind to another per-

[13]A. Almaney, "Communication: Is It the Transmission of Information?" *Journal of Technical Writing and Communication*, 4 (Spring 1974), 107–15.

[14]P. Drucker, *Management: Tasks, Responsibilities, Practices* (New York: Harper & Row, Pub., 1973), p. 483.

son: (1) the words, which may have different meanings to different people at different times, and (2) the nonverbal component—from the appearance of your paper to the tone of your voice—which many experts claim constitutes the majority of the message. Finally, there are the ideas, emotions, attitudes, and experiences that receivers add when they interpret the message.

The last part of the definition is **produce responses**. A response may include more than what we deliberately hope for—more than just an answer to a letter or participation in a staff meeting. For one thing, we may produce responses even though we do not receive a direct, overt answer: a reader may appreciate a congratulatory memo, but not write back to tell you; someone at a staff meeting may understand and agree with your point, but not speak aloud. All kinds of responses are going on every time people act and react—talking, seeing, feeling, listening, thinking, observing, impressing, doubting, or agreeing. People are constantly responding to one another, to their own experiences, and to their environment.

If we put this definition all together, we find that the main goal of business communication is to influence—to control our audience's responses in the way we had intended, so that we can fulfill certain aims for ourselves and our organizations. Effective business communication, of course, results in our eliciting the response we desire—both in the short term, such as having our audience obey an order, and in the long term, such as having our audience continue to follow the spirit of the policy. Secondary goals—such as self-expression, social relationships, and career advancement—also involve producing change in knowledge, attitude, or action.

With all these complicated variables going on in the communication process, no wonder communication is imperfect. It is imperfect for many reasons, which we shall explore in the next section.

Why Is Communication Imperfect?

We have seen that communication is an extremely complex process. Even if you work hard to understand a subject and to write or speak effectively about it, you cannot be sure that your meaning has been received exactly. In fact, since no two people think alike, no message but the most simplistic is ever perceived precisely as it exists in the communicator's mind.

This loss of meaning, which may block communication, is often called *noise*. We already saw that this is the term used in the electronic model of communication for static, loss of power, or other conditions that distort the signal as it travels from one point to another. Other communication experts call these conditions *communication falloff*. Still others call them *distortion* or *interference*. Regardless of what you call them, unavoidable barriers exist even in the best of situations. I am not referring here to lack of skill—although bad organization, bad delivery, or bad grammar would certainly block communication. Instead, I mean those barriers that may exist despite your skill, barriers over which you have no control, barriers that make communication necessarily imperfect.

Even though we rarely communicate absolutely perfectly, learning about the various barriers to communication can make us aware of and help us avoid certain pitfalls. Specifically, we should beware of possible psychological, semantic, and physical barriers.

Psychological barriers

Psychological barriers to communication include people's emotions, perceptions, and selectivity.

EMOTIONAL: One possible psychological block is emotional. For example, you might be emotionally blocked if you are announcing a new policy you know will be unpopular, giving the first major presentation on your job, or writing to someone you dislike. The people with whom you are communicating are also subject to emotional blocks. They may feel indifferent or hostile toward you or your subject, or be biased against you (perhaps because of your youth, sex, race, relatives, friends, or even clothes) or against your subject (perhaps because they think it's illogical, perhaps simply because "That's not the way we've always done things here").

PERCEPTUAL: Even if there are no emotional blocks, every person perceives things differently. Although we all live in the same objective world, we all live in different subjective worlds. Communication involves perception, and perception is never precise. A second psychological block, then, is perceptual.

One perceptual problem is that people perceive things differently. Given precisely the same data, people see, interpret, or respond to them differently. Figure 1.1 illustrates how people see things differently. What do you see when you look at this picture? Some people see an old woman; some see a young woman. Try to find the one you didn't see. The old

FIGURE 1.1

What do you see in this picture?

woman is looking down and to the left; she has a large, prominent nose and chin. The young woman is looking away; you see only one eyelash, the tip of a small nose, one ear, and the jut of her jaw. The old woman's nose is the young woman's jaw. The point here is that when presented with the same data, people see them differently.

As a business example of this perceptual problem, imagine everyone in a company receiving a copy of the annual report. An accountant may concentrate only on one footnote in the financial statement; a sales person may look at nothing but the marketing charts; and a public relations officer may respond only to the quality of the brochure itself. Each reader received the same data; each reader perceived them differently.

A second perceptual problem is caused by people "filling in" information without checking its accuracy. The following figure shows another example. What appears in this figure is a Roman number 9. Adding one line to this Roman numeral, make a 6 out of it.

If you tried to create a Roman number 6, then you "filled in" missing information. Reread the instructions; they do not specify Roman numerals. The correct answer is to place an *S* in front of the *IX* to create the word *SIX*.

As a business example, your boss might ask you to turn in a report "right away." You work late that night because you assume she means as soon as humanly possible; in fact, she meant before the end of the week. In this case, you "filled in" information.

A final perceptual problem is that people's perceptions are based on their own experiences. We perceive what we expect to perceive. People don't necessarily resent or dislike the unknown or unexpected; they simply don't perceive it at all. For example, imagine this scene: A father and his son are driving to work one morning when suddenly they're involved in a terrible car crash. The father is killed instantly and the son is badly hurt. An ambulance rushes the son to a hospital. In the admitting room, the nurse says, "We've got to take him straight into surgery or he may die." They rush him down the hall to surgery. The surgeon walks in, takes one look at the boy, and says, "I can't operate on him. He's my son." How can this be? Students come up with all kinds of ingenious answers: the "father" is a priest; the son was adopted. The correct answer is that the surgeon was the boy's *mother*. Many people don't think of this answer because their experiences have convinced them that surgeons are male. Similarly, people in business may not take in information because it runs counter to their expectations.

The following figure illustrates this perceptual problem. Read aloud the sentences in the three triangles:

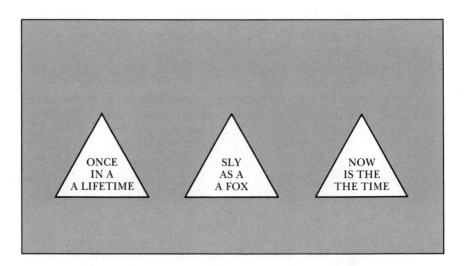

Did you notice the repeated words in each sentence? If not, then your experiences (that is, your familiarity with the phrases) were controlling your ability to perceive.[15] As a business example of this kind of psychological problem, you may find people perceiving your alma mater on the basis of their experiences with your school or with people from your school instead of their experiences with you.

SELECTIVITY: A final set of psychological barriers exists because of competition for people's time and attention—the selectivity block. We are all bombarded with information sources, such as newspapers, magazines, technical journals, reports, memos, letters, meetings, radio, television, videotapes, computer printouts, terminal displays, and electronic mail. We simply cannot absorb all this information flowing our way, so we must screen it selectively.

One factor in the way people select is timing. Some messages that may be effective at one time might be blocked, or even detrimental, at another time. For example, a letter of congratulation or condolence sent out immediately after the event is more effective than one sent later; a meeting about accident prevention gets more attention if it follows an

[15]The "six," hospital, and triangle examples appear in many sources, among them R. Huseman, J. Lahiff, and J. Hatfield, *Business Communication* (New York: Holt, Rinehart & Winston, 1981).

accident than if it precedes one; a report turned in late may have a highly negative effect if your supervisor has been anxiously awaiting it or may have little effect if he is busy with other matters; a rush typing assignment may affect your secretary differently at 4:45 P.M. than at 9:30 A.M.

Another selection factor is context. In one research experiment, subjects were shown two identical pictures of a railroad train in a station, one captioned "parting" and the other "arriving." On a scale ranging from "sad" to "happy," the subjects tended toward "sad" for the first picture and "happy" for the second. The subjects received the same data, but the suggestiveness of the context—the captions—influenced the way they perceived the picture. In the business world, you might be more apt to read an article if it appears in a magazine you respect, or a report if it is accompanied by a cover memo from your boss. Similarly, you might tend to pay more attention to a presentation if it is held in a boardroom or a well-appointed conference room, or listen more attentively to a sales talk in an elegant restaurant or hotel.

One more aspect of selectivity: we tend to remember the extremes and forget the middle ground. Think about comments you may have gotten from a teacher, a coach, or a boss. Most people remember the most positive and the most negative, and forget the neutral or middle-ground comments. Therefore, your communication may be blocked, or "selected out," simply because it does not contain startling positive or negative news.

Semantic and physical barriers

The first set of barriers we just discussed has to do with what is going on in our audience's minds, as a result of their psychological state. The second set of barriers has to do with what goes on in their minds as a result of the words you choose and the way things look.

SEMANTIC BLOCKS: Words, of course, are symbols, and therefore limited because they cannot have precisely the same meaning for everyone. Since words can mean different things, their different meanings may block communication. The study of word choice is called *semantics*, so the kinds of blocks that arise from word choice are called semantic blocks.

Even if you are skilled enough to avoid problems such as incomprehensible jargon and overly pompous words, you may still run into semantic problems because of the different shades of meaning between words. Semanticists call this difference—the impression or aura associated with a word—its *connotation*, as distinguished from its *denotation*, or explicit formal definition. Consider, for example, the difference between *inexpensive* and *cheap: cheap* has a more negative connotation. Consider the differences between *heavy* and *weighty*, *soiled* and *filthy*, *divide* and *sever*.

We find a more subtle connotative difference between, say, *hold* and *accommodate: accommodate* has a more positive connotation. Consider the subtle differences between *chronic* and *inveterate*, *stately* and *majestic*, *command* and *direct*, *compute* and *calculate*.

Another semantic barrier may occur even if you have considered connotation. A word may be misunderstood because it has one meaning for you and another for someone else. Each person filters words through his or her own memory, extracting meanings that are somewhat different in every case. For example, consider the possible connotations of these words to the following pairs of people: the word *pig* to a farmer and a police officer; the word *profit* to a shareholder and a consumer activist; the word *credit* to an accountant and a school registrar; the word *bear* to a stockbroker and a camper. Problems with people perceiving the same word in different ways are especially likely any time you use (1) abstract words such as *honesty*, *liberal*, *conservative*, *immoral*, *democracy*, or *discrimination*, or (2) indefinite terms such as *as soon as possible*, *in a timely manner*, *effectively*, *when you have a chance*, *moderate*, or *several*.

PHYSICAL BARRIERS: Communication does not consist of words alone. Another set of barriers is caused by your own physical appearance, your audience, or the context of the document or the presentation. Your ideas, however good and however skillfully imparted, are at the mercy of various potential physical barriers.

For writing, there is a whole barrage of possible physical blocks. No matter how well you write it, for example, a document may be illegible for various reasons: jammed or jagged margins, fingerprints or smudges, a faulty typewriter ribbon, unclear photocopies, unreadable word-processor printout, water or coffee spots, or messy corrections. Another set of physical barriers might be caused by the paper itself: a poor quality of stationery, for example, or inappropriate use of cheap stationery when a glossy printed brochure might be needed to imply prestige, or inappropriate use of a glossy brochure when a simple photocopy might be needed to imply haste.

For speaking, alas, just as many physical barriers abound, besides those caused by lack of skill, such as mumbling, not enunciating, speaking too quickly, or using distracting gestures. Noises may occur inside the room itself—such as hissing ventilation, blowing air conditioning, clattering typewriters, ringing telephones, slamming doors—or outside the building—such as traffic, construction, or airplanes. Finally, your message may be blocked because the people in your audience are uncomfortable: they cannot hear because of bad acoustics or a bad sound system; they cannot see because of inadequate lighting; they are too warm or too cold; or they lack comfortable seating.

To summarize the various barriers to communication, let's look at a simple example. Imagine you are trying to communicate the idea that no smoking is allowed near a certain machine. You might avoid semantic barriers by choosing for your sign the words "No smoking." You might avoid physical barriers by making the sign visible and well illuminated. You might avoid psychological barriers by doing your best to make sure the workers cannot easily ignore the sign. That these barriers exist is unavoidable; becoming aware of them and trying to overcome them is part of your job if you want to be successful in business.

I hope this chapter has convinced you not just that communication is imperfect, but that business communication is both important and complex. With those basic assumptions in mind, then, we can proceed to analyzing how you can improve your abilities to succeed at this important, complex activity.

REVIEW QUESTIONS

To check your understanding

1. List at least three reasons why communication is important in the business world.

2. List at least three bodies of knowledge on which skilled communicators must draw.

3. List at least three ways a business communication course differs from other communication courses.

4. What is the importance of the following aspects of communication: (a) accuracy, (b) social environment, (c) rhetoric?

5. In what way is communication circular?

6. Why should communication be considered a process?

7. How is communication a *sharing*?

8. What is included in the concept of a *message*?

9. What is the main goal of business communication?

10. Explain these psychological barriers to communication: (a) emotion, (b) perception, (c) selectivity.

11. What is a semantic block?

12. List three physical blocks to communication.

APPLICATION QUESTIONS

To apply your knowledge

1. How has the method of communication in the business world changed during your lifetime? What special skills do you need to communicate effectively while using the new technology?

2. Assume that you are working for a company that markets personal computers. Name five different groups of people you may have to communicate with in an average day. What are the types of language appropriate to each?

3. Assess your specific goals in studying business communication. Which skills need further development? How will developing these skills aid you in a business career?

4. Why are sociology, psychology, and graphic design fundamental areas of business communication?

5. Think of a classroom situation you have recently experienced. How does it illustrate the circularity of communication?

6. Explain how the social environment of that same classroom setting affected communication.

7. What are four communication situations you might encounter in a typical business setting? Describe the form the communication might take (such as a memo), the audience you are addressing (for example, your boss), and the response you desire (say, an evaluation of a new program).

8. Describe an experience you have had that shows how two people can interpret the same message in two different ways. How could more effective communication have avoided this situation?

9. Why must emotion be taken into account when we are communicating? How are the emotions of the communicator as important as those of the receiver?

10. Give an example of a magazine or television advertisement that relies heavily on the connotations of the words or visual images that it uses. How can a similar awareness of semantics help you influence a business audience?

CASES

To practice what you learned

1. You are called upon in a staff meeting to give a presentation on the company's new health insurance program for employees. The pro-

gram includes expanded coverage of eye and dental care, but also a 10 percent decrease in the total amount the policy will pay for hospitalization and lab work. You know the changes in insurance coverage will not be well received; it is also your first oral report to the full staff. What psychological blocks may you expect to confront, both in yourself and in your audience? How might you try to overcome them?

2. You would like to get approval for a budget increase for a project you are working on. The project is going well and you feel your request is justified. However, you also know that your boss has been under pressure lately, particularly regarding other projects undertaken by your department. How would social environment influence the wording and timing of your memo to your boss?

3. You are in charge of a group that is studying the procedure by which customer credit applications are evaluated. The study is in response to numerous complaints from customers that the existing procedure is unfair. Your group is ready to make its report to a group of upper-level supervisors. The report includes recommendations for revamping the credit system and making it more fair. What is the process of communication that has taken place in this situation? (Consider the circularity of communication and the *sharing* of a message.)

4. To market a new brand of bath soap, your department has decided to enlist the aid of a well-known sports figure. Magazine advertisements will show the sports star enjoying a shower using "Freetime" soap, along with a picture of him bathing his infant daughter with the same soap. The style of the ad will be nostalgic, in the manner of Norman Rockwell. Analyze the *message* of the ad, especially its emotional and nonverbal aspects.

5. You work as an accountant for a large company. Much of your work you perform independently—researching clients' accounts at a computer terminal, at your desk, and at the files. And yet communication is a major aspect of your job: for one thing, you must file a report every Friday detailing the week's activities. What are some of the forms of communication that your job includes? List the special languages you had to learn to perform your job, and the various audiences you might come in contact with.

2

The Environment:
Business Organizations and Channels

Analyze Your Organization.
How people work together • *What goals people work toward*

Analyze Changes in the Business Environment.
Electronic communication • *International communication*
• *Nondiscriminatory communication*

Analyze the Channels of Communication.
Directional flow • *Communication channels*

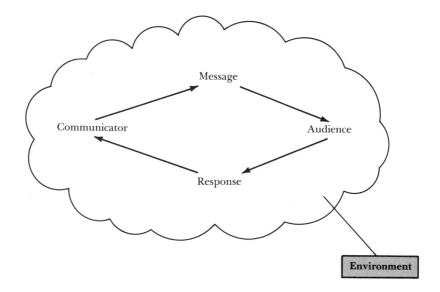

Message

Communicator   Audience

Response

Environment

IN the previous chapter, we built a model of communication that includes the five variables you see in the illustration: the communicator, the
audience, the message, the response, and the environment. In chapters 2
through 6, we shall discuss how you can translate that communication
model into a communication *strategy*. In other words, these five chapters
cover how you can make the most effective use of each of the five
variables, so that you can come up with a method to set a strategy for your
business communication.

Why should we look at communication strategy before we look at
communication skills (such as grammar and punctuation)? The answer is
that communication strategy always comes first. All the great skills in the
world are not going to do you any good if you—for example—write or
speak to the wrong person, don't have your ideas structured, don't think
about how to motivate your audience, or neglect any other aspect of your
strategy. Although we will look at each communication strategy variable
in a separate chapter, remember that they are not totally separate ideas.

They all depend on one another. For example, the communicator's goals and credibility depend on the nature of the audience; a message depends on the nature of the goals; and so forth.

Keeping that interdependence in mind, then, let's begin our discussion of communication strategy by looking at the context in which you will communicate. The steps are: (1) analyzing your organization, (2) analyzing the changes in today's business environment, and (3) analyzing the channels of communication.

Analyze Your Organization.

All business organizations depend on communication. Communication is the glue that binds various elements, allows structure to develop, coordinates activities, allows people to work together, and accomplishes results. Not only is communication essential for the success of businesses, however; understanding the business organization to which you belong is equally essential for your success in communicating within the business world. One of the big differences between business communication and other kinds of communication is this different environment. Writing a report in a business environment, for example, is different from writing a term paper in a college environment.

Before we discuss business organizations, think for a moment about nonbusiness groups you have worked with—such as a fraternity, sorority, church group, community group, student government, or club. Different communication behaviors were undoubtedly appropriate in these different groups. In student government, for instance, meetings are probably more formal than in student clubs; in a church group, you are more likely to discuss matters with your local youth group leader than with the worldwide religious leader.

These kinds of written and unwritten group rules of how and with whom people communicate become even more complex in business organizations. How can you go about analyzing your organization? Look at: (1) how people work together and (2) what goals they work toward. These concepts are summarized in Table 2.1.

How people work together

The first thing most of us think of when considering how people work together in business is formal structure. When you are working for a company, what does its organizational chart tell you?

TABLE 2.1		
How to analyze your organization		
Figure out:	*By looking at the:*	
How people work together	Formal structure → Organization chart	
	Informal structure → Networks Political coalitions	
What goals people work toward	Formal goals → Brochures Policies	
	Informal goals → Myths Atmosphere	

FORMAL STRUCTURE: The first question to ask yourself about is its overriding structure. Is it organized by function or by product (or, in a *matrix*, by both)? Here is an example of functional organization:

Functional organizations tend to be stable, are typical of companies where technology doesn't change fast, and allow people to specialize. They present at least two communication problems to be aware of: (1) they may be bureaucratic and resistant to change, and (2) they don't allow many people to see the "big picture," so that rivalries between groups may be high and decisions may pile up at the higher levels.

A product or project organization looks like this:

These kinds of organizations work better in fast-changing environments because people integrate many tasks around one project. The main communication drawback to be aware of is that the various groups responsible for the different products or projects may have to compete for pooled resources—such as computers or purchasing.

Besides the overriding structure of the organization, think about how hierarchical the organization is.

On one hand, you might find yourself in a hierarchical and authoritarian structure. If so, you'll find clearly demarcated divisions, clear job descriptions, and work standards. Incentives in hierarchical organizations are usually monetary, such as bonuses. What are the communication patterns within such an environment? You will probably see an emphasis on downward communication; you will find yourself reporting, not sharing, upward; you may find you cannot communicate except to the level directly above you; you will probably find that informal meetings are not the norm.

On the other hand, you may find yourself working within a less hierarchical organization. This kind of organization tends to have a much "flatter" design, and not as many levels of command. Instead of pay schemes as the chief motivator, you find the much talked about incentives of individual growth and job enrichment. In this kind of environment, you can expect much more group consensus. You will probably share more with people above you. And you may feel frustrated because decisions take so long to make.

Another thing you can find out from an organizational chart, of course, is various reporting relationships. Who reports to whom? What level are you on? What level are the people with whom you communicate on? Does your boss want to be informed, or sent copies of, your communications? Will other people's bosses or subordinates need to be informed about certain communications?

Finally, an organizational chart lets you know where people are located. Location has enormous influence on communication. You will reach people housed in your office building differently than, say, people located in an international division. You will reach people connected with you by electronic mail differently than people connected with you only by telephone or regular mail.

You can learn a lot from an organizational chart about the overriding structure, the kind of hierarchy, reporting relationships, and where people are located. Analyzing the organizational structure alone, however, is not enough. "Organizations," says organizational theorist Hal Leavitt, "are not the static structures depicted in organization charts, . . . They are constantly changing networks of tasks, structures, information systems, and human beings, that are both simple and complicated, orderly and disorderly, placid and volatile."[1]

[1]H. Leavitt, *Managerial Psychology*, 4th ed. (Chicago: University of Chicago Press, 1978), p. 282. Professor Leavitt's book is excellent—well written and practical.

INFORMAL STRUCTURE: Therefore, when you think about how people work together, don't forget to analyze the informal structure—sometimes called *networks* or *political coalitions*. Informal networks and coalitions don't show up on organizational charts, but they are just as important. For example, say you had a formal organizational chart like this:

If you analyzed this formal structure, you would conclude that the secretaries are subordinate to you and equal to one another. If you analyzed the informal structure, however, it might look like this:

In this case, your boss's secretary has the power to deny you access to the boss, to screen your boss's mail, or to decide whether or not to interrupt him or her.

As another example, say you and four others of equal rank report to the same boss. The formal organizational structure would look like this:

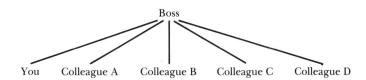

Again, the informal network structure might be quite different. On one hand, you might have:

Here, A and B are *opinion leaders*. They might have more credibility, more competence, more power, or more access to information or to the boss. For whatever reasons, knowing who the opinion leaders are within your organization is just as important as knowing who the supervisors are.

On the other hand—with the same formal structure of you and four others reporting to the same boss—the informal structure might look like this:

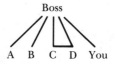

Here, C and D form a political coalition. They tend to stick together and agree. Knowing informal political coalitions is as important as knowing formal divisions.

Finally—still with that same formal structure of you and four others reporting to the same boss—the informal structure might look just like the formal structure, like this:

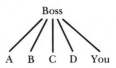

In this case, you and your colleagues work in isolation from one another. In this kind of informal structure, the boss has a great deal of control over information and decision-making.

What goals people work toward

Analyzing how people work together, as we just saw, includes analyzing both the formal and the informal structures. Similarly, analyzing what goals people work toward includes analyzing both the formal and informal goals.

FORMAL GOALS: Figuring out a company's formal goals is relatively easy, because formal goals are officially published. A good place to start looking is at your college placement office; such offices often have recruiting brochures, annual reports, and other documents available. Another good source of information about formal goals is the library: libraries often have annual reports, 10-K's, the *F & S Index of Corporations and Industries*, and other sources listed on pages 464–69. Finally, you can discover a good deal about formal goals from company policies, procedures, and your job description—usually from the company personnel department.

From any of these sources, look for the company philosophy— sometimes called *mission statement* or *credo*. Think about what the company chooses to emphasize; look at the document both for what it says and how it looks (photographs and illustrations). Finally, think about the kind of *image* the company projects in its official documents.

INFORMAL GOALS: Just as organizations have informal structures, they also have informal goals. These goals are often called the *culture* of an organization—that is, the values, expectations, and beliefs the group members share. The unstated cultural goals of an organization may not show up among official published policies and procedures. They tend to surface in what people say and in the atmosphere of the organization.

Figuring out informal goals or culture is less straightforward than reading the formal goals. First, listen to the stories people tell about the company. Often, these stories are called company **myths**. Here is an example of such a myth from Data General, the computer company in Tracy Kidder's Pulitzer Prize–winning book *The Soul of a New Machine:*

> a company called Keronix accused Data General's officers of arranging the burning of a factory . . . . In time, the courts found no basis for those charges and dismissed them. Indeed, it seemed preposterous that the suddenly wealthy executives of Data General would risk everything, including jail, and resort to arson, just to drive away what was, after all, a small competitor. . . . many years later, some veteran employees would say privately that they believed someone

connected with the company had something to do with that fire . . . . They had no basis for saying so, no piece of long-hidden evidence. It seemed to me that this was something they wanted to believe . . . . In a land of tough and ready companies, theirs, some of Data General's employees seemed to want to think, was the toughest and readiest around.[2]

That tough cowboy culture also comes out in the language the engineers use. The author notes this cowboy language in at least three places in the book:

To some of the engineers, . . . what ensued was a "war," and the first open battle, which was fought at a Howard Johnson's motor inn down south, was "the big shoot-out at HoJo's." . . .

There was talk of *wars, shootouts, hired guns* and *people who shot from the hip* . . . . From the vocabulary alone, you could have guessed that . . . these engineers were up to something. . . .

he'll simply ignore what one or two of them have to say and eventually they'll get angry and go elsewhere. In local parlance, he's a "gunslinger," one who "shoots from the hip." . . .[3]

In summary, listen to the stories people tell and the language they use for your first clues about the organization's informal goals.

A second clue to these unwritten informal goals is the company's **atmosphere**. How can you analyze your organization's atmosphere? Perhaps the easiest way is to think about decor, dress, and security procedures.

For example, consider company A: You enter a large, old, impressive lobby with a high ceiling, glass and steel walls, and modern sculpture. The security guard requires you to sign in and wear a badge. As you walk down the hushed halls, you occasionally see people dressed in blue or gray suits come out from rooms with closed doors.

Contrast that scene with company B: You enter a wood-paneled lobby with a low ceiling, hanging plants, and comfortable chairs. Instead of a guard, you are greeted by an outgoing receptionist who calls people by their first name. You walk through an open office space, noticing people talking in small groups, wearing various styles of dress.

Obviously, the communication patterns would be different in these two companies. But the atmosphere is just one part of your organizational

[2]J. T. Kidder, *The Soul of a New Machine* (New York: Avon Books, 1981), pp. 23–24.
[3]Ibid., pp. 38, 46, and 190.

analysis. The main point is this: find out whatever you can about the company's formal and informal structures, and its formal and informal goals. The context, or environment, in which you communicate influences how you communicate—your communication strategy.

Analyze Changes in the Business Environment.

People who communicate effectively in business have always analyzed their organization. Recently, however, people who communicate effectively in business have also had to be aware of several major changes in the business environment that have drastically influenced business communication: (1) electronic communication, (2) international communication, and (3) nondiscriminatory communication.

Electronic communication

As you examine the environment in which you will be communicating as a professional, certainly one of the most obvious upheavals you see taking place involves recent trends and developments in electronic communication. It's hard to believe that only a century ago, business people were writing letters with a pen and ink, and filing in vertical stacks—one document on top of the other filed simply in the order they were written. As recently as a decade ago, communication technology in business involved little more than the electric typewriter, copy machines, horizontal file cabinets, and the telephone and telegram. Even as recently as a few years ago, most business people were not using personal computers at all.

You can see the same sort of progression in business communication textbooks. As the twentieth century began, textbook examples consisted of longhand letters. By the mid twentieth century, the examples were typewritten. As recently as a few years ago, textbooks simply added a chapter on "the office of the future." Nowadays, the "office of the future" is the "office of the present," and electronic communication is more than a separate unit: it permeates business communication courses. In this book, you will see significant changes: computerized research sources when we discuss research, techniques for composing at the word processor when we discuss composition, computer graphics packages when we discuss visual aids—to take just a few examples.

What are the important changes that electronic communication has forced your generation of business people to face? Certainly, one change is in the way business people can now gather information. Other changes affect the way business people write: word processing and electronic mail. The final set of changes involves the way people speak in business: computer graphics and teleconferencing. Let's look at each of these in turn.

GATHERING INFORMATION: First, electronic data bases and storage systems have significantly influenced how you gather information in business. Through various data bases, you now have access to much more information much faster. For example, on a computer you can call up stock prices, abstracts of business articles, or information about the current standing of a company or product. You can also perform much of your "library" research right from your computer terminal: for example, with on-line "card catalogs." Not only will you have access to more information on various communication and analysis tools, but some programs print out data-base information directly on spreadsheets; others incorporate graphs derived from spreadsheet analysis directly into your reports. Finally, you will be able to file data much more efficiently. The main troubles with traditional files are space and categories. With electronic storage, of course, you need not fill your office with cabinets, because the information is stored in the computer. Further, you can file a piece of information under various headings. For example, you could file information on an item a customer bought under both the customer's name and the item purchased.

WRITING: Electronic communication will affect not only the way people gather information in business, but also the way they actually write.

Word processors are having a tremendous influence on business writing. They are made up of five components: (1) a keyboard or *mouse* for entering information, (2) a monitor (a cathode-ray terminal—CRT— or television screen), (3) some way to load information, (4) a printer, and (5) some way of powering the machine—either its own power source, if it is a *micro* or *personal* computer, or a larger source if it is connected with a *mini* or *mainframe* computer. Word processors are used in many ways in business. You may have one at your desk. Your company may have them for certain clerical or nonclerical people to use. The machines may be *stand-alones* having no connections with other people or machines, or they may be *networks*, connected with other people or machines.

How do word processors affect the way people write? For one thing, they influence the way people compose. Instead of composing in long-hand, business people can now compose—and even jot down ideas—directly into their word processor. Some software programs help people get started writing or get organized before they start writing. Second, word processing affects the way business writers revise. Instead of the laborious process of having something typed, correcting it, and having it retyped, writers can now revise directly into the computer. Not only does this save time, it also makes revising easier. Furthermore, some software packages check your spelling, punctuation, wordy expressions—and much more. Finally, word processing affects the final product. The machine's printer can offer various type faces and sizes—as well as bold and italic print.

Electronic mail is a second way in which your business writing is different than it was a few years ago. Electronic mail is a method by which you type messages into your computer and send them to someone else's computer. For example, if you wanted to set up a meeting, you might do so by locating the schedules of a group of people by electronic mail. You could see at a glance what times all the people had free. As another example, if you wanted to leave a message for someone, perhaps someone you cannot reach by phone, you could leave it in the "electronic in-box." As a final example, you could make a general announcement by sending it to various receivers. The electronic mail in this case takes the place of a poster in the halls. *Facsimile transmission* is a more sophisticated version of electronic mail. You transmit not only words but also images electronically—including a facsimile of the actual document or a photograph or other illustration.

SPEAKING: The way you speak in business will also be affected by changes in electronic communication. One major change that has taken place is the change in the kinds of graphics you can use for your oral presentations (and for written documents, as well). Software packages can print out pie charts, bar charts, or line graphs, for instance. Other programs can print various sizes and shapes of lettering. Still others can give you predrawn pictures to incorporate into your visuals. And yet others let you draw your own pictures, and then print them out.

Another change in the way you may speak comes from the field of teleconferencing. Teleconferencing includes—at its most simple—a telephone conference call, in which three or more people are all hooked into the same telephone line to talk at once. Slightly more advanced is still-picture teleconferencing, in which a series of still pictures are transmitted as you speak. *One-way live* teleconferencing occurs if only one location transmits a presentation to other locations, which receive only. Finally, the most sophisticated teleconferencing is *two-way interactive*, in which people at two locations can see and speak to each other at the same time.

Teleconferencing will never replace face-to-face communication. Instead, it provides another alternative channel of communication. For example, if you were to demonstrate a new product to all the sales representatives in the field at the same time, you might use teleconferencing. On the other hand, if you wanted to have all the sales representatives in the field meet to brainstorm or to establish more personal relationships with one another, you would probably choose a face-to-face meeting.

The same is true of all the other forms of electronic communication. Instead of completely replacing older channels of communication, they will give business people an additional form of communication. As a historical example, imagine what people may have thought when the telephone was invented: "People won't talk with each other anymore. They will talk *only* through that machine!" This is not true, of course; people use both face-to-face communication and the telephone for conversations, depending on the circumstances.

A final thought to keep in mind as you consider electronic communication. Just because all this technology exists does not mean that all business people or all companies will use all of it. People may unconsciously balk at change or consciously choose nonelectronic forms. Companies may find some electronic forms useful for what they do—and others unnecessary or wasteful.

So, the so-called office of the future is with us today. But that office will vary, depending on the people and the company where you end up working.

International communication

A second trend you can readily see in the business environment is an increasing international presence. Although business has been conducted between people in different countries for centuries, it has never occurred on the same scale as in the last decade. Companies now establish plants in other countries: Japanese cars are manufactured in the United States; American cars are manufactured in France. Large multinational firms are without doubt a dominant force in today's business environment.

What does this imply for your career? For one thing, you have an increasing chance of working overseas. Or, you may work in America for a multinational firm. Even if you do not work directly for a multinational company, you will certainly have dealings with these kinds of companies or with people from other countries. Therefore, unlike your business predecessors, you will have to be aware of the communication implications of communicating with people in different cultures.[4]

Sensitivity to the complex and delicate nature of cross-cultural communication is a first step toward this awareness—if only to pinpoint possible communication problems. Similarly, if you can avoid a "right versus wrong" attitude toward cultural differences, you will be well on your way toward success. It's only natural for people of all cultures to think their own is right and everyone else's is wrong; that their own culture, race, or group is superior to others. For example, Americans may believe that Europeans are dirty because their cities are older than ours. On the other hand, Japanese may believe Americans are dirty because we bathe, soak, and rinse in the same bath water. As another example, Americans may believe another culture is primitive or backward; people in other cultures may just as unfairly see Americans as rude, loud, and disrespectful.

One way to bypass this instinct to set up "right versus wrong" cultures is to analyze and describe—rather than to impose American value judgments on—other cultures with which you interact. Anthropologists Clyde and Florence Kluckhohn have come up with the following list of questions that get at the root of any culture's value system: (1) What is the attitude toward the innate character of human nature? (2) What is the proper relation of human beings to nature? (3) What is their sense of time? (4) What is their attitude toward activity? and (5) What is their attitude toward social relationships? These questions and values are illustrated in Table 2.2. Using analysis like this one is at least a start toward identifying where possible communication problems may lie.

Once you realize the increased chances for problems in cross-cultural communication and that American values are not the only "right" values, then you can begin to change your communication behavior when necessary. Many common problems in cross-cultural communication stem from both what you say and how you say it. Here are some examples.

1. Language, obviously, varies across cultures. Many more business students today are studying a foreign language, either hoping or expecting to be working in the international arena. Even if you do not learn a language, however, you should beware of possible pitfalls

---

[4]Three older, but classic, sources of more information on international communication are E. Hall, "The Silent Language in Overseas Business," *Harvard Business Review*, (May-June 1960), 87–96; E. Hall and W. White, "Intercultural Communication: A Guide to Men *[sic]* of Action," *Human Organization*, 19 (1960), 5–12; and E. Hall. *The Silent Language* (New York: Doubleday, 1959).

TABLE 2.2 Cultural value systems*			
Attitude toward	Range		
Humanity	Basically evil ↓ Initial lack of trust	Mixture of good and evil ↓ Initial choice	Basically good ↓ Initial trust
Nature	Submit to nature ↓ Life determined by God/fate	Harmony with nature ↓ Live in harmony with nature	Mastery over nature ↓ Control and challenge nature
Time	Past tradition	Present moment	Future goals
Activity	Being, not accomplishing, most important	Inner development most important	Future and accomplishments most important
Social relations	By rank or class ↓ Authoritarian decision-making	By entire group ↓ Group decision-making	By individual ↓ Individual decision-making

*Adapted from F. Kluckhohn and F. Strodtbeck, *Variations in Value Orientations* (Evanston, Ill.: Row, Peterson, 1961), quoted in L. R. Kohls, *Survival Kit for Overseas Living* (Chicago: Intercultural Network/Systran Publications, 1979), Appendix A. This Kohls book is a good one to read if you will be working overseas.

in translation. Words don't always carry the same connotations in other languages. American businesses have suffered from several examples of mistranslation. General Motors' slogan "Body by Fisher" was translated into Flemish as "Corpse by Fisher." "Come Alive with Pepsi" became "Come Out of the Grave" in German and "Bring Your Ancestors Back from the Grave" in certain parts of Asia.[5]

2. Not only the words themselves, but also how directly you express yourself, differ among cultures. In America, people tend to value frankness and directness. To "say what you mean" is generally a positive attribute. In other cultures—Japan, for instance—people may avoid saying something unpleasant to avoid embarrassment or to save face.

[5]See D. Ricks, *Big Business Blunders* (Homewood, Ill.: Dow Jones-Irwin, © 1983), pp. 83, 85.

3. Gestures also vary across cultures. For example, in France the American sign for "okay" means "zero"; thumbs up means "okay." In Germany, speaking to someone with your hands in your pockets is a sign of disrespect. In Greece, an upward nod of the head means "no," not "yes." And in India, the left hand is considered unclean. You might also unknowingly use an obscene or improper gesture. In Australia, the American sign for hitchhiking is obscene, as is using your index and middle finger to form a V in Scotland. In England, back slapping is improper, as is pumping your hand more than once in a French handshake.

4. Americans usually suppress emotions in business communication. In the Middle East, on the other hand, expressing feeling—including shouting, weeping, even jumping up and down—is considered appropriate adult behavior. Middle Easterners may interpret American self-control as a dishonest hiding of feelings.

5. Americans also usually discourage touching between adult business colleagues. In Latin America, on the other hand, greetings may range from a handshake to a two-handed handshake to an *abrazo*, or double side-to-side embrace. At the other extreme, any touch whatsoever may be seen as an insult in Java.

6. The physical distance between American business colleagues is typically about two feet, and usually not closer than ten inches. If you stood two feet away from a Latin American, he or she would feel the same way a North American would feel if someone were standing five feet away.

7. Finally, place and things differ among cultures. In America, we discuss business virtually anywhere except at church—at home or at parties, for instance. In India, though, it's impolite to discuss business in someone's home. In America, many people judge status by the new possessions surrounding someone; in England, people might be inclined to judge status by possessions that seem old-fashioned.

What does this trend toward the increasingly international nature of business mean? First, that to communicate effectively, you should analyze and empathize with the culture of the people with whom you are communicating. Second, that you should observe and follow both the linguistic and the nonverbal patterns you see. Differentiate between those practices that are necessary for business and unnecessary American habits that can block communication.

Nondiscriminatory communication

Another big recent change in the business environment has been the increasing effort to alleviate discrimination, as indicated by legislation such as the Civil Rights Act, the Equal Pay Act, and the Rehabilitation Act. Here are some suggestions for avoiding bias in your business communication.[6]

First, beware of **racism** in these three ways:

1. Avoid any word, image, or situation that suggests that all or most members of a racial or ethnic group are the same.

   Anglos: prim, cold, stuffy, rational
   Asians: sinister, inscrutable, serene, industrious
   Blacks: childlike, shuffling, lazy, athletic

2. Avoid qualifiers that reinforce racial stereotypes.

You wouldn't say	*So don't say*
Bob, a well-groomed white man. . . .	George, a well-groomed black man. . . .
He's not what you'd call shy. Bob Jones puts on quite a sales presentation.	She's not what you'd call shy. Connie Wang puts on quite a sales presentation.

3. Avoid racial identification except when it is essential to communication.

You wouldn't say	*So don't say*
Martha, an outgoing white woman, . . .	Sylvia, an outgoing Latino woman, . . .
Leo McCarthy, noted white legislator, . . .	Willie Brown, noted black legislator, . . .

Beware also of **sexism** in your business communication. Be sensitive to these common pitfalls.

---

[6]For more on nondiscriminatory communication, see *Without Bias: A Guidebook for Nondiscriminating Communication* (New York: John Wiley, 1982).

1. Avoid generic (or general) terms that imply men are the only people on earth.

Avoid	*Prefer*
man-made	artificial, synthetic
man-hours	working hours
workmen's compensation	workers' compensation

2. Avoid job titles that end in the word *man*.

Avoid	*Prefer*
salesman	sales representative
workman	worker, employee
businessman	executive, manager

3. Avoid expressions that seem to value men over women.

Avoid	*Prefer*
man-sized job	large job, sizable job
manly effort	valiant effort
manpower	work force

4. Avoid letter salutations that automatically imply an unknown reader is a man, such as "Dear Sirs" or "Gentlemen." Here are five ways to overcome this problem:

   a. Use a descriptive term.
   Dear Customer:
   Dear Colleague:
   Dear Subscriber:

   b. Use a job title.
   Dear Sales Representative:
   Dear Permissions Editor:

   c. Use a formal asexual salutation.
   Dear Recipient:
   Dear Sir/Madam:
   To whom it may concern:

   d. Use an informal asexual salutation.
   Dear Reader,

> Dear Friend,
> Greetings (or regional variations, such as "Howdy" or "Aloha")

    e. Omit the salutation altogether.

5. Beware of overusing third-person singular pronouns. For example, the clause "Each employee must ask himself" is correct grammatically, but overusing third-person singular pronouns such as *he* or *him* to describe both men and women can sound sexist. Here are four alternatives to consider.

    a. Reword the sentence.

Avoid	*Prefer*
Typically, a manager at XYZ Company will call monthly meetings with his staff.	Typically, the manager at XYZ Company will call monthly staff meetings.

    b. Recast the sentence into plural.

Each employee must ask himself. . . .	Employees must ask themselves. . . .

    c. Replace pronouns with *one, you, he or she,* or *hers or his.*

his staff	his or her staff

    d. Alternate male and female examples.

The job-interview form might include statements like these:	The job-interview form might include statements like these:
"He's not the right person for the company" or "He lacks the necessary qualifications."	"He's not the right person for the company" or "She lacks the necessary qualifications."

6. Avoid referring to women as children.

Avoid	*Prefer*
my girl	my secretary
the gals	the women

7. Avoid comments that stereotype women. Judge your audience as individuals, not as a sex group.

Avoid

Are we boring you ladies with all this business talk?

I know you gals probably aren't too interested in these technical matters.

Pardon the rough language, ladies.

We all know how *she* got promoted. (wink)

8. Avoid secretarial assumptions. Do not assume that any woman within twenty feet of a copy machine, a coffee pot, or a telephone is a secretary.

Finally, be sensitive to the way you write and talk about **disabled** people.

1. Avoid mentioning an impairment when it is not pertinent.

Avoid	*Prefer*
The deaf accountant completed the audit.	The accountant completed the audit.

2. Separate the person from the impairment.

Avoid	*Prefer*
Dan, an epileptic, has no trouble with the new job.	Dan, who has epilepsy, has no trouble with the new job.

3. Avoid using words that would offend you if you were impaired.

Avoid	*Prefer*
deaf and dumb	hearing- and speech-impaired
fits, spells	seizures, epilepsy
crippled	disabled
spastic, retarded (unless, of course, used to describe precise conditions)	

Analyze the Channels of Communication.

Once you have considered the organization itself—and how it is changing today—think about the channels of communication open to you: (1) directional flow and (2) communication channels.

Directional flow

The directional flow in which you send a message—whether it is, say, being sent within the organization or outside of it, whether it is being sent up or down the hierarchy—also affects the communication. For example, some research evidence shows that information gets distorted as it flows upward; other evidence shows that most information gets lost as it flows downward; still other research shows that lateral communication may be blocked by rivalry and jealousy among peers.[7] Therefore, it is important for you to consider how to avoid the common pitfalls inherent in downward, upward, lateral, and external types of communication.

DOWNWARD COMMUNICATION: Within an organization, you will probably find a great deal of downward communication—that is, information flowing from higher levels to lower levels. Examples of such

---

[7]See J. Koehler, K. Anatol, and R. Applbaum, *Organizational Communication*, 2nd ed. (New York: Holt, Rinehart & Winston, 1981), chap. 4, for a summary of the research on the flow of information in hierarchies.

communication include: staff meetings, manuals, procedures, policy statements, instructions, job descriptions, newsletters, announcements, letters to commemorate occasions or achievements, memos, telephone conversations, performance appraisals, counseling sessions, interviews, and even chance meetings in the hall.

All this downward communication is typically used for four purposes: (1) to explain set standards, such as informing an employee about specific job instructions or general company policies, (2) to provide feedback to employees, such as giving a performance appraisal, (3) to encourage participation, such as eliciting new ideas or upward feedback on current policies, and (4) to motivate or inspire, such as showing how an employee's job fits into the big picture or the company's general mission.[8]

One of the biggest dangers in downward communication is that information may get garbled on the way. One study of downward communication in 100 firms determined how much of what top management said actually permeated the organization. The researchers found that vice-presidents understood 65 percent of the message, general supervisors 56 percent, plant managers 40 percent, foremen 30 percent, and production-line workers only 20 percent. Other studies show that there is a loss for each level a message descends.[9]

How can you reduce this loss of meaning in your downward communication? First, remember that just because communication is downward does not necessarily mean it is one-way. In some situations, you will be conveying information—such as when you are explaining specific instructions or announcing a meeting. In these cases, you might ensure two-way communication by requesting that the instruction sheet be initialed and returned, or by asking your subordinates to call and confirm if they'll be attending the meeting. In other situations, you will be trying to elicit information from other people. For example, you might be holding a brainstorming session to discuss new products, or sending around a questionnaire to uncover potential problems. Remember that to increase two-way communication in these situations, you may need to ask for a response; traditionally, downward communication will not receive a response unless it is specifically requested. Finally, beware of subordinates' natural tendency to tell you what they think you want to hear.

Second, your tone is crucial. On one hand, you want to avoid an overbearing or patronizing attitude toward people who work for you; on the other hand, you want to avoid an artificial warmth or friendship.

[8]D. Katz and R. Kahn, *The Social Psychology of Organizations* (New York: John Wiley, 1966), pp. 239−43.

[9]R. Nichols, quoted in Koehler, Anatol, and Applbaum, *Organizational Communication*, pp. 86−87.

Also avoid insults, personal references, and inappropriate sarcasm, since you are representing management, and perhaps even the organization itself.

Third, downward communication must be clear. Here I am talking about something beyond clear sentences or visual aids. I mean that your desires, wishes, or required actions must be clearly understood. If you are, for example, instructing subordinates about a task, you must clearly identify the procedure you want them to implement. As another example, you must clearly explain to your audience whether you are looking for minor suggestions or for complete revisions.

Finally, downward communication must be based on mutual trust. If you don't trust your employees, your prejudice will stand in the way of true communication with them. If your employees don't trust you, they may not try to understand you; they may lose their job enthusiasm; they may purposely delay action.

UPWARD COMMUNICATION: One of the most noticeable changes in the business communication environment in the past few years has been the increased emphasis on upward communication: the flow of information from subordinates to their supervisors. The most typical forms of upward communication are reports, memos, meetings, and interviews. Upward communication is typically used to accomplish three purposes: (1) to report on activities or accomplishments of a person or a division, (2) to offer suggestions and opinions, and (3) to increase participation in management functions, such as planning or controlling. Your boss (and, in turn, the organization itself) will benefit from your ability to communicate upward: he or she will be able to make better decisions with better information, learn from past mistakes and successes, exercise more efficient control, and plan more effectively for the future.

The biggest problem to overcome in honest upward communication is that of trust. Various studies have shown that employees tend to conceal their opinions, ideas, and problems from their supervisors. One study showed people felt they would get in "a lot of trouble" if they were honest with their supervisors. Another showed that employees fear their bosses might perceive them as lacking independence. A third study demonstrated employees' fear of being "penalized" for honesty. And a final study showed people's belief that managers are not really interested in their problems.[10]

In order to overcome these kinds of problems, you must establish a relationship with your boss. If you have a supervisor who doesn't want to

---

[10]See Koehler, Anatol, and Applbaum, *Organizational Communication*, chap. 4.

hear your opinions or your problems, that's one thing. But you shouldn't assume all bosses are like that. Establish guidelines with your boss; find out how much she or he wants to know, how often, and under what circumstances. It's just as important to manage this relationship as it is to manage your relationships with subordinates.

Once you have established how much upward communication you and your boss want, be aware of the two most common pitfalls of this kind of communication: tone and detail. Avoid, on one hand, an impolite tone—too brisk, argumentative, or insulting. On the other hand, avoid being smarmy, showing too obvious a desire to please. Be sure to include the appropriate amount of detail. Consider how much detail your boss wants, based on the specific assignment and on his or her personality.

LATERAL COMMUNICATION: Communication between people at the same hierarchical rank, but in different functional areas (such as a supervisor in the marketing department and a supervisor in the research and development department), is called horizontal, or lateral communication. This flow of communication is becoming increasingly important as businesses become more large, complex, and specialized. Even in small companies, however, lateral communication is essential in order to coordinate various functions by encouraging teamwork among peers. Major blocks to lateral communication include: departmental isolation, lack of time and communication opportunities, and jealousy or rivalry between groups. These problems are certainly surmountable, especially when you consider the benefits of teamwork: coordinating tasks, solving problems, sharing information, resolving conflict, and increasing interpersonal rapport.

The main thing to keep in mind is that it's in your best interest—and the best interest of your company—to keep this flow of communication open. Very often, young people starting their business careers neglect this form of communication, because lateral flow is not a part of the usual structured pattern of reports and meetings. Imagine, for example, that you have been hired in the accounting department and that your group is designing a new set of travel expense forms. How might your ability to communicate laterally help you? For one thing, you might want to discuss the forms with your peers in other departments. After all, they are the people who will be filling them out. For another, you might join with people in other departments that have large printing orders coming up, and save money by having everything printed at the same time. Finally, you might avoid possible conflicts or bottlenecks in printing if you have already established a relationship with your peers in the printing department.

OUTWARD (EXTERNAL) COMMUNICATION: In addition to communication within the company or organization, of course, you will also be communicating to many different audiences outside the firm. These external audiences include suppliers, dealers, vendors, manufacturers, prospective customers, current customers, former customers, government agencies and bureaus, and community groups. Much external communication—such as advertisements, press releases, and large direct mailings—is handled by a company's public relations or corporate communication office. But even if you do not work for the communication office, you will be representing your company every time you write or speak to external audiences.

The most common external writing is usually in the form of letters—to answer questions, deal with complaints, request information, or sell products as just a few examples. Sometimes business people write reports to external audiences as well; a representative from a subcontracting firm might write a report to the contracting firm, for instance. Oral communication to external audiences might include presentations to trade or professional associations, to community groups or clubs, or to prospective or current customers.

Communication channels

All communication—regardless of its directional flow—uses one or more of the three channels of communication: writing, speaking to a group, and speaking to one person. Of course, communication within these channels may vary—from formal to informal, from domineering to passive. Nevertheless, each channel has certain inherent characteristics. What are the differences among the three channels?

Sometimes, of course, you do not choose the channel. You must write, obviously, if you are told to answer certain letters, or to write a report. Even if you do not make the strategic choice whether to write or speak—if it has been decided for you—think about the characteristics of each channel so you can overcome any possible weaknesses in your communication.

In other cases, your analysis of the organization will dictate your channel choice. In a hierarchical organization, for instance, you would probably write instead of dropping by the president's office. In an informal corporate culture, you might talk to someone in the hall instead of writing.

Finally, in some cases you might have to decide which channel to use. In these cases, choose the most appropriate channel according to the following discussion.

ANALYZE: Whether you choose the channel or have the channel chosen for you, analyze the three channels in terms of time, cost, place, detail, privacy, relationships, permanent record, and response. These considerations are summarized in Table 2.3.

First of all, consider the three channels in terms of time. A writer's time is usually high: you need time for drafting and editing. The exception, of course, is if you dash off a quick note to someone either on paper or by electronic mail. When you speak to a group, your time is usually fairly high because of preparation, practicing, and arranging. When you speak to one person, your preparation time is usually lower. You cannot conclude, however, that speaking to one person takes the least amount of time. Why not? You must take into account your audience's time as well. A reader's time is usually shorter than a listener's—because people can read faster than you can talk.

Besides your time and your audience's time, consider two other aspects of time. When you write, you do not control if, when, and how thoroughly your message will be read. When you speak, however, you do control when and how much the listeners will take in. Finally—unless you use electronic mail—transmission may be slower with writing, because of the mailing time.

The main cost associated with each channel of communication is everybody's time. Again, for writing your time is longer; your readers' time is shorter. For speaking, your listener's time is longer than your readers' time would be. Other possible costs associated with writing include secretarial help, materials, filing, and possibly postage. Other possible costs associated with speaking are travel, facility, teleconferencing, and telephoning costs.

One of the biggest differences among the channels has to do with detail. Writing is the most effective channel for very detailed information. As we shall be discussing in chapter 6, people simply cannot take in as much information when they listen as they can when they read.

Another difference is place. Readers, of course, need not be in the same place as you. For most presentations—that is, unless you are using teleconferencing—your listeners must be in the same place. For one-to-one speaking, you may be face to face with your listener, or on the telephone.

A major consideration is privacy. Both writing and speaking one to one may be very private; speaking with a group, of course, is not.

The relationships that evolve from each channel are somewhat different. Writing may be impersonal—especially if you're not careful—and is certainly less spontaneous than the other channels of communication. Speaking one to one is more spontaneous and may help build rapport and individual relationships. Speaking with a group has the

TABLE 2.3

Channels of communication

	Writing	Speaking	
		To a group	*To one person*
Time	Writer's preparation time usually high: drafting, editing.	Speaker's preparation time varies: practicing, preparing, arranging.	Speaker's preparation time usually low.
	Reader's time usually shorter: reading takes less time than listening.	Listener's time usually longer: listening takes more time than reading.	
	Writer does not control if, when, and how thoroughly message will be read.	Speaker controls when and how thoroughly message will be heard.	
	Transmission time may be slow (except with electronic mail or teleconferencing).		Transmission time may be faster.
Cost	Writer's time.	Speaker's time.	
	Reader's time: relatively short.	Listener's time: relatively long.	
	Secretarial, materials, filing, and possible postage expenses.	Possible travel and facility expenses (except with teleconferencing).	Possible telephone expenses.
Place	Readers need not be in same place.	Listeners must be in same place (except with teleconferencing).	Listeners may be either face to face or on the telephone.
Detail	May be very detailed.	May be moderately detailed.	Usually less detailed.
Privacy	May be very private.	Not private.	May be very private.
Relationship	May be impersonal.	May build group relationships.	May build individual relationships.
Record	Permanent, legal record.	Usually no permanent record (except with videotape).	Usually no permanent record (except with audiotape).
Response	May be delayed.	Immediate.	
	Does not include nonverbal.	Includes nonverbal.	May include nonverbal.
	Writers may be unaware of reader response unless they build in a response mechanism.	Depending on the style of presentation, may range from limited to extensive.	May be extensive.

added possible advantages of building group relationships and consensus.

One of the big advantages of writing, on the other hand, is that it creates a permanent record. When you speak, you have no permanent record unless you use video or audio tape.

Finally, consider the channels in terms of your audience's response. When you write, their response may be delayed. A written response does not include nonverbal communication. In fact, you may not even know your readers' response unless you build in a way for them to reply. Speaking, of course, provides more immediate response, usually includes nonverbal response, and may be more extensive.

CHOOSE: What can we conclude from this kind of analysis? When you have the choice, choose according to these guidelines.

Write if:

1. you have the time to prepare;
2. your audience's time is limited;
3. secretarial, material, and postage costs are not prohibitive;
4. you need to communicate a great deal of detailed information;
5. you need a permanent record;
6. you do not need an immediate response; or
7. you do not need a response at all—such as to clarify, to confirm, to announce, or to report.

Speak to a group if:

1. you have time to prepare and arrange;
2. your audience has the time to attend;
3. the cost of getting the group together is not prohibitive;
4. you need a group of people to hear or discuss the same information at the same time;
5. you want to build a group identity or relationship; or
6. you want group response, which includes nonverbal response, and may include consensus.

Speak to a person individually if:

1. you do not have much time to prepare;
2. you need a very fast answer;

3. telephone costs are not prohibitive;

4. you do not need to communicate a great deal of detailed information;

5. you want to build your individual relationship;

6. you do not need a permanent record; or

7. you need extensive, immediate feedback.

PITFALLS: Even if you do not have the choice, try to overcome the following possible pitfalls.

For writing: (1) Since you cannot control if, when, or how thoroughly your audience will read your message, be sure to make your writing not only clear so they can understand it, but focused on their interests so they will *want* to read it. (2) Since writing may become overly impersonal, work hard to keep in mind the person or people to whom you are writing. (3) Your reader's response will not be immediate, and may not be forthcoming at all. If you are writing about a matter that does not require a response (such as to announce, to confirm, or to clarify), this characteristic of writing does not pose a problem. If, however, you do want a response, make it easy for your reader to respond. End your written document with a "response mechanism," such as:

I will call you next Tuesday to confirm this appointment.

If I do not hear otherwise from you, I shall assume these changes meet with your approval.

Please fill out the attached response sheet by May 3.

If you are interested in receiving more information about this product, please fill out and return the enclosed postcard.

For speaking to a group *or* to one person: (1) Since it takes your listeners longer to hear your information than it takes your readers to read it, avoid wasting their time talking to them if you don't need to. (2) Since speaking usually provides no permanent record, consider writing such a record afterwards—for example, a summary of a telephone conversation or minutes of a meeting. For speaking to a group: (3) Since your listeners can't take in as much detail as your readers can, avoid overloading them with facts. For speaking to one person: (3) Since most people spend less time preparing for a phone call or a visit than they do for writing or speaking to a group, avoid the mistake of wasting time and being unorganized through lack of preparation.

In conclusion, this chapter shows some of the ways the environment influences your communication strategy. Three analyses will help you understand your environment. First, analyze the organization. Second, analyze changes in today's business environment. Third, analyze the flows and channels of communication. You will be writing and speaking within an ever-changing business environment; all the brilliant writing or speaking in the world won't be of any use to you unless you can work effectively within that environment.

REVIEW QUESTIONS
To check your understanding

1. How do you analyze "how people work together"?
2. What four things can you learn about from an organizational chart?
3. What is an *opinion leader*?
4. How do you analyze "what goals people work toward"?
5. List, and give an example of, each of the three aspects of business communication that electronic communication has affected.
6. What two major kinds of analysis and observation do you need to keep in mind in the increasingly international business environment?
7. List three ways you can avoid writing "Dear Sirs."
8. What are the two most common pitfalls in upward communication?
9. What channel of communication takes the most time?
10. List three ways to overcome possible pitfalls in writing as a channel of communication.

APPLICATION QUESTIONS
To apply your knowledge

1. The five variables in the communication strategy are interdependent. Think up an example of that interdependence (other than the two listed at the beginning of the chapter).
2. Find and turn in a copy of a real-world example of an organizational chart. Analyze each of the four points outlined in Table 2.1 that you can learn from such a chart.
3. Analyze a student, community, religious, or business group you have been involved with. What was the formal structure? What was the informal structure (networks and coalitions)?

4. Find and turn in a copy of a published example of a company's formal goals.

5. Analyze the atmosphere of your school's main entrance.

6. Interview someone who has used electronic communication of some sort in business. Find out, and report back on, how the technology affected the way he or she gathered information, spoke, or wrote.

7. If you are male: interview a female student about a situation in which she felt discriminated against, and discuss what kinds of behavior you might avoid in business. If you are female: interview a male student about a situation in which he was surprised or bewildered to be accused of being sexist.

8. Analyze a situation from your life in which you received downward communication. How well did your superior deal with the four dangers (discussed in the chapter) typical of downward communication?

9. How would you give "upward" feedback to one of your teachers?

10. Describe a business situation in which lateral communication would be important.

11. Describe a business situation in which writing would be preferable to speaking.

12. Find and turn in a copy of a real-world example of business writing. How successful was the writer at overcoming each of the three possible pitfalls in writing?

CASES

To practice what you learned

1. Pick two companies you would like to work for. Using sources available on pages 464–69, in your library or placement office, analyze and compare the formal organization and formal goals of the two companies.

2. Interview someone with business experience—an alumnus, friend, or family friend. Based on the interview, analyze both the formal organization and goals *and* the informal organization and goals of his or her company.

3. Interview a foreign student at your school or someone who has worked or lived in a foreign country. Prepare a brief report (written or oral) on what you learned about cross-cultural communication.

4. You are a supervisor. On three different occasions, three different trusted employees have complained to you about another employee accusing him of sexist behavior. Prepare notes for an interview with the accused employee.

5. Write a one-paragraph mini-case describing a realistic work situation in which it is unclear whether the main character should (1) write, (b) speak to a group, or (c) speak to an individual. Leave your "answer" unclear. Bring the mini-case to class for discussion.

3

The Communicator:
Objectives
and Credibility

What Do You Want to Accomplish?
Your objective • Your style • Your tone

How Does Your Audience Perceive You?
What is credibility? • How can you enhance it?

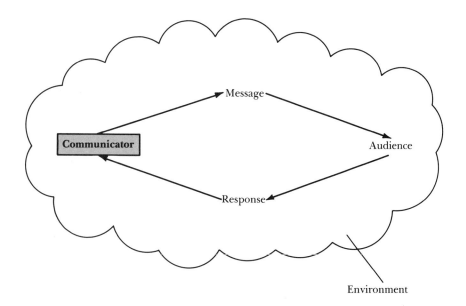

Message

Communicator

Audience

Response

Environment

YOU, the communicator—as either writer or speaker—are clearly one of the variables in your communication strategy. In this chapter, we will look at how you can become purposeful, appropriate, and believable for your audience. Before you actually begin writing or speaking, then, answer the two questions posed in this chapter. First, what precisely do you want to accomplish? In other words, state your communication objective. Then, you will be able to choose the appropriate style and tone to accomplish your objective. Second, how does your audience perceive you? Consider your credibility and how you can increase it to become more persuasive.

What Do You Want to Accomplish?

Before you start to write or speak, you must define what you are trying to accomplish. This sounds fairly obvious. And yet, much ineffective business communication stems from writers and speakers neglecting to clarify their aims. Moreover, even when ineffective communicators do specify their aims, they do not consider the appropriate style and tone for reaching those aims. By stating your objective and choosing the appropriate style and tone—as described in this section—you will gain a sense of purpose and appropriateness that will make you more effective.

Your objective

The first step toward analyzing what you want to accomplish is to set your objective. "I know my objective, all right," ineffective communicators might insist; "I want to tell my potential customers all the great features of this product" or "I want to report to my boss about all the problems we're having with this project."

To communicate effectively, however, these vague notions of objectives are not enough. People who communicate in business need to specify both (1) the response they desire from their audience, and (2) specific means by which they plan to achieve that response. So, instead of saying

I want to describe all the great features of this product,

they need to specify the desired response,

I want ten customers to purchase this product this month,

and the means to achieve that response,

I will describe the three features my potential customers will find most attractive.

Instead of saying

I want to report on all the problems we are having on this project,

they need to specify the desired response,

I want my boss to understand the reasons for the delay,

or,

> I want my boss to change our current procedures so we can avoid future delays,

and the means to achieve that response,

> I will report on the four problems that most concern my boss.

Coming up with these kinds of specific objectives, instead of working from vague notions of your goals, offers you two enormous benefits. First, a specific definition will save you time, making you more efficient. Just the thought of listing every single feature of a product or every single problem you encountered on a certain project may be overwhelming. By cutting your topic down to a manageable size, you will find it is no longer too big, too abstract, or too difficult to handle. Sometimes, of course, you will need to get across a great deal of detailed information. My point here is simply that you will waste time if you include *unnecessary* detail. Besides being able to start faster, you will be able to work faster if you know specifically what you are trying to cover. You can also avoid wasting time writing unnecessary letters or calling unnecessary meetings; if you don't have a specific purpose, you don't need to communicate.

Second, having a specific objective will make your message more effective. Since effective business communication is defined in terms of audience response, you must know what that response is supposed to be. That way you can be sure to build toward and stress your purpose.

How can you gain all these benefits? The process of setting objectives is a relatively simple one. Start with your **general goal,** which is usually a broad statement about what you are doing, for example,

> to provide mail service throughout the organization,

or what you hope to be doing, for example,

> to increase the number of women hired,

or what problem you're trying to solve, for example,

> to exchange defective supplies you were sent.

These general goals are necessary, of course. They usually describe your job, trigger your need to communicate, and start you thinking. But knowing general goals alone is not enough to make you an effective communicator. So don't stop here.

Instead, define your **communication objective.** Decide precisely how you hope your audience will respond. Be as specific as possible: quantify anything that is measurable, such as

two mail deliveries, ten newly hired women, four boxes of supplies,

and specify anything that is dated, such as

each day, by next year, by the end of next week.

To define your communication objective, complete this statement:

As a result of this message, my audience will _____.

Fill in the blank with a specific action, dated if possible.

Using that formula, let's look at some examples that show the difference between general goals and specific communication objectives.

To reach the general goal of "to provide mail service throughout the organization," set a communication objective of "As a result of reading this memo, the mail delivery staff will follow the procedure for picking up and delivering twice each day."

The general goal of "to increase the number of women hired" could be made more specific by stating, "As a result of attending this presentation, ten women at this college will sign up for a job interview with my company."

For the general goal "to exchange defective supplies," you might say "As a result of reading this letter, the vendor will exchange these four boxes of defective supplies by the end of next week."

The time it takes to set a communication objective varies. On routine matters, you may be able to do it in a matter of seconds. More complicated matters, of course, will take longer. Avoid the temptation to skip the crucial step of specifying your objective, however; the time you save in efficiency and in results will more than make up for the time it takes to think through your purpose for communicating.

Your style

Once you have defined your communication objective, you will know the appropriate communication style. In this context, *style*, of course, does not mean fashion or personality. Instead, it means the various styles available to you when you communicate in business, styles that are similar to the various *leadership styles* or *management styles.*[1]

Here are the four basic communication styles:

Tell   Sell   Confer   Join

Let's look at each in turn.

On one end of the continuum, you see the TELL style. Here, you are trying to explain or instruct. You know the "answers"; you want to TELL your audience the "answers." Just because you are TELLING, however, does not mean you are being authoritarian. In fact, the TELL style is often used in upward communication—a report to your boss on your department's activities for the month, for example. The TELL style is also often used in external communication—a letter explaining a policy to a customer, for example. The point is that you are informing someone. Here are some sample communication objectives for which you would use the TELL style:

> As a result of reading this memo, the employees will understand the benefits program available in this company.

> As a result of attending this community presentation, my audience will understand how the zoning rules in this town work.

> As a result of reading this report, my boss will learn what this department has accomplished this month.

> As a result of reading this letter, my customer will understand the reasons why we turned down his request for credit.

Moving over one notch, you will see the SELL style. When you use this style you are trying to get your audience to do something differently—not just to learn, but to change their actions. You know the "answers"; you want them to act differently because of these "answers."

---

[1]The material on what I am calling *communication style* is adapted from the literature on management and leadership style. Most importantly, the TELL/SELL/CONFER/JOIN continuum is a simplification of R. Tannenbaum and W. Schmidt, "How to Choose a Leadership Pattern," *Harvard Business Review,* 36 (March-April 1958), 95–101. Other versions of this continuum include R. Blake and J. Mouton, *The New Managerial Grid* (Houston: Gulf Publishing Company, 1978); R. Likert, *The Human Organization* (New York: McGraw-Hill, 1967); and V. Vroom and P. Yetton, *Leadership and Decision-Making* (Pittsburgh: University of Pittsburgh Press, 1973).

Sample objectives for this SELL style might be:

As a result of reading this letter, my client will sign the enclosed contract by next Tuesday.

As a result of attending this presentation, the committee will approve my plan.

As a result of reading this memo, my boss will approve my travel budget.

The third style, CONFER, is appropriate when you are trying to consult or interact with your audience—to gather information or opinions. You do not know the "answer"; you want to learn the "answer" from them. Examples here include:

As a result of reading this survey, at least 50 percent of the employees in this organization will respond by answering the questionnaire.

As a result of this telephone call, my customer will list precisely what products she wants us to send her.

As a result of this question-and-answer session, my audience will voice their concerns about the policy.

Finally, for those times when you need or want high audience involvement, the style is JOIN. In these situations, both you and your audience act together; you collaborate or brainstorm to discover the "answer." Examples of this style include:

As a result of reading this agenda memo, my audience will come to the meeting prepared to offer their thoughts on this particular idea.

As a result of attending this presentation, my audience will come up with solutions to this particular problem we're encountering.

Of the four styles for communicating, none are either "good" or "bad." Every one of us must use every one of these styles in our job: sometimes we want to get information from people; sometimes we want to give information to our audience. So the point is to specify the appropriate style for your objective. As general rules of thumb, use the TELL/ SELL styles when you: (1) have all the information you need, (2) can understand that information without any help from others, and (3) are concerned primarily with a logical, orderly, quick decision. Generally, use the CONFER/JOIN styles when you : (1) need more information, (2) need critical evaluation, opinions, and ideas from other people, and (3) are concerned about people feeling involved and carrying out decisions effectively.[2]

Your tone

Your tone should be appropriate for your objective and style. The concept of *tone* is hard to define precisely. And yet, as readers or listeners ourselves, we all feel the communicator's tone. You know when your boss is using a threatening tone, or when your instructor is using a humorous tone, or when an irate customer is using an angry tone. Similarly, your audience will always pick up on your tone—no matter how impersonal you may feel you are being when you write a report or speak to a large group.

Tone, then, is the way your speaking or writing sounds, the feeling it conveys, the mood you set. Like a mood, your tone can vary indefinitely: from placid to agitated, from playful to somber, from modest to proud, from thankful to bitter, from whimsical to factual, from pleading to ordering, from fanciful to factual. In business communication, however, you will usually rule out the extremes of rapture and rage.[3]

There are no hard and fast rules regarding tone. In part, this is because your tone will vary enormously with your personality. People have, and should have, different personalities. In business, however, since you are trying to achieve a result through your audience—and not simply trying to express your own personality to its fullest—you must analyze the effect of your tone on them. Therefore, your tone also varies enormously with your audience and your relationship to them: you might be sympathetic for one audience, more hard-line for another; you might be the friend of one colleague, a distant associate of another; you might be an adviser in one situation, an advisee in another. Finally, your tone varies with your subject and objective. You might be serious about one topic, humorous about another; extremely worried about one topic, less concerned about another; giving orders to accomplish one objective, eliciting ideas to accomplish another. All these variations make it impossible to develop an absolutely right or wrong tone. Instead, you develop an appropriate or inappropriate tone.

Based on those variables (your personality, your audience, and your topic and objective), let's take an example of a communication situation

[2]For a more complex discussion of how to choose the appropriate style, see Vroom and Yetton, *Leadership and Decision-Making.*

[3]For an excellent discussion of tone, see F. Crews, *The Random House Handbook,* 4th ed. (New York: Random House, 1983), pp. 5–8.

and the range of tones available to you. Say you were trying to communicate the necessity for keeping a certain work area clean. On one end of the range, you could adopt a *light* tone: "Let's all pitch in and get rid of the garbage we've all been wading through in the work area!" On the other end of the range, you could adopt a *formal* tone: "This is to inform you that anyone found leaving garbage in the work area will be docked one hour's pay." Somewhere in between, you could adopt a *middle* tone: "To increase productivity, we must work together to clean up the work area."

Again, none of these tones is the right or wrong one in any absolute sense; their appropriateness is based on your analysis of the situation. In most business situations, the middle tone is appropriate. Watch out for lapsing automatically into an overly friendly, cutesy light tone or an overly pompous, overly official formal tone. Make your tone a choice, not a habit.

As you make this choice, consider at least three guidelines for achieving an appropriate tone. (1)Base your tone on your *communication strategy* (the context, audience, and message)—not just on your own personality or on some tone you have automatically used for all business communication up to now. (2) Base your tone on *sound*. Try reading your writing out loud. Can you comfortably read what you've written? Does it sound stilted and stodgy? Can you imagine actually saying it to someone? Practice your presentation aloud. Does it sound artificial and impersonal? Does it sound patronizing? Most students can detect their mood and attitude more easily if they read aloud than they can if they read silently. (3) Base your tone on a *positive* attitude. This does not mean you should always be cheery and amusing; obviously, you would not want to be flippant or jaunty as you gave someone a criticism or a refusal. Instead, it means showing the warmth, respect, and goodwill you feel toward your audience. A positive attitude does not mean you should never communicate bad news, either. Instead, it means showing consideration for your audience as you impart bad news. Here are two examples: "You failed to enclose your check, so it's impossible to send your order" (negative tone) versus "As soon as your check arrives, we'll be happy to send your order" (positive tone); "There will be no exceptions to this rule" (negative tone) versus "This rule must apply equally and fairly to everyone" (positive tone).[4]

Occasionally, you may find it appropriate to adopt a *humorous tone*. Humor in business communication plays a strictly subordinate role: a business presentation is not a night-club act; a business letter is not a comic

---

[4]For a helpful discussion of positive tone, see R. Huseman, J. Lahiff, and J. Hatfield, *Business Communication* (New York: Dryden Press, 1981), ch. 6.

book. Humor in business is likely to be occasional rather than continuous, smile-provoking rather than side-splitting.

Since your goal in business communication is certainly not to have people rolling in the aisles with laughter, why use humor at all? You can use humor to attract and keep your audience's interest; unless you have their attention, you cannot accomplish your business goals. You may also use humor if you wish to establish a more relaxed atmosphere, to break down barriers, to diffuse tension. Finally, you may use humor to vary the mood. As communication teacher Roger Wilcox says, "Given a momentary respite, a change of pace, your audience feels mentally refreshed, ready to settle down again to another period of close concentration. Used in this way, humor has somewhat the effect of a seventh inning stretch, or of a coffee break in the middle of a conference."[5] So, you see, if you use humor to keep your audience with you, you are using it for business purposes, not just for fun.

How Does Your Audience Perceive You?

Once you have formulated what you want to accomplish (that is, once you have stated your objective and chosen both the appropriate communication style and tone to accomplish that objective), consider your audience's perception of you. In other words, consider your own credibility: their belief, confidence, and faith in your power or reliability or trustworthiness. Their expectations of you have a tremendous impact on how you set your communication strategy.

The importance of the audience's perception of the communicator has been demonstrated in various studies. For instance, in one experiment, separate audiences heard the same tape-recorded speech favoring leniency toward juvenile delinquents. The speaker on this tape was identified differently to each group: one group was told it was a judge, the other that it was an ex-delinquent out on bail. The results showed that the "judge's" talk was received favorably by 73 percent of the audience, in contrast with only 29 percent for the "delinquent."[6] In another study, an

[5]R. Wilcox, *Oral Reporting in Business* (Englewood Cliffs, N.J.: Prentice-Hall, 1967), p. 218.

[6]H. C. Kelman and C. I. Hovland, " 'Reinstatement' of the Communicator in Delayed Measurement of Opinion Change," *Journal of Abnormal and Social Psychology*, 48 (1953), 327−35.

industrial psychologist interviewed 137 executives and purchasing directors about how they selected their suppliers. A key finding was that the audience's perceptions of the suppliers themselves was by far the most important consideration: "At the very top of the list, . . .mentioned two and a half times more often than. . .price, stands 'Personal Relations': a good working relationship with the suppliers as people."[7]

What is credibility?

Most people use the term *credibility* to refer to an audience's perceptions of the communicator. Let's take a look at five factors that affect credibility.[8]

The most obvious kind of credibility in business is based on position or **rank**. Imagine you heard someone in your company say, "We are going to paint all the walls in this building with purple and orange stripes." You would probably find that statement more credible if you heard it from the president than if you heard it from the janitor. Similarly, if someone says, "You'd better do this—or else" or "If you do this, I'll raise your salary," you will believe it only to the extent that the person has the rank or status to punish or reward you. Credibility by virtue of rank—which is related to what some theorists call the audience's *perceived dependency* or the communicator's *coercive/reward power*—is certainly important. But remember that even if you are not immediately promoted to company president, you can gain credibility in other ways.

For instance, another aspect of credibility is the audience's sense of the communicator's **goodwill**. People will tend to listen to you or read what you write more favorably and believe you if you have, for example, done them favors or established a personal as well as professional relationship with them. Imagine being given precisely the same advice—not to apply for a certain position—by two people: a colleague with whom you

[7]H. Lazo, "Emotional Aspects of Industrial Buying," in *Dynamic Marketing for a Changing World*, R. Hancock (Chicago: American Marketing Association, 1960), pp. 258–65.

[8]For the five factors that affect credibility, I have synthesized two sets of research by social-power theorists. The terms *coercive/reward power, expert power, referent power,* and *legitimate power* come from J. French and B. Raven, "The Bases of Social Power," in *Studies in Social Power,* ed. D. Cartwright (Ann Arbor: University of Michigan Institute for Social Research, 1959), pp. 150–67. This article, or an abridgment of it, appears in many anthologies on group behavior and power. The terms *perceived dependence, personal obligation, expertise,* and *identification* come from J. Kotter, "Power, Dependence, and Effective Management," *Harvard Business Review,* 54 (July–August 1977), 125–36.

eat lunch and a colleague who is applying for that same position. Naturally, you would place more credibility in the person whom you felt had your best interest at heart, the person toward whom you felt goodwill.

Another very important source of credibility is the audience's sense of the communicator's **expertise**. Imagine talking to the person sitting next to you on an airplane about the aircraft. How would your opinion of what that person had to say change if you found out he or she were: vice-president of the airline? an aeronautical engineer? a first-time flyer? The point here, of course, is that even without knowing your seatmate personally, your opinion might be swayed by your perception of her or his expertise, achievement, or competence.

Although expertise is certainly important, audiences often grant credibility to communicators with no expertise whatsoever on a certain subject. For example, why do you suppose the American public responds to an endorsement of avocados by an actress or an endorsement of an after-shave lotion by a baseball player? It's not because these people are seen as experts in agriculture or grooming, but because of their **image**. Image—sometimes called *identification* or *referent power*—is based on attractiveness and energy, the audience's desire to *be like* the communicator. In the case of the endorsements, people want to be thin like the actress or athletic like the baseball player. In business, admiration for someone's social grace or attractiveness might increase that person's credibility— even though these attributes have nothing to do with the topic at hand. Image is not only a matter of looks, but a matter of dynamism. Think back, as another example, to your first day of classes in any term. How are you influenced by the lively, energetic teachers as opposed to the dull, boring teachers? The very people with the most expertise, the very people from whom you may eventually learn the most, may have to overcome a credibility problem if they are not dynamic.

Although—like it or not—image contributes to credibility, credibility is not a fake or artificial phenomenon. In fact, the final contributing factor is the audience's perception of the communicator's **morality and fairness**—that is, his or her values and objectivity. Imagine a dinner-table conversation with your relatives. Regardless of how dynamic and handsome Uncle Anthony may be, if he is stubborn and unyielding on every issue, his lack of objectivity or fair-mindedness may decrease his credibility. Aunt Alice, on the other hand, may be a comparatively bumbling speaker, but if you agree with her values and standards, her sense of morality may increase her credibility.

In conclusion, credibility stems from at least five factors. These factors—and their connections with the work of three of the most important theorists on social power—are summarized in Table 3.1.

TABLE 3.1 **What makes credibility**		
What this book calls:	*Is similar to what social-power theorists call:*	*Is based on your audience's perception of your:*
Rank	Perceived dependence or Coercive/reward power	Position, power, status in organization
Goodwill	Personal obligation	Personal relationship
Expertise	Expertise or Expert power	Competence, achievement
Image	Identification or Referent power	Attractiveness, dynamism
Morality and fairness	Legitimate power	Values, objectivity

This table synthesizes both French and Raven's and Kotter's theories. Naturally, I have simplified their ideas somewhat. I am especially aware that *perceived dependence* is not equal to *rank*.

How can you enhance it?

Once you understand these five factors, you can enhance your credibility by stressing your initial credibility and increasing your acquired credibility.

INITIAL CREDIBILITY: *Initial credibility* refers to your audience's perception of you before the communication itself ever takes place, before they ever read or hear what you have to say. Your initial credibility, then, may stem from their perception of who you are, what you represent, or your previous relations.

Based on the five factors we have just analyzed, let's look at some examples of situations in which your initial credibility is likely to be high. (1) Rank: Obviously, your initial credibility would tend to be higher if you are higher in rank than those with whom you are communicating—for example, if you are their supervisor or are in some other position of power. (2) Goodwill: If you are on good personal terms with a client, you would have higher initial credibility than another salesperson who didn't know the client at all. (3) Expertise: If you have a reputation for your ability in chemistry, your initial credibility in a discussion of the chemical components of a product is likely to be high. On the other hand, if you are seen as a manufacturing specialist, you would have higher initial credibility when it came time to discuss the setup for the production line. (4) Image: You would tend to have higher initial credibility if your audience identified with your attractiveness in some way. Or, you might have image credibility by association if you are linked somehow with a group your audience respects—such as a powerful committee or a well-regarded company. (5) Fairness: Finally, your initial credibility may be high based on the values and standards the people in your audience perceive that you hold in common.

As part of your communication strategy, then, you may want to stress or remind your audience of your initial credibility. Here are some techniques for doing so, based on the examples cited in the previous paragraph. (1) Rank: You could stress your rank by handing out business cards at a conference or by stating your title on the front page of a report. (2) Goodwill: You could open a sales letter or presentation by referring to the personal relationship you have with your customer. (3) Expertise: A short biography, résumé, or list of your experiences might emphasize your expertise. (4) Image: To stress image by association, use your company letterhead or mention a respected association or person with whom you're working. (5) Fairness: As a final technique, you could open a meeting or a letter by mentioning specific values you and your audience share.

In addition to stressing initial credibility in your communication strategy, in those lucky cases in which it is high you may use initial credibility in any of three ways. First, you may use it as a "bank account." If the people in your audience regard you highly, they may trust you even in unpopular or extreme decisions or recommendations. Just as drawing on a bank account reduces your remaining balance, however, drawing on your personal credibility reduces the balance of your audience's trust. Therefore, don't waste your credibility by spending it extravagantly or on unimportant issues; remember to deposit to your account, perhaps by goodwill gestures or with further proof of your expertise.[9]

Second, you may use high initial credibility to back up threats. On rare occasions, you may need to threaten. For example, as a boss, you may need to "crack down" on employees, or as a subordinate you may

---

[9]R. Wilcox, *Communication at Work* (Boston: Houghton Mifflin, 1977), p. 300.

need to "get tough" with your boss. In general, threats are not a good persuasive technique (as we shall see when we discuss audience motivation in chapter 4), but on those unusual occasions when you need to threaten, you can do so only from a position of high credibility.

Finally, you may use high credibility when your audience must "take your word for it," accept what you say on blind faith. For example, your boss may have to bow to your expertise in certain technical matters he or she does not understand. Or your staff may have to trust you in a situation where they cannot see the big picture or the long-term goals you are aware of.

Those, then, are some ways in which to use high initial credibility. But what about situations in which you have low initial credibility? You must try to gain or acquire it.

ACQUIRED CREDIBILITY: *Acquired credibility*, unlike initial, refers to your audience's perception of you after the communication takes place, after they have read or heard you. Even if your audience knows nothing about you in advance, your good ideas and your persuasive writing or speaking will help you earn or derive credibility. The obvious way to acquire credibility, therefore, is to do a good job on your analysis and communication in general.

Besides doing a good job in general as part of your communication strategy, you can use other techniques to increase your credibility. The following four techniques are especially useful in those situations where your initial credibility is low. First, you can increase your credibility by citing ideas or benefits that match your audience's views, needs, and goals. For example, stress cost savings to a cost-conscious customer; stress luxury to a prestige-conscious customer. Another technique to increase credibility is to identify yourself with your audience's goals and needs. As examples, mention your summer construction job when you are dealing with construction workers, or the stock you own through your company's stock-option policy when you are talking to stockholders. A third technique is to use quotations from authorities your audience wants to be like. For example, cite well-regarded scientists to an engineering group, or well-regarded consultants to a management group. A final technique would be to associate yourself somehow with well-regarded people. Have your letter or report countersigned by your boss, for example, or have someone your audience respects introduce you at a presentation. Methods for increasing your credibility are summarized in Table 3.2.

In some senses, the goal of the rest of this book—and, indeed, any business communication course—is to increase your acquired credibility by improving your communication skills. More particularly, though, hav-

	Initial credibility	*Acquired credibility*
Factor	*Stress by:*	*Increase by:*
Rank	Emphasizing your title or rank (e.g., including your full title)	Associating yourself with high-ranked person (e.g., by counter-signature or introduction)
Goodwill	Referring to personal relationships	Citing benefits or ideas that match your audience's goals and needs
Expertise	Including a biography, résumé, or list of experiences	Associating yourself with or quoting from someone your audience sees as expert
Image	Emphasizing attributes that your audience finds attractive	Identifying yourself with benefits or ideas that match your audience's goals and needs
Fairness	Mentioning values you share with your audience	

TABLE 3.2

How to enhance credibility

ing read this chapter, you should be aware of how to : (1) set your objective, style, and tone, and (2) analyze and enhance your credibility before you ever start actually writing or speaking.

REVIEW QUESTIONS
To check your understanding

1. Who is "the communicator"?

2. As a communicator, you should become purposeful, appropriate, and believable. In order to do this, what two major questions should you ask yourself?

3. What two benefits accrue from specifying a communication objective?

4. What statement should you complete to form a communication objective?

5. With what should you fill in the blank in that statement?

6. Who knows the "answer" in the TELL/SELL styles? In the CONFER/JOIN styles?

7. What is *tone*?

8. As you make the choice for tone, what three guidelines should you consider?

9. What are five factors that make up your *credibility*?

10. What is the difference between *initial* and *acquired* credibility?

APPLICATION QUESTIONS

To apply your knowledge

1. For each of the following general goals, invent a possible communication objective (using the formula in this chapter). Include the desired audience response. Be specific; include dates if possible.

    a. "to maintain good customer relations"

    b. "to increase the customer's understanding of this product"

    c. "to improve morale in this company"

2. For each of the following objectives, choose an appropriate style. In each instance, explain why.

    a. "As a result of reading this memo, management will understand our progress on the construction project."

    b. "As a result of this telephone call, my customer will let me know how satisfied he or she is with our service."

    c. "As a result of this letter, at least ten people will order this product."

3. Analyze a situation in which someone used a tone you felt was inappropriate. Explain why.

4. Find and turn in a copy of an advertisement in which someone had *image* credibility.

5. Describe a situation in which you—as of *today*—would have high *expertise* credibility.

6. Imagine you want your parents to give you an extra $100. How might you use one of the four techniques for increasing your credibility (described at the end of the chapter)?

CASES

To practice what you learned

1. Write a one-paragraph mini-case describing a situation in which you had to communicate to achieve a specific result. Using the definitions for the three terms introduced in this chapter, state (1) the *communication objective,* (2) the *communication style,* and (3) the *tone* that would be appropriate.

2. Choose a person who has or had some kind of authority over you, for example, a teacher, parent, or boss. Analyze that person's communication style in terms of the four part continuum introduced in this chapter. Analyze your reaction to that style. What lessons do you learn that you might use in business communication?

3. Think of someone's behavior—your roommate's, officemate's, brother's, sister's, whomever—that has bothered you. Write three paragraphs asking them to change the behavior—each paragraph saying essentially the same thing, but using a different tone.

4. Prepare to discuss two situations: (1) one in which your initial credibility was high and how you stressed it or might have stressed it, and (2) one in which your initial credibility was low and how you enhanced it or might have enhanced it.

4

The Audience:
Motivation

Analyze Your Audience.
Who are they? • *What do they know and feel?*

Motivate Your Audience.
Punish or reward them. • *Appeal to their growth needs.*
• *Use people's need for balance.* • *Perform a cost/benefit analysis.* • *Be sensitive to character traits.*

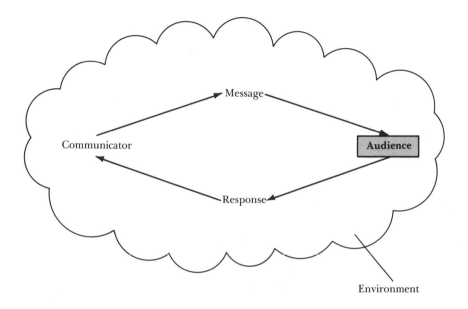

Message

Communicator

Audience

Response

Environment

NO matter what your communication objective may be—having your audience buy a product, pay a bill, approve your plan, work harder, or promote you—it involves motivating someone to respond in the way you desire. To accomplish your objective, therefore, you must center on your audience, not on yourself. Rhetorical theorists refer to this ability as becoming *reader- or listener-based, audience-centered,* or using the *you* approach. Whatever it is called, the theory boils down to being persuasive by aiming your message toward your audience's needs and desires. This ability to analyze and motivate your audience may very well be the most important strategy of all for your success in business communication, and, by extension, for your success in business.

Analyze Your Audience.

The first step toward motivating your audience is to analyze them. Ask yourself (1) who they are and (2) what they already know and feel. Here are some more specific considerations for each of these two main questions.

Who are they?

First of all, who will actually receive your message? For example, to whom is your letter addressed or to whom will you be speaking at the meeting? This person or these people constitute your **primary audience**. Visualize and think about them. Obviously, your persuasiveness will depend on how much and how well you can relate to these people.

Besides your primary audience, in business communication you may often have a **secondary audience**, sometimes called a *hidden audience*. Even though this audience may not be the person or people to whom you are actually writing or talking, you need to keep them in mind because they may be somehow affected by, or involved with, your message. Examples of secondary audience members include: someone who receives a copy of your memo, someone who will be affected by decisions made at your meeting, or someone who may have to approve or sign the letter you write. In these cases, you need to write or speak appropriately for your secondary audience as well as for your primary audience.

Finally—especially if your primary and secondary audiences are in conflict—think about the **key decision maker** in your audience. Often, young business people neglect or avoid thinking about powerful audience members because they're afraid or embarrassed. Clearly, if you want to be successful, you must keep these people in mind. For example, if you are writing to several people, and you know the leader of the group prefers short notes, consider keeping the memo short. As another example, if you know that the person you feel is the key decision maker in a group is a "morning person," consider scheduling your presentation for the morning, even if it interferes with your own schedule.

Now, in the best of situations you can analyze these primary, secondary, and key audience members based on your personal knowledge of them **as individuals**. You can analyze their specific background, including their ages, educational levels, training, opinions, interests, and attitudes. As examples, you would certainly approach a young inexperienced person differently than you would someone older and more experienced; someone with a Ph.D. in electrical engineering differently than an amateur electrician; an experienced administrative assistant differently than a newly hired secretary; a person whose hobby is collecting stamps differently than someone who uses them only on letters; a person who loves television differently than a person who hates it. The more you know or can find out about the person or people with whom you are communicating, the better your chances are for being persuasive.

Unfortunately, however, in many business situations you must communicate with people you do not know personally—as when you write to unknown potential customers, or speak to an unknown audience. In these cases, you can analyze what you know about them **as a group**—including their group characteristics, norms, traditions, standards, rules, and values. You might, for example, approach a group of research people differently than a group of salespeople. Or, you might approach customers buying toasters differently than customers buying spark plugs.

Once you have analyzed as best you can who your listeners or readers are, the next step is to think about both their knowledge and their attitudes.

What do they know and feel?

First, think about their knowledge of the topic. By doing this, you can avoid one of the most widespread problems in business communication: speaking or writing over the heads of your audience—that is, using words and phrases, or assuming technical expertise, with which the people in your audience are unfamiliar. You can also avoid another harmful problem: writing or speaking on too low a level—that is, sounding patronizing because you laboriously explain terms or detailed background they already understand. For example, if you are discussing computer software with potential customers, avoid using jargon only a computer expert can understand. On the other hand, if you are describing the software to computer engineers, avoid explaining rules and procedures they already know. In short, consider their knowledge so you can talk their language and provide them with just the appropriate amount of detail.

You need to understand more than what your audience members know, however. You also need to understand what they feel: their inclinations, dispositions, opinions, or attitudes. These include not only their perception of you (that is, your credibility, as we discussed in the previous chapter), but also their attitudes toward what you're about to tell them. Do they want to hear what you have to say? Are they in favor of, against, or indifferent to your message? Will it either benefit or threaten them in any way? Guess their probable reactions in advance, so you can structure your

---

TABLE 4.1
Audience inventory

Who are they?

Primary:	Who, exactly, are the people receiving your message? Visualize and name them all.
Secondary or Hidden:	Besides those actually receiving it, name anyone whom you will inform (such as by sending a copy) or who must approve what you write or say.
Key Person:	Who is the leader or key decision maker in your audience?

What do they know and feel?

Knowledge:	What kind of wording will they understand? How much detail do they need?
Attitudes:	Are they in favor of, against, or indifferent to your message? Will it benefit or threaten them in any way?

---

message appropriately (as we shall discuss in the next chapter). Remember to consider their attitudes as well as their knowledge.

Effective communication is based on a systematic audience analysis. Table 4.1 summarizes the steps in this inventory. Only by knowing or learning who they are, what they know, and what they feel can you imagine what it would be like to *be* your audience. Put yourself in their shoes: empathize with them. Then, you can make your message audience-based, and therefore persuasive and successful.

Motivate Your Audience.

Once you have taken your audience inventory, you need to figure out how best to motivate the people you've just analyzed. Some of the concepts we have already discussed will make you more persuasive. You should try to increase your credibility (as we discussed in the previous chapter). You should also try to structure your message persuasively (as we shall discuss in the next chapter). So, keeping in mind that persuasion includes the environment, the communicator, and the message, we will now look specifically at a fourth aspect of persuasion: psychological techniques for motivating your audience.

Understanding psychological theories of motivation is just as important for your success in business as understanding internal-combustion theories is for a car mechanic. Without a theory, neither of you could keep things running or fix them when they break down. And, like the car mechanic, you will apply theoretical background in practical, down-to-earth situations. However, you will find that people are more complex and unpredictable than cars.

So, then, let's enter this discussion of psychological theories not as students might in a psychology course—to *learn* the concepts—but rather as potential business communicators should—to *apply* the concepts. We will consider what theorists believe to be five techniques for motivating people: (1) punish or reward them; (2) appeal to their growth needs; (3) use people's need for balance; (4) perform a cost/benefit analysis, and (5) be sensitive to character traits.

Punish or reward them.

Many students believe they will be able to influence people in business—especially their subordinates—by using **threats and punishment**. Certainly, threats and punishment are one way of motivating people, but this method is more limited than you might initially guess. Researcher Walter R. Nord has found six reasons why threats may not work.[1] Let's look at them in a business situation.

Imagine one of your employees spends too much time talking on the phone to friends during the work day. So you write him a memo or call him in for an interview and say: "If you don't stop talking on the phone to friends, I'll fire you." First, your threat may work only when you are actually watching over your employee's actions. Therefore, his compliance will be sporadic, since you can't possibly watch him all the time. Second, threats may get rid of one response (in this case, talking to friends on the phone), but not produce the desired response (such as getting more work accomplished). Third, threats may stop the inappropriate action even when it is appropriate: he might stop talking in friendly ways

---

[1]W. Nord, "Beyond the Teaching Machine: The Neglected Art of Operant Conditioning in the Theory and Practice of Management," *Organizational Behavior and Human Performance*, 4 (1969), 375–401, noted in K. Locker, "Justifications for Reader Benefits," *Journal of Business Communication*, 19 (Summer 1982), 51–65. I am indebted to Locker's analysis for the first part of this chapter.

to customers, not just to friends. Fourth, threats produce tension, making the work place less pleasant and productive in general. Fifth, threats tend to make people dislike you. This may make it hard for you to enlist your employee's support on your next new project or to help him improve his performance. Finally, threats provoke counteraggression. Feeling that your orders and nagging reduce his freedom, he may respond by asserting his freedom in other ways: "I'll come in late from lunch today because my boss is so unfair!"

So, although sometimes they are clearly necessary, use threats and punishment with caution. Instead, consider using **rewards** as a way to change behavior. Many psychologists would argue that rewards, or what they call *positive reinforcement*, are the most effective way to shape behavior.[2]

Rewarding certain behaviors is an extremely powerful way to get the response you want. You are likely to be successful if your rewards include these following four characteristics. First, they must be important to the person who is being rewarded. Some people might react to group acceptance, some to money, and others to recognition of achievement. Second, rewards must be appropriate and sincere. A special lunch would be too much of a reward for a staff member who typed a letter successfully or a customer who placed one order; on the other hand, a mere "Thanks" is too little of a reward for a staff member who completed a terrific job on a three-month project or for your largest annual customer. Third, effective rewards must be immediate. If you wait to recognize achievements, your recognition won't be as effective in getting people to repeat the behaviors you want. Finally, remember that rewards don't have to be elegant. Plaques, pens, and trophies are fine, but the research shows that even simple verbal recognition is an effective reward.

One effective reward technique consists of breaking down large projects or tasks into smaller components, and rewarding the participants at each step. For example, if you were teaching someone how to play tennis, you wouldn't teach all the strokes on the first day. Instead, you might start with several sessions on the forehand volley. After the person got the hang of that skill, you might introduce the backhand volley, and so forth. Similarly, in persuasive business communication, you might break down a large project into smaller units. For example, if you were trying to

---

[2]I have chosen to deal only with positive rewards, not with negative rewards. Non-laboratory experiments haven't shown negative rewards to be of much use; positive rewards seem to produce much better results in most studies of persuasive communication. See E. Bettinghaus, *Persuasive Communication*, 3rd ed. (New York: Holt, Rinehart, & Winston, 1980), p. 32. This book contains a very thorough summary and analysis of the research into persuasive communication. I am indebted to this book for my discussion of rewards, growth needs, and balance needs.

explain how to run a complicated computer program, you could break down the instructions into a series of short steps and have "Good job!" or "Well done!" flash on the screen to reward each step. The more complex your communication objective—that is, the more complex the action with which you want your audience to respond—the more you may want to use this breaking-down technique.

In general, most business communicators could be more successful if they used punishment less and rewards more often.

Appeal to their growth needs.

Given the overwhelming evidence that positive reinforcement (or rewards) is a powerful agent for influencing people, let's discuss further how to reward people effectively. When most students think of rewards, they think of tangible items, such as "more money," or "a bigger office." Obviously, however, in most situations you simply won't be able to reward your audience with tangible prizes. You cannot, for example, offer your boss money for accepting your proposal, offer your customers free products, or offer your subordinates free vacations.

One helpful set of theories in our search for effective rewards is Maslow's needs hierarchy and Herzberg's related research. As you can see from Figure 4.1, both Maslow and Herzberg have identified two sets of

FIGURE 4.1

Appeal to their growth needs.

Maslow's Needs Hierarchy		Herzberg's Research
Personal Growth	**Growth Needs**	Work itself (achievement)
Self-esteem		Advancement (recognition)
Group affiliation		Working relationships
Safety	**Deficiency Needs**	Working conditions
Survival		Safety

needs that motivate people: *deficiency needs* and *growth needs*.[3] Deficiency needs are needs without which we cannot survive—such as food, water, sleep, and shelter. Growth needs, on the other hand, are needs that enhance our lives—such as affiliation, esteem, accomplishment, and advancement. As you can also see in Figure 4.1, Maslow's and Herzberg's sets of needs roughly parallel each other: both sets of deficiency factors have to do with survival and safety; group affiliation is similar to working relationships, self-esteem to recognition, and personal growth to achievement.

At first glance, you might guess that **deficiency needs** are the most basic needs, and therefore the ones to appeal to most effectively. Not so. For one thing, in most business communication they simply do not apply. You cannot say, for example, "If you aren't persuaded by this memo or letter, I'll kill you!" Also, Herzberg's business research shows that deficiency needs seldom motivate people. Security, physical needs, and even working conditions might be perfect, but this alone won't motivate people. They need things like good relationships and recognition. In fact, you can probably think of many situations, especially in the high-tech industry, in which people are extremely motivated despite knowing their jobs are insecure and despite working in dirty cubbyholes—because they feel such a high sense of mission and achievement.

Herzberg's research, then, shows that the **growth needs** are the positive motivators. He cites pride in achievement, recognition by others, enjoyment of the work itself, and responsibility as important persuasion factors. Herzberg's findings have been extended by much subsequent research. Weger, for example, found that money was not the most important motivator for supervisors: recognition, achievement, and interpersonal relations were all more important.[4] As another example, a research team from Columbia recently found that salary and other status symbols were not rewarding to computer professionals; the opportunity to learn new skills was far more important to them.[5]

What all this research bodes for business communication is this: if you want to motivate someone with rewards, consider the extraordinary

---

[3]See R. Maddox, "The Relation between Maslow's Need Hierarchy and Herzberg's Research," cited in M. Weisbord, "Organizational Diagnosis: Six Places to Look for Trouble with or without a Theory," *Group and Organization Studies*, 4 (December 1976), pp. 430–47. The growth and deficiency models, of course, are based on the old classics: A. Maslow, *Motivation and Personality* (New York: Harper & Row, Pub., 1970); and F. Herzberg, *Work and the Nature of Man* [sic] (Cleveland: World, 1968).

[4]J. Weger, *Motivating Supervisors* (New York: American Management Association, 1971), pp. 53–54.

[5]E. K. Warren, L. Roth, and M. Devanna, "Motivating the Computer Professional," *Faculty R&D*, a publication of the Columbia Business School (Spring 1984), p. 8.

persuasive power of the growth needs. For example, if you are trying to get people to work together to devise a new plan, you might appeal to their esteem or recognition needs by pointing out how much you value their suggestions; if you are writing a report, you might appeal to their affiliation or relationship needs by pointing out the pride they may take in the accomplishments of the division as a whole. Stress, as much as possible, how your message ties into your audience's growth needs.

Use people's need for balance.

Using growth needs can be even more effective if you couple the ideas underlying them with balance theory.[6] According to proponents of this theory: (1) people prefer a state of psychological balance (called *consistency*, or *equilibrium*, or *freedom from anxiety*); (2) when they hear ideas conflicting with what they already believe, people lose that state of balance and feel anxiety; and (3) when they feel anxiety, people attempt to restore their sense of balance.

Although I assume everyone can agree with the first point—that people prefer to feel balanced and free of anxiety—the second and third points may need some illustration. How does that second step occur? How do people lose their sense of balance? They do so when confronted with information that conflicts with what they currently believe. For example, they think they are good writers and you tell them their sentences are unclear; they think they did a great job on an oral presentation and you tell them their visual aids are incomprehensible; they think they're helpful and you tell them they're no longer wanted on a certain committee; they think they're doing a good job in their sales region and you tell them they're among the worst performers. Notice that in these examples, the new information conflicts with important beliefs (such as those we saw in the growth and deficiency models—esteem, achievements and so forth). If, on the other hand, people hear conflicting new information that doesn't threaten their self-concept or belief system—if they learn, for example, that Reno is farther west than Los Angeles, or that Minnesota is farther north than Maine—they probably will not feel anxious.

The third step, according to this theory, is restoring equilibrium. You should be aware that your audience may do so in any one of three

---

[6]Balance theory goes by different titles: Festinger calls it *consonance and dissonance*, Osgood *congruity and incongruity*, Abelson and Rosenberg *consistency*, and Heider *balance and imbalance*. Once again, for our purposes it's not important what you call the theory, but how you use it. For more information on balance theory, see any standard textbook on social psychology.

ways. First, they may resist or deny the new information. Be aware that in cases where the new information conflicts with people's important and well-established beliefs, they are likely to resist your attempts at persuasion. As one psychologist says: "As people move through life they build up a wardrobe of ideas and points of view. These ideas are comfortable. They fit well. They suit the taste of the individual and he feels at ease with them. Like an old shoe, they have become shaped to his contour. . . . He's reluctant to discard any of these ideas for something new. When he tries on new ideas they feel awkward. They're not cut quite right for him. He misses the security of the old ideas."[7] A persuasion expert concurs: "The more central the belief, the more resistant individuals will be to change the belief."[8] A second possible audience reaction is to devalue the information, thinking something along these lines: "He has no right to give me advice"; or "She must be out to get me, so I don't need to listen to what she says"; or "They obviously don't know the facts, so I just don't believe what they have to say." Finally, if you have been successful, your audience will neither *resist* nor *devalue* the new idea; instead they will *accept* it and establish a new equilibrium.

How can you use people's need for balance to get them to accept your idea? One way is to emphasize an anxiety or a problem they have that is causing them "imbalance," then offer a solution that will make them feel balanced. For example, say you are trying to persuade your boss, who is dead set against staff meetings, to hold them. You might emphasize the anxiety ("Department morale is low; turnover is high; absenteeism is increasing"), and then provide balance by solving the problem ("Therefore, we should hold weekly staff meetings").

What can you do if you are trying to convince people to do something that conflicts with their current beliefs—that is, something that will cause them "imbalance"? In these situations, tie the potentially "unbalancing" information to their needs. For example, if you are trying to persuade members of the budget committee to purchase new equipment for your office, and you know their basic state of mind is cutting back, not increasing spending, tie your request to what is important to them: increased productivity, cost savings, perhaps even a time savings for the committee.

A third application of balance theory involves encouraging active participation. Think of situations in which you have seen this principle work: the more people get involved with social, religious, or political groups, the more they tend to agree with these groups' ideals—to bring

---

[7]J. Nirenberg, *Getting Through to People* (Englewood Cliffs, N.J.: Prentice-Hall, 1963), p. 114.

[8]Bettinghaus, p. 24.

their beliefs into balance with their actions. Sometimes, if you can get people participating (in other words, change their behavior first), they will seek balance by convincing themselves they are participating in something worthwhile (in other words, change their minds second). In business communication, for example, if you wanted to persuade a customer to buy a home computer, you might encourage him to get involved with using it. As another example, if you wanted to persuade an employee to cut utility costs, you might invite her to join the Energy Awareness Committee.

A final application of balance theory is to concentrate on key features. Anyone with sales training will recognize this one. If people are sold on two or three key features of your proposal, they will tend to sell themselves on the other features as well, to bring their perceptions into balance. Therefore, consider presenting key points with which your audience will agree before you throw the whole idea at them.

In summary, don't underestimate people's need for balance. Beware of how this need may block your good ideas; consider using balance-theory techniques to improve your persuasiveness.

Perform a cost/benefit analysis.

Another way of thinking about what motivates people is to apply economic ideas to psychology. Just like money, goods, and services, behavior can be offered for exchange. The communicator (like a seller) and the audience (like a buyer) take into account both the cost and the benefit of the behavior. Therefore, a strong benefit will motivate your audience, and a high cost may have the opposite effect. In essence, the communicator performs a *cost/benefit* analysis.[9]

For example, imagine you have a great plan for a new advertising brochure. The benefit seems obvious to you: your company will sell more of its product. The costs, however, might include time and money to print the new brochure, the waste throwing away all the old brochures, hurting the feelings of the person who designed the old brochure, and additional time and bother for your boss even to consider the idea when the old brochure has seemed to work well enough—not to mention simple inertia.

As another example, imagine you want a new personal-computer

---

[9]What I call *cost/benefit* analysis, theorists call *social exchange* theory. For more information on social exchange theory, see J. Chadwick Jones, *Social Exchange Theory: Its Structure and Influence in Social Psychology* (New York: Academic Press, 1976).

system for your work group. Again, although the benefit of increased productivity seems obvious, what are some of the workers' costs? Fear of the unknown, time and effort to change and learn a new system, and perhaps even fear that they might be rendered obsolete and lose their jobs.

Using this approach, you might try the following three tactics to increase your persuasiveness. (1) Analyze both the costs and the benefits of the idea itself. Many of us tend to look only at the potential benefits without thinking of the potential disadvantages. Perhaps you should not even send the message. (2) Analyze both the costs and the benefits for your audience. Again, many times we see just the potential rewards for ourselves without thinking about the potential costs for our readers or listeners. (3) Specify the benefits your audience will gain. Too often, we assume people will see the benefits, when we should make a conscious effort to emphasize what's in it for them.

Naturally, people are not as simple as the numbers in a financial cost/benefit analysis. You should not assume everyone will act the same way when confronted by the same situation. People will perceive costs differently: some people are more likely to take risks; loyalty, timing, fear, or tradition may influence some people to act against what might seem to be in their best interest.

Therefore, in addition to considering the techniques we've examined so far (all of which suggest ways to motivate people in general), effective communicators must take into account persuasion techniques that might apply to their individual audience members specifically. The next section, on character traits, offers some suggestions for doing just that.

Be sensitive
to character traits.

We seem to be a nation of amateur psychologists. We take character quizzes in the Sunday papers; surveys interpret why people vote, dance, or buy what they do; various magazines are devoted to analyzing behavior. We use psychological terms often and casually: "Denise, try to have an open mind on this subject," "Jeff has such an inferiority complex," "What an extrovert Brad is!"

Making these generalizations about ourselves or other people can be dangerous. We infer character traits through behavior we perceive, and we may either perceive or infer incorrectly. Worse yet, we may then categorize people based on an incorrect inference. It may be more helpful, then, to equate character with *traits*, not with *people*. In other words, don't pigeonhole people into one category; everybody's character is more complex than one simple trait.

Given those cautions, though, remember that effective communication is partially based on what will motivate and persuade your individual reader or listener. For example, you would certainly want to write or speak differently to a backslapping sales manager than you would to a methodical accountant. (Or, to avoid the kind of stereotyping I just cautioned you against, perhaps I should say a backslapping accountant and a methodical sales manager.)

The point is that different people are convinced by different things. And, just as engineers use electrical theory to predict how machines work, communicators must use psychological theory to predict how people work. Effective communicators analyze what will motivate the people with whom they are communicating.

There are many ways to go about this analysis.[10] Instead of discussing all the possible personality theories, it would be more useful, I think, to present a model to help you analyze the kinds of character traits you will probably have to deal with most often in business. More important, I'll suggest how you can appeal to each of these types and be most persuasive. Keep in mind, though, that everyone displays each of these traits at times, and the traits may change for any specific person with the situation.

Figure 4.2 shows the Four C's Model—one way to analyze the character traits of the people with whom you will be working in business. These typical business character traits are described along two dimensions. The first dimension involves people who are interested in changing the status quo (either to achieve results or to accomplish a "dream") versus those who believe in keeping things the way they are now (either through maintaining current procedures or through maintaining their group affiliation). The second dimension involves people who tend to work alone (either carefully or competitively) versus people who tend to work in a group (either toward change or toward maintaining the status quo).

To explain each of the Four C's, let's imagine a typical business communication situation. You have been asked to write a report that includes research on what's been done in the past, and recommendations about what to do in the future. Let's say you have finished your research: you know what has been done and you have some ideas about the future. You sit down to write. Naturally, since you took a course in business

---

[10]According to Freud, for example, people are driven by their pleasure principle (the *id*), their reality principle (the *ego*), and their conscience (the *superego*). His notions have been more recently popularized as the internal *child, adult,* and *parent.* Another theorist, Jung, classified people as *introverts* and *extroverts.* And one psychologist even categorized people by body type: even-tempered, fat *endomorphs*; vigorous, athletic *mesomorphs*; and high-strung, skinny *ectomorphs*.

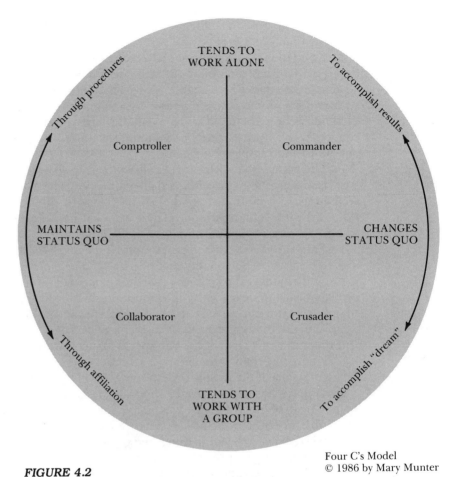

FIGURE 4.2

Four C's Model
© 1986 by Mary Munter

The Four C's Model: Business personality traits

communication, you analyze your audience first. Here are four different cases illustrating how you might report exactly the same information to each of four bosses.

AUDIENCE 1: Your boss is what you would call "bureaucratic," preferring to work alone and carefully. She is very consistent, and you've noticed she likes facts and statistics. She is not a "mover and a shaker"; in fact, she is slow to decide and doesn't seem to like change. According to Figure 4.2, what character type is she? *The comptroller.* To motivate her, write in a matter-of-fact tone. Incorporate a good deal of information, including methods and data. Instead of just stating one conclusion, offer various options and your conclusion from among them. Emphasize tradition, process, and system.

AUDIENCE 2: Your boss is enthusiastic, idealistic, a "cheerleader" almost. He is creative and is eager to change things based on his ideals. Because of his great enthusiasms, he is sometimes prejudiced. What character type is he in Figure 4.2? *The crusader.* To persuade a crusader, adopt an enthusiastic and informative tone. Emphasize how your ideas tie to his ideals or "dreams." Because he is motivated by ideas, you might include many points of view and a lot of information. Remember, crusaders will be persuaded by the value of the idea itself.

AUDIENCE 3: You hate to use such a cliché, but you think of your boss as a real "people person." He almost always works as part of a team. He does not like to make decisions to change things, and will avoid conflict and risk. What character type is he in Figure 4.2? *The collaborator.* To persuade a collaborator, adopt a trusting and nonthreatening tone. As you would for the crusader, you might include various options, but since the collaborator is less interested in ideas themselves, you would avoid long, detailed, enthusiastic explanations. You might use testimonies from people you know he respects, or back up your argument with statements from the organizational policies and goals you know he agrees with.

AUDIENCE 4: Your boss is the quintessential "business person." She likes action and results, and bases decisions for change on results, not ideals. She is decisive and efficient—sometimes, alas, even domineering. In Figure 4.2? She's *the commander.* To persuade her, adopt an efficient and results-oriented tone. Here you might prefer a short summary format, stating your own conclusions and recommendations clearly. Since commanders are motivated by results and power, emphasize the outcome for the company as well as "what's in it for them."

Most students recognize these character types. Perhaps you've dealt with a commander editor on your school newspaper, or a crusader art-history teacher, or a collaborator coach, or a comptroller secretary.

Many students imagine, however, that people in business will be commanders. Although CEOs tend to be commanders or crusaders, any one of the traits might be exhibited by your immediate supervisor, your subordinate, or someone else with whom you must work closely. So don't be surprised when your brilliant ideas seem blocked by someone saying: "That's not the way we do things here," (comptroller) or "Well, I can't really decide until I find out where Mary Lou stands on that issue," (collaborator) or "What's the bottom line on that?" (commander). In fact,

TABLE 4.2
The four C's model for business personality traits

	Comptroller	Commander	Crusader	Collaborator
Likes	Facts and systems	Action and results	Ideas and information	People and group affiliation
Wants	Status quo based on procedures	Change based on results	Change based on ideals	Status quo based on affiliation
Strengths	Consistency Due process	Decisiveness Efficiency	Creativity Inspiration	Teamwork Loyalty
Weaknesses	Bureaucratic Territorial	Domineering Power-hungry	Indecisive Prejudiced	High need for approval Avoids conflict and risk
Work Style	Alone and careful	Alone and competitive	With group and dominant	With group and passive
Use this tone:	Accurate and factual	Efficient and results-oriented	Enthusiastic and informative	Trusting and nonthreatening
Stress:	Organizational tradition Process and system Task well done	Their achievement Results for company Power	Their ideals Information Value of ideas	People they respect Organizational goals

the constant interaction among these different personality types allows organizations to succeed: organizations need both tradition and change. It's your job, then, as a communicator, to figure out which of these types you are writing or speaking to—if you want to be persuasive. Table 4.2 summarizes the Four C's model and its communication implications.

In summary, you have many tools to motivate the people in your audience. As a first step, of course, you must analyze who they are and what they feel and know about you and your topic. Based on that analysis, choose one or more of the various techniques we have discussed in this chapter: (1) Use threats and punishments cautiously, for the reasons we discussed; instead, try the kinds of rewards we examined. (2) Stress how your message contributes to their growth needs. (3) Use people's need for balance by solving their problems, tying your idea to their needs, getting them to participate, or selling them on key features of your proposal. (4) Try a cost/benefit analysis from your audience's point of view; then, stress their benefits. (5) Be sensitive to their character traits and vary what you say accordingly, as outlined in Table 4.2.

REVIEW QUESTIONS
To check your understanding

1. What three groups of people should you include in a business audience analysis?
2. Why should you analyze what your audience knows? What they feel?
3. List at least four reasons why threats and punishment may not work.
4. List the four characteristics of an effective reward.
5. What are growth needs?
6. Why can balance needs block communication?
7. What four ways can you use balance needs to increase your persuasiveness?
8. Explain three tactics for using a cost/benefit analysis to communicate effectively.
9. Why should you take character traits into account in motivating your audience?
10. What are the Four C's of character traits?

APPLICATION QUESTIONS
To apply your knowledge

1. Find and turn in a copy of a magazine or newspaper advertisement that appeals to a secondary audience as well as a primary audience. What is the relation of the two groups? Why does the ad not appeal merely to the primary audience?

2. Is the key decision maker always a member of the primary audience? Describe a business situation in which he or she is a member of the secondary audience.

3. Assume you have been asked to speak before a group you know nothing about. How would you go about learning what your audience knows and feels? What sources of information would you use and what sort of questions would you ask?

4. Give an example of a business situation in which you feel it would be appropriate to use threats or punishment. Give an example in which rewards would be more appropriate.

5. What kind of rewards might you use in boosting office morale? In carrying out an advertisement campaign? Give specific examples and explain why they would achieve your objective more effectively than threats.

6. Analyze your own growth needs as a student of business communication. If you were in your teacher's position, how would you use these growth needs to help your class progress?

7. Why can an understanding of people's growth needs aid you in restoring their equilibrium when their sense of balance is threatened? In your answer, cite a specific example in which fulfilled growth needs can help counteract the anxiety your message may cause.

8. Why can a cost/benefit analysis be useful? Give two examples from your own experience that show how such an analysis persuaded you to take a certain course of action.

9. Assume you are marketing a new type of personal calculator. Describe the type of appeal you would make to each of the four C's.

10. What type of verbal reward do you think would appeal to each of the four C's?

CASES
To practice what you learned

1. You work for a toy manufacturer in the publicity department. Your newest product is a minicomputer designed exclusively for children. The computer comes equipped with educational programs designed to help children learn basic mathematics, spelling, and grammar. Also included are a computer-games package and a graphics option. The computer features a colorful console, an easy-to-read instruction pamphlet narrated by the magic "mouse" Marvin, a washable surface, and a fifty-dollar rebate offer. Write an advertisement that will appeal to the primary audience (children) and the secondary audience (their parents).

2. You work for a bank and have been asked to speak before the Greater Popperville Athletic Association. The topic of your lecture is IRAs. You know that your audience is united by a common interest in sports, and in order to persuade its members of the importance of early planning for retirement, you want to draw on that interest to make your point. How would you use the language of your audience to discuss your topic, using the various techniques of motivation?

3. You have recently taken over supervising a small accounting department whose former head left things in a dismal state of disarray. Job efficiency is down: your employees are hopelessly behind in their monthly accounts, causing some friction with other departments of the company. Personal tensions are also obvious in the office, and beyond that, you must contend with the employees' lack of attention to the appearance of the office and the kitchen facilities. Using the motivating techniques you have learned in this chapter, outline the ideas you would write or say to them.

4. You must mediate between your company, a small newspaper publisher, and the lithographers' union, to which most of the employees belong. At issue is the new equipment soon to be installed—a computerized typesetting system that will render many of the union members' existing jobs obsolete. Although your company has pledged to retrain all employees and, as a goodwill gesture, give all a modest raise, the union remains suspicious of the change and unrest threatens. In writing or speaking to the union, how would you satisfy their need for balance, and what sort of cost/benefit analysis would you provide in order to win their cooperation?

5. You have been asked to draw up a list of recommendations for streamlining the expenditure-approval process in your organization. Until now, five signatures have been needed on every expenditure over $500, a requirement you feel is responsible for the lengthy delays in getting checks issued and the poor relationship with creditors that has resulted. You are in favor of requiring three signatures on every expenditure over $1000. Outline what you would write to your boss, a copy of which would go to the company president. Your boss exhibits "comptroller" character traits, and the president is a "crusader."

5

The Message:
Structure

Thinking Versus Structuring

Thinking
Be aware of your assumptions. • *Draw valid conclusions.*
• *Avoid logical defects.*

Structuring
Provide a hierarchy for your ideas. • *Put your ideas in order.*

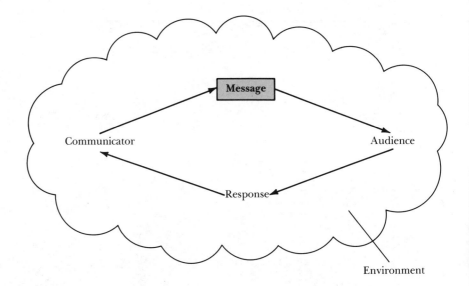

Communicator

Message

Audience

Response

Environment

THE last chapter emphasized becoming *audience-centered*, or using the *you* approach by analyzing and motivating your readers or listeners. This chapter continues with the concept of being audience-centered, but now we will look at how to structure *what* you write or say to make it appropriate, useful, and persuasive for your audience.

Thinking Versus Structuring

In business communication, too many people simply write or speak in the order that ideas occur to them—not in the order that would be most persuasive. Thinking and structuring a communication are two different processes. When you think, naturally, all different kinds of ideas occur to you—some good, some bad, some complete, some fragmented. The result of the thinking process is your conclusion. When you communicate, on the other hand, you don't want your audience to have to wade through all the false starts and disjointed ideas you went through; instead, you want to structure your ideas to make your conclusions clear.

As a simple example, imagine that you got this note from the moderator of a student committee on which you were serving:

> We have to reserve the rooms for the Speakers Series through Office Services at least two weeks in advance. I'm worried about getting all the speakers on the agenda by then. We also need to print up posters announcing who's speaking. Will you take care of these arrangements? Don't forget that the poster should include the room numbers, too.

How much easier even this simple example would be if the writer had structured the message for you, instead of just writing as he or she thought up ideas. For instance:

> I just wanted to remind you about the three arrangements you agreed to handle for the Speakers Series:
> 1. Invite the speakers and set the time.
> 2. Reserve the rooms by November 15.
> 3. Print up the posters (including the names of the speakers, the times, and the room numbers) for distribution by December 1.

The same kind of message structure—or lack of message structure—occurs in business communication. Imagine you got this memo or phone call from an employee:

> Those delivery people from ABC Trucking are making life miserable for us. They've been at least two hours late every day this week. We can't package the materials on time with this kind of service. Besides, most of the packagers are on early shift, and once they've gone, some of the delivered material actually spoils. I think we better do something because we're losing 15 percent of the material. Maybe we should call the manager at ABC Trucking. But I've called over there so many times, I think it's useless. I've heard all the reasons, and I honestly think they're stuck with what has now become a regular 2:00 P.M. delivery time. We might change our packagers' shifts, but we'd have to have a meeting and explain the situation because they're not necessarily going to like the change.

Again, this message would have been more likely to get results if it had been structured properly. For example:

> I recommend we call a meeting to discuss the possibility of changing the packagers' shift hours. ABC Trucking is consistently delivering at 2:00, instead of noon, as they used to, which is creating a spoilage loss of 15 percent. To avoid that loss, we need to change our schedule.

The process of thinking through ideas, then, is different from the process of structuring those ideas. When you think, you work through a hodgepodge of data. Being disorganized during this stage is perfectly natural. When you communicate, however, you don't simply present that hodgepodge of data. Instead, you stress your conclusion and order your data.

Figure 5.1 is a simplified illustration of this difference between thinking and structuring. Of course, the two steps shown in that figure are difficult and complicated, as the rest of the chapter will show. This

FIGURE 5.1

Thinking versus structuring

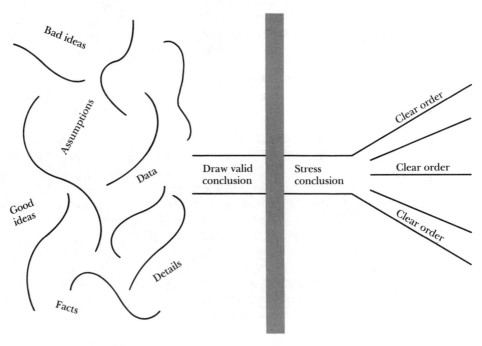

chapter, then, will show you how to go through these two steps of, first, thinking logically and, second, structuring your message effectively.

Thinking

The thinking process may be compared to an assembly line. Your assumptions, which form the basis for your thinking, are like assumptions about what will be produced: we will manufacture cars; we will manufacture toothbrushes; we will manufacture fuzzy wallpaper. You can see how a change in assumptions means you must change the entire assembly line. The facts you have gathered are like the raw materials: we have steel; we have plastic; we have wood. You also can see how a change in available facts must influence what it is you can "manufacture," or think. Drawing valid conclusions is like setting up the assembly line correctly. You wouldn't want it to be upside-down or on the ceiling, just like you wouldn't want to think incorrectly. Finally, avoiding logical defects is like having the assembly line workers watch for defective products and toss them off the line.

As you are thinking, then, remember to: (1) be aware of your assumptions ("What should you be manufacturing?"); (2) draw valid conclusions ("Construct that conveyor belt properly"); and (3) avoid logical defects ("Get rid of defective products"). This section will show you some techniques for using logic and reasoning to accomplish these three steps.

Be aware of your assumptions.

Assumptions are the basis for all the rest of your thinking. You assume the sun will rise tomorrow, so you plan your day; you assume your car will start, so you plan a trip. You can imagine how differently you would feel if these assumptions changed: if you knew this were your last day on earth or that your car had been blown up, you would change the entire basis of your thinking.

Similarly, in business communication you make assumptions. Here are three cases. Case 1: "This program will increase our profits" assumes you want to make a profit. Case 2: "I better finish this report tonight or I'll get fired" assumes you want to keep your job. Case 3: "In this letter, I'm going to try to calm down this irate customer" assumes that you don't want your customers to be angry. These assumptions seem obvious and uncontroversial at first glance. Yet only when you are aware of them can you question them. In case 1, the assumption that you want to make profits may not hold true in a situation where long-term community relations are more important than short-term profits. In case 2, you may have legal or moral reasons why you want to quit your job. In case 3, you may have to ignore one angry customer for the sake of twenty-five happy customers who need your attention first.

Here are three more examples of business statements. Try to figure out their assumptions. (1) "Consolidating our Chicago plant is the essential first step toward streamlining production." The assumption is that you want to streamline production; aware of that, you can question the assumption, in which case you might conclude "Yes, we want to streamline production," or "No, that is not our main concern right now." (2) "We need to hire two new sales reps to expand our division." The assumption is that you want to expand the division. (3) "An increase in the advertising budget is worthwhile because this will be such an effective campaign" assumes you need an effective campaign right now. In any situation, awareness of your assumptions allows you to question them.

Besides being able to question them, you will gain a second benefit from knowing your assumptions: later on, when you communicate your ideas, you can decide whether to state those assumptions explicitly or not. "Yes, streamlining production is a stated department goal, so I'll remind my audience of that"; "No, expanding our division is not an agreed-upon policy. I'll have to prove my assumption"; or "My audience clearly disagrees with the assumption that we need a new advertising campaign. Either I'll have to convince them, or I should save this idea for later."

Draw valid conclusions.

Assumptions and facts are what you start out with when you're thinking; conclusions are what you end up with. If you assume it will be sunny tomorrow, you may conclude, "I'll go to the beach and sit in the sun." If you observe various facts (the sky is cloudy; the wind is blowing; the temperature is dropping), you may conclude, "I won't go to the beach because a rainstorm is coming." How do you draw conclusions? Only two valid methods exist: deduction (based on an assumption, as in the sunny-day example) or induction (based on facts, as in the rainy-day example).

Deduction means starting with a main principle or assumption, applying it to a specific case, and drawing a conclusion. You start with a main principle, such as "Business communication is important"; apply a specific case, such as "Writing is a part of business communication"; and come up with a conclusion, "Therefore, writing is important." As you can see, in deduction it's crucial that your main principle be correct. If you started with an incorrect main principle, such as "Accounting is unimportant in business," then you'd have to conclude (logically, but not truthfully), "Balance sheets are unimportant."

Here are two on-the-job examples of deduction. "Manufacturing problem X will result in decreased production" (main principle); "Plant Y exhibits manufacturing problem X" (applied specific case); "Therefore, plant Y will suffer from decreased production." Another example: "Storing certain parts in temperatures over fifteen degrees will ruin them" (main principle); "Someone left these parts out overnight at twenty degrees" (applied specific case); "Therefore, these parts must be ruined."

Let me emphasize that all these examples show how you *think*, not how you communicate. If you were communicating, you would show the results of your deduction: "Plant Y will suffer from decreased production because of manufacturing problem X" or "These parts are ruined because they were left out overnight at twenty degrees."

The only other valid way to draw conclusions is by **induction**. Induction means starting with specifics and generalizing to a main principle. You start with a series of specifics, such as "I'll be spending a lot of time in business participating in meetings," "I'll be spending a lot of time writing letters," "I'll be spending a lot of time talking on the telephone," and "I'll be spending a lot of time writing memos to people within the organization," then draw a generalization: "Therefore, I'll be spending a lot of time communicating."

In induction, it's crucial that your specifics be reliable, relevant, and representative. Say you started with specifics such as these: "Joe says he never has to balance books in his job"; "Carole says she can get people to do the accounting she needs done in her job." You might conclude, "Therefore, I'm not going to bother to study accounting." These specifics may not be reliable: Joe and Carole may not be reliable sources of information. The specific facts may not be relevant: Joe's and Carole's jobs may be very different from what yours will be. And these specifics may not be representative: if you asked 300 business people whether they used accounting techniques in their jobs, Joe and Carole might be the only two who would say "No."

To take a business example of inductive reasoning, you might think: "We can distribute product X through existing channels"; "We can capitalize on name-brand recognition for product X"; "We can promote product X in conjunction with the Olympics." "Therefore, we can readily market product X." Again, this is how you might *think*, not communicate. When you communicate that idea, you would state: "We can market product X successfully because we can (1) distribute it through existing channels, (2) capitalize on name-brand recognition, and (3) promote it in conjunction with the Olympics.

Although induction and deduction are two different (and opposite) procedures, in practice we often combine them. We cannot gather specifics without some organizing principle; we cannot choose relevant main principles without some knowledge of specific problems or issues. The point is not that you must separate your thinking into either deduction or induction, but that you must use valid reasoning as you think through your ideas.

Avoid logical defects.

To return to the assembly-line analogy for thinking, imagine your idea is like a product moving down the conveyor belt. Your correct deductive or inductive reasoning means the belt is correctly built and operating. As your idea moves along, however, it can go wrong in many ways. Watch for and get rid of these defects in thinking, which are sometimes called *logical fallacies*. You can avoid these defects by remembering three main rules.

First, don't jump too fast to conclusions. (1) One defect resulting from a breach of this rule is called *hasty generalization*, or jumping to a conclusion based on too little evidence. For example, you might think: "Marketing strategy X increased sales 13 percent in Atlanta supermarkets. Let's try that same strategy in Fairbanks." In this case, it may have been hasty to jump from one example (in Atlanta) to a generalization about all others (such as Fairbanks). The situations may be completely different. As another example: "The woman we hired in the Engineering Department quit, so let's stick to hiring men." Again, that thought shows a hasty jump from one example to a huge generalization. (2) Another kind of jump is called drawing *false causes*. This happens when you jump to the conclusion that event 1 caused event 2 simply because event 1 preceded event 2. "The new sales director is fabulous. Sales increased 42 percent as soon as we hired him." In this example, the thinker does not examine other possible causes for increased sales—such as the economy, advertising campaigns, or even the weather. Connecting *unrelated ideas* (sometimes called a *non sequitur*, a Latin expression that means "does not follow") involves using causal terms—such as *therefore, because, thus,* or *so*—to make a leap between statements having no causal connection. "Ms. Jaspers works for an international firm, so I'm sure she can't be prejudiced against foreigners." This thought leaps to the implication that a prejudiced person cannot possibly hold an international job.

Second, don't hide: don't hide your ideas themselves and don't hide behind illogical false ideas. (1) Avoid hiding *questionable assumptions*. For example, "We are marketing product X in trade journals because we marketed product Y in trade journals." This conclusion is based on the hidden questionable assumption that you should market product X *exactly* the same way you marketed product Y. (2) Avoid hiding the main point by *skirting the issue*. Skirting the issue means evading the main point by focusing on a minor point. "The overseas workers allege that the managers require them to work in unsafe weather conditions. Perhaps we should increase their pay to mollify them." This example ignores issues of management misconduct and the workers' allegations by focusing on pay as a means of silencing the protest. (3) Avoid hiding from a *false analogy*. False analogies assume that because something is like something else in some way, the two must be alike in other ways. "The more floors in a skyscraper, the more likely it is to be hit by lightening. Similarly, the more hierarchical levels in an organization, the more likely that organization is to be struck down by economic disaster." This statement extends the height analogy confusingly, and blurs the distinctions between natural and economic disasters. (4) Avoid hiding behind exaggerations, or *exaggerating the point*. This defect occurs when you argue by extending an idea to such extremes that it appears ridiculous. "Mr. Palmer suggests that we try to recapture market share by lowering our price seventeen cents per unit. By that reasoning, we might as well go for a 100 percent market share and start giving products away. Or perhaps he'd like us to pay people to buy them." This argument ignores the possible validity of the seventeen-cent price decrease by extending the idea of price reduction absurdly. (5) Avoid hiding behind *irrelevant attacks* (on the person, not the idea) or *popular appeals* (to a general truism instead of the specific case). An example of an irrelevant attack on a person might be: "Anne mishandled the budget last year, so she can't be expected to run that meeting well." Anne's accounting ability has nothing to do with her ability to run a meeting. An example of a popular appeal: "It's un-American to buy that product." This appeal to patriotism ignores the specifications of the product.

Finally, don't oversimplify. (1) Avoid the *either/or defect*. This occurs when you set up two alternatives and do not allow any others. For example, "We must open a new plant by spring or we will go bankrupt" ignores other possible alternatives to bankruptcy. "If you don't like your boss, then quit!" ignores other alternatives, such as changing the situation. (2) Avoid the *catchall explanation*. This oversimplification occurs when you isolate one factor and treat it as if it were the sole cause. "The Edsel failed because consumers weren't ready for a push-button gear shift." This idea ignores other possible reasons or combinations of reasons for the Edsel's failure.

Structuring

Thinking and structuring, as I stated at the beginning of the chapter, are two different processes. So far, we have been discussing thinking. Thinking is what goes on in your head. Communicating is getting your ideas into someone else's head: you communicate by providing an *audience-based* or a *you*-approach *structure*. In the words of *Harvard Business Review* editor David Ewing: "One of the most common misconceptions is that the reader wants a blow-by-blow account of how the writer came to his or her conclusions. When you make this error, . . . you lead off with what you saw and heard in the first phase, and then you describe what the next series of tests or interviews produced, then you give the highlights of what you learned in the next phase, and sooner or later you come to your conclusions or recommendations."[1] (Ewing's ideas about writing, as well as those of the other experts quoted in this chapter, apply equally well to speaking.)

The rest of this chapter deals with how to come up with an effective structure instead of just mirroring your thought process. Specifically, an effective structure is based on: (1) providing a hierarchy of ideas for your audience, and (2) choosing the appropriate order for those ideas.

Provide a hierarchy for your ideas.

An effective structure is based on your providing a hierarchy of ideas for your audience—in other words, dividing ideas into groups and differentiating among the levels of those groups. To show what I mean by a hierarchy, I shall use two relatively simple analogies: a business organization chart and a family tree. At the end of the chapter, I'll summarize with a more difficult business communication example.

To see what happens when you do not provide a hierarchy of ideas, look at the examples in Figure 5.2. Imagine trying to run the organization in Figure 5.2 with no hierarchy: the president could not possibly supervise all of those positions. Imagine trying to explain the family tree with no hierarchy: no one could possibly understand how the people are related to one another. And yet, this lack of hierarchy is exactly the way in which

---

[1] D. Ewing, *Writing for Results in Business, Government, the Sciences and the Professions*, 2nd ed. (New York: John Wiley, 1979), pp. 38–39. This is an excellent book on professional writing in general, and on persuasive writing in particular. I am indebted to it for the ideas both in this chapter and in Part II.

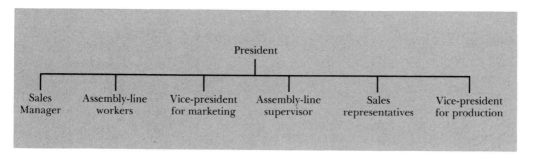

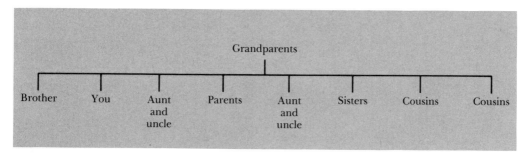

FIGURE 5.2

No hierarchy: Examples

ineffective communicators present their ideas. They simply list all their ideas in any order, without any attempt to show groups or levels.

Now, to see what I mean by providing a hierarchy, take a look at the examples in Figure 5.3. Just as the organizational chart and the family tree in Figure 5.3 are easier for you, as a reader, to comprehend, your ideas will be easier for your audience to comprehend if you establish some kind of hierarchy for your communication structure.

To provide a clear hierarchy, you need to: (1) stress your conclusion (or first-level idea), (2) divide your writing or speaking into main points (or second-level ideas), and (3) subdivide these into supporting points.

STRESS YOUR CONCLUSION (TOP-LEVEL IDEA): Your conclusion, of course, is the most important idea in your communication. It's the result of all your time, effort, analysis, and thinking. It's closely tied to your communication objective. (As we discussed in chapter 3, your communication objective is stated in this form: "As a result of this message, my audience will _____.") Sample conclusions might be: "follow this procedure," "buy this product," or "approve my recommendations."

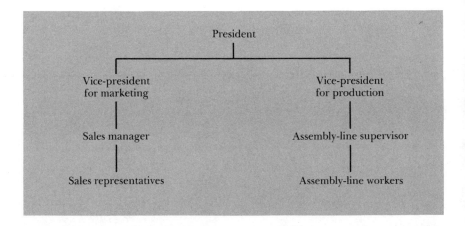

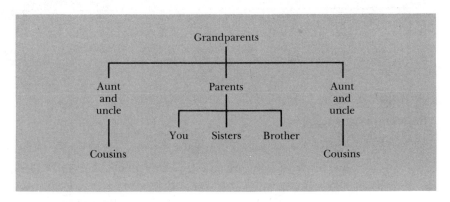

FIGURE 5.3

Clear hierarchy: Examples

Your conclusion, then, is your top-level idea, the general idea from which all the rest of your message stems. In our organization chart example, the conclusion would be represented by the president; the rest of the chart shows how everyone in the company relates to him or her. In the family tree example, the top-level idea or conclusion is represented by your grandparents: the rest of the chart shows how everyone in the family relates to them.

If your conclusion, then, is the top-level idea, how can you stress it in your message structure? To answer that question, consider the Audience Memory Curve:

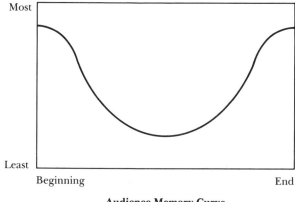

Audience Memory Curve

As its name implies, the Audience Memory Curve demonstrates what people in your audience are likely to remember. In any communication, they are likely to recall what you state at the beginning and at the end. The implication for stressing your conclusion is clear: stress it by stating it either at the beginning or at the end of your message. Never bury your conclusion in the middle. Buried conclusions are one of the most typical problems in business communication. If your conclusion is in the middle, your audience is likely to skip it, miss it, or—at best—have to work hard to find it. Later, when we discuss choosing an order for your ideas, I'll point out when to put your conclusion first and when to put it last. For now, just remember to stress your conclusion by placing it prominently: at the beginning or the end—not in the middle.

DIVIDE INTO SECOND-LEVEL POINTS: You want your conclusion to stand out the most prominently, so you state it first or last. Your next level of prominence is made up of your second-level points. If you think of your conclusion as the top-level idea, then the next level down is made up of your second-level ideas. In the organizational chart example, your second-level ideas are represented by the three vice-presidents. In the family tree example, your second-level ideas are represented by your parents' generation. In business communication, your second-level points would be the main division into which you divide your writing or speaking, such as "four steps in the procedure," "five reasons to buy this product," or "three recommendations for approval."

How can you figure out what your second-level ideas are? To quote David Ewing again: "You need to do the same thing that practically every good writer [or speaker] has done since the first cogent stone tablet was written by a caveperson: Step back mentally from the details and try to see the essence of the message."[2] Specifically, Ewing suggests three possible methods. First, imagine you meet your reader or listener on the street. He or she is in a great hurry, so you must explain your ideas within two minutes. What would you say? Second, imagine you had to send a telegram to your reader or listener. At some outrageous price per word, how would you encapsulate your main ideas to save money? Finally, try asking yourself: "What does my audience need to know most? If someone were to skim my writing or pay partial attention to my presentation, what is the absolute minimum he or she should learn?"

Another expert, Linda Flower, refers to this process of dividing into second-level ideas as "nutshelling and teaching your main ideas." She suggests: "In two or three sentences—in a nutshell—try to lay out the whole substance of your paper. Nutshelling practically forces you to distinguish major ideas from minor ones and to decide how those major ideas are related to one another. . . . Once you can express your idea in a nutshell to yourself, think about how you would *teach* those ideas to someone else. . . . Like nutshelling, trying to reach your ideas helps you form concepts so that your listener gets the *point*, not just a list of facts."[3]

SUBDIVIDE INTO LOWER-LEVEL POINTS: Your second-level ideas are, in turn, supported by your lower-level points. Most experts today agree that using visual charts—just like the company's organizational chart or your family tree—is a more effective way to subdivide your ideas than using traditional outlines.[4] Idea charts look like upside-down trees or pyramids; therefore, they have been termed *idea trees* or *idea pyramids*. Whatever you choose to call them, these sketches will help you organize your thoughts. Figure 5.4 shows some simple examples of idea charts.

When you put together an idea chart, you can get your ideas down in an informal way. Also, you can group your ideas by similar subject matter: "This is problem X; that is problem Y." "This is reason X; that is reason Y." "This is recommendation X; that is recommendation Y." Then, you

[2]Ibid., pp. 49–50.

[3]L. Flower, *Problem-Solving Strategies for Writing* (New York: Harcourt Brace Jovanovich, Inc., 1981), pp. 86–87. Professor Flower has contributed a great deal to our understanding of how to write more effectively; however, she suffers from an unfortunate propensity to use nonverbs, such as *nutshelling*.

[4]Two of the most influential writers on idea trees are Linda Flower and Barbara Minto. Flower's work is based on research she and her colleagues have conducted at Carnegie-Mellon University on how the writing process actually works. Minto's work is based on years of experience as a consultant in business writing. I am indebted to a book by each of them for my discussion of structuring in this chapter: L. Flower, *Problem-Solving Strategies for Writing*; and B. Minto, *The Pyramid Principle: Logic in Writing*, 2nd ed. (London: Minto International, 1978).

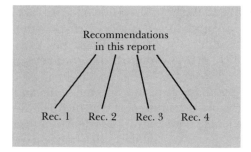

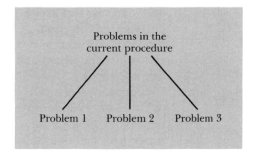

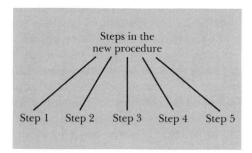

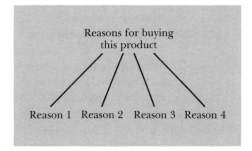

FIGURE 5.4

Sample idea charts

can develop key overarching concepts that summarize and label each grouping: "What I have here is a series of problems (reasons, recommendations)."

Idea charts offer you at least three advantages over traditional outlines. First, they let you see the whole picture and how the parts fit: they are more visual than an outline. They also allow you to change, add, or omit information that does not fit: they are more flexible than an outline. Finally, they can actually help you come up with ideas. As Flower says: "A traditional outline, written before you start, only arranges the facts and ideas you already know. An issue tree highlights missing links in your argument and helps you draw inferences and create new concepts."[5]

What should you keep in mind as you are sketching your idea chart?

First, make sure that any higher-level idea summarizes or generalizes about all the lower-level ideas branching out below it. In the organization chart example, the vice-president of marketing "summarizes" the entire marketing department; an assembly-line worker shouldn't be included

[5]Flower, *Problem-Solving Strategies for Writing*, p. 88.

below the marketing vice-president because he or she is not in the marketing department. In your family tree, your parents "summarize" you, your brothers, and your sisters, and therefore you belong below them. Your cousins, on the other hand, do not belong below your parents; they belong below their own.

Second, make sure all branches on the same level are the same kind of idea. For example, one level in the organization chart is made up of the same kind of idea, all vice-presidents; neither the president nor the supervisors belong at the vice-presidents' level. Similarly, in a family tree, everyone in your parents' generation belongs on the same level; neither your grandparents (one generation), nor you, your brothers, your sisters, or your cousins (another generation) belong at your parents' level. In business communication, instead of dealing with generations, you may be dealing with reasons, steps, problems, recommendations, or changes.[6]

Third, limit the number of branches on your upside-down tree. Your audience's short-term working memory—conscious attention—can handle only five to seven main points.[7] This means you should group together a maximum of five to seven main branches on any level. If you were communicating about the organization chart example, you would want to restrict yourself to the main branches, not overwhelm your audience with a list of every single employee in the firm. If you were communicating about your family tree, you would want to present only five to seven branches that your audience could comprehend, not list every ancestor you know of.

Put your ideas in order.

Once you have sketched your idea tree, you need to decide the order in which to present your supporting ideas. Again, to use the organizational structure example in Figure 5.3, should you discuss the marketing or the production department first? In the family tree example, should you discuss yourself, your sisters, or your brothers first?

To make these decisions, you must first ask yourself: "Am I trying to *explain* something or to *change* something?" As writing consultant Barbara Minto says (once again, her ideas on writing apply equally well to speaking): "It is useful to know that you can make only two kinds of statements in writing: those that tell the reader *about* something and those that tell the reader to *do* something."[8]

---

[6]Minto, *The Pyramid Principle*, bk. 1, pp. 12–13.

[7]Flower, *Problem-Solving Strategies for Writing*, p. 133.

[8]Minto, *The Pyramid Principle*, bk. 6, pp. 2–3.

FOR EXPLANATORY IDEAS: If you are writing or speaking in order to explain something, you shouldn't have much trouble deciding where to place your top-level idea. I can't imagine your explaining a process and waiting until the end to say "And so that's how you use the copying machine" or explaining a policy and waiting until the end to say "So that's our benefits package." Place your top-level idea first.

Once your top-level idea is placed first, how should you order the rest of your ideas? When you are explaining something, you may choose to order your ideas in any of three ways.

First, you can order by **time**. This is an effective ordering to use for historical background or for steps in a process. For example, if you were explaining a payroll procedure, you would order by time: (1) submit withdrawal forms a month before payday; (2) submit time reports two weeks before payday; (3) pick up paychecks on the first of the month.

Second, you can order by **components**. This order is the most useful if you are describing existing classifications, such as geographical or spatial divisions. For example, if you were reporting on profit analysis for divisions, you might order: (1) West Coast region, (2) Midwest region, and (3) East Coast region; if you were explaining the layout of your office building, you might order by describing what they would find on the: (1) first floor, (2) second floor, (3) third floor, and so on.

Finally, you might order by **importance**. Ordering by importance is more difficult than ordering by time or components. When you order by time, most people agree on the sequence. When you order by components, you are not implying any priorities (in the case of west to east, you're not implying that the West Coast is more important; in the case of first to third floors, you're not implying any floor is more important than any other). When you order by importance, however, you must make a value judgment. In these cases, you want to show priorities or a ranking of ideas. For example, you might analyze the causes for a mechanical breakdown: (1) most important cause, (2) second most important cause, and (3) third most important cause. As another example, you might analyze the problems in your current inventory system: (1) most important problem, (2) second most important problem, (3) third most important problem, and so forth. Since you are making judgments, be sure to use the strategies in chapter 4 to analyze how your audience will assess the importance of these ideas.

FOR ACTION IDEAS: Explanatory ideas are relatively easy to order. You place your top-level idea first, then order the supporting ideas based on the topic: by time, by components, or by importance. Action ideas are trickier to put in order. If you are recommending a change, you need to consider not only the topic, but also your own credibility (as we discussed in chapter 3) and your audience's attitude (as we discussed in chapter 4). Basically, you make your decision based on your audience's likelihood to agree or to disagree.

First, let's consider situations in which your audience is **likely to agree** with your proposed action. People might be agreeable for many reasons. They may be so busy or distracted with many other projects that they are likely to accept your ideas readily. They may have delegated the question to you or asked you to come up with a solution. They may see you as an expert in this particular area, someone with high initial credibility. Finally, the topic may be so uncontroversial that they have no strong opinions one way or the other.

In these cases, your audience will want to see your ideas clearly. Therefore, you should structure the message: (1) with your top-level idea first, where they can see it easily, and (2) with your strongest evidence first, where they will be more likely to hear or read it. This strategy is called the *direct approach*. For example, you might state: "I recommend we install this new machine," follow with your strongest argument, and end with your weakest. Or you might state: "Let's work together to keep the staff lunch room cleaner," follow with the most important argument, and end with the least important.

The direct approach has two major benefits. First, research shows that people can take in your ideas and understand you more easily when they know the top-level idea first. Perhaps more important, the direct approach saves your audience time. Business readers do not want to waste time with mysterious endings or suspense. On the contrary, they usually want to read as efficiently as possible to get through that ever-growing pile of reading material on their desks.

Despite its advantages, I find that many of you, as students, feel uncomfortable using the direct approach. Perhaps you want to avoid taking a stand. More likely, you have not been trained in using the direct approach. Perhaps most of your writing and speaking training before you took this class was for academic—not business—communication. This means you have been rewarded for emphasizing the logic of your argument or the expression of yourself—not the results of the action. One of the biggest transitions between successful academic and successful business life will be your ability to work with a different kind of audience, and structure your messages appropriately given that audience.

Although you don't want to assume automatically that your audience will disagree, occasionally you will have to deal with people who are **likely to disagree**. For example, they might be hostile or threatened. The topic might be so controversial or delicate that they feel anxious. They may see you as someone with very low initial credibility.

In these cases, your audience needs to be convinced. Research shows at least three ways to structure a convincing case for such an audience. (1) State your least controversial points first. If people agree with the first thing they read or hear, they are more likely to agree with the rest. (2) Present rejected alternatives first; state your recommendation last. You will be more persuasive if you present a series of rejected alternatives than if you allow the audience to think up all the alternatives themselves; naturally, people are less likely to reject ideas they come up with themselves. Also, you may be perceived as more fair-minded if you state all the options first. (3) Use your strongest evidence last. Use the beginning to arouse audience interest. Get them to "buy in" on ideas you know they believe or problems you know they need to solve. Once you have gotten their agreement, they will be more likely to accept your strongest evidence at the end.

This strategy is called the *indirect approach*. Use it sparingly, since it wastes audience time: use it only if your audience is likely to disagree with your ideas or if your audience is interested in your analytic process. You might, for example, structure a message differently for a research and development audience—who want to know about your analysis—than for a management audience—who want to know your results. You would certainly structure a message differently for an audience openly hostile to your ideas than for an audience that is indifferent or basically favorable toward your ideas.

Here's an example of a simple one-point recommendation, showing the difference between structuring for audiences likely to agree and structuring for audiences likely to disagree.

CASE 1: Your busy boss has asked you to come up with a recommendation to either expand or cut back on the widget product line. She has delegated this decision to you and wants a clear-cut solution. In this case, you might state:

> I recommend that we cut back on the widget line. The main reason for this recommendation is that widgets lack the potential for long-term growth. (followed by your analysis)

Note that the recommendation is stated first and clearly; your strongest evidence is stated at once.

CASE 2: Your boss is more concerned about the widget line. She has been personally involved with its current success. She is also concerned with the future of the company, of course, and has asked for your tentative opinion. In this case you might say:

We don't want to sacrifice our future profits for the sake of short-term gains. Therefore, although widgets contribute enormously to our current profits, we must consider cutting back on that line because of its lack of long-term growth potential. (followed by your analysis)

Note that the opening states an idea with which you know she will agree ("We don't want to sacrifice our future profits. . . . "). The rejected negative argument ("although widgets contribute enormously to our current profits")—which also ties to her pride and achievement in the current line—precedes your recommendation and strongest point, which appear at the end.

In summary, this chapter has dealt with how to structure your ideas for your audience. Instead of presenting ideas in the disorganized way they occur to you, think through those ideas, and then structure them clearly. Obviously the steps involved in thinking and structuring are not totally separate; as you compose, you circle back and forth between them. But the finished product should be structured clearly. That's your job as a writer or speaker—and no doubt it's a hard job.

REVIEW QUESTIONS
To check your understanding

1. What is the difference between thinking and structuring?
2. What three guidelines should underlie the thinking process?
3. Explain the difference between deductive and inductive thinking.
4. What is crucial to deductive thinking? inductive thinking?
5. What is the basis of an effective structure?
6. List three steps in providing a clear hierarchy.
7. Where should your conclusion be placed?
8. What is an idea chart and how can it help you?
9. What three guidelines should you remember as you make an idea chart?
10. What are three ways of ordering explanatory ideas?
11. What are two ways of ordering action ideas? When would you use each?
12. What is the difference between a direct and an indirect approach?

APPLICATION QUESTIONS
To apply your knowledge

1. What are the assumptions underlying the following statements?

   a. The best solution to the problem of employee absenteeism would be to limit the number of sick days.

   b. Doris deserves a bonus because she has achieved impressive results with her program and has put in a lot of overtime.

   c. If I study business communication I will increase my job effectiveness and brighten the prospects for my career.

   d. Stan's recommendation for diversifying our market is to begin a nationwide advertising campaign.

   e. Second-quarter gains point to the health of the corporation and the probability of a high rate of annual growth.

2. Indicate whether the following statements are inductive or deductive.

   a. Robert has studied agricultural economics, so he knows a lot about the development of wheat as an international commodity.

   b. The Midwest market has slowed down considerably in the past year, making it a bad time to introduce this new product.

   c. Common sense rules out the need for long-range goals during retirement.

   d. Because widgets are a cold-weather product, they will sell best north of the Mason-Dixon Line.

3. Give examples of the following logical fallacies: (a) hasty generalization (b) false cause (c) unrelated ideas (d) false analogy (e) popular appeal (f) catchall explanation.

4. What does it mean to communicate with an *audience-based structure?* Select a magazine advertisement as an example, and explain how it is audience-based rather than structured according to some other system.

5. Construct an idea chart of this chapter, using the table of contents on page 91 as your starting point. Be sure to include the top-level idea, main points, and supporting points, arranged in hierarchical order.

6. Suppose you have determined that the only way to increase employee productivity is to raise wages, increase vacation time, and enhance the benefits package. How would you present this conclusion to an audience that is likely to agree? unlikely to agree?

7. From your own experience, describe a book or a lecturer that was particularly effective at teaching you something, telling you something, or getting you to do something. What was the basis of that effectiveness? Consider the strategies discussed in this chapter, especially providing a hierarchy for ideas and then ordering them.

CASES
To practice what you learned

1. Your company manufactures ladies' apparel, and there has recently been a downward trend in the number of blouses produced each day. Your boss asks you to put together a memo, based on the field reports from various supervisors, that deals with this situation. Supervisor A attributes the poor performance to inadequate training of the seamstresses. Supervisor B claims that the material has been of inferior quality, causing delays in the production of each blouse. Supervisor C recommends higher wages to attract better workers. Supervisor D mentions that the working conditions could be improved. Structure this information into a brief memo supporting your boss's main contention that the rate of production can be increased only with major expenditures.

2. You would like to take some time off from work for personal reasons. You are due some vacation time and feel that it would be better to take it now rather than next month, when the annual budgets are due. You are tired, having just completed a major project, and want to be rested for the big push to resolve complex budgetary controversies when the need arises. Most important, if you don't take your vacation days within the remaining six weeks of the year, you will lose them. You do not think your boss will be well disposed toward your request for leave. How would you structure your message to him?

3. You have come up with some recommendations for improving consumer awareness of your product. Specifically, you feel that a catchier advertising slogan, redesigned packaging, and a national advertising campaign could increase sales as much as 30 percent—a conclusion based on the results of a scientifically conducted survey. You must present your ideas at the next staff meeting. Describe how you would go about putting them in a logical and convincing form, and what kind of format and supporting ideas you might include.

4. You have been asked to review a new piece of machinery your boss is thinking of buying, which can fold documents, and stuff, address, stamp, and bundle envelopes all at once. One person can operate the machine, which will handle mail in half the time taken by your existing machinery. How would you structure your review of this equipment differently to stress (a) the process it can accomplish, and (b) its benefits for the company?

6

The Response:

Feedback

Listening Skills
How you look • How you feel and think • What to say

Reading Skills
Reading comprehension • Reading speed

Feedback Skills
Giving feedback • Receiving feedback • Peer feedback in this class

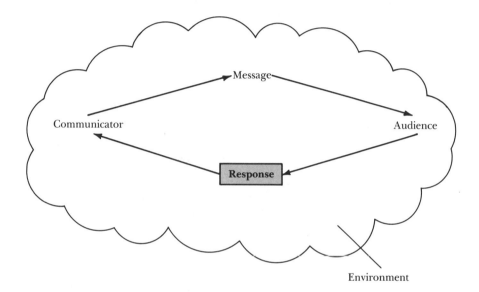

S O far, we have looked at how to improve your ability to increase your credibility, analyze your audience, and structure your message effectively. These techniques are useful when you are sending messages to your audience. Communication in business, however, involves more than just sending messages; you must respond to other people's messages as well. In this chapter, we will discuss some techniques to help you respond more effectively. First, we will look at the two communication skills necessary for understanding other people: listening and reading. Then, we will analyze another kind of response skill that serves to affect and change other people: giving and receiving *feedback*.[1]

---

[1] I don't particularly like the term *feedback*, but I can't think of a better one. *Response* is too broad: for example, listening is a response directed primarily at understanding someone; feedback is a special kind of response directed at changing someone's behavior. *Evaluation* and *appraisal* imply more of a process value judgment than *feedback* does.

Listening Skills

Listening is an extremely important and surprisingly difficult communication skill in business. Why is it important? Various studies show that business people spend from 45 to 63 percent of their time listening.[2] You will need to be an effective listener, for example, when you are brainstorming ideas with others, interviewing or being interviewed, appraising or being appraised for reviews, collecting data, talking on the telephone, resolving conflicts, and attending meetings.

Not only will you spend a lot of time listening, you will also stand to benefit from effective listening. You will be able to gather more detailed information when you need it for decision-making or problem-solving. You will learn new ideas or concepts you may have never thought of by yourself. You will understand people better so you can react to employee or client needs—perhaps even increase cooperation to enhance employee or customer relations.

Given that listening is so important, why is it so difficult for most of us? One reason listening is hard is that there are various **internal blocks** to concentration. A major internal block stems from your ability (as a listener) to think so much faster than a speaker can possibly talk. The person to whom you're listening is probably talking at about 125 words per minute; you can probably process information, on the other hand, at about 600 words per minute. With all that extra time available in your brain, no wonder your mind may wander to completely unrelated topics, such as lunch plans, football predictions, or office plants you suddenly notice need watering. Another internal barrier may occur if you have gotten into the habit of "tuning out" noise. Because you are constantly bombarded with sounds (such as radio and television noise), you may automatically turn off noise in your head even when you have no need to. A final internal block to listening is emotional. It's hard to resist jumping to conclusions, defending your own positions, contesting new ideas, and judging concepts with which you disagree. I don't mean to imply that you should never disagree, of course; but rather, you'll be a more effective listener if you make the conscious effort to hear the speaker out *before* you judge or evaluate.

Listening may also be difficult because of a variety of **external blocks**. You may be distracted by ringing telephones, clattering typewriters or computer printers, conversations you can hear in the hall, a change in the weather you see through the window, or a glance at papers

[2]W. Keefe, *Listen, Management!* (New York: McGraw-Hill, 1971), p. 10.

on your desk reminding you of other work you should be doing. Of all the external blocks, time is probably the most important. "I don't have time to listen to all this!" may be running through your head. Although you certainly don't want to have your time monopolized by constant chatting, you must set aside blocks of time for listening. Remember that people may take their problems or ideas elsewhere: subordinates may complain to others if they feel you're not hearing them; colleagues may stop sharing their ideas; customers may take their business to someone who seems more responsive.

To overcome these blocks to good listening, consider enhancing your listening ability by improving how you look, how you think, and what you say.

How you look

As a good listener you can show your interest in a variety of ways. First of all, consider your posture. Stand or sit with what nonverbal experts call an *open posture*—that is, facing the other person and looking alert. On the other hand, avoid what might be perceived as a *closed posture*: slumping, keeping your arms crossed, turning away, or bowing your shoulders. Also, avoid aggressive postures, such as thrusting out your chin or keeping your hands on your hips.

Second, analyze your gestures. Research shows that open, expressive gestures will tend to make the talker feel comfortable. Nervous gestures—such as cleaning your fingernails, drumming your fingers, or keeping your hands on or near your face—will tend to make the talker feel uncomfortable.[3] Therefore, get rid of any physical objects that might distract you: pencils for doodling or tapping, papers for shuffling, objects or jewelry for examining.

Your facial expression is also important. Avoid a deadpan, stony face. Instead, look interested: raising and lowering your eyebrows, occasionally smiling, or nodding can help establish rapport.

Perhaps the most important signal of your attentive listening is your eye contact. Obviously, you want to avoid the extremes: you don't want to appear to be in a staring contest, which could be interpreted as aggressive; you don't want to constantly look away, down, up, or out the window, which could be interpreted as uninterested. There has been quite a bit of interesting research on eye contact and its relationship to listening.[4] In

[3]A. Mehrabian, *Nonverbal Communication* (Chicago: Aldine, 1972).

[4]All the studies discussed in this paragraph are cited in M. Knapp, *Essentials of Nonverbal Communication* (New York: Holt, Rinehart & Winston, 1980), pp. 186–89.

one experiment, people who thought they were receiving less eye contact judged the listener as "less attentive." In another study, subjects who saw actors in a film maintaining either 15 percent or 80 percent eye contact perceived the actors with more eye contact as "friendlier." In normal conversation, we maintain eye contact about 40 percent of the time when we are talking and about 75 percent of the time when we are listening. Effective listeners, of course, do not stare constantly, but they do maintain more eye contact than ineffective listeners. One more word of warning on eye contact: experiments show that people have less eye contact when they are not interested in the speaker or when they are higher in status than him or her. So, any lack of eye contact might be perceived as standoffish or snobbish.

The distance between you and the person talking also communicates your interest and involvement. Furniture is one consideration. You may want the separation implied by a four-foot-wide desk between the two of you; you may want the closeness implied by side-by-side chairs. The amount of space around you is another consideration. As we shall be discussing in more detail in chapter 11, most people consider the area from eighteen inches to four feet around them their "personal space." This distance may be appropriate for conversational listening. Most people consider the area up to eighteen inches around them "intimate space." This distance, therefore, may be appropriate only for more intimate conversations, such as comforting someone.[5]

In general, however, get close enough to the other person to indicate your concern and attention. At the same time, be sensitive enough to avoid moving in too close. Let the person to whom you are listening be the guide. If the distance is too close, he or she will back off, lean back, or tilt his or her head back. If, on the other hand, someone opens up and becomes more animated as you lean in, she or he probably feels comfortable with the distance.

Altogether, the important thing to keep in mind about nonverbal signals of listening is how they make the speaker feel. You may very well think: "Just because I'm turned away or just because I'm drumming my fingers doesn't mean I'm not listening." And you may be correct. The point is, however, that even if you are listening, inappropriate nonverbal cues may mistakenly—but nonetheless damagingly—make the other person feel you're not interested.

---

[5]E. Hall, *The Silent Language* (New York: Premier Books, 1971).

How you feel and think

So far, we have been discussing ways to look interested. But just looking interested is not enough. You cannot fake good listening by merely mechanically nodding and maintaining eye contact. Good listening, in other words, must be sincere. You need to control your own feelings and thoughts as well.

Controlling your **feelings** is often difficult. You may want to interrupt or disagree before the person speaking is finished. Instead, be patient and give the speaker time. Good ideas are not necessarily spoken quickly and concisely—or even clearly. Avoid interrupting; hold your fire; do not block communication by arguing, criticizing, or becoming angry too soon. Listen first. One of the best ways to control your feelings is to *empathize* with the talker: try to put yourself into his or her shoes instead of contrasting that position with your own vantage point.

To control your feelings, you must avoid prejudging either the topic or the speaker. If you convince yourself that a meeting is going to be dull or that the person sitting in your office has nothing to teach you about a topic, you are likely to fulfill your own prophecy. Give new topics a chance. One way to do this is to think of aspects of a topic that might have specific value for you or your company. Besides the topic, give the talkers themselves a chance. Don't be overly affected by the initial impressions they make on you—such as the way they look, the way they dress, the color of their skin, or their sex. Don't be overly affected by their delivery either. Useful ideas may not be beautifully phrased. Good listeners are aware of their own prejudices and biases so they can consciously battle to overcome them as they listen.

Besides controlling your feelings, try to **think** objectively and analytically—hearing the speaker out before you judge. Analyze content, listening for and organizing key words and main ideas as you go along. Some helpful methods for analyzing content include: (1) trying to anticipate what the other person is getting at, (2) mentally summarizing what he or she has said so far, and (3) taking notes in your head, weighing the evidence. As you listen objectively, don't tune out difficult or technical matters. Force yourself to concentrate. If you need to ask for clarification, it's always better to have a specific idea of what you don't understand than to admit you didn't hear anything that was presented.

As you are listening for the speaker's content, don't take overly detailed notes. Some listening experts insist you should not take notes at all because it will distract both you and the speaker. Others recommend taking notes so you can organize and remember ideas. The decision depends on the situation: if you were interviewing twenty people the same day, you might decide in favor of taking notes; if, on the other hand, someone came into your office to discuss a serious personal problem, you would probably decide against taking notes. If you do take notes, however, avoid overzealous note-taking that distracts you from listening. Instead of constructing elaborate outlines and writing out complete sentences, just jot down main points, key phrases, and abbreviations.

Besides listening for the speaker's content, analyze her or his feelings. Listen not only to what the other person says, but how she or he says it. Be aware, in other words, of the other's voice, volume, facial expression, and body movement. Sometimes, people say one thing but a good listener can hear that they really mean something else. Consider, for example, the different tones of voice with which someone might say, "Yeah, that's a great idea, all right." What does this person really mean? What is he or she really trying to tell you?

What to say

Obviously, most of the time you are listening you are not saying anything. In fact, the most important step toward becoming an effective listener is to stop talking yourself. Although many of us naturally prefer talking to listening, we must at times be silent. A key to good listening is learning to tolerate silence. Instead of feeling uncomfortable with silence, think of it as a chance to let the other person be heard.

Besides silence, though, you might say a few things to encourage the other person to talk. First, ask questions. Ask general questions—such as "How do you feel about this project?" or "What are your thoughts on this matter?"—to get the speaker started. Ask for clarification or detail to make sure you understand. Second, reflect back to the speaker what she or he said. Restate or rephrase ideas so both you and the speaker know that you heard and comprehended. Finally, use brief phrases, such as "I see," "Uh-huh," and "Go on." These kinds of phrases tend to encourage people to talk more, just as attentive body language does.

Try these three techniques of looking interested, thinking nonjudgmentally until the speaker has finished, and paraphrasing or remaining silent instead of arguing. You will find that if you do, your career will be more personally, intellectually, and professionally rewarding—and that you will be more effective during the many hours you will spend listening during your career.

Reading Skills

Reading is to writing what listening is to speaking; clearly, your ability to read effectively will also be important in business. Because reading, too, is a response skill, many of the benefits you will gain from it are similar to those you gain from listening: you will acquire information, learn new ideas, and increase your understanding. Also, as with listening, effective reading involves controlling your feelings: do not stop reading just because you initially disagree. Good reading means avoiding prejudging the topic or the writer: give new topics and even bad writers a chance. Finally, like good listening, good reading involves anticipating, summarizing, and concentrating.

Despite the similarity in benefits, however, the processes are quite different. Here, then, are some suggestions for improving your reading comprehension and speed.

Reading comprehension

The main difference between reading and listening—indeed, a major block to reading comprehension—is that when you read, you do not have any human contact with the writer; the writer is not there on the spot with you. Since you normally do not speak to the writer as you read, it becomes vitally important to engage yourself in a mental dialogue with him or her instead. This kind of dialogue is often called *active reading*—becoming actively involved instead of passively detached. Many reading experts feel that active reading is the key to increasing comprehension, improving concentration, overcoming boredom, and stimulating creativity. Two methods for active reading are: (1) asking questions, and (2) using recall techniques.[6]

ASK QUESTIONS: The first way to become an active reader is to ask questions as you read. **What kind** of questions might you ask? Questions can range from simple memory quizzes to complex evaluations and deci-

---

[6]For more on active reading and other concepts discussed in this section on reading, see K. Baldridge, *Seven Reading Strategies* (Greenwich, Conn.: Baldridge Reading Instruction Materials, 1977). I am indebted to this book—as well as to reading lab materials used at the Stanford Learning Assistance Center and at DeAnza Community College—for many ideas in the reading comprehension and reading speed sections of this chapter.

sions. Imagine you are reading a memo from a colleague outlining her proposal for a new accounts-payable procedure. In order from simple to complex, here are some kinds of questions you might ask as you read. (1) The simplest kind of question is a memory question. Memory questions require just the recall of information: for example, "What are the four steps outlined in the memo?" (2) Translation questions involve changing the ideas into some different form: for instance, "How would the transition between step 2 and step 3, in fact, work?" (3) Application questions transfer the concept into everyday terms: for example, "How would this procedure affect each secretary's workload?" (4) Analysis questions identify the logical steps in the thinking process: the reader might ask, "How did she arrive at the conclusion that we need a new accounts-payable procedure?" (5) Synthesis questions bring together information to create new ideas: "How do the ideas in this memo fit with the previous complaints I've received about the current procedure and with Dudley's suggestion about last Thursday's staff meeting?" (6) The most complex kind of questions, evaluation questions, require judgment: "Should we try to change the accounts-payable procedure?"

When might you ask these questions? Effective readers do so before, during, and after they read. Before you start reading, ask yourself what your purpose is for reading. Develop questions based on the title, subtitles, and introduction. Questioning before you start reading will increase both your anticipation and your interest.

As you are reading, turn headings and topic sentences into questions. For example, if you are reading the sentence "We have many competitors in this market," you might ask yourself, "Who are these competitors?" or "What do I know about them?" or "What are our advantages and disadvantages compared with them?" Or, as you are reading, imagine you are talking with the writer. Ask questions such as "What is the basis for your opinion?" or "What should we do if this happens instead of that?" If you ask questions as you read, you can then read for the answers to those questions. (This process is especially useful when you are reading something that is uninteresting or difficult for you.) Asking these questions will help maintain your interest and increase your understanding.

Finally, question when you are through reading. Only after you have finished the piece should you raise questions about its validity, its application, and its relationship to what you already know. Questions asked after you read will help you evaluate your understanding of and further your reflection on the topic.

USE RECALL TECHNIQUES: The second way to become a more active reader and thus increase your comprehension is to use recall techniques. These techniques can be either mental (such as a summary you make to yourself) or written (such as notes or underlining). Recall techniques may include any of these three components: structuring, annotating, and summarizing.

To recall anything, you must **structure** it in some way. This means determining the different levels of meaning: the conclusion, main ideas, and supporting details. Structuring in reading is the response side of what we discussed in the previous chapter about structuring your writing—figuring out an idea chart for the reading material even if the writer hasn't stated it explicitly. To do so, figure out the conclusion or objective. To locate main points, look for subheadings or paragraphs that introduce new topics. The bulk of the reading material is usually details. Sometimes you need to remember them; sometimes you do not. But you must have a sense of how those details fit into the main structure.

How can you structure? You can do so mentally; this is the quickest method, but you will have the least recall. Or, you can write out a quick idea chart on another piece of paper; this will probably provide the most recall, but it is too time-consuming to do with everything you read. Finally, you can mark on the piece itself; this is faster than a written diagram, but still provides something you can review.

Annotation is a second recall technique. When you annotate as you read, you make the structure visible by using symbols. Many readers underline points in their reading with a pencil or felt-tip pen. One problem with underlining is overkill. Ineffective readers outline almost every sentence; you've probably seen fellow students almost cover each page of their texts with their yellow highlighting pen. Even if they don't overdo the underlining, ineffective readers underline to show only one level of importance. Effective readers, on the other hand, somehow show at least three levels of importance.

Differentiating levels not only makes the structure more apparent when you review, but it forces you to analyze constantly instead of merely underlining everything in sight. For example, you might: (1) circle the conclusion or objective (in some cases you may not be able to do this unless you have completed your reading and annotation), (2) underline the main points, and (3) bracket the important supporting details. You don't need to follow that procedure exactly, but you do need to find some combination of circles, underlines, brackets, stars, check marks, and so forth in order to differentiate among levels of importance as you annotate.

The final recall technique is to **summarize**. An ideal summary is written in your own words, and includes the conclusion and main ideas. Summaries check your comprehension, facilitate review, and strengthen retention. In fact, some research shows that retention over time is almost impossible without periodic summarizing.[7] Summaries may be mental, oral, written, or a combination—depending on how important the material is. Write down your summary only if it is very important; remember, though, that a mental summary is much more effective than no summary at all.

If you use these techniques of asking questions and recalling information, you should be able to increase your reading comprehension. You should also be able to overcome some of the main reading problems—such as a tendency to wander from the material or jump to conclusions, and even distracting noises and other blocks to concentration. The main problem that these techniques will not solve is the lack of time for reading. For skills to make you a faster reader, take a look at the next section.

Reading speed

Think about the amount of reading you will be doing each week when you start working:

	Approximate number of words
Memos, letters, reports	120,000
30 percent of two daily papers (*New York Times, Wall Street Journal*)	435,000
80 percent of three trade journals (specific to your business)	150,000
50 percent of two newsmagazines (*Time, Newsweek, Business Week*)	45,000
25 percent of one book (fiction or nonfiction)	35,000
50 percent of one pleasure magazine (*Sports Illustrated, New Yorker*)	30,000
	815,000

The average reading rate is 250 words per minute. If you read a week's worth of reading (815,000 words) at 250 words per minute, it would take you fifty-six hours each week, or eight hours each day. Obviously, you cannot spend this amount of time reading. What you need to do is develop new approaches to reading.

[7]Baldridge, *Seven Reading Strategies*, p. 54.

The key to effective reading is flexibility—that is, you should read different kinds of material at different speeds. Don't try to speed-read everything (especially, of course, this very book!); on the other hand, don't bother with a detailed and careful reading of everything. Remember, when you move from college to business, you don't have to read everything as if you were studying. One method for developing this flexibility, the SARAS Method, is illustrated in Figure 6.1.

SURVEY: The first step in the SARAS Method is to survey. Surveying does *not* mean speed-reading. Surveying *does* mean previewing the material by reading certain items very carefully and completely skipping all the rest. When you survey, you read three things only: the beginning, the end, and the structural clues. For a book, you would read: the beginning (cover and preface or introduction), the end (summaries or conclusions), and the structural clues (the table of contents). For a chapter or an article, you would read: the beginning (title and introduction), the end (summary or conclusion), and the structural clues (headings and subheadings). Yes, this means that in business reading—unlike pleasure reading, such as mystery stories—you should survey the end *before* you read the entire piece.

What will you gain from this survey? Surveying allows you to understand quickly the overall organization and major points before you read the material. Both your comprehension and your retention will improve because you will grasp this structure before reading thoroughly. After surveying, you will also be able to define your purpose, rate, and time.

ANALYZE: The second step, then, is to analyze. Based on your survey, you will be able to decide if it is worth your time to: (1) read the entire selection, (2) read only certain parts of the selection, or (3) not read it at all. This decision will save you time by allowing you to avoid unnecessary reading. *If* you decide to read, you will be able to define your purpose. Are you reading for the main idea? for specific details? just one part of the article? After defining your purpose, you can decide on the appropriate rate at which to read the entire selection.

READ AT THE APPROPRIATE SPEED: The third step is to read at the appropriate speed. Figure 6.1 shows the three basic reading speeds: speed-reading (or *skimming*), general reading (or *accelerating*), and careful reading (or *phrase-reading*). Although this book and your business communication course are not about reading, let's quickly touch on how each of these works and look at some exercises for improvement.

The first speed is called **speed-reading** or *skimming*. Unlike survey reading (which is a selective and careful sampling of any *key parts* of the text), skimming involves a rhythmic flowing over the *entire text*. The goal

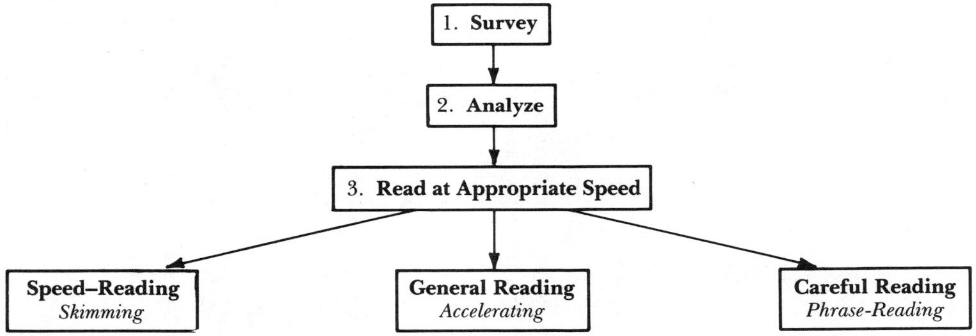
1. Survey
2. Analyze
3. Read at Appropriate Speed
Speed–Reading
Skimming
General Reading
Accelerating
Careful Reading
Phrase-Reading

	Speed–Reading	General Reading	Careful Reading
Read for:	Main ideas	Main and subordinate ideas	Main and subordinate ideas and details
Reading unit:	Page or column	Line	Phrase
Examples:	Some magazine or newspaper articles	Some texts or cases	Some texts or reports
Skills used:	1. Finger patterns 2. Externally imposed rhythm	1. Acceleration devices 2. Internally imposed acceleration	Efficient use of eye fixations
Possible uses:	1. Skimming for main idea 2. Previewing 3. Warming up	1. Reading general material 2. Increasing concentration	Reading difficult material

SARAS Method
© 1986 by Mary Munter

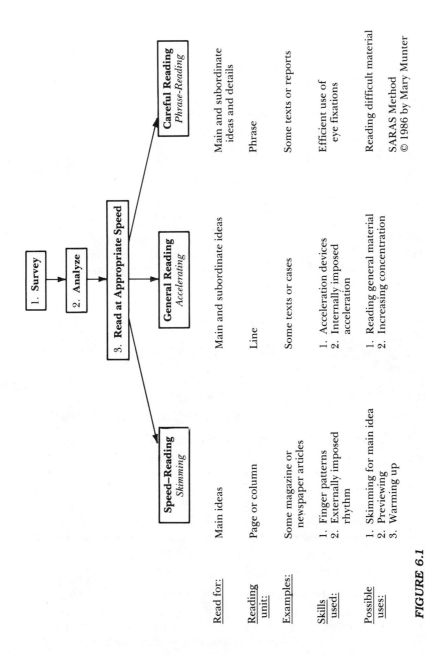

FIGURE 6.1

The SARAS method for reading flexibility

of skimming is to gain a general sense of the contents by reading at extremely high speeds—about 800 to 8000 words per minute. Although some commercial reading courses claim that you can skim at these speeds for full comprehension, both research evidence and common sense indicate that, in fact, you cannot.[8] (In the words of comedian Woody Allen, "I used speed-reading to complete *War and Peace* in ten minutes. It's about Russia.") Sometimes, however, you'll find it necessary to read for partial comprehension. For example, you might want to review quickly material you have already read. Or you might want to skim when you don't need thorough comprehension but just a general idea of the contents. Finally, you might skim when you don't have time for detailed reading; skimming is better than giving up and skipping the material altogether.

To skim, you must overcome two possible problems. The main problem most people have with skimming is psychological. We are so used to reading for full comprehension that we feel guilty or uncomfortable reading for only partial comprehension. In business, you *must* skim some material, or you'll get bogged down. You must learn to relax your mind and accept the idea that it is all right to read for half comprehension in those situations you have deemed less important. The second problem is to avoid stopping. A key to successful skimming is to keep moving quickly. When you first try skimming, remember that you are learning new eye movements and processes that run counter to all your previous reading experience. As you continue to practice, you will probably pick up key words and phrases. From these fragments, you will eventually start to pick up the general meaning of the text.

To keep moving quickly, use two techniques at once to read each page or column at one time. One technique is called *finger patterns.* Figure 6.2 illustrates the most common finger patterns. Finger patterns are devices for keeping yourself looking down the entire page. Concentrating on and around your finger helps you do this. Using the pattern with which you feel most comfortable, move down the page (or column) of print, using your finger as an aid for disciplining your eyes and mind. At the same time you are using a finger pattern, use the second technique, *externally imposed rhythm.* This means that when you skim, you choose a rhythm and stick to it—no matter what.

Figure 6.3 consists of two exercises for improving your skimming ability.

If you have decided that you have the time and the need to read for better comprehension, use a second reading speed called **general reading** or *accelerating.* As opposed to skimming, where you read by the page or

---

[8]R. Carver, "Speed Readers Don't Read; They Skim," *Psychology Today*, August 1972, pp. 22 ff.

numeros et sidera tractabant et unde omnia orirentur et quo discederent. Socrates autem primus philosophiam devocavit e caelo et in urbibus hominibusque collocavit et coegit eam de vita et moribus rebusque bonis et malis quaerere. Ego vos hortor ut amicitiam omnibus rebus humanis anteponatis. Sentio equidem, excepta sapientia, nihil melius homini a deis immortalibus datum esse. Divitias alii anteponunt; alii, salutem; alii, potestatem; alii, honores; multi, etiam voluptates. Illa autem incerta sunt, posita non tam in consiliis nostris quam in fortunae vicissitudinibus. Autem in virtute summum bonum ponunt, bene illi quidem faciunt; sed ex ipsa virtute amicitia nascitur nec sine virtute

Move straight down the center of the page.

tilem vitae? Isque ipse se diligit non ut aliam. Eiqui studia in contemplatione rerum ponebant sapientes appellabantur, et id nomen usque ad pythagorae aetatem manavit. Hunc aiunt docte et copiose quaedam cum leonte disputavisse; et leon, cum illius ingenium et eloquentiam admiratus esset, quaesivit ex eo qua arte maxime uteretur. At ille dixit se artem nullam scire sed esse philosophum. Tum leon, admiratus novum nomen, quaesivit qui essent philosophi. Phythagoras respondit multos homines gloriae aut pecuniae servire sed paucos quosdam esse qui cetera pro nihilo habeerent sed naturam rerum cognoscere cuperent; hos se appellare studiosos sapientiae, id est enim philosophos. Sic

Move from the upper left-hand corner directly to the lower right-hand corner.

orirentur et quo discederent. Socrates autem primus philosophiam devocavit e caelo et in urbibus hominibusque collocavit et coegit eam de vita et moribus rebusque bonis et malis quaerere. Ego vos hortor ut amicitiam omnibus rebus humanis anteponatis. Sentio equidem, excepta sapientia, nihil melius homini a deis immortalibus datum esse. Divitias alii anteponunt; alii, salutem; alii, potestatem; alii, honores; multi, etiam voluptates. Illa autem incerta sunt, posita non tam in consiliis nostris quam in fortunae vicissitudinibus. Autem in virtute summum bonum ponunt, bene illi quidem faciunt; sed ex ipsa virtute amicitia nascitur nec sine virtute amicitia esse potest. Denique ceterae res, quae

Move from side to side down the page.

Eiqui studia in contemplatione rerum ponebant sapientes appellabantur, et id nomen usque ad pythagorae aetatem manavit. Hunc aiunt docte et copiose quaedam cum leonte disputavisse; et leon, cum illius ingenium et eloquentiam admiratus esset, quaesivit ex eo qua arte maxime uteretur. At ille dixit se artem nullam scire sed esse philosophum. Tum leon, admiratus novum nomen, quaesivit qui essent philosophi. Phythagoras respondit multos homines gloriae aut pecuniae servire sed paucos quosdam esse qui cetera pro nihilo habeerent sed naturam rerum cognoscere cuperent; hos se appellare studiosos sapientiae, id est enim philosophos. Sic pythagoras huius nominis inventor fuit. Ab anti-

Move down the page in a spiral motion.

numquam intempestiva, numquam molesta est. Itaque non aqua, non igne in locis pluribus ultimur quam amicitia; nam amicitia secundas res clariores facit et adversas res leviores. Est qui velit in omnium rerum abundantia ita vivere ut neque diligat quemquam neque ipse ab ullo diligatur? Haec enim est tyranndrum vita, in qua nulla fides, nulla caritas, nulla benevolentia potest esse; omnia semper metuuntur, nullus locus est amicitia. Uis enim aut eum diligat quem metuat aut enum a quo se metui putet? Multi autem si ceciderunt, ut saepe fit, tum intellegunt quam inopes amicorum fuerint. Vero stultius quam cetera parare quae parantur pecunia sed amicos non parare, optimam et pulcherriman quasi supellec-

Hesitate briefly over about ¼ to ⅓ of the page at a "block."

vitiae, ut eis utaris; honores, ut lauderis; salus, ut dolore careas et rebus corporis utaris. Amicitia res plurimas continet; nullo loco excluditur; numquam intempestiva, numquam molesta est. Itaque non aqua, non igne in locis pluribus ultimur quam amicitia; nam amicitia secundas res clariores facit et adversas res leviores. Est qui velit in omnium rerum abundantia ita vivere ut neque diligat quemquam neque ipse ab ullo diligatur? Haec enim est tyrannorum vita, in qua nulla fides, nulla caritas, nulla benevolentia potest esse; omnia semper metuuntur, nullus locus est amicitia. Uis enim aut eum diligat quem metuat aut enum a quo se metui putet? Multi autem si ceciderunt, ut saepe fit, tum intellegunt quam

Sweep across several lines at once.

FIGURE 6.2

Finger patterns for skimming

FIGURE 6.3
Skimming exercises

New-page skimming drill

Skim a total of forty pages: first, ten pages at five seconds per page; then, ten pages at ten seconds per page; then, ten pages at fifteen seconds per page; finally, ten pages at twenty seconds per page. After you have done this drill about three times, you should understand the main ideas when you "slow down" to skim at twenty seconds per page (which is probably about 1000 words per minute).

Repeat-page skimming drill

Skim the same ten pages three times: at three, then five, then ten seconds per page. Then, read the same ten pages as quickly as possible for complete comprehension. If you continue to read new material, you should find that you are reading much faster because of this drill.

---

column for main ideas only, in general reading you read line by line for main and subordinate ideas. General reading rates are usually about 400 to 500 words per minute. Although you're reading for good comprehension at this rate, you are not reading for every last detail. You will probably read many memos and letters at this rate.

To use this rate, you must overcome the problems of ingrained reading habit and lack of concentration. The key to effectiveness is to push yourself constantly as you read line by line. The two main techniques for pushing yourself are *acceleration devices* and *internally imposed acceleration*. Acceleration devices are mechanical aids for reading slightly faster than feels comfortable. They include a series of machines—such as controlled readers and reading accelerators—that may be available at your school's learning lab or bookstore. Probably the most useful (and inexpensive) device is an index card. Use a card to *cover up* each line as you finish it and to push your rate. The other acceleration technique is an internally imposed rhythm. Unlike skimming, where the rhythm is set externally (at a certain number of seconds per page), in general reading the rhythm is set internally. Concentrate on reading slightly faster than you usually do. Figure 6.4 outlines two drills for this reading rate.

Use the final rate, **careful reading**, only when you have decided the occasion warrants detailed reading. In these cases, you can still improve your reading rate a bit by using *phrase-reading* techniques.

The key to effective phrase-reading is called *eye fixations*. As an experiment, find a partner and take turns watching each other's eyes as

---

FIGURE 6.4

Acceleration exercises

Rate-acceleration drill

In this exercise, read for one minute at your current comfortable rate. Calculate and record the number of words you read: multiply the number of lines you read by the approximate average number of words per line. Then, read for ten to twenty minutes, constantly pushing yourself to read faster than is comfortable—perhaps by using an index card. Now, read for one minute at your new comfortable rate, and calculate the number of words you read. This rate should be higher than your starting rate because of the effect of the ten- to twenty-minute practice session.

Eight-passage drill

This drill starts the same way: read for one minute at your current comfortable rate. Instead of calculating your rate, however, measure the amount of material you finished (a page and a half, three fourths of a page, or whatever), and divide the next section of your book into eight adjoining passages of that same length. Then, read the first two passages in fifty-five seconds each, the next two at fifty seconds each, the next two at forty-five, and the final two at forty seconds each. You will probably lose comprehension by the time you're reading at forty seconds, but you will learn how it feels to force acceleration.

---

you each read. What you will see is that people's eyes do not move smoothly across the line; instead they move in a series of little jumps, or *fixations*, during which you take in the material. Most people jump or fixate about four to six times across each line. The idea behind phrase-reading is to cut down the number of fixations to two or three across each line. Figure 6.5 presents some phrase-reading exercises.

Try these techniques, then, to increase your reading comprehension and speed: become an active reader by asking questions and using recall techniques; become a flexible reader by using the SARAS Method of differing reading speeds. These techniques should help you cut down on the enormous amount of time every business and professional person spends reading.

Both reading and listening are the same kind of response skill; that is, they are aimed at furthering an understanding of what someone else has written or said. Now, let's look at a second kind of response skill.

FIGURE 6.5

Phrase-reading exercises

Mechanical phrase-reading

In these exercises, you mechanically, or automatically, stop a certain number of times, as shown in this "visual swing." In this simple warm-up exercise, you "read" across the lines, fixating first three, then two times per line.

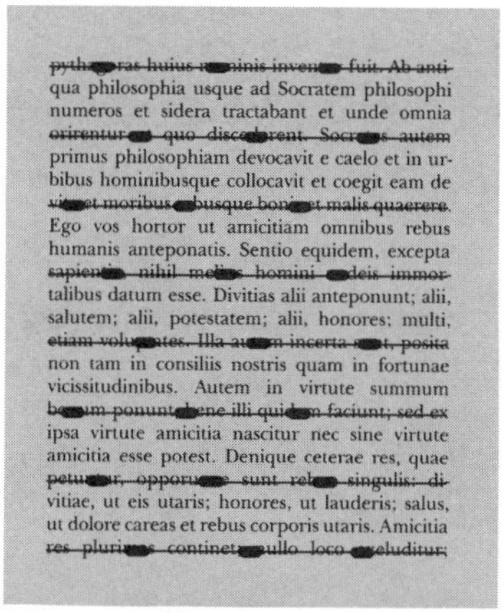

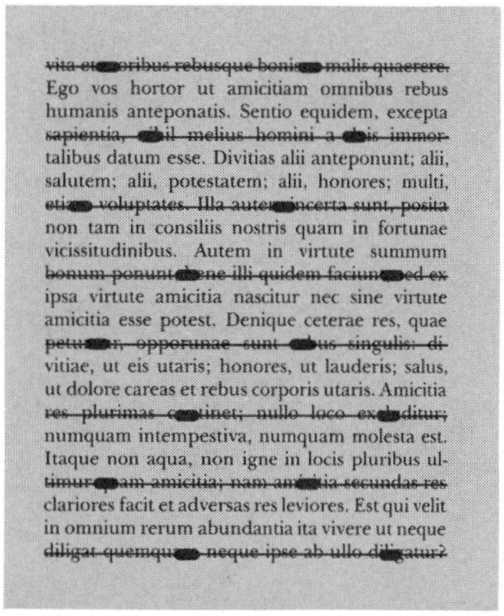

A second mechanical exercise is called the *divided-page exercise*. Using a light pencil, mark and divide the pages of your book into two or three columns of about five words each. Then, read across each line, fixating once in the middle of each column, slightly above the line of print.

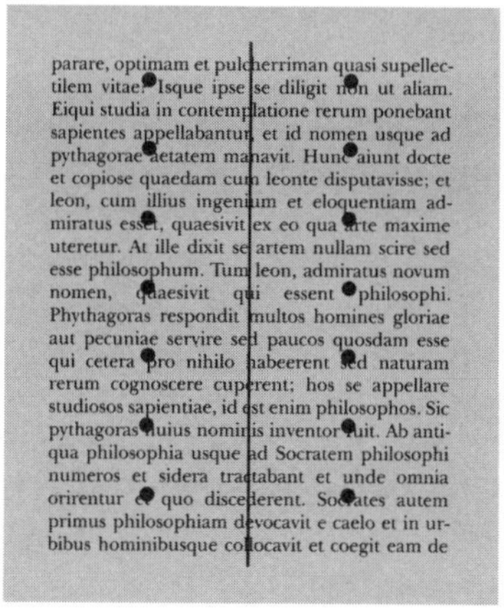

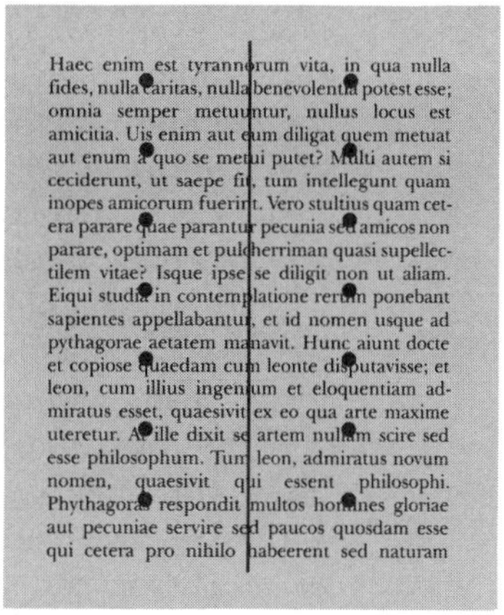

FIGURE 6.5 *(cont.)*

Conceptual phrase-reading

In fact, true phrase-reading does not consist of an automatic number of stops per line. You actually read in phrases of words that make sense together. The following paragraph shows how you might read in conceptual phrases. When you practice this exercise, try to stop only two or three times per line, but realize you will stop more often if the wording demands it.

In fact, true phrase-reading does not consist

of an automatic number of stops per line. You actually read

in phrases of words that make sense together.

This paragraph shows how you might read

in conceptual phrases. When you practice this exercise,

try to stop only two or three times per line,

but realize you will stop more often if the wording demands it.

Feedback Skills

What do all the following activities have in common? Reading your instructor's comments on a paper you wrote for this class. Hearing comments as you watch yourself on videotape. Editing a draft of a group report. Working with a group of colleagues to prepare your presentation for an important meeting. Receiving suggestions from your customers on how to improve your product or service. Evaluating your subordinates for their yearly performance appraisals. The answer is: they all involve giving and receiving feedback.

Feedback skills are essential to your success—both as a communicator and as a business person. That's why peer feedback is included in so many business communication courses.

By *feedback* I mean a certain kind of response. When you read or listen, your goal is to *understand* what the other person is writing or saying. When you give feedback, however, your goal is to *change* or affect what the other person is doing. Imagine that I told you: "You should stand on your head." You may read and understand that sentence, but you probably won't change your behavior as a result. If I could get you to accept and understand why you should stand on your head, and you proceeded to stand on your head, then you would have accepted my feedback. The point is that feedback is worthless unless the person receiving the feedback accepts, understands, and acts on it.

Effective feedback skills are crucial for your success in any business or organization. By learning how to *give* good feedback, you may lighten your own work load by reducing the time wasted by misunderstandings, repetitions, and unnecessary corrections. You may also create a more pleasant work environment by reducing needless, unwanted, or inappropriate behavior. Finally, if you learn to give feedback now, then later on when you are promoted to supervisor you will be able to give more effective performance appraisals to your employees.

By learning how to *receive* feedback, you will gain three additional benefits. First, you will be more effective, because you will have more information. Second, you will gain understanding of the several ways in which you come across to various people. Finally, you may find that others are more likely to accept your feedback if you are willing to accept theirs.

All in all, effective feedback skills will allow you to do a more effective job, increase group participation, and maintain better working relationships. Let's look at some techniques of giving and receiving feedback in general[9] and then apply these techniques specifically to business communication.

Giving feedback

Although essential for your success, giving feedback is quite delicate and difficult. We all know how hard it can be to have someone criticize our work, so we must be compassionate and tactful to others. On the other hand, we know how frustrating it can be when people are too nice and seem unwilling to help, so we must be detailed and specific. Perhaps the most difficult task involved in giving feedback is denying our natural inclination to point out every single problem we can possibly see and instead to zero in on the important problems we hope to change. Denying this inclination marks the difference between giving feedback (that is, helping the other person learn to change him- or herself) and simply fixing it or doing it yourself. For example, you wouldn't want to retype a letter for your secretary, visit clients for your sales staff, or personally resolve all conflicts for your work group. Instead, by giving feedback, you

---

[9]Many of these principles are based on an old classic article, J. Anderson, "Giving and Receiving Feedback" in A. Athos and J. Gabarro, *Interpersonal Behavior* (Englewood Cliffs, N.J.: Prentice-Hall, 1963), pp. 83–89.

want to help these people perform these actions more successfully for themselves in the future.

The best feedback involves both oral and written comments. (As we discussed in chapter 2, writing and speaking have different advantages and disadvantages.) The advantages of talking with people instead of just writing include the following: (1) you can ask them open questions (such as "What do you see as your strengths and weaknesses on the job this year?") to elicit their problems instead of just telling them what their problems are; (2) you can "read" their nonverbal behavior when they don't understand or when they disagree; (3) you can clarify right on the spot any questions they might have; and (4) you can end on a positive note. Written feedback has its own advantages: (1) you can take more time to choose precise wording; (2) you can be more detailed; (3) you can give someone a permanent record; and (4) you can give someone the opportunity to consider your comments at his or her leisure.

Whether you speak or write, giving effective feedback is based on two criteria: trust and understanding.

TRUST: Feedback clearly will not work if the other person does not trust you. You could offer brilliant suggestions to no avail if the other person mistrusts your motives or becomes defensive. To gain trust, consider these three steps to help you establish a climate of emotional acceptance.

First, examine your own motivation. You need to be in a frame of mind designed to help, not to show off or to get even. Your motivation will come through—in your tone of voice, in your expression, in your word choice—and unless the other person feels a sense of "I value you and I want to help you reach your goals," she or he is not likely to trust you or accept your feedback.

Second, gain trust by describing specific actions, instead of seeming to judge the entire person. This means avoiding "loaded" and clearly judgmental terms such as *terrible, lousy, great,* or *terrific.* When you use these "loaded" terms, the other person feels as if you think he or she is completely horrible or completely wonderful. Obviously, this is untrue. You are not trying to summarize the person's entire being or entire performance; instead, you are trying to deal with certain specific behaviors. So, instead of evaluating the entire person, describe a specific behavior. For example, instead of saying, "That was a bad memo," say "Your main idea was not clearly stated." Instead of saying "Your presentation was good," say "Your presentation was clearly structured."

Third, if you want someone to trust you, be sure to include positive as well as negative comments. You probably know that people will not accept completely negative feedback: if they get overwhelmed, they may feel threatened and may not change their behavior. Perhaps you aren't aware, however, that people also tend not to trust completely positive comments. So be sure to include a balance. And, in many cases, you might want to open and close a feedback session on a positive note.

UNDERSTANDING: In addition to the emotional side of giving feedback—gaining trust—there is also a logical side—gaining understanding. To do this, you should, first of all, preview the general pattern of your remarks. Show the other person the broad picture, such as "Here are your three strengths; here are two areas for improvement." Don't overload his or her mind with a barrage of unrelated details. Give some kind of agenda to start.

Once you've established the broad areas, be as specific as possible. The more specific you can be, the better your chances of being understood clearly. For example, say "I feel uncomfortable when you look away and don't answer my questions" instead of "I feel uncomfortable about your actions this morning." Or, say "I appreciate the way you remained calm when all the phones rang and five visitors arrived at once," instead of "Way to go this afternoon!"

Finally, avoid overkill. Since the goal of good feedback is to change and improve behaviors, do not feel obligated to tell the other person every single thing you can think of. There is a limit to what people can take in and change. Focus on the most significant issues.

Receiving feedback

Your ability to receive feedback is also important for your success in business. You will never improve, grow, or change unless you can accept feedback. The keys to receiving feedback are: to avoid defensiveness and to encourage response.

Defensiveness is one of the major blocks to receiving feedback and to keeping lines of communication open. Often defensiveness results when we try to save face or to avoid looking silly. At its worst extreme, defensiveness is a constant assumption that we must attack, that relationships are based on mutual antagonism, that interactions are struggles. Defensiveness is thus based on a false premise. Because people in business must compromise and learn from one another, they must attempt to maintain "win/win" attitudes instead of "win/lose" attitudes. Even if you do want to beat out an opponent, however, defensiveness will usually harm your ability to do so: the attitude makes you appear unpleasant and unconfident.

AVOID DEFENSIVENESS: You can avoid defensiveness by maintaining four attitudes. One, exchange of information and ideas is a positive experience. Unless you have a specific reason to expect real hostility (such as dealing with an angry client or employee), assume your audience will enjoy and benefit from communication with you, and vice versa. Only by exchange and interplay of ideas can we and our businesses improve.

Two, don't take criticism of your ideas as criticism of yourself. If you think about it, naturally you can't go through life with *none* of your ideas *ever* criticized. Even if your ideas are rejected, you have at least participated in the communication process. More important, remember that rejection of your idea is not a rejection of you as a person.

Third, remember that other people share your uncertainties and insecurities. When people feel defensive, they may think that everyone else is confident and clear. This is a common anxiety resulting from the difference between the inner self we know and the outer self we present in public. We know our inner self better than anyone else's, and therefore we know our weaknesses and insecurities far better than we know anyone else's. But, just because we cannot know other people's insecurities as well as our own doesn't mean other people don't have them. In fact, some uncertainty is almost a necessity for an intelligent, questioning, aware person.

Finally, when someone disagrees with you, don't immediately and automatically defend yourself. Instead of dodging or denying the feedback, judge it and possibly use it to improve yourself or your ideas. Ask yourself if the feedback is justified. If you think it is correct, express your agreement; if partially correct, qualify your agreement; if completely incorrect, try to respond with questions and more interaction to clear up the disagreement.

ENCOURAGE RESPONSE: Besides avoiding a defensive attitude, you can improve your ability to receive feedback by using specific techniques to encourage response. First, ask for it. If you tell people something like "I'd like your ideas on this" before you present your ideas, you will emphasize how important you think their thoughts are and encourage them to read or listen to you more carefully, thus becoming more actively involved.

To ask for a response, specify a method or channel (how you want them to respond) and specific questions. Specifics not only make it easier for your audience to reply, they also demonstrate the sincerity of your request. In writing, for example, specify a method (such as a tear-off sheet, a questionnaire, or a follow-up phone call) and specific questions you would like ideas about (such as agenda items, confirmations, or answers to a list of questions). In speaking, avoid abrupt endings such as

"Does everybody understand?" or "Any questions?" People are not likely to admit they're too dumb to understand or to come up with questions on the spur of the moment. Instead, specify the method, such as, "Please feel free to interrupt with your thoughts or questions as we go along," or "Please hold your ideas until the end of the presentation, when we will have a discussion period."

Another way to ask for response when you are speaking is to be alert to your audience's nonverbal signals. If, for example, someone's facial expression looks quizzical, you might ask, "Tom, you look concerned about what I just said." If someone gives a sudden start, you might say, "Beth, you look uncomfortable about that last idea." Clearly, this kind of request varies with the audience and the situation: it is probably most appropriate in two-way discussions; you don't want to put someone on the spot in a group session, so you might speak with that person later in private.

Second, give time for feedback. If you want a response, schedule time for it. Do not, for example, ask for questions after having spoken for fifty-nine minutes at an hour meeting. You may want to set up special feedback sessions after giving a presentation or writing a memo. Besides scheduling time for people to respond, give them time to think. Everyone, from teachers to managers, seems to find it hard to wait through more than about three seconds of silence. Wait at least fifteen seconds; don't be afraid of silence. It takes time for your audience to formulate ideas. You may also want to give your audience a few days to consider responses.

Third, reward feedback. As we discussed in chapter 4, rewarding behavior is one of the most powerful ways to encourage it. In speaking, show your interest in the other person's ideas by asking questions to make sure you understand and by complimenting him or her for constructive responses. In writing, acknowledge effective feedback with a specific response or a thank-you note. Let people know you appreciate their time and effort.

Peer feedback in this class

So far, we have been discussing giving and receiving feedback in business situations. Since giving and receiving feedback will be so crucial for you in business, many business school courses may offer you the opportunity to practice feedback skills. In some courses, you may practice role-playing a performance appraisal; in others, you may practice dealing with problem employees. In many business communication courses, you may practice by giving your peers—that is, classmates—feedback on their writing and speaking skills. In these kinds of exercises, you not only practice your feedback skills, you also improve your communication skills.

Let's switch gears, then, here, and examine giving and receiving feedback in a business communication course.

You will gain at least four benefits from giving and receiving peer feedback on writing and speaking. First, many students report that giving feedback to others actually helps them improve their own writing or speaking: by spotting, correcting, and suggesting improvements for others, they improve themselves as well. Second, you will necessarily get more extensive comments. No one person—even your professor, however skilled he or she may be—can ever recognize all the possible ways to improve. Third, you will hear a different perspective; as you know, business communication often involves reaching various audiences simultaneously. Finally, you will have the chance to practice receiving feedback gracefully.

Since the rest of this book—and, indeed, the rest of the course you are using it in—deals with standards for good speaking and writing, we won't go into them in complete detail here. Instead, let me just give an overview of the main points you will want to watch for when you are giving someone feedback.

Since you always make it easier for someone to understand your feedback if you use some kind of a checklist or agreed-upon criteria, refer to the checklists on pages 142 and 254. Your instructor may use them or other checklists for feedback in this course.

WRITING: As you can see from the checklist on page 142, effective feedback on someone's writing includes comments in three areas: (1) the entire document, (2) each paragraph, and (3) each sentence. As you watch for those three areas, here are some techniques to keep in mind. For one thing, use a light pencil on the paper itself. Avoid the negative associations of a red pencil or of overly bold, aggressive lines. Instead, be gentle with your pencil marks: for example, use brackets to show sentences that need work, instead of slashing four thick lines through them. If you see patterns in someone's writing, you may want to use a color code to indicate them: for example, if you notice a tendency to be wordy, underline all the wordy phrases in blue instead of writing "WORDY" each time the problem occurs. Another technique is to provide some (but not all possible) rewrites. Suggest ways to improve by reconstructing an example or two: for example, if someone uses the passive voice habitually, rewrite a couple of sentences in the active voice. Do not, however, rewrite the entire document (unless, of course, your goal is to edit—not to give feedback).

Again, the goal of feedback is to help the other person learn to change his or her behavior by providing a model, not to do the job yourself.

Finally, make your suggestions tactfully. When you are making suggestions for improvement, use comments couched in terms designed not to hurt people's feelings. Here are some samples of tactful written comments: "Make sure your main idea stands out for reader," "A bit 'jumpy'; provide transitions between these paragraphs," "Make your good ideas visually clear to your reader by using highlighting," "Would this tone offend your reader?" "Paragraphs 2 and 5 lack topic sentences," "This sentence is too specific for a topic sentence," "Overuse of prepositions? See my green circles in first three paragraphs," "Sentences too long? 52, 61, and 58 words."

SPEAKING: Effective feedback on someone's speaking may include comments in these three areas: (1) structure, (2) delivery, and (3) visual aids. I suggest you decide in advance what you're analyzing. Unlike writing feedback, where you have the chance to read and reread, speaking feedback usually occurs after only one listening (unless, of course, you have access to videotape). Unless you can watch the presentation several times, then, decide in advance what you are giving feedback on. For example, you could assign one person or group of people to each of the areas (structure, delivery, visual aids); you could comment on only one of the areas; or you can attempt to cover all three yourself. The third alternative is fairly difficult; even trained speech instructors need lots of practice before they can comment on all three areas simultaneously. But it is possible. Be sure to comment on the structure first: you can comment on the delivery at any time, but you must catch the opening and preview at the beginning—or you've lost your chance to do so.

And, as in writing feedback, you must make suggestions tactfully. Here are some typical speaking comments, couched in terms designed not to hurt feelings. "Watch out for slouch," "Watch sway," "Watch for distracting gestures," "Use hands conversationally," "Avoid reading," "Add variety to pitch," "Use pauses for emphasis," "Watch voice drop at the end of sentences," "Add opening to grab audience's attention," "A bit hard to follow. Preview (or visual aids or more explicit transitions) would help here," "Avoid looking at screen; look at audience."

By taking time to develop effective listening, reading, and feedback skills as part of this course, you will be laying the groundwork for work in other courses as well as your career.

REVIEW QUESTIONS
To check your understanding

1. List three reasons why you might experience internal blocks to listening.

2. What are five types of nonverbal signals that can show you are a good listener?

3. What are three characteristics of a good attitude to develop toward the talker in order to be a good listener?

4. Cite two techniques you can use to become an active reader.

5. What are the six kinds of questions you can ask about what you read?

6. Explain the three possible components of recall.

7. What are the main steps in the SARAS Method?

8. What are two reasons why it is important to read at the proper speed?

9. What is feedback and what are three reasons why giving it is important?

10. What are the two keys to giving feedback effectively? What are the two keys to receiving feedback effectively?

11. What are the three areas of writing that are the focus of effective feedback? What are the three areas of speaking?

APPLICATION QUESTIONS
To apply your knowledge

1. Think of a situation you've experienced in which you know the person you were talking to was not listening closely. Describe how you felt at that time and how similar feelings might affect a business situation.

2. Assume you are interviewing someone who seems particularly tongue-tied. What sort of techniques would you use to get the person talking and keep him or her going so you can find out what you need to know?

3. Imagine that you have been asked to outline a critique of a proposal for new lighting installations in the city's parks. List five questions you might ask of the proposal that illustrate the kinds of questions characteristic of active reading.

4. Why is structure essential to effective recall? In your answer, make a comparison between the role of structure in writing and responding.

5. Select a brief article from one of your favorite magazines and read it according to the SARAS Method. Make a record of your specific response at each step: your survey of the article, the type of reading you select, and your reading technique.

6. What type of reading material in general lends itself to skimming? to general reading? to careful reading? List two examples in each category that you are likely to encounter in a business situation.

7. How is feedback different from criticism? Assume you are dealing with a co-worker who is late in meeting a deadline, and give an example of each.

8. Assume you have been giving someone well-meant feedback and he or she responds in a highly defensive way. What do you consider the most effective response on your part to defensive behavior?

9. What kinds of benefits for your own writing and speaking can learning to be a good reader/listener provide?

WRITING CHECKLIST

1. Have you used standard business elements and formats correctly?
   (See chapter 7.)
   > **Letter elements and format**
   > *(See pages 152–56, 158–63.)*
   > **Memo elements and format**
   > *(See pages 157, 164.)*
   > **Report elements and format**
   > *(See pages 165–73.)*

2. Are your document and paragraphs effective?
   (See chapter 8.)
   > **Unified (on one subject) and emphatic (main ideas placed prominently)**
   > *(See pages 183–90.)*
   > **Organized (ordered clearly) and highlighted (organization visually apparent to reader)**
   > *(See pages 190–97.)*
   > **Connected (clear transitions between ideas)**
   > *(See pages 198–201.)*
   > **Of appropriate length (not too long or too short)**
   > *(See pages 201–3.)*

3. Are your sentences effective?
   (See chapter 9.)
   > **Arranged clearly (important words emphasized, verb near subject, modifiers placed correctly)**
   > *(See pages 210–16.)*
   > **Of appropriate length (not too long, too short, or too monotonous)**
   > *(See pages 216–21.)*
   > **Using vigorous verbs (avoiding overused nouns, weak verbs, elongated verbs, passive verbs)**
   > *(See pages 222–29.)*

4. Is your word choice effective?
   (See chapter 10 and appendixes.)
   > **Brief (avoiding overused prepositions and repetitions)**
   > *(See pages 235–40.)*
   > **Simple (avoiding pompous words and unnecessary jargon)**
   > *(See pages 240–48.)*
   > **Correct (using correct wording and grammar)**
   > *(See pages 248–51 and Appendixes A, B, C, and D.)*

7

Introduction to Business Writing

The Composing Process
Stage 1: Prewriting ● *Stage 2: Drafting* ● *Stage 3: Editing*
● *Avoiding writer's block*

Business Formats
Letters ● *Memos* ● *Reports*

GOOD writing is based on clear objectives, effective audience analysis, and effective structure. Unless you have gone through the steps outlined in part I, all of the carefully crafted paragraphs and sentences in the world are not going to make you an effective business writer.

After you have set your strategy, then, let's look at some techniques to use when you sit down to write, during the composing process itself. Then, we will look more specifically at the kinds of writing you will be doing in business.

The Composing Process

Just as many business speakers suffer from stage fright, many business writers suffer from writer's block. Most of us have, on occasion, stared helplessly at an empty page or an empty computer screen—or plunged recklessly into our writing with only "an outline in our head"—just to get the job of writing over. Over the past several years, however, researchers have examined the ways effective writers work—and the ways they avoid writer's block. In this section, we will look at a three-stage plan for efficient composing: (1) prewriting, (2) drafting, and (3) editing. Finally, we will review techniques for avoiding writer's block.

Stage 1: Prewriting

The first step in an effective composing process is not to start immediately generating a page full of perfect words. Instead, think of the prewriting stage as being just what its name implies: "before writing." During this stage, focus on your assignment (from, say, your boss at work or your teacher at school), and gather information.

You yourself might provide one source of information for some business writing. For example, you might have the information in your head on how to deal with certain customers, answer certain questions, or solve certain problems. You have a choice of several **intuitive** methods for getting in touch with that information.

1. Free writing is a technique for forcing yourself to prewrite. You can do free writing with a pen or pencil on paper, or on a computer terminal, or on a computer terminal with a program that does not allow what you've written to show on-screen (usually called *invisible writing*). Decide on a time limit in advance. Keep your pen or pencil moving, or your fingers moving at the keyboard. If you cannot think of anything to say, write "nothing to say" over and over until you do think of something. Be as spontaneous as possible: don't edit; don't analyze.

2. Note-keeping is another way to generate material. You might keep a journal or notebook with you over a period of time. As ideas occur to you (in the car, in bed, after you shower), jot them down. Or you might keep notes on a computer, again jotting down ideas when they occur to you instead of forcing yourself to write at certain scheduled times.

3. Brainstorming is a method you can use by yourself or with other people. Successful brainstorming is based on maintaining two distinct stages. In stage 1, agree on a time limit in advance, and always record all ideas either by writing them down or taping the session. First, define your general topic. Then, blurt out or jot down any and every association that comes to mind, always recording. Continue to associate freely and follow up on ideas, without worrying about reaching a conclusion. Do not criticize any ideas. In stage 2, review the list of jottings, grouping related ideas into categories and striking irrelevant ones. Finally, experiment with statements that express the essence of each category.

    Other methods are more **analytic** than the intuitive methods just described. Analytic methods are generally more orderly and quick than the intuitive approaches. They may, however, produce more mechanical or less original results.

4. Focusing is an example of an analytic prewriting technique. First, define your general topic. Then, focus on one aspect of your topic. Break this aspect into more specific subtopics. Focus on the second aspect of your topic. Break the second aspect into more specific subtopics. Continue in this way for each aspect of your topic.

5. Journalists' questioning is another possibility. Answer this set of questions: who? what? where? when? how? why?

6. Rhetorical questioning focuses on any of the standard rhetorical questions that apply in your specific case. What does X mean? How can X be described? What are the component parts of X? How is X made or done? How should X be made or done? What are the causes of X? What are the consequences of X? How does X compare with Y?

The other major source of information comes from outside your own head. For example, you might need to consult your files or consult another person. The two main **synthetic** prewriting techniques for gaining information from outside sources are interviewing and reading. (See chapter 6 for more detailed information on both interviewing and listening. See appendix E for more detailed information on business research and documentation.)

7. For interviewing, use good body language: appropriate eye contact; an open, relaxed posture; energy in your voice, gestures, and facial expression. Use encouragements to talk. Try nonverbal encouragements, such as nodding, and verbal encouragements, such as "I see" or "Uh-huh." To generate the most information, ask open-ended questions—those that cannot be answered "Yes" or "No." Paraphrase or summarize to show you are listening, to make sure you have understood, and to elicit further information. Ask for details, examples, or clarification to encourage more specific information.

8. For reading, be flexible. Skim irrelevant sections; slow down for important sections. Read actively, scribbling in the margins, underlining, and taking notes. Beware of plagiarism; always acknowledge your sources.

The point in this chapter is not to go into the specifics of gathering information from outside sources. Instead, the point here is that you should gather together all your information *before* you start writing.

Once you have your information, think it through, arrive at a conclusion, and sketch an idea (as we discussed in chapter 5). Don't start writing without an idea there. You risk wasting your time and confidence, and losing your reader's comprehension. Of course, your ideas may change as you write; naturally, you may change your structure as you go along. But to start writing without any idea chart is to invite disaster.

Stage 2: Drafting

Perhaps the most important thing to remember as you are drafting is to adopt a **drafting attitude**. This attitude means not allowing yourself to be a perfectionist as you draft. Instead, think of drafting as a creative gushing forth of ideas. You will be analytical and even picky during the editing stage, but you should stifle perfectionism as you draft. Just get it down on paper.

To maintain that attitude, avoid editing during the draft stage. Do not worry about specific problems. As examples, if you cannot think of a word, leave a blank space; if you cannot decide between two words, write them both down; if something sounds awkward, leave it and go on. Circle or put a check mark in the margin for these unclear or awkward sections; you will come back to them later.

With that drafting attitude in mind, get your draft down on paper: handwriting, **typing or word processing, or dictating.** You will save time if you avoid handwriting: you write in longhand at about fifteen words per minute; you can type at twenty to sixty words per minute; you can dictate at sixty-five to ninety-five words per minute. Furthermore, you will find it much easier to spot and correct errors later if you can edit from a typed copy. Your draft copy should be typed on one side only, double- or triple-spaced, with wide margins.

Since typed drafts are both faster to prepare and more efficient to edit, consider the ways you can get a typed draft. First of all, you might type it yourself on a standard typewriter. As we discussed in chapter 2, however, more and more business and professional writers are composing directly on a word processor. We even have a new verb creeping into the language to reflect this change in behavior: although secretaries still *type*, managers *keyboard*. Regardless of what you call it, however, word processing is one way to save a lot of time in the composing process because you can make changes later without typing the entire piece—or waiting for someone else to retype it.

Dictation is another method for drafting rapidly and getting a typed copy. New technology is making dictation increasingly easy: such devices as telephone hookups to word-processing centers and portable recording machines are replacing the personal secretary. Not only are these devices more flexible in terms of time and place, but studies show that typists can transcribe at an average of thirty-five words per minute from taped dictation, which is faster than typing from shorthand transcription (twenty-five words per minute) or handwritten text (fifteen words per minute). With all these advantages, the biggest danger in dictation is that you will ramble: so stick to your idea chart.

Most of us probably have not dictated before, and it takes some getting used to. It requires practice, but with attention to a few points, it should eventually come easily.

Keep in mind, then, these six points as you dictate. (1) Begin by explaining the format. Give the transcriber all the format details first. In some firms, you'll need only to identify the standard formats. In other cases, you might want to prepare standard formats yourself for your own reference. Also, include instructions on the number of copies you'll need and whether you are dictating a rough draft or a final copy. (2) Speak in a normal, relaxed voice. Try not to be flustered by the machine. Speak normally, enunciating clearly and not talking too rapidly. (3) Identify needed punctuation and paragraph breaks. Most people let their voice inflection indicate a comma, but specify end-of-sentence punctuation (such as "period," or "question mark") and other punctuation (such as "dash," "semicolon," "parentheses"). Indicate paragraphing by saying "new paragraph." Indicate capitals by saying "initial cap" or "all caps" before you say the word. (4) Spell out unusual words, proper names, and possibly confusing words. Be particularly careful to spell out people's names; you know how it feels to have your name misspelled. See Figure 7.1 for a list of the most commonly confused words for dictation. See Figure 7.2 for the phonetic alphabet telephone operators use to clarify specific letters. (5) Correct as clearly as possible. If you are using a machine, rewind and tape over. If you are phoning it in, say "correction" and then specify the unit of thought you are revising; say, for example, "Correction. Begin sentence again." (6) End with thanks and possibly revisions. Some people play back the tape and add changes at the end of the tape. Be sure to tell your transcriber at the beginning if you're going to do this. It's proper and friendly to thank the transcriber at the end of the tape, even though you may feel funny thanking a machine.

Regardless of how you choose to get your draft down quickly into a typed copy (by typing, word processing, or dictating), another hint for effective drafting is this: **don't necessarily force beginning to end** composition. Many writers get bogged down with their introduction or first section. Besides, writers often have to change their introduction because they modify their ideas or organization as they compose the rest of the draft. Writing your introduction last will help you avoid both of these problems. In chapter 8, we will analyze exactly what you should include in your introduction. Right now, however, as you think about the composing process, consider writing your introduction last.

Stage 3: Editing

An important hint for effective editing is to schedule a **time gap** between the drafting and editing stages. I guarantee that you will do a better job of editing if you leave some time between the two stages. For important or complicated writing, separate the two stages by several days, or at least overnight. If you are extremely busy or if you are writing on less important, more routine matters, leave a shorter time gap. For example,

accede, exceed	forth, fourth
accept, except	incidence, incidents
access, excess	its, it's
addition, edition	legislator, legislature
affect, effect	loose, lose
allusion, illusion	maybe, may be
already, all ready	miner, minor
altogether, all together	new, knew
anyone, any one	no, know
assistance, assistants	ordinance, ordnance
bare, bear	passed, past
brake, break	personal, personnel
capital, capitol	practical, practicable
cease, seize	precedence, precedents
cite, sight, site	principal, principle
coarse, course	residence, residents
complement, compliment	respectfully, respectively
correspondence, correspondents	rite, right, write
council, counsel, consul	some one, someone
decent, descent, dissent	stationary, stationery
deference, difference	their, there, they're
disapprove, disprove	therefore, there for
eligible, illegible	through, threw
era, error	waive, wave
everyone, every one	whose, who's
finally, finely	your, you're
formally, formerly	

FIGURE 7.1

Most commonly confused words for dictation

you might give yourself a few hours, a lunch break, or even a five- to ten-minute coffee break.

Only after this time gap should you embark on the final step in the writing process. When you start editing, don't immediately begin to agonize over detailed issues such as commas and precise wording. Instead, save yourself time by analyzing the **larger issues first**, so you can cut or modify sections before you have wasted time perfecting them. These larger issues include the following questions: Does this document accomplish my communication objective? Is it written in the appropriate style? Is it written appropriately for my audience? Does it emphasize my main idea(s)? Is it structured persuasively? Should it be in written form at all? (See part I of this book if you are unclear what any of these questions

A	Alice	N	Nellie
B	Bertha	O	Oliver
C	Charles	P	Peter
D	David	Q	Quaker
E	Edward	R	Robert
F	Frank	S	Samuel
G	George	T	Thomas
H	Henry	U	Utah
I	Ida	V	Victor
J	James	W	William
K	Kate	X	X ray
L	Lewis	Y	Young
M	Mary	Z	Zebra

FIGURE 7.2

Phonetic alphabet for spelling as you dictate

mean.) Then, and only then, should you edit the document, paragraphs, sentences, words, and punctuation, as we shall be discussing in the next several chapters. Again, don't fine-tune your writing until you have checked for overall strategy.

One good way to edit is to spread out your draft—which, of course, should be typed, double-spaced, and on one side of the paper only—and analyze it. Examine its plans, logic, and flow. Adjust it and regroup it where necessary. If you're using a standard typewriter, cut and tape sections to move them (and avoid wasting your time retyping). If you're using a word processor, you can move sections electronically.

The final step in editing is to **fine-tune** your writing. Unfortunately for many ineffective writers, this fine-tuning step is where they start, instead of where they end, the writing process. More fortunate and effective writers edit last.

What should you check for as you edit? Basically, you check: (1) the document and paragraphs, and (2) the sentences and words. The second part of this chapter and chapter 8 cover the document and paragraphs; chapters 9 and 10 cover sentences and words.

Avoiding writer's block

If you use these techniques for drafting and editing, you should find that you can alleviate problems with writer's block. Writing is difficult work.

No formula, alas, will free you from that work. However, here are some suggestions to help you avoid the most common pitfalls in the writing process.

1. Remember that it is a myth that writing is easily inspired in everyone else. Writing is a complex process involving various stages, not a one-step magic formula.

2. Schedule your time. You don't have to write in one session. Plan so you can separate your prewriting, drafting, and editing stages. Allow a gap of days or at least one night between drafting and editing for important and complicated documents; allow hour-long lunch, or coffee breaks for less important or routine documents.

3. Separate the thinking process from the ordering process. Clear thinking and clear writing are related, but they are not identical. Order your ideas appropriately for your reader; don't just write in the order that the ideas occurred to you.

4. Separate the ordering process from the drafting process. Never start to write without an idea chart. Order your ideas before you start to put them into paragraph and sentence form.

5. Separate the drafting process from the editing process. Do not try to edit during the drafting stage. During the drafting stage, let your creativity flow. Do not worry about specifics; you can come back and fix them later. Do not necessarily write straight through from beginning to end. Do not try to "finish one thing at a time"; you can revise later.

6. If you bog down during the editing stage, try: imagining you are talking to your reader; free-writing for a while; or talking into a tape recorder, typing that, and revising it.

7. Edit a typed copy. Whether you use a typewriter, word processor, or dictation, get a typed copy. Use one side only, double- or triple-spaced. Typed copies are much easier to correct.

8. Move sections around if necessary. Do not waste time rewriting or retyping sections that do not need to be changed. Instead, move them around—by machine if you're using a word processor, with scissors and tape if you're using paper.

9. Expect to rethink. Although we have been discussing the different stages in the writing process separately, in fact the stages are not completely separate; as a writer, you do not actually move in lockstep from generating information to drafting to editing. You might, for example, find and fix flaws in your organization when you are

editing and fine-tuning. Or, you might find and fix problems with your strategy as you are organizing. By expecting this kind of continual rethinking, you can avoid some of the frustrations that occur when it happens.

Business Formats

What makes business writing different from the academic writing you have spent most of your life doing? One major difference has to do with the conventional formats used in business writing—such as letters, memos, and reports—which differ from the formats you use in school, such as term papers and essays. In the rest of this chapter, we will look at these three business formats: (1) letters, (2) memos, and (3) reports.

Letters

Letters are the major form of external communication—that is, communication to people outside your own company. Business letters include seven **standard elements:**

1. The heading includes either your return address in the company letterhead, followed by the date, or (as in the following example) your return address and the date, typed in:

   > 122 Brook Hollow
   > Lexington, CT 95540-9876
   > March 28, 1992

2. The inside address includes your reader's name, title, and address, typed at the left margin like this:

   > Ms. Helen Pellegrin, Director
   > Personnel Department
   > Digimax Corporation
   > 100 Southington Avenue
   > Corvallis, OR 34567-0021

   See Figure 7.3 for a list of state abbreviations.

3. The salutation may be formal:

   > My Dear Ms. D'Aunno:
   > Dear Mr. Chairperson:

semiformal:

> Dear Mr. Leavitt:

or informal:

> Dear Scott:
> Dear Scott,

The salutation is usually punctuated with a colon, never with a semicolon. Use a comma only for informal letters. (See chapter 2 for ways to avoid sexist salutations, such as "Dear Sir.")

4. The subject line (optional) serves as a topic heading for your reader:

> SUBJECT: ADJUSTMENT TO CLAIM #4563

FIGURE 7.3

Abbreviations for U.S. states

Alabama	AL	Montana	MT
Alaska	AK	Nebraska	NB
Arizona	AZ	Nevada	NV
Arkansas	AR	New Hampshire	NH
California	CA	New Jersey	NJ
Colorado	CO	New Mexico	NM
Connecticut	CT	New York	NY
Delaware	DE	North Carolina	NC
Florida	FL	North Dakota	ND
Georgia	GA	Ohio	OH
Hawaii	HI	Oklahoma	OK
Idaho	ID	Oregon	OR
Illinois	IL	Pennsylvania	PA
Indiana	IN	Rhode Island	RI
Iowa	IA	South Carolina	SC
Kansas	KS	South Dakota	SD
Kentucky	KY	Tennessee	TN
Louisiana	LA	Texas	TX
Maine	ME	Utah	UT
Maryland	MD	Vermont	VT
Massachusetts	MA	Virginia	VA
Michigan	MI	Washington	WA
Minnesota	MN	West Virginia	WV
Mississippi	MS	Wisconsin	WI
Missouri	MO	Wyoming	WY

5. The body.

6. The closing and signature may be formal, including your full name and title:

> Very truly (or Sincerely) yours,
> WIDGET CORPORATION
>
> *Hilda Morales*
>
> Hilda Morales,
> Training Assistant

semiformal:

> Yours truly (or Sincerely yours, or Sincerely),
>
> *Patrick Maloney*
>
> Patrick Maloney
> Sales Representative

or informal:

> Cordially,
>
> *Bret Bero*
>
> Bret Bero
> Assistant to the Director

7. The references (if necessary) at the bottom-left margin indicate the writer's uppercase and the typist's lowercase initials, enclosures, copies (indicated both to readers receiving the letter and to readers receiving copies), or blind copies (indicated only to those readers receiving copies):

> MM:ab (or MM/ab)
> Encl.
> cc
> bcc

Standard formats for letters are semiblock, modified-block, and full-block. Use whichever form your company or audience prefers. Semi-block is usually the most popular, but use any format as long as you are consistent within the letter. These formats are illustrated in Figure 7.4.

Now that we've seen the standard elements and formats for letters, let's discuss what they say. Letters usually fall into one of **three categories.** Figure 7.5 shows examples of these different kinds of letters. Don't use these examples as formulas, however. Base your decisions about how to organize a letter on your communication strategy.

First, some letters are about routine or pleasant matters: for example, routine claims, routine credit, routine orders, and other requests for information. Naturally, in these kinds of situations, you would usually choose a direct approach to emphasize the good news—making it clear right away what you are writing about, then providing the necessary details, and closing with the main idea or a look toward the future.

Other letters convey less pleasant information—so-called "bad news" letters—for example, saying no to an adjustment request, a credit request, or to someone who has ordered merchandise. Again, because of the reasons we discussed in part I, in these situations you would probably choose an indirect approach to lead up to the "bad news"—opening with a *buffer* (a pleasant or neutral statement), then providing the facts or reasons that led to the negative decision, then stating the bad news, and finally ending with a pleasant or neutral statement.

Third, some letters are written to convince: for example, sales letters or collection letters. Again referring back to the strategy we discussed in part I, in a sales letter you want to open with an attention getter, use the motivational techniques we discussed in chapter 4 to describe the product you want your readers to buy or the action you want them to take, and close with the action step you hope they will take.

FIGURE 7.4

Standard formats for letters

Full-block
Each line begins flush with left margin.

```
Date

Name
Address
Address

Salutation:

xxxxxxxxxxxxxxxxxxxxxxxxxxxxxxxxxxxxxxxxxxxxxxxxxxxxxxx
xxxxxxxxxxxxxxxxxxxxxxxxxxxxxxxxxxxxx.

xxxxxxxxxxxxxxxxxxxxxxxxxxxxxxxxxxxxxxxxxxxxxxxxxxxxxxx
xxxxxxxxxxxxxxxxxxxxxxxxxxxxxx.

Closing,

Signature
```

FIGURE 7.4 (cont)

Modified-block
Date, closing and signature begin at the center of the page

```
                                        Date


      Name
      Address
      Address

      Salutation:


      xxxxxxxxxxxxxxxxxxxxxxxxxxxxxxxxxxxxxxxxxxxxxxxxxxxxxxx
      xxxxxxxxxxxxxxxxxxxxxxxxxxxxxxxxxxxxxxxx.


      xxxxxxxxxxxxxxxxxxxxxxxxxxxxxxxxxxxxxxxxxxxxxxxxxxxxxxx
      xxxxxxxxxxxxxxxxxxxxxxxxxxxxxx.


                                        Closing,


                                        Signature
```

Semi-block
Paragraphs are indented five spaces.

```
                                        Date


      Name
      Address
      Address

      Salutation:


          xxxxxxxxxxxxxxxxxxxxxxxxxxxxxxxxxxxxxxxxxxxxxxxxxxxx
      xxxxxxxxxxxxxxxxxxxxxxxxxxxxxxxxxxxxxxx.


          xxxxxxxxxxxxxxxxxxxxxxxxxxxxxxxxxxxxxxxxxxxxxxxxxxxx
      xxxxxxxxxxxxxxxxxxxxxxxxxxxxxx.

                                        Closing,

                                        Signature
```

Memos

Memos (*memo* is short for *memorandum*) are the form people use to write to one another within a company. The standard elements of a memo are fairly simple. They include: (1) the date; (2) the "to" line with your reader's name or readers' names; (3) the "from" line with your name, and (4) the "subject" line.

Usually, the subject line is the element that causes the most problems. Think of the subject line as a headline in a newspaper. Imagine your reader shuffling through mounds of paperwork. Choose the headline that would be most useful for him or her. Your subject should be neither too broad, such as

Incorrect: Subject: Announcement

nor too specific, such as

Incorrect: Subject: Announcement about the meeting at 2:00 P.M. on Friday, October 15, to discuss three items

Further, it should not be either a sentence or a paragraph.

Incorrect: Subject: We will be holding a meeting next Friday at 2:00 P.M. in the conference room.

Instead, it should be a headline phrase, such as:

Correct: Subject: October 15 Meeting Agenda

Finally, standard practice for memo writing dictates that you sign your name at the top of the page, next to the "from" line, like this:

Correct: From: Bob Zimmerman

not add a closing and signature at the end, as you would in a letter.

Incorrect: Sincerely yours,

Bob Zimmerman

Bob Zimmerman

FIGURE 7.5

Sample letters

Letters about routine or pleasant matters

Sample letter of inquiry

WIGGETT COMPANY

165 South Marshland Avenue
Houston, Texas 77262–3122

February 15, 19____

Ms. Nancy Harsha, Manager
Lakeview Conference Center
Forty Post Road
Houston, TX 77262–2306

Dear Ms. Harsha:

Direct opening

   We at the Wiggett Company are currently planning our training seminars for next month. We are considering the Lakeview Conference Center as a possible site. Will you please send me the following information about your hotel?

Clearly stated inquiry

1. What is your room charge for a group of 20 people?
2. What is your meal charge for 3 meals a day for 20 people?
3. What kind of meeting rooms do you have available? at what costs?
4. What kinds of visual aids do you have available? at what costs?

Polite closing

   We will be choosing our location on March 15, so I would appreciate hearing from you before then.

Sincerely,

Alex

Alexander Paine
Personnel Coordinator

Sample letter of response

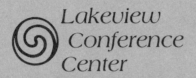

Lakeview
Conference
Center

RIVER ROAD
LIVINGSTON, TX 77351–7602

March 1, 19____

Mr. Alexander Paine
Personnel Coordinator
Wiggett Company
165 South Marshland Avenue
Houston, TX 77262–3122

Dear Mr. Paine:

Direct opening

I am happy to answer your four questions regarding the Lakeview Conference Center as a possible location for your training sessions.

1. We can offer you our discounted rate for any group over 10 people. Therefore, the room charge per night is $50.
2. The standard charge for three meals a day is $35. We can make arrangements for more or less expensive meals if you wish.
3. We have one large meeting room, seating 50, and three small rooms, each seating 25. One of these small rooms would probably meet your purposes. There is no extra charge for use of the meeting room.
4. We have flip charts, overhead projectors, and slide projectors available at no charge. We can also rent videotape equipment for you at $20 per day.

Clear response

Polite closing

Please don't hesitate to call if you have further questions.

I look forward to welcoming you to our hotel.

Sincerely,

Nancy

Nancy Harsha
Manager

Letters saying "no"

Samples letter of credit denial

CAMPION'S CLOTHING STORE

905 Birch Street • Concord, NH 03301−1848

April 22, 19____

Mr. George Stromeyer
411 Alton Woods Drive
Nashua, NH 03061−5236

Dear Mr. Stromeyer:

Buffer

We sincerely appreciate your interest in opening an account with us at Campion's Clothing Store.

Indirect structure

Polite closing

The results of the routine credit checks you authorized, however, permit us to serve you only as a cash customer. In that capacity, we look forward to seeing you in the store again soon.

Sincerely,

Sherri Carroll

Sherri Carroll
Assistant Manager

Sample letter of merchandise-exchange denial

Grocery Store

3412 South Main Street
Iowa City, IA 52240—4764

June 9, 19____

Ms. Julia Rabkin
835 Midvale Avenue
Iowa City, IA 52240—4761

Dear Ms. Rabkin:

Buffer

What you said in your May 17 letter is correct: we want to keep our customers happy.

Indirect structure

That is why we maintain our 90-day return policy. Potato chips will become stale after 90 days, and we don't want to sell another customer a stale product. Therefore, we hope you will understand why we cannot accept returns after 90 days.

Polite closing

Thank you for this opportunity to explain. We look forward to continuing to do business with you.

Sincerely,

John Casesa
Produce Manager

Letters to convince

Sample sales letter

Maloney Insurance Company

11 Middlefield Road, Suite B
Minneapolis, MN 55401-4764

December 3, 19___

Mr. Allen Dietrich
52 Fruitdale Street
Minneapolis, MN 55401-4652

Dear Mr. Dietrich:

Attention grabber

Do you know how the new tax laws will affect you this year?

Explanation

We are offering a free seminar explaining the changes caused by the new tax laws. After the seminar, you may sign up—if you wish—for an individual consultation with one of our representatives.

Action step

Please join us on Saturday, December 15, at 10:00 A.M. at the Sunset Hotel conference room to learn more about how you can benefit from the new tax laws.

Sincerely,

Ardis Olson

Ardis Olson

Sample collection letter

wholesale fabrics
11245 paseo grande/glendale, AZ 85301-5664

November 3, 19____

Ms. Rebecca Cunningham
Rebecca Dress Shop
4556 Diana Road
Glendale, AZ 85301-5677

Dear Ms. Cunningham:

Attention grabber

    As a business woman, you realize that your credit rating is one of your most valuable assets.

Explanation and action step

    Yet you are jeopardizing your credit rating for $96.75, the balance of your past due account with us. Please maintain your good credit reputation by sending your payment today. Otherwise, we shall have to report your account as delinquent to the local credit bureau. Your check will make it unnecessary for us to make such a report.

Sincerely,

John Krieder

John Krieder

FIGURE 7.6

Memo formats

**Most companies have their own memorandum forms.
Here are some typical examples:**

Date_____

To: _____

From: _____

Subject: _____

Date: _____

Subject: _____

To: _____

From: _____

To: _____   Date: _____

From: _____   Subject: _____

Figure 7.6 shows some conventional formats for a memo. Most companies provide memo forms with blanks for you to fill in.

When do you write memos? In general, any time you would write a "letter" to someone within your company. Typical occasions for memo writing include: (1) announcing something, such as an event or policy, (2) confirming something people have agreed on, or (3) clarifying something in writing, thereby providing a permanent record.

Reports

A final set of business writing conventions has to do with reports. There are many kinds of reports—some formal, others informal; some sent to audiences within the company, others sent to audiences outside the company; some conveying information or summarizing activities (what we called the TELL style in chapter 3), others making recommendations (the SELL style); some *interim* or *current-status* reports, others *final* reports. Obviously, reports will vary in these different situations.

In general, however, reports include preliminary information, a body, and supplementary material. See Figure 7.7 for an example of each element.

The **preliminary information** may include four items:

1. The title page includes, of course, the title—usually four to eight words long—your name and position, your reader's name and position, and the date.

2. The cover letter (if you're sending the report outside the company) or cover memo (if you're sending it within the company) usually discusses the authorization for the report or the occasion for writing the report, the scope, any acknowledgments, and a polite closing.

3. The *abstract* or *executive summary* is a stand-alone document that summarizes the content, not just the organization, of your report. For example, instead of saying the report covers three trends, summarize what each of those trends is. Think of this summary as a condensed version of your report so busy readers can get the gist of your ideas quickly. Your headings on the summary should be *exactly* the same as those on your report, so your readers can easily skim back and forth between the two. Your executive summary is crucial, because the research shows that most managers read it, although fewer than half of them read the entire body of your report. The executive summary is usually written last and is usually no more than one page single-spaced.

4. The table of contents lists the sections in your report. Number the pages in the body of the report with Arabic numbers: 1, 2, 3, and so

forth. Number the pages of the preliminary information with small Roman numerals: i, ii, iii, and so forth. Appendixes are usually letters: Appendix A, Appendix B, and so forth. Exhibits are usually numbered with large Roman numerals: Exhibit I, Exhibit II. The table of contents *may* also include a list of illustrations or exhibits.

The **body of the report** comes next:

5. The introduction is *not* a synopsis or summary. (Remember, the synopsis was included in your executive summary or abstract in the report's preliminary-information section.) Instead, the introduction states what current situation exists, why you are writing, and how your report is organized. (We shall discuss introductions in more detail in the next chapter, pages 184–86.)

6. The conclusions, for a TELL style, or the recommendations, for a SELL-style report, usually come next.

7. The detailed development and support provides the main body of descriptive, explanatory, or analytic information. It should be organized clearly, with headings and subheadings, as we shall discuss in the next chapter.

The **supplementary material** at the end *may* include three items. Whenever appendixes and exhibits are short enough, include them in the body of your report instead of making your reader go back and forth to the supplemental information.

8. Appendixes stand on their own. Examples include tables of data, samples of forms, copies of questionnaires, explanatory articles, or financial statements.

9. Exhibits are charts and graphs. (We shall discuss these in chapter 13.)

10. Reference materials—bibliography and footnotes—usually come last. See Appendix E for details on research and documentation. Figure 7.7 shows a sample report.

In conclusion, this chapter has served as an introduction to business writing. In business, you will need to compose effectively and efficiently. You will also need to use different formats—letters, memos, and reports—from the ones you use in other situations. In the chapters that follow, we shall apply various business writing criteria to these various business formats.

FIGURE 7.7

Sample report

CORPORATE ARTS SUPPORT AT HIGH TECH CORP.

[handwritten: how info. is presented]
[handwritten: Title]
[handwritten: Heading]

Executive Summary

This report outlines how High Tech Corp. can contribute to the arts in a manner that combines the company's philanthropic motives with the aim of promoting its own interest. It concludes that a well-developed program of arts funding can be a highly effective way to improve our company's image as a business led by enlightened and forward-looking management, a good community member, a producer of good products or services, and a good place to work. The report shows how we can develop such an effective program by: (1) developing goals and messages for our donations; (2) targeting an audience; and (3) developing a method to establish and implement the program. The report ends with four examples of corporations that have developed highly effective programs to fund the arts and serve the business's interest at the same time.

[handwritten: what concl.]
[handwritten: key points]
[handwritten: how org., concl.]

Steps for program development

[handwritten: Sub heading, Sub/sub heading]

1. Developing goals and messages for our donations

Examples of goals a business might establish for its arts donations are to improve its public image as a good citizen, neighbor, and place to work, increase consumer awareness in a new market, improve the quality image of its products, and increase sales. Messages that might achieve these goals are that the company is run by enlightened and creative management, that the business takes the same care and discipline with its work as does an artist, and that the consumer can help the arts by buying its products or services.

[handwritten: basics, facts & concl.]

2. Targeting our audience

A corporation can target the audience it wants to reach through its donations to the arts. Because arts audiences are generally of higher income and education than normal, arts funding can be especially helpful if this is the audience the business wants to reach. Other targets that can be isolated through arts donations are international, national, and local audiences.

3. Developing a method to implement our plan

To create an effective arts-funding program, management should take advantage of opportunities to consult experts in public relations, advertising and marketing, and corporate philanthropy and foundations. These people can help both in developing and in implementing the program.

Examples of other companies

Examples of successful arts-funding programs are those of American Express, Ciba-Geigy, Amway, and General Mills.

[handwritten: add key points about these co.]

CORPORATE ARTS SUPPORT AT HIGH TECH CORP.

As the arts continue to rely increasingly on corporations for support, many businesses are learning to structure their gifts so that they in turn can benefit from the arts. While a business can still maintain philanthropic motives in its support of the arts, there are many sophisticated methods it can use to couple these motives with its own interest. According to Jerry C. Welsh, an American Express marketing executive: "The wave of the future isn't checkbook philanthropy, it's a marriage of corporate marketing and social responsibility."[8]

Business donations to the arts have been steadily increasing in the United States for the last thirty years. According to a survey by the Business Committee for the Arts, business support for the arts exceeded $500 million per year in 1982. This figure is three times higher than subsidies provided by the National Endowment for the Arts.[11] The increased reliance on corporate support first started in this century as much of the wealth in the United States shifted from a few powerful families to the many stockholders of corporations. Another increase came in the 1970s as a result of a burgeoning economy and business's heightened sensitivity to social responsibility. The most recent impetus for increased donations to the arts has been recent federal budget cuts in arts programs.

The purpose of this report is to explain some of the methods High Tech Corp. can use to choose among the numerous requests for donations to the arts and how we can assure that our gifts will also serve its self-interest. The report begins by outlining three important aspects of corporate donations to the arts: (1) developing the goals we wish to achieve through donations and the messages that will achieve them; (2) targeting the audience we want to reach; and (3) developing a method we can use to establish and implement an arts-support program. The report concludes with four examples of successful arts-support programs developed by corporations in the United States.

Steps for program development

1. Developing goals and messages for our donations

The first step toward more effective use of donations is to determine goals we wish to achieve from our support of the arts and the messages that will achieve them. Corporations can often attain several goals through arts support and send a variety of messages to the public. Examples of messages, as well as the goals they intend to accomplish, are as follows:

* Enlightened company that cares about society as a whole and the community where it does business. Goals are to improve public image and business.

* Similarity between the excellence and care seen in art and the company's products or services. Goals are to sell more products, reach a different market, and attract investors.

* Good place to work, sophisticated management and art as part of the corporate environment. Goals are to improve employee morale and attract new talent.

* Forward-looking and creative management that aligns itself with the artistic ideas of today. Goals are to improve public image and attract investors.

* Good product or service to buy, because for each new transaction the corporation promises to donate a predetermined amount of money to a specific arts organization. Goal is to increase sales.

important items

2. Targeting our audience

backward ref.   *forward ref.*

After establishing goals and messages, we should determine the audience we wish to reach through our donations. Because arts audiences are traditionally of higher income and education than the general public, corporations can use this to their advantage if this is the audience they wish to reach. In 1978 the National Endowment for the Arts published a survey of 272 audience studies. The results showed that the median income of arts audiences was 15 percent to 30 percent above the population median; that about 85 percent of the audiences had been to college whereas only 26 percent of the population had; that 56 percent of the audiences were in professional occupations whereas only 15 percent of the labor force were; and that blue-collar workers constituted 7 percent of the audiences and 47 percent of the labor force.[2] American Express feels this is the upscale audience that uses its travel-related services, and, consequently, it has developed highly sophisticated marketing techniques through the arts.

We might also target an international, national, or local audience through arts donations. If we wish to receive national recognition for High Tech Corp.'s gifts, we can either support big-ticket items that automatically command national recognition, such as the Metropolitan Opera or televised art, or we can nationally advertise its contributions. In addition, we can reach an international audience by supporting American performing-arts groups that tour abroad. Many corporations, however, are more concerned with reaching a local audience where their business is located or targeting a specific geographic region where their business or image needs improvement.

3. Developing a method to implement our plan

The method we use to determine our goals, messages, and target audience and then implement our program will vary according to what the management decides to devote to this project. Whenever possible, however, the program should involve people with skills in public relations, advertising and marketing, and corporate philanthropy and outside foundations. Management should realize that all donations will have a public relations effect, whether they want it or not, and that any discussions regarding contributions should include someone with public relations experience. The public relations expert can give realistic opinions about recognition the corporation can achieve through different programs. A person with advertising and marketing expertise should also be included to help define the message the company wants to send, the target audience, and the method and costs of reaching them. Some corporations hire specialists to guide their arts programs. This is especially true of companies that have private art collections. A curator, whose yearly salary will vary between $25,000 and $40,000, can assemble a valuable collection with a consistent theme, as well as maintain and publicize the collection.[10] Other outside sources that can help plan arts programs are foundations such as the New York–based Business Committee for the Arts.

Examples of Other Companies

Ciba-Geigy Corporation

Under the direction of President and CEO A. M. MacKinnon, the Ciba-Geigy Corporation has purchased an extensive collection of art representing the

New York School of Abstract Expressionism and Geometric Painting. By focusing on a particular theme in its collection—an in-depth study of the New York School—the company has achieved national recognition. The company started the collection when it moved from its Manhattan headquarters to its new suburban location in Ardsley, New York. MacKinnon felt a commitment to modern art symbolized the company's break with the past and its attitude that its business melds both art and science. Because the company is one of the oldest producers of dyes, its art collection also emphasizes the use of color to further stress the meeting of science and art.

Ciba-Geigy reaches a national audience because of the quality and depth of its collection, but its primary targets are its employees and the communities where it has offices. Through extensive exhibits both on Ciba-Geigy's property and in the community, the firm promotes its image as a good community member and employer.

General Mills

General Mills has hired a special curator, Donald B. McNeil, to assemble a collection of art as well as to promote it along with the company's reputation in exhibits around the country. The 1100-piece collection consists of works by living artists because, McNeil says, the artists are responding to the same currents in society as General Mills.[10] McNeil arranges exhibits at museums, universities, and community art centers around the world. In addition, the company regularly organizes exhibits for its employees.

Amway Corporation

A strong and regular supporter of the arts, Amway Corporation used its 1982 donation to the National Symphony Orchestra to help the firm reach a European audience where its business was beginning to expand. Amway sponsored a seventeen-concert tour of Europe for the orchestra. The chairman of Amway, Jay Van Andel, accompanied the orchestra on its tour and took advantage of the opportunity to invite distributors and foreign dignitaries to the concerts and receptions afterwards. In addition to improving the company's image with European distributors and the public, Van Andel had daily speaking engagements before heads of state and influential executives in conjunction with the orchestra tour. To show his appreciation, the conductor of the orchestra, internationally renowned cellist Mstislav Rostropovich, gave a private concert for Amway's employees at the Ada, Michigan plant.

American Express

American Express has what is now perhaps the most innovative program of corporate support for the arts. In thirty-two cities throughout the United States it has used a tremendously successful program that links its donations to a local art organization with use of the American Express card in that area. In Tulsa, Oklahoma, for example, American Express agreed to donate to the Tulsa Ballet Theatre one cent each time an American Express card was used in that area and $1 when a new card was issued. William M. McCormick, president of the firm's consumer and financial services group, says that agreements like this one are "as successful if not more successful as any marketing program we've ever done."[8] In addition to the funds it receives, the arts organization also benefits from the extensive advertising American Express does to promote the campaign. According to Michael Sudbury, the development director of the Tulsa Ballet Theatre: "American Express did all the work for promoting the campaign through its marketing and advertising department. All we had to do for advertising was approve copy and minor details. We could never afford to undertake such a professional and extensive campaign on our own."[18] A similar agreement with the San Jose Symphony resulted in $30,000 in donations and $205,000 in advertising for the symphony. American Express transactions in the area increased by 25 percent.

Through its campaign in Tulsa, American Express also wanted to increase the number of businesses that accept their card for purchases. To achieve this, they asked the ballet company to give an informal performance at the newest and largest shopping mall in Tulsa, where American Express wanted more business. American Express promoted this event with its own advertising and publicity. In addition, the company hosted a reception after a performance by the Dance Theatre of Harlem, a special visiting performance sponsored by the Tulsa Ballet. American Express used the power of the Tulsa Ballet Board of Directors and the attraction of the Dance Theatre of Harlem to entice retailers to their reception. In this way, company officials were able to gain important introductions with business leaders they wanted as clients.

Conclusions

We have a variety of creative ways to combine our philanthropic motives in supporting the arts with our desire to promote our own interest. Corporate support of the arts can be a highly effective means of improving our image as a good company with creative management, a good community member, a good place to work, and the producer of a good product or service. To develop an arts-support program that meets our needs, management should realize the valuable contributions they can make by consulting with experts in public relations, advertising and marketing, and corporate philanthropy and foundations.

Bibliography

[1] "American Express Shows Way to Benefit from Giving." *Business Week,* 18 October 1982, pp. 44–45.

[2] "Art for Subsidies Sake." *The Wall Street Journal,* 5 May 1984, p. 14.

[3] "Business Can Benefit by Giving to the Arts." *The Wall Street Journal,* 11 January 1982, p. 26.

[4] "The Corporate Bottom Line: It's Better to Give than to Receive." *Esquire,* March 1984, pp. 255–256.

[5] "Corporations and Culture." *Advertising Age,* 6 October 1980, p. 17.

[6] Dardenne, P. "Budweiser Program Teams Sports and Art." *Public Relations Journal,* February 1983, pp. 32–33.

[7] "Getting the Best from Corporate Philanthropy." *International Management,* April 1984, p. 5.

[8] "Helping Hands: Companies Change the Way They Make Charitable Donations." *The Wall Street Journal,* 21 June 1984, p. 1.

[9] Joseph, James. "Directing the Flow of Corporate Largesse." *Business and Society Review,* Summer 1982, pp. 40–43.

[10] "Keepers of Corporate Art." *Fortune,* 21 March 1983, pp. 114–121.

[11] MacKinnon, A. "Business and the Arts: A Productive Alliance Comes under Stress," *Management Review,* October 1982, pp. 63–71.

[12] Marth, D. "Contributions to Culture," *Nation's Business,* July 1982, pp. 58–59.

[13] McKinley, J. K. "Business for Art's Sake," *Management World,* February 1983, pp. 63–71.

[14] Milmo, S. and Pfaff, C. "Culture, Sports Draw Sponsors." *Advertising Age,* 22 June 1981, p. 38.

[15] Pirozzolo, R. D. "Support for the Arts." *Public Relations Journal,* September 1982, p. 23.

[16] Reynes, R. A. "Gift Horses and Hobbyhorses." *Barron's,* 28 March 1983, pp. 38–40.

[17] "Small Charities Hit Hard by Recession." *The Wall Street Journal,* 24 February 1982, p. 33.

[18] Sudbury, Michael. Personal interview. 20 February 1985.

This report was written by Mark Floyd and is used with his permission.

REVIEW QUESTIONS

To check your understanding

1. What is meant by a *drafting attitude?*
2. What are two advantages of a typewritten draft?
3. What six points should you remember as you dictate?
4. What is the first stage of editing?
5. List four tips for avoiding "writer's block."
6. List the seven elements of a business letter. Which two are optional?
7. Letters usually fall into one of three categories. The opening differs for each of the three categories. List the three openings you would use for each of the three categories.
8. List three characteristics a memo heading should *not* exhibit.
9. What is the difference between a report's *executive summary* and *introduction?*
10. Place these report elements in the correct order: the introduction, the reference section, the abstract, the cover letter, the appendixes, and the table of contents.

APPLICATION EXERCISES

To apply your knowledge

Rewrite the following memo, using the standard business-memo format.

Subject: Revisions
From: Leslie Baxter

Dear Mr. Harmon,
The new procedures manual is now available in final form. Mr. Michael Free and Ms. Anne Jones, who compiled the revised manual, will be conducting seminars with each division to answer any questions concerning the revisions.
The meeting with the Receiving Division is scheduled for March 16, 10:30–11:30 A.M. in Room 200. Please arrange for your entire staff to attend. Individual copies of the manual will be distributed at the meeting.
Thank you for your cooperation.

Sincerely,

Leslie Baxter

Leslie Baxter

Rewrite the following letter from Daniel Long (Sales Representative, Southwest Sprinkler, 160 Freedom Parkway, Phoenix, Arizona 95026–0523), using the standard business-letter format.

> Mr. Wilson Hewitt
> Appleby Agricultural Supply
> 116 Grove Avenue, Tulare, CA 93671–2340
> April 18, 1994.
>
>
> Mr. Hewitt,
> I am sorry to inform you that we are unable to fill your order #10016AA for ten solid-state Dynaflow sprinkler-system control panels right now. The demand for this unit has simply exceeded our expectations and it will be at least sixty days before any more units are ready for shipment.
>   If you would like us to hold your order and ship the units when they are ready we would be more than pleased to do so. Just return the enclosed order form and we will rush you the control panels as soon as possible. Appleby Agricultural Supply is one of our most valued customers and we hate to cause you any inconvenience. We hope to be of service to you again in the future. I remain,
>   apologetically yours,

CASES

To practice what you learned

> *NOTE:* **The twenty letter-writing cases, ten memo-writing cases, and ten report-writing cases that follow are designed to be used throughout part II of this book, as exercises for the various writing skills covered in chapters 7–10.**

Letter cases

1. You work for a manufacturer of farm machinery. The recent fall in grain prices has cut retail sales and, as a result, new orders from your distributors. One of them, A&M Equipment, has an outstanding bill of $27,000. The payment is six months overdue. You will allow A&M to pay the bill in three equal parts, with the first payment due one month from the date of your letter. Write to Bill Schwartz, A&M Equipment, 299 Main St., Popperville, IN 47568-2583.

2. You are a sales representative for a toy manufacturer and would like to propose a new promotional package to your retail outlets. Beginning in October, shoppers who purchase two toys above ten dollars in price will be able to select a third toy free. You would like retailers to display the free toys shoppers may choose from in a prominent location; you will provide signage and other materials for the display. You feel the promotion will attract business for the retailers in the pre-Christmas season. Write a form letter to your retailers.

3. You handle claims for a large mail-order firm. A Mrs. Irma Watson writes that two months ago, she sent a check for $120 along with an order for twelve widgets at $10 each. She has not yet received the widgets, although your company has cashed the check. You must write her asking for proof of payment (a photocopy of her check) and stating that six months ago the price of widgets went up to $12 each. As a goodwill gesture, however, you will send her twelve widgets as ordered when a copy of both sides of the canceled check is received. Mrs. Irma Watson, 12 Main St., Brookhaven, IL 62910-8936.

4. You work for a software firm and recently ran across the name of an old school friend in a directory of free-lance programming consultants. You want to renew the acquaintance in the hopes that he may be able to aid you in getting some troublesome kinks out of a new program your firm is developing. Before you make him an offer, however, you want to check on his experience and expertise. Write him suggesting lunch when you visit his town next month. Larry Weiss, 1458 S. Hawkins, Omaha, NE 68112-4573.

5. You need to order new office equipment for your accounting firm. You would like to take advantage of a special offer advertised by Brown Furniture, whereby a 10 percent discount will be deducted from every order placed before January 1. You would like the equipment as soon as possible and hope to arrange a night delivery. Your order is for three executive desks, six swivel chairs, and a six-foot bookcase. Brown Furniture, 11943 Washington Place, Los Angeles, CA 90052-5716.

6. You are helping to organize a conference on business ethics, which your company considers a vital issue in today's changing business climate. You want to solicit participation in a panel discussion from six prominent members of the legal, financial, and corporate worlds. The panel will take place at 8:00 P.M., May 12, in the State University Auditorium. A banquet will precede the discussion. Draft a letter to the potential participants.

7. Your company obtained legal counsel from the firm Latham, Watkins, & Smith in September. You would like an itemized account of the services the firm provided before sending payment for its October 18 bill for $19,280. Mr. Joseph Popp, Latham, Watkins, & Smith, 1800 G Street, Suite 203, Utica, NY 13504-7682.

8. To kick off the spring season, your tour and travel company is offering a special tour package to local corporations. Any ten-day cruise in the South Pacific booked with thirty people or more will be discounted 20 percent between March 1 and April 15. The prices (before discount) are included in the enclosed brochure; they cover meals, tips, and local transportation (but not air fare to the port of departure). The tours are an ideal bonus incentive for outstanding managers. Draft a letter to companies encouraging them to take advantage of this offer.

9. You work for customer relations in a large rug-manufacturing company. Write to a customer denying her credit request of September 2. Explain you would be happy to reconsider her application if she resubmits after six months. Ms. Sarah Cullen, 8693 Dogwood Avenue, Midvale, MA 02332-3090.

10. You would like information about the latest products of the Allied Corp. A brochure or catalog will do; you would also like price lists, ordering instructions, and information about discounts for bulk orders. Sales Manager, Allied Corp., Highway 101, Grantville, MO 64456-7406.

11. On the basis of submitted bids, your company has decided to award a construction contract to Sampson Building & Construction. The project, a new parking lot at your Hoboken plant, is scheduled to begin in the fall, probably October 1. Write Mr. Arthur Sampson, president, informing him of the decision and telling him that a formal contract will be drawn up by your lawyers soon. 2100 Motter Avenue, Hoboken, NJ 07030-6445.

12. Your supervisor is not satisfied with the quality of the food served in the employee cafeteria and has asked you to draft a letter of complaint. Specifically, cite the frequent shortages at lunchtime, complaints of unsanitary conditions, and excessive energy use. Inform the supplier that your company will have to consider not renewing the contract if the level of service is not improved. Mr. T. Thiemann, Superfoods, Inc., 111 Lincoln Blvd., Miami, FL 33152-9411.

13. Your accounting office needs a word processor—a piece of equipment you know nothing about. You employ three typists, who must enter many contracts needing multiple revisions, as well as spread-

sheets and other tabular material. You would like advice about which of three models marketed by ABC Compuware would best suit your needs. Perhaps an ABC representative could call on you at your office. ABC Compuware, The Haverford Bldg., 21 Knowle St., Philadelphia, PA 19014-0987.

14. Before you can settle a customer complaint, you need a copy of all correspondence exchanged between the customer and your company about the purchase in question—of twelve model XD-3 collapsible drawing boards. Unfortunately, the person who had your position before you did not keep detailed records, and you must request a copy from the customer of her original order, which you believe was dated September 22. Anna Graham, Associated Graphics, 22 Sawyer St., Lexington, KY 40511-1320.

15. You need a copy of the June statement of your company's account with the Haven Restaurant. Bobby Owens, Owner, Haven Restaurant, 11856 Benny St., Frederick MD 21701-1042.

16. You are considering hiring Mr. Leonard Hunter, a financial analyst. His résumé lists employment in 1983 with Mark & Mark, Ltd., a London firm. Among his references are Mr. G. Eddington of Mark & Mark. Write him asking for a description of Mr. Hunter's duties and an assessment of his talents as an analyst. Mr. G. Eddington, Mark & Mark, Ltd., 21B Baker St., London, England.

17. Write to Mr. Leonard Hunter telling him you have decided to hire him as an assistant budget manager. His annual salary will be $25,000, with full benefits and two weeks' vacation each year. You hope he can begin work May 11. You look forward to receiving a written acceptance from him. Mr. Leonard Hunter, 79 Smith Way, Apt. 22B, Rockville, CA 95677-3024.

18. You would like to engage the services of a famous design firm, known for its classic look. Your department's recruiting brochure is almost finished and you need a rough layout by the end of the month. In addition, future projects include a new logo and several other brochures. You would like to arrange an exploratory meeting. Gary Graphics, 1212 Howard St., Percyville, IL 62272-2583.

19. You are sending a check for $1430.23 to the Shuttleville Supply Co. for services rendered. This payment, dated February 27, should close your company's account with the firm. Shuttleville Supply Co., Accounts Payable, 780 Bayou St., Biloxi, MS 49309-1332.

20. You need to reorder your letterhead—forty reams of 8½-by-11-inch bond. In addition, you need 1000 memo pads and 5000 No. 7 envelopes. Place an order with Young Paper Corp., 8117 Lucy Avenue, San Antonio, TX 78284–2253.

Memo cases

1. You work in your company's accounting department and need information about the contract with Petersen Architectural Associates—specifically, the date of the contract and the schedule of payment for the new wing on the company headquarters. Bill Lustig of the Legal Division handled this account; address your memo to him.

2. Your boss, Joe Frasier, has asked you for suggestions to increase employee productivity in your office. Your suggestion is a new seating arrangement, which would bring supervisors closer to their employees (supervisors now are grouped together in a separate suite). In addition, you think that the typists should be moved to another room to reduce the noise level. You are attaching a plan of your proposed rearrangements.

3. You want to remind all Publicity Department members of next Tuesday's staff meeting. The meeting will take place at 3:00 in Room 2B. Everyone should be prepared to discuss the results of the fall marketing campaign. An agenda will be circulated Monday morning.

4. Lately the office kitchen facilities have been neglected, and you want to encourage your staff to keep them neat, especially since visitors are frequently in the building. You don't want to appoint clean-up duty, but may have to if employees are not more conscientious about cleaning up after themselves. Also, you want to announce that all food left in the refrigerator Friday afternoon will be thrown away.

5. You need to report to your supervisor, Mr. Green, about your meeting today with the representative from Standard, Inc., Stuart James. Standard is prepared to take over production of all paper packaging for your company's products, but James suggests redesigning several packaging models to cut down on the amount of paper required. You need a go-ahead to get estimates from designers so you can determine whether this measure would really be cost-effective.

6. You want to attend a seminar on management that will be held in St. Paul on two consecutive weekends next month. You feel participation in the seminar will enhance your performance in your present situation as assistant supervisor, and may also prepare you for more advanced responsibilities. You are willing to pay for your transportation, but are writing your boss, Phyllis Sawyer, to ask whether the company might cover the $250 registration fee.

7. In response to your co-worker Rosemary Delaney's request, you have checked your files and verified that the St. John account is inactive. The last business between St. John Chemical Corp. and

your company was in 1979. Suggest that she contact Joe Dwyer at the Pittsburgh branch for more complete information about the St. John dealings—he last handled that account. Copy to Joe Dwyer.

8. You have met with Marion Baker of the Human Resources Department and want to confirm the results of your meeting. Employees in your department who have been employed for more than one year are now entitled to the full range of benefits; part-time employees will receive hospitalization only. Additionally, you need to know the maximum length of time an employee may receive disability pay, and would also like clarification of the company's policy for maternity leave.

9. You have prepared a budget for next month's sales meeting/banquet for field representatives. Items in the budget include the dinner, flowers, gifts, the speaker's fee, and transportation to and from the hotel. The estimated total cost is $5000 over budget. You are sending the itemized costs to Sue Osmond, the meeting organizer, and asking her what can be eliminated so that the budget is not exceeded.

10. You want to commend the performance of one of your co-workers, Sandy, at a recent meeting with a client. You think she made a superb presentation, which probably clinched the million-dollar contract with the Omega Corporation. You want her boss, Ed Burns, to know how much you valued her help. Copy to Sandra Day.

Report cases

1. You have completed a survey of consumer reactions to Tastytime, a new brand of cookie that your company hopes to introduce to retail markets in the spring. The survey measured consumer preference for a large versus a small cookie, along with the most popular flavors of cream filling. The report you are submitting to the marketing group includes a methodological description of the survey, quantification of its results, and conclusions about Tastytime's chances on the market. Appendix A gives the questions asked of consumers in the survey. Draft an introduction to the report.

2. Your annual report to shareholders details the company's fiscal condition during the past year. Expenditures and gains are tabulated, and are accompanied by descriptions of new projects, key personnel, and major policy trends. The report concludes with an account of the company's goals for the coming year and a special salute to the chairman of the board of directors for the last thirty years, Marvin Zucker. Draft a cover letter.

3. Your boss has asked you to analyze three markets—the South, the Midwest, and the Northwest—for perfume consumption. Your study shows that each of the regions has distinctly different purchasing patterns, which can be broken down according to sex and, further, three age groups within each sex: teenagers, twenty-five- to forty-year-olds, and those forty years old and over. You intend to give a detailed discussion of each of these groups. How would you highlight the sections of your report to make its structure stand out?

4. You have completed a cost/benefit analysis of the latest guided missile developed by the Heedlock Corp. The analysis covers the many stages of the project and its high overhead. In addition, it details the demands put on Heedlock by its Defense Department contract. You conclude that the missile is a costly, high-risk project. Draft an executive summary that reflects how you might present your material.

5. You are writing a report on your company's acquisition, a high-tech firm in Helium Valley. The firm manufactures computer chips and has produced net revenues of $1 million since 1981. The prospect for the coming year is a 24 percent growth rate and diversification into foreign markets. The report is directed to the board of trustees, who want to know the yield of the company's investment in the firm. You have chosen to order your data according to the following headings: history of firm's production, history of firm's sales, worldwide market outlook. Which of these aspects of your report would you summarize in your introduction? in your executive summary?

Note: The following cases involve primary research. You will be interviewing business people or analyzing business documents to gather your data.

6. Write a report on the use and effect of some aspect of electronic communication on one or more real businesses. Include live interviews, as well as library research.

7. Write a report comparing the writing and graphics in five or more current annual reports. (See chapter 13 for graphics information.)

8. Write a report on how one or more businesses have dealt with a crisis. (See F. Corrado, *Media for Managers* [Englewood Cliffs, N.J.: Prentice-Hall, 1984].)

9. Write a report on the kinds of communication that actually take place in a typical day of one or more business people. Compare your data with studies of what other researchers have found.

10. Write a report on the effects of office design and layout on communication patterns in one or more businesses. Compare your results with studies other researchers have made.

8

Business Documents and Paragraphs

Unity and Emphasis
For the document as a whole • For paragraphs

Organization and Highlighting

Connection

Appropriate Length

NOW that we have looked at the composing process, and the basic formats for letters, memos, and reports, let's get down to the nuts and bolts of what you look for as you edit *any* of those kinds of documents. This chapter will deal with editing your documents and paragraphs. The following two chapters will deal with editing your sentences and words.

To define the terms, the *document* is the entire piece you are writing: a letter, a memo, a report, or whatever. A *paragraph* is an essential unit of thought signaling to your reader a new step in your structural development. Although it may—very rarely—consist of a single sentence, a paragraph is almost always a group of four to eight sentences, or about 100 to 250 words.

Why should we discuss the documents and paragraphs together? Because they both should exhibit the same characteristics. In some senses, a well-constructed paragraph is like a document in miniature. A writer who can put together an effective paragraph can probably put together an effective document. The four principles that apply to documents and paragraphs are: (1) unity and emphasis, (2) organization and highlighting, (3) connection, and (4) appropriate length.

Unity and Emphasis

Unity means your writing has a quality of *oneness*: it is unified around a central idea; it is all on the same subject. *Emphasis* means that your main ideas are placed prominently, emphasized, that is, for your reader. These sound like easy concepts, but they are not always so easy to carry out. How can you make sure your writing is unified and emphatic? Let's look first at some pointers for unity and emphasis for the document as a whole, then at some similar—but not identical—pointers for each paragraph.

183

For the document as a whole

For the document as a whole, you can achieve unity by thinking back to your communication objective: "As a result of this message, my audience will _____ ." A unified document will deal only with ideas that relate to that objective. You can also achieve unity by thinking back to your idea chart. Ruthlessly cut out any information that does not relate to your main points. For example, if you are writing about one procedure, don't tack on information about another—unless, of course, you have set out to write a two-part document about two procedures. Besides cutting irrelevant ideas—making sure your document is unified around your objective and ideas—you should also make sure the document is unified around the correct *assignment*. Just as you would answer the exact question a teacher might ask you on a test, you should answer the exact question your boss or your customers, for example, might have requested you to answer in that piece of writing.

If cutting unrelated information makes your document unified, then stressing important information makes your document emphatic. As you recall from the Audience Memory Curve in chapter 5, the beginning and the end are the two places your reader is most likely to remember. Therefore, your introduction and conclusion are crucial.

INTRODUCTION: What should you include in an introduction? First, build reader interest and receptivity. Most writers accomplish this by referring to an existing situation or to familiar ideas the reader shares with them—for example, "We need to increase market share," "XYZ is a growing firm," or "As we discussed last Thursday." This statement about the situation familiar to your audience might be called the *what exists*. Second, your introduction should explain the *why write*—the changes, issues, or reasons for your writing. For example, "We have discussed possible methods with our staff," "Several problems have arisen," or "Someone suggested we do X." Finally, include the *how organized*—point your reader toward your conclusion and organization. If you are using the direct approach, state your solutions in the same order you use in the body of the document. If you are using the indirect approach, open with a question or list of options; again, use the same order for those options in the body of the document. Figure 8.1 includes examples of the three parts of an introduction.

Although an effective introduction includes each of these elements, you may present them in any order, depending on your credibility and your audience's needs. If you have high credibility or your audience wants to see your solution quickly, state the *how organized* first; if your audience is

FIGURE 8.1

Effective introduction

An effective introduction includes:

	The *WHAT EXISTS* What exists, is familiar, is shared	The *WHY WRITE* Why you are writing— change, issues, reasons	The *HOW ORGANIZED* Direct approach: or Indirect approach:	
			State solution	Ask questions
Examples:	Every employee must understand company policies.	You are a new employee.	Here are five policies.	What should you know?
	Business people must communicate with an increasing number of audiences.	Present legislation demands that you report X to the government.	This memo outlines four steps in reporting process.	How should you deal with reporting X?
	The copying machine serves the entire third floor.	It has been breaking down daily.	I recommend purchase of a new machine, for three reasons.	What should be done? Here are four options.
	Your time is valuable.	You have become more busy lately.	I recommend you take a time-management program.	What can you do? Here are some possible solutions.

more interested in the project itself, state the *why write* first; if you have lower credibility or are less sure of your audience's agreement, state the *what exists* first.

Here are three examples of the same introduction written in three different orders:

What exists first: The current eating facilities of XYZ Company have come increasingly under attack (what exists). The committee has now completed its survey of employee attitudes toward the service (why write). This memo outlines the three strong employee preferences that became apparent from that study (how organized).

Why write first: The committee has just completed a company-wide survey of employee attitudes toward the eating services at XYZ (why write). This survey was conducted because the services have been increasingly attacked (what exists). This report outlines the three major findings (how organized).

How organized first: The committee recommends that XYZ Company adopt three proposals: redecorate the lounge, offer a wider variety of food, and change the lounge hours (how organized). These proposals are based on a company-wide survey of employee attitudes toward the eating services (why write) inspired by the increasing attacks on those services (what exists).

How long should an introduction be? At the most, write three paragraphs—one each for the *what*, the *why*, and the *how*. At the least, open with one sentence that accomplishes all three aims, such as: "As you requested last Tuesday, I have summarized my objections to the new marketing plan," or "In response to your letter of March 28, I am glad to answer your questions about our new claim-adjustment policy."

CONCLUSION: At the end of your document—your conclusion—is the other place to emphasize your main points. Avoid restating your main idea in pompous words: "Thus it becomes readily apparent that due to the fact that we have. . . ." Avoid introducing a completely new topic; this not only diverts your reader's attention from your communication objective, it spoils your document's unity. Finally, avoid apologizing or undercutting your argument at the end; remember, the ending will leave a lasting impression in your reader's mind.

Instead, you may choose one of three endings. (1) Restate your main ideas if you are using the direct approach and the document is long. Obviously, you don't need to reiterate three points in a one-page memo or letter. (2) State your conclusions or recommendations if you are using the indirect approach. (3) State an *action step* or *feedback mechanism*. Typical action steps include; "I'll call you next Thursday to discuss this matter," "Please let me know if I can be of further help," or "Once I have your approval, I'll go ahead with this plan."

All right. So you can achieve unity and emphasis in your document by unifying all ideas around your communication objective, and by emphasizing your main ideas in your opening and closing. Now, how can you achieve unity and emphasis in your paragraphs?

For paragraphs

You unify a paragraph by unifying all the ideas in the paragraph around one topic sentence. The topic sentence is the dominating idea of the paragraph; it contains the essence of the paragraph. A good topic sentence contains: (1) a generalization and (2) a controlling idea that is (3) definable. Let's look at each of those specifications.

A good topic sentence is always a **generalization** relative to the other sentences in the paragraph. Here are three examples demonstrating the difference between generalizations (appropriate for a topic sentence) and specifics (not appropriate for a topic sentence).

1. Our customers prefer highly fashionable clothing styles. (general) I noticed a customer rejecting this coat because it was not fashionable enough. (specific)

2. This new system confuses our operators in several ways. (general) One operator reports having trouble understanding how to use her command key. (specific)

3. Sarah's presentation was marred by three problems. (general) I could not read the print on Sarah's visual aids. (specific)

In addition to always being generalizations, topic sentences always contain a **controlling idea**. A controlling idea is not simply the subject of the sentence. The controlling idea describes or evaluates the subject. To continue with the same three examples, here are some illustrations of the difference between topic sentence *subjects* and topic sentence *controlling ideas*:

1. Our customers prefer highly fashionable clothing styles. (subject: customers; controlling idea: highly fashionable clothing styles)

2. This new system confuses our operators in several ways. (subject: the system; controlling idea: confuses in several ways)

3. Sarah's presentation was marred by three problems. (subject: Sarah's presentation; controlling idea: marred by three problems)

Finally, keep in mind that your controlling idea, although a generalization, can't be too vague. The generalization must be limited enough to be **readily defined**. For example, contrast our three topic sentences once again, this time noting the difference between effective, definable generalizations and ineffective, vague generalizations:

1. Our customers prefer highly fashionable clothing styles. ("Highly fashionable" is definable.)
   Our customers prefer great clothes. ("Great" is too vague.)

2. This new system confuses our operators in several ways. ("Confuses in several ways" is definable.)
   This new system is outrageous. ("Outrageous" is too vague.)

3. Sarah's presentation was marred by three problems. ("Marred by three problems" is definable.)
   Sarah's presentation was horrible. ("Horrible" is too vague.)

Once you have a topic sentence made up of a generalization and a definable controlling idea, you will find it easy to ensure paragraph unity. Simply unify all the other sentences in the paragraph around the topic sentence. Every other sentence in the paragraph should amplify your topic sentence; no other sentence in the paragraph should stray from the point of your topic sentence. Therefore, all the other sentences in your paragraph are called *supporting sentences:* they **support** your topic sentence. To return once again to our three examples:

1. Our customers prefer highly fashionable clothing styles. (For good unity, do not include information on other customer considerations—such as price or service—in this particular paragraph.)

2. This new system confuses our operators in several ways. (For good unity, do not include information about the strengths of the new system in this particular paragraph.)

3. Sarah's presentation was marred by three problems. (For good unity, do not include information about the good points in Sarah's presentation in this particular paragraph.)

Paragraph unity, then, means unifying your supporting sentences around the controlling idea of your topic sentence.

For paragraph emphasis, place your topic sentence *first*. One difference between business writing and other kinds of writing is that in virtu-

GOOD

Think of a paragraph as an inverted pyramid:

Or think of it as an I shape:

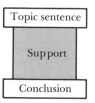

BAD

In business writing, avoid paragraphs whose main idea comes last:

And avoid a paragraph whose topic sentence is buried like this:

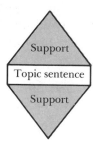

FIGURE 8.2

How to visualize a paragraph

ally all business writing, your topic sentence comes first. Obviously, you don't want to bury your topic sentence in the middle; in business writing, you usually don't want to save it up until the end. Since you are often dealing with a busy audience, your readers should be able to skim your writing by reading the first sentence in each paragraph—and still understand your main ideas.

Figure 8.2 illustrates what a paragraph looks like. The topic sentence is broader than the supporting sentences. It looks almost like an umbrella. To achieve unity, make sure all the support sentences fall under the idea in the umbrella. To achieve emphasis, make the umbrella sentence the first one in the paragraph.

Very occasionally, you may use one-sentence paragraphs to provide emphasis, transition, or variety. Writers who consistently use one-sentence paragraphs, however, usually have not grouped their ideas together for their readers.

Organization and Highlighting

Unity and emphasis are not enough to make your business writing completely effective for your reader. Your document and paragraphs must also be well organized. Organization means dividing your ideas hierarchically and ordering your ideas persuasively. One of the main differences between business writing and other kinds of writing, however, is the use of highlighting to *show* that organization to your reader. If organizing is what you do in your head, highlighting is what you do to make your thoughts visually apparent to your reader.

What do I mean by making your ideas *visually apparent*? I mean using the way your document appears on the page to show your organization. Highlighting techniques include: headings, subheadings, capitalization, underlining, indentations, lists, and so-called bullet points. (We'll discuss each of these shortly.)

Highlighting provides two benefits for your reader: (1) it shows your organization and (2) it stresses your key points. An example of highlighting to show your organization is:

RECOMMENDATIONS: ROLE OF THE CHAIR

This title shows your reader that what follows is a list of recommendations. Here is another example that shows organization:

PROCEDURE FOR MAIL—DELIVERY SYSTEM

This title shows your reader that what follows is steps in a procedure.

Besides showing your organization, highlighting can also stress your main points. For example,

Provide legal counsel

might be a main point under RECOMMENDATIONS: ROLE OF THE CHAIR.

Collect mail by 2 P.M. daily

might be a main point under PROCEDURE FOR MAIL–DELIVERY SYSTEM.

RULES: Whether you are using highlighting to show your structure or your main ideas, remember these four rules:

One, **be consistent**. If you are going to capitalize your main ideas, capitalize main ideas only throughout. If you are going to underline your secondary ideas, do so throughout. If, for example, you have capitalized a main heading, such as

MINUTES OF THE JULY 16 MEETING,

do *not* capitalize the topics discussed at the meeting, such as

PROGRESS REPORT FROM THE ABC DIVISION.

The progress report is a subset of the minutes of the meeting, so it (and other such subsets) should be highlighted differently than the main heading. Being consistent also means always indenting consistently, including indenting or not indenting paragraph openings. As a final example of consistency, always label consistently, using either numbers, letters, decimals, or typography in the same way throughout.

Two, **use idea headings**, not category headings. By *idea headings* I mean stand-alone headings that capture the essence of your ideas—headings a reader can skim and understand without referring to the rest of the text. Examples of idea headings include:

BENEFITS OF THIS PRODUCT
1. You will save time.
   (Followed by section on time savings)
2. You will save money.
   (Followed by section on money savings)

Ineffective headings, on the other hand, are simply vague categories. Your reader could skim these and have no idea what you're writing about. Examples of these ineffective category headings include:

BACKGROUND
BENEFITS
RESULTS
ORGANIZATION

Three, **don't overdo highlighting**. Many students get so carried away with the idea of highlighting that they start underlining or capitalizing almost every line on the page. Obviously, having *everything* highlighted is just as useless for your reader as having nothing highlighted. This technique works only if used judiciously.

Besides limiting the amount of material you highlight, also limit the wording of the sentences or phrases that you do highlight. For example, don't highlight

In order to grow, we should consider decentralizing for the following reasons:

Instead, keep it short:

Benefits of decentralizing:

Don't highlight

To increase production of this product, I submit that we should continue to buy, rather than to produce, component Y.

Instead, say

Continue to buy component Y.

Limit the wording of your headings and subheadings.

Four, **show ideas of equal importance**, such as ideas in a list, in the same grammatical form. In other words, use *parallelism* in wording each group of headings and subheadings. You might have a list consisting of a series of action verbs (such as *improve*). You must, however, be consistent within the list—all verbs, or all nouns, or whatever. (See pages 425-26 for more on parallelism.) For example, you might choose to start each subheading with a noun:

The ABC acquisition would result in loss of:

freedom in product development,

morale for employees, and

independence as a division.

As another example, you might start each subheading in the list with a verb:

Steps to organize internally:

> *establish* formal sales division;
>
> *define* production responsibilities; and
>
> *improve* accounting system.

FORMATS: Keeping in mind those four rules, choose the appropriate format for highlighting. Figure 8.3 shows five of the most frequently used formats. Use any of these formats, any combination of them, or any format prescribed by your organization. Just be sure to use the same format—the same kind of headings, subheadings, indentations, and so forth—consistently throughout your document. If you do select one of the five formats in Figure 8.3, consider their differences, strengths, and weaknesses.

In the outline format, you place increasingly subordinate ideas ever further to the right of the page. This format uses number and letter labels, as in a formal outline.

The modified outline format uses typography—such as capital letters, underlining, and italics—instead of the numbers and letters used in a more formal outline format.

In the decimal format, like the other outlining formats, you place increasingly subordinate ideas ever further to the right of the page. In this format, however, you label with numbers and decimals. This format is useful for scientific and government reports, or any report in which you want to be able to refer back to specific sections by specific numbers. Sometimes, however, this format can be somewhat unwieldy.

The bullet format is far less formal. The name *bullet* presumably stems from the ● mark, which looks as if you had shot a bullet through the paper. "Bullets," however, can be typed as a dash -- or as an asterisk * as well as inked in lowercase as ●. This format is appropriate especially if you do not want to imply a ranking or priority of ideas, as you might in a list.

Another informal format is the indented-list format. Here, you simply indent groupings of similar ideas, and then underline your topic sentences or subheadings. This format is useful for short memos or letters.

Regardless of the format, or consistent combination of formats, you choose, keep in mind the document-design guidelines illustrated in Figure 8.4.

FIGURE 8.3

Highlighting formats

Outline format

> ### I. TITLE HEADING I
>
> IIIIIIIIIIIIIIIIIIIIIIIIIIIIIIIIIIIIIIIIIIIIIIIIIIIIIIIIIIIIIIIIIIIIIIIIIIIIIIIIII IIIIIIIIIIIIIIIIIIIIIIIIIIIIIIIIIIIIIIIIIIIIII.
>
> #### A. PRIMARY SECTION HEADING A
>
> AAAAAAAAAAAAAAAAAAAAAAAAAAAAAAAAAAAAAAAAAA AAAAAAAAAAAAAAAAAAAAAAAAAAAAAAAAAAAAA.
>
> > 1. Secondary Heading 1
> >
> > IIIIIIIIIIIIIIIIIIIIIIIIIIIIIIIIIIIIIIIIIIIIIIIIIIIIIIIIIIIIIIIII IIIIIIIIIIIIIIIIIIIIIIIIIIIIIIIIIIIIIIIIIIIIIIIIIIIIIIII.
> >
> > > a. Third-level heading a
> > >
> > > aaaaaaaaaaaaaaaaaaaaaaaaaaaaaaaaaaaaaaaaaaaaaaaaaaaaaa aaaaaaaaaaaaaaaaaaaaaaaaaaaaaaaaaaaaaaaaaa.

Modified outline format

> ### TITLE HEADING I
>
> IIIIIIIIIIIIIIIIIIIIIIIIIIIIIIIIIIIIIIIIIIIIIIIIIIIIIIIIIIIIIIIIIIIIIIIIIIIIIIIIII IIIIIIIIIIIIIIIIIIIIIIIIIIIIIIIIIIIIIIIIIIIIII.
>
> #### PRIMARY SECTION HEADING A
>
> AAAAAAAAAAAAAAAAAAAAAAAAAAAAAAAAAAAAAAAAAA AAAAAAAAAAAAAAAAAAAA.
>
> > Secondary Heading 1
> >
> > IIIIIIIIIIIIIIIIIIIIIIIIIIIIIIIIIIIIIIIIIIIIIIIIIIIIIIIIIIIIIIIII IIIIIIIIIIIIIIIIIIIIIIIIIIIIIIIIIIIIIIIII.
> >
> > > *Third-level heading a*
> > >
> > > aaaaaaaaaaaaaaaaaaaaaaaaaaaaaaaaaaaaaaaaaaaaaaaaaaaaaa aaaaaaaaaaaaaaaaaaaaaaaaaaaaaaaaaaaaaaaaaa

Decimal format

1. TITLE HEADING I

I.1 PRIMARY SECTION HEADING A

AAAAAAAAAAAAAAAAAAAAAAAAAAAAAAAAAAAAAAAA
AAAAAAAAAAAAAAA.

   I.1.1. Secondary Heading 1

   11111111111111111111111111111111111111111111111
   11111111111111111111111111111111111111.

      I.1.1.1. Third-level heading a

         aaaaaaaaaaaaaaaaaaaaaaaaaaaaaaaaaaaaaaa
         aaaaaaaaaaaaaaaaaaaa.

Bullet format

TITLE HEADING I

PRIMARY SECTION HEADING A

AAAAAAAAAAAAAAAAAAAAAAAAAAAAAAAAAAAAAAAA
AAAAAAAAAAAAAAAAAAA.

● Secondary Heading 1

   111111111111111111111111111111111111111111111111111111
   111111111111111111111111111111111.

   --Tertiary heading a: aaaaaaaaaaaaaaaaaaaaaaaaaaaaaaaaaaaaaaaaaaa
   aaaaaaaaaaaaaaaaaaaaaaaaaaaaaa.

● Secondary Heading 2

   2222222222222222222222222222222222222222222222222222222
   2222222222222222222222222.

Indented-list format

TITLE HEADING I

IIIIIIIIIIIIIIIIIIIIIIIIIIIIIIIIIIIIIIIIIIIIIIIIIIIIIIIIIIIIIIIIIIIIIIIIIIIII
IIIIIIIIIIIIIIIIIIIIIIIIIIIIIIIIIIIIIIIIIIIIIIIII.

1. Item 1: 111111111111111111111111111111111111111111111
11111111111111111111111111111.

2. Item 2: 22222222222222222222222222222222222222222222222
222222222222222222.

3. Item 3: 3333333333333333333333333333333333333333333333333
33333333333333333333333333333333333333.

FIGURE 8.4

Highlighting: Document design

Make your document design as easy as possible on your reader's eyes.

1. Place increasingly subordinate ideas farther and farther to the right:

Preferred:

MAIN TITLE HEADING

AAAAAAAAAAAAAAAAAAAAAAAAAAAAAAAAAAAAAA
AAAAAAAAAAAAAAAAAAAAAAAAAAAAA.

Secondary Idea Heading

IIIIIIIIIIIIIIIIIIIIIIIIIIIIIIIIIIIIIIIIIIIIIIIII
IIIIIIIIIIIIIIIIIIIIIIIIIIIIIIIIIIIIIIIIIIIIIIIII
IIIIIIIIIIIIIIIIIIIIIIIIIIIIIIIIIIIIIIIIIIIIIIIII
IIIIIIIIIIIIIIIIIIIIII.

Not
preferred:

MAIN IDEA HEADING

AAAAAAAAAAAAAAAAAAAAAAAAAAAAAA
AAAAAAAAAAAAAAAAAAAAAAAAAAAAAA
AAAAAAAAAAAAAAAAAAAA.

Secondary Idea Heading

IIIIIIIIIIIIIIIIIIIIIIIIIIIIIIIIIIIIIIIIIIIIIIIIIIIIIIIIIIIIII
IIIIIIIIIIIIIIIIIIIIIIIIIIIIIIIIIIIIIIIIIIIIIIIIIIIIIIIIIIIIII
IIIIIIIIIIIIIIIIIIIIIIIIIIIIIIIIIIIIIIIIIIIIIIIIIIIIIIIIIIIIII
IIIIIIIIIIIIIIIIIIIIIIIIIIIIIIIIIIIIIIIIII.

2. Place the entire subordinate section father to the right, not just the initial line.

Preferred:

> MAIN IDEA HEADING
>
> AAAAAAAAAAAAAAAAAAAAAAAAAAAAAAAAAAA AAAAAAAAAAAAAAAAAAAAAAA.
>
> > Secondary Idea Heading
> >
> > IIIIIIIIIIIIIIIIIIIIIIIIIIIIIIIIIIIIIIIIIIIIII IIIIIIIIIIIIIIIIIIIIIIIIIIIIIIIIIIIIIIIIIIIIII IIIIIIIIIIIIIIIIIIII.

Not preferred:

> MAIN IDEA HEADING
> AAAAAAAAAAAAAAAAAAAAAAAAAAAAAAAAAAAAA AAAAAAAAAAAAAAAAAA.
>
> > Secondary Idea Heading
>
> IIIIIIIIIIIIIIIIIIIIIIIIIIIIIIIIIIIIIIIIIIIIIIIII IIIIIIIIIIIIIIIIIIIIIIIIIIIIIIIIIIIIIIIIIIIIIIIII IIIIIIIIIIIIIIIIIIIIIIIII.

Preferred:

> MAIN IDEA HEADING
>
> AAAAAAAAAAAAAAAAAAAAAAAAAA.
>
> > • Bullet point 1. 1111111111111111111 1111111111111111111111111111111 111111111111111111111111.
> >
> > • Bullet point 2. 222222222222222222 2222222222222222222222222222222 222222222222222222222.

Not preferred:

> MAIN IDEA HEADING
>
> AAAAAAAAAAAAAAAAAAAAAAAAAA.
>
> > • Bullet point 1. 1111111111111111111
> 111111111111111111111111111111111111111111 11111111111111111111111111111111111111.
>
> > • Bullet point 2. 222222222222222222222
> 2222222222222222222222222222222222222222222 2222222222222222222222222222222222222222.

Connection

Your unified, emphasized, organized, highlighted writing must also "flow" or "connect" clearly. This quality of connectedness is often called *coherence* in writing; that is, your ideas cohere. You can connect your ideas to achieve coherent writing by using: (1) transitions, (2) highlighting, (3) identity signals, or (4) parallelism.

Perhaps the most familiar way to connect your ideas is to use **transitions**. These are words and phrases whose sole function is to stick your ideas together so your reader can see how they connect. For example, here is an executive summary from a report, with the transitions italicized:

> XYZ Company must attempt to clear up its financial crisis. *First,* cut back drastically on labor, outside services, and manufacturing overhead expenses. *Second,* do not approach shareholders for more capital. *Finally,* renegotiate short-term liabilities with the bank.

Figure 8.5 lists the most common and useful transitions.

A second method to connect your ideas is **highlighting**. As we discussed in the previous section, highlighting is using headings and subheadings, lists, bullet points, and indentations to emphasize your organization and main ideas. Highlighting provides connection by showing how your ideas relate to one another. For example, if you number three items in a list, you don't need to use the transitional words *first, second,* and *third.* Here is another way of writing the same executive summary, this time using highlighting instead of transitions:

METHODS TO CLEAR UP FINANCIAL CRISIS
- Cut back drastically on:
    - - labor,
    - - outside services, and
    - - manufacturing overhead expenses.
- Do not approach shareholders for more capital.
- Renegotiate short-term liabilities with the bank.

A third method to connect your ideas is to use **identity signals.** These are words that assert: "The issue already mentioned is still under discussion." Pronouns can serve as identity signals. (See pages 433–39 for more on pronouns.) For example, you might write:

To signal	
Addition or amplification	and, besides, in addition, and then, also, too, first, second, further, furthermore, moreover, next, subsequently, finally, last, again, equally important, similarly
Contrast	but, or, nor, yet, still, however, on the contrary, on the other hand, conversely, although, and yet, in contrast to, at the same time, nevertheless, nonetheless
Example or sequence	for example, for instance, that is, first, second, third, in the first place, in the second place, finally, last
Conclusion	therefore, thus, then, hence, in conclusion, to sum up, to summarize, in sum, all in all, in short, in brief, consequently, as a result, accordingly, to this end, for this purpose
Time or place	before, earlier, formerly, so far, until now, in the past, meanwhile, in the meantime, now, at the same time, simultaneously, soon, in a few days, afterwards, later, subsequently, here, near, nearby, there, opposite, beyond, above, below, further on

FIGURE 8.5

Transitions to connect ideas

On Monday, the divisional supervisors will meet to plan the XYZ proposal. *They* will discuss bids, schedules, and contracts.

The pronoun *they* connects back to *the divisional supervisors* in the first sentence. As another example, you might write:

The vendor from ABC Supply Company is coming by next Wednesday at 3:00. *He* will be bringing the product samples you wanted to see.

In this case, *he* connects back to *the vendor* in the first sentence.

Similarly, demonstrative adjectives can serve as identity signals. (See pages 440–41 for more on adjectives.) For example:

Each profit center showed significant improvement in its bottom line. *These* profits did not surprise the controller because she had changed the overhead allocation.

Here *these* connects back to *bottom line*. Take the sentence:

We introduced Mushmeal Cereal in 1986. *That* product is now our most successful.

Here, *that* refers back to *Mushmeal Cereal*.

Besides pronouns and adjectives, you can use repeated words as identity signals. For instance:

The secretary's primary *concern* is with the overhead on the switchboard. The sales representatives share his *concern* because they have had to deal with client complaints.

Those sentences are connected by the repeated word *concern*. As another example:

We should increase introductory training programs for all new employees, so each supervisor won't have to repeat company policies. Those *new employees* will appreciate learning about the company and meeting one another.

Those sentences are connected by the repeated phrase *new employees*. If you don't want to repeat the word or phrase exactly, you can use an implied repetition, such as:

Twenty salespeople tripled their previous sales record this year. Twelve *more* doubled their previous record.

The word *more* implies a repetition or connection back to *salespeople*.

A fourth and final method to achieve coherence is **parallelism**. Parallelism, as we discussed under the section on organization, is stating equally important ideas in the same grammatical form. Here's an example of parallelism in which we connect a series of equally important concepts by starting each with a verb:

> To receive disability insurance, you need to do three things. Fill out the form. Send it to the personnel office by February 14. Send a copy to your supervisor.

Here's another example, this one connecting equally important ideas with the phrase *perhaps we should*:

> We face several possible solutions. Perhaps we should sell out. Perhaps we should pare down certain departments. Or perhaps we should refinance.

Appropriate Length

Most books on writing—and business writing especially—exhort writers to keep their writing concise. You may have heard people quote formulas such as these: "If you can't fit your idea on the back of my calling card, then you don't have a clear idea," or "Remember the K.I.S.S. formula: 'Keep It Short, Stupid.'"

To imply that the shortest document is *always* the most effective document, however, is just plain silly. You need to edit your documents and paragraphs to the appropriate length—sometimes long and sometimes short. On one hand, of course, you should respect your readers' time: don't make them wade through unnecessary information. On the other hand, though, you don't want to cut out essential information.

How long should your document be? There is no one answer. Base your length on: (1) the topic (a report on all the word processors available might be longer than a report on three employees' vacation leave), (2) the audience (a memo to a boss "who refuses to read anything over one page" should be shorter than a memo to a boss who likes a lot of detail), and (3) what was called for (a letter replying to one easy, specific question should be shorter than a letter replying to several complex questions).

How long should each paragraph be? Again, there is no definite answer, but shortness is not always a virtue. Paragraphs are usually at least three to four sentences long: one topic sentence and at least two supporting sentences to back up your controlling idea. Avoid a series of one-sentence paragraphs; in fact, use one-sentence paragraphs extremely sparingly. On the other hand, watch out for overly long paragraphs—that is, over 300 words or eight sentences. Use long paragraphs extremely sparingly. Think of how formidable long paragraphs look to your reader. As writing experts Strunk and White point out: "Enormous blocks of print look formidable to a reader. He has a certain reluctance to tackle them; he can lose his way in them."[1]

The following examples illustrate the problems associated with inappropriate paragraph length. Here is a series of poor paragraphs that are **too short**:

> If you consistently write in very short paragraphs, you will find they do not develop your ideas.
>
> Short paragraphs also tend to give the impression that you can't group your ideas together logically. Of course the preceding sentence belongs in the first paragraph along with a topic sentence about the drawbacks of short paragraphs.
>
> Perhaps after that topic sentence, you could list the drawbacks.

An improved version might read:

> Consistently writing very short paragraphs presents several drawbacks for your reader. First, your paragraphs will lack development. Second, they will lead your reader to think you cannot group your ideas together logically.
>
> The preceding paragraph is now the correct length for the amount of information it contains. The topic sentence introduces the idea of the drawbacks; the subordinate sentences list them. Naturally, that list could have been extended to include several more items.

Here is a poor paragraph that is **too long:**

> If you consistently write very long paragraphs, your reader may just look at the page and say "Forget it! Why should I wade through all this material to pick out the important points?" And why should your reader do that work? Isn't it your job as a writer to decide what you want to emphasize and to make that stand out? Besides which, the format, or the way your ideas appear on the page, is very important psychologically to your reader—or lack of reader. You may want to show the creative gushing process you go through as a writer and just go on and on writing as ideas come into your head. Your psychologist, your friends, or your family might possibly be

---

[1]W. Strunk and E. B. White, *The Elements of Style*, 3rd ed. (New York: Macmillan, 1979), p. 17.

very interested in how this process works. On the other hand, I doubt very much that the person reading your memo cares too much about your internal processes. The business reader wants to see your main ideas quickly and to have the work of sorting out done for him or her. Didn't you find just the look of this paragraph rather put you off? Did it make you want to read on? Or did it make you want to give up?

A more effective paragraph might look like this:

Medium-sized paragraphs are easier for your readers to comprehend. Their comprehension increases because you have emphasized your main idea; shown specific ideas, not an unrelated thought process; eliminated repetitious ideas; and showed your organization (in the paragraph you're reading now, through parallel structure).

Place ideas that don't relate to the topic sentence in another paragraph, making sure each paragraph has:

- unity and emphasis,
- organization and highlighting,
- connection, and
- appropriate length.

This chapter has covered the "larger issues" to look for as you edit. Always edit your document and paragraphs before you edit your sentences and words. Otherwise you may waste time with "smaller issues" in sections of your document that you end up cutting out altogether. The "larger issues," again, are: (1) unity and emphasis, (2) organization and highlighting, (3) connection, and (4) appropriate length.

REVIEW QUESTIONS

To check your understanding

1. What four principles underlie a well-written document or paragraph?
2. In what two ways can you make sure your document is unified?
3. Explain the three elements of an effective introduction.
4. Describe a good topic sentence.
5. What is the relation between the topic sentence and the rest of the paragraph?
6. Name two benefits highlighting provides for your reader.
7. List four rules for effective highlighting.

8. Name four techniques to achieve coherence, or connection, in writing.

9. On the basis of what three variables should you decide how long your document should be?

10. All paragraphs should be clearly structured and easy to comprehend. *About* how long are *most* paragraphs?

APPLICATION QUESTIONS

To apply your knowledge

1. Determine whether the following are general (and therefore appropriate for a topic sentence) or specific (and therefore inappropriate for a topic sentence).

   a. At Dirko Inc., earnings per share have increased an average of 8 percent per year over the last five years.

   b. Few managers devote enough time to strategic planning.

   c. Fifty-nine percent of the sample population responded to the survey.

   d. Terms such as *recession* and *economic slump* have replaced the feared term *depression*.

   e. Euphemisms reflect our fears and desires.

   f. Our new advertising campaign will focus on our bargain line of clothing.

   g. We will feature our sweaters and blouses retailing under $30 in the Sunday newspaper's color supplements.

   h. National Bank's Executive Account is specially geared to the needs of today's active executive.

   i. The minimum checking balance required is $450.

2. Provide two specifics to illustrate the following general statements.

   a. American auto companies were unprepared for the turn to economy in consumer taste.

   b. Accounting is a complex subject.

   c. Considerations other than just starting salary will influence my job decision.

   d. An effective orientation and training program tends to increase worker confidence on the job.

   e. Women are far from having true equality in the job market.

   f. Your credibility is based on various considerations.

3. Rewrite this section from a memo so as to highlight the main ideas.

    We can offer you three cost advantages that you cannot obtain on your own. We offer a central clearinghouse for those hard-to-find supplies. Currently, to trade stock with another plant, you waste time finding one with needed supplies, and then you waste more time negotiating a swap. Using the headquarters as a central clearinghouse, you have a one-stop shopping point for all your supply needs. This will free your time so that you can attend to more important matters. In addition, we can offer discounts. We will pass along the savings of larger-quantity discounts. This will help cut your costs. Finally, as a unified block, we will have greater market power to deal more forcefully with suppliers. As a larger customer, your needs will be more important to the suppliers.

4. Read the paragraph and answer the questions about it. Each sentence is numbered so you can refer back to it.

    (1) What is the proper length for a paragraph? (2) This question has no simple answer. (3) Primarily, you should be guided by coherence. (4) That is, your paragraph length should reflect the number of supporting and explicating statements needed to develop your main idea. (5) However, certain size considerations are relevant regardless of the coherence of the paragraph. (6) If your paragraphs frequently exceed one third of the typed page (or about 100 to 150 words), you will tire your reader. (7) Similarly, overly short paragraphs will seem choppy even if you are enumerating a series of briefly developed ideas. (8) In either case, you can achieve balanced paragraphs without sacrificing paragraph coherence. (9) Most lengthy paragraphs can be divided into two related, but separate paragraphs. (10) In the same manner, extremely short paragraphs almost always fit logically with an adjacent paragraph or require further development.

    a. In sentence (2), the identity signal is
       (1) a pronoun
       (2) a repeated key word
       (3) a demonstrative adjective
       (4) an addition or amplification
    b. In sentence (4), *that is* refers back to
       (1) the model paragraph in question
       (2) business writing in general
       (3) the idea that paragraph length should be guided by coherence
       (4) the phrase "this question"

   c. In sentence (3), the transition word, *primarily*, signals
      (1) sequence in terms of priority
      (2) addition or amplification
      (3) contrast
      (4) time or place

   d. In sentence (5), *however* signals
      (1) example or sequence
      (2) addition or amplification
      (3) contrast
      (4) conclusion

   e. In sentence (7), *similarly* signals
      (1) example or sequence
      (2) addition or amplification
      (3) contrast
      (4) time or place

   f. In sentence (5), the phrase *regardless of the coherence of the paragraph*
      (1) qualifies the idea expressed in the first part of the sentence
      (2) provides an example of the concept defined by the first part of the sentence
      (3) provides a transition to the subject of coherence
      (4) refers back to the topic sentence to reinforce paragraph unity

   g. In sentence (8), the phrase *in either case* signals
      (1) contrast
      (2) example or sequence
      (3) time or place
      (4) addition or amplification

   h. In sentence (9), the phrase *but separate*
      (1) is a demonstrative adjective
      (2) signals an illustration or example
      (3) qualifies the adjective *related*
      (4) prepares for the transition to short paragraphs

   i. In sentence (10), *in the same manner* signals
      (1) time or place
      (2) contrast
      (3) conclusion
      (4) addition or amplification

   j. Throughout this paragraph, the key unifying pronoun is
      (1) *it*—referring to the model paragraph
      (2) *you* and *your*—referring to the reader

(3) *this*—referring to the idea of paragraph length

(4) *they*—referring to experts on writing

5. **Read this paragraph and answer the questions about it.**

   (1) The *either/or* logical fallacy is a particularly common fallacy, founded as it is on Occidental dualism. (2) The error in either/or thinking is to assume there are only two alternatives of thought or action in a given situation, for example: "We must acquire the Handee Bottling Plant or give up all hope of becoming more than a regional brewery." (3) In this example, the writer or speaker is arguing for the proposal by assuming it is the only method of expansion. (4) Thus, it is easy for the writer or speaker to predict dire consequences if the action isn't implemented. (5) This logical fallacy has two distinct disadvantages: it ignores other possible alternatives, and it refuses to allow a rational evaluation of the original proposal on its own merits. (6) Very few decisions are as black-and-white as either/or thinking suggests. (7) Therefore, the either/or formulation is rarely logically justified.

   a. What does the pronoun *it* in sentence (1) refer to?

   b. What transition word appears in sentence (2) and how does it function?

   c. Which sentences contain demonstrative adjectives?

   d. What are the transition words in sentences (4) and (7)? How do they function?

   e. What key terms or phrases are repeated in this paragraph?

6. Answer the following questions regarding appropriate length.

   a. The following paragraph is too short and needs to have its ideas developed. How would you improve it?

      We based our advertising campaign on a national poll of consumers. The poll helped us find out what they thought.

   b. The following paragraph is too long and needs to be made more concise. How would you improve it?

      We based our advertising campaign on a national poll of consumers. It was hard to find people willing to conduct the telephone survey at first, though we had already determined that that was the best method to contact people representing a cross-section of American households. Respondents were asked twenty questions about their use of kitchen appliances. The questions were composed by Bill Green and Dennis Haley in our office. The results showed that 90 percent of the American public uses a can opener regularly and 76 percent look for space-saving qualities in an appliance. These statistics have a margin for error of ± 3 percent, which we thought was a fairly good rate of accuracy and something to be proud of. As a result of our survey we decided to market an electric can opener you can hang on your wall.

c. Suppose you had to condense an eight-page document into one page for your boss. How would you go about deciding what to include? What aspects of the document would you focus on?

d. The topic of your memo is your annual vacation. You are writing two versions—one to your boss and one to your secretary. What do you imagine each would want to know about your vacation? Discuss the appropriate length for each.

e. Why should one-sentence paragraphs be used sparingly? When might they be used effectively? Give an example of an effective one-sentence paragraph.

CASES

To practice what you learned

See cases at the end of chapter 7, pages 175–81.

9

Constructing Businesslike Sentences

Watch Your Sentence Arrangement.
Emphasize important words. ● Place the verb near the subject. ● Place modifiers correctly.

Watch Your Sentence Length.
The problems ● The solutions ● Variety and rhythm

Use Vigorous Verbs.
Avoid overusing nouns. ● Avoid overusing weak verbs.
● Avoid elongated verbs. ● Avoid overusing passive verbs.

WRITING is hard work. Not only do you need to think through your strategy, use business formats, and compose an effective document and paragraphs—you also need to construct clear sentences. In this chapter, we'll examine how to decide on sentence arrangement, sentence length, and vigorous verbs.

Watch Your Sentence Arrangement.

The way you position your words can change the emphasis, and even the meaning, of a sentence. Consider how the different arrangement of words in these two somewhat fanciful sentences changes their emphasis:

> My boss rode a camel down Main Street and through the park.
> Down Main Street and through the park, my boss rode a camel.

In the next two sentences, changing the arrangement changes the entire meaning:

> Slipping on a banana peel, my boss laughed at Groucho Marx.
> My boss laughed at Groucho Marx slipping on a banana peel.

> Placing your words in the appropriate order or position in a sentence to achieve the emphasis and meaning you desire is what sentence arrangement is all about.

Emphasize important words.

First, let's consider emphasis. If you want to emphasize a word in the sentence, place it in one of the emphatic positions we discussed in chapter 5—**first or last**. For example, if you want to emphasize Kathy, write:

Kathy sent a memo outlining the new hiring procedure recently adopted by the company.

In that sentence the procedure is "buried" in the middle of the sentence. If, on the other hand, you wanted to emphasize the procedure, you might write:

The new hiring procedure that the company recently adopted was the topic of Kathy's memo.

Besides choosing the position of the words—by placing important words at the beginning and the end—you also may use a word's grammatical function in the sentence for emphasis. Grammatically, sentences have: main part(s) and subordinate part(s). Just as a private is subordinate to a general, and a hotel clerk is subordinate to a hotel manager, the subordinate parts of your sentence are less important than the main parts. Obviously, then, you want to place your most important idea in the **main part**.

The main part—called the *main clause* or the *independent clause*—is the subject and the verb. In the sentence

My boss tossed the badly written report into the wastebasket

the main clause is "boss tossed" (subject/verb). On the other hand, "After tossing the badly written report into the wastebasket" is *not* a main clause: it has no subject. "My angry, frustrated boss" is *not* a main clause either: it has no verb. So, your main clause is your main subject and a verb: put your most important idea in your main clause.

Other, less important information goes in the subordinate, or less important, parts of the sentence. In the sentence

Before jumping out of the window, my boss tossed the badly written report into the wastebasket

the phrase *before jumping out of the window* is subordinate to *my boss tossed* because it is not the main subject/verb. In the sentence

After tossing the report in the wastebasket, my boss jumped out the window

the emphasis is different: now *my boss jumped* is in the main clause. How about this sentence?

Whenever I write a bad report, my boss screams.

The main clause: *my boss screams.* The subordinate idea: *Whenever I write a bad report.* One more example:

Because my boss was shouting at me, I jumped out the window.

The main clause: *I jumped.* The subordinate idea: *Because my boss was shouting at me.*

You can probably tell intuitively which are the main and which are the subordinate sentence parts. Main parts can stand alone: *I jumped* and *my boss screamed* are complete sentences, completed ideas. Subordinate parts sound incomplete, as though something is yet to come: the phrases *whenever I write a bad report, . . .* and *because my boss was shouting at me, . . .* leave the reader waiting for what comes next.

If you are in doubt, however, study the following. It contains some widely used *subordinators*—words signaling that the less important parts of the sentence are coming up:

Subordinators

after	so that
although	supposing
as	that
as if	though
as soon as	till
as though	unless
because	until
before	when
even though	whenever
if	where
inasmuch as	wherever
in order that	whether or not
insofar as	which
in that	while
no matter how	who
no matter what	whoever
now that	whom
provided	whomever
since	whose

Place the verb near the subject.

A second major concern in sentence arrangement is **avoiding large gaps** between your subject and verb. To explain what I mean by *gaps*, first think about what the normal sentence pattern is in English. Here is an example of a typical sentence pattern:

Lindsay smashed the projector.

The subject, *Lindsay*, is followed by the verb *smashed*. So the normal sentence pattern is subject/verb.

Subject/verb gaps occur when the writer puts something between the subject and the verb, as in:

Lindsay, the vice-president for marketing, smashed the projector.

That sentence, with a gap of five words (unlike *this* sentence with a much longer gap of seventeen words), is still easy to read. The problem occurs when a writer does what I did to you in the previous sentence: stretches the reader's endurance by inserting large gaps between subject and verb. For example, this sentence has a thirteen-word subject/verb gap:

Managers, in addition to having to make significant commitments to following through with recommendations, must also act quickly to achieve success.

Possible rewrites include:

Managers' commitment and quick action are essential for implementing recommendations.

In addition to committing themselves, managers must act quickly.

Place modifiers correctly.

Closing the subject/verb gap will make your sentences *easier* to read, but your third choice in sentence arrangement will make your sentences *possible* to understand. This third choice has to do with where you place your modifiers. A modifier is a sentence part that attaches or connects to another part. For example, in the sentence

Bill, who is my uncle, fell out of the tree

the phrase *who is my uncle* refers to *Bill*, not to the tree. Although in this case, you could figure out that Bill, not the tree, is your uncle, you could also figure it out grammatically—because *who is my uncle* is close to *Bill*. The third rule, then, is to place your modifiers as close as possible to what they modify.

Let's look at some business examples. Take the sentence

I have asked for permission to get away from my boss.

Here, the modifier *from my boss* is too far away from what it *should* modify—that is, *asked for permission*—and too close to what it should not modify—that is, *to get away from my boss.* The sentence should read:

I have asked my boss for permission to get away.

As another example, in the sentence

She explained the mainframe computer in her letter

the phrase *in her letter* modifies *mainframe computer.* Since a mainframe computer is obviously not inside the letter, the modifier is misplaced. The sentence should read:

In her letter, she explained the workings of the mainframe computer.

Students often point out that the reader can figure out with common sense that the computer is not inside the letter. True enough. At best, if you misplace modifiers, your reader will still be able to understand. (The reader may laugh at you, or perhaps send the example into a magazine as a funny juxtaposition, but still understand.) At worst, however, your reader will not even understand.

Here are two examples of misplaced modifiers where the reader can't even figure out what's going on:

He had a plant on the file cabinet that was right in the center.

Is the plant on the center of the file cabinet or is the cabinet in the center of the room?

You can telephone the people in the Houston office and tell them about your new expense account for ten dollars.

Is the expense account for ten dollars or does the telephone call cost ten dollars?

One special kind of misplaced modifier is called a **dangling modifier.** The term *dangling* refers to its solitary, unattached position at the beginning of the sentence. The opening phrase must refer to the following subject. For example, take this sentence:

> Knowing your interest in this research, you will soon receive a copy of the report.

The phrase *knowing your interest in this research* dangles because it does not refer to the following subject, *you*. To make that modifier cease dangling, the sentence should read:

> Knowing your interest in this research, I shall send you a copy of the report.

Now *knowing your interest in this research* no longer dangles: it refers to the following subject, *I*.

As another example, take the sentence

> As employees at the Bayshore Company, full medical-insurance coverage applies.

The opening phrase, *as employees at the Bayshore Company*, does not refer to the following subject, *full medical insurance*. (The medical insurance is not an employee!) The sentence should read:

> As employees at the Bayshore Company, we are covered with full medical insurance.

Now the opening phrase, *As employees at the Bayshore Company*, does refer to the following subject, *we*.

One more example:

> Young and inexperienced, the task seemed easy to Bartholomew.

The opening phrase does not refer to the following subject. (The task is not young and inexperienced.) The sentence should read:

> Young and inexperienced, Bartholomew thought the task seemed easy.

Now the opening phrase, *young and inexperienced,* does refer to the following subject, *Bartholomew*.

Sentence arrangement, then, is no easy task. Arrange your words carefully: (1) emphasize key ideas by placing them first or last, and by placing them in the main part of your sentence; (2) avoid overly long gaps between your subject and verb; (3) place your modifiers as close as possible to what they modify. See Table 9.1 for a summary of these ideas.

TABLE 9.1	
Watch your sentence arrangement.	
What to do	*How to do it*
Emphasize important words.	Place them first or last in the sentence.
	Place them in the main clause.
Place verbs near subjects.	Avoid long subject/verb gaps.
Arrange modifiers correctly.	Place them as closely as possible to what they modify.
	Remember that an opening phrase must modify the following subject.

Watch Your Sentence Length.

In general, long complicated sentences are harder for your reader to comprehend than shorter, simpler sentences. A sentence could be as long as 80 or 100 words, and still make grammatical sense. Grammatical sense, however, is not the only important issue to consider. Another important issue is making your writing easy to read by avoiding overly long sentences.

How long is too long? One well-known and often-quoted specialist, Rudolph Flesch, recommends that sentences average 17 words.[1] Most business communication experts recommend an average sentence length of about 20 to 25 words. And most writing experts agree you should reconsider sentences over 40 or 50 words. But, writing is not like accounting; you cannot judge your sentences by any hard-and-fast numerical rule. Your sentence is too long any time its length makes it confusing.

The problems

Beware especially of two kinds of sentences that tend to extend to ponderous lengths: overly compound and overly complex sentences. **Compound**

---

[1] R. Flesch, *The Art of Plain Talk* (New York: Harper & Brothers, 1946), p. 38.

sentences join two or more main ideas together with a coordinator, usually *and*. For example:

> He walked into the building and the guard asked to see his identification badge

is a compound sentence; it joins two main ideas (*he walked into the building* and *the guard asked*) with *and*. Although this sentence is compound, it is not too long. However, here is a compound sentence that is too long:

> Sufficient computer technology exists for our needs, and we should direct our efforts toward applying such technology efficiently, and the emphasis should be on the accounting system and the inventory of the warehouses.

This sentence would be clearer to the reader if rewritten:

> Since sufficient computer technology exists for our needs, we should direct our efforts toward applying such technology efficiently. We should emphasize two applications: the accounting system and the warehouse inventory.

One way to spot overly long sentences, then, is to watch out for too many *and*s. Usually, but not always, more than one *and* is too many. Get rid of the *and*s that your reader cannot easily follow.

Another problem with overly long sentences has a different cause: **overly complex** sentences. By *complex,* I am not referring to a sense of *complication,* but rather to a specific grammatical meaning: a *complex sentence* has at least one main clause and at least one subordinate clause. Of course, there's nothing more wrong with a complex sentence than there is with a compound sentence. The problem occurs when you write *overly* complex sentences.

Sentences that are overly complex pile up phrases, parenthetical ideas, and qualifiers to the point where the reader has trouble excavating the main idea. For example, here is a sentence that is too long because it is overly complex:

> The effect of foreign competition also shows up in the downward trend for widget exports, which, during the first four months of this year, averaged about 433 per capita, compared with an average of 628 per capita during the same period last year.

Rewritten, the sentence reads:

> The effect of foreign competition also shows up in the downward

trend for widget exports. During the first four months of this year, we sold 433 widgets per capita. During the same period last year, we sold 628 widgets per capita.

The solutions

Let's imagine you have written a sentence that is overly compound, overly complex, or just plain overly long. For example, say you had written this:

Regardless of their seniority, all employees who hope to be promoted will continue their education either by enrolling in the special courses to be offered by the ABC Company, scheduled to be given on the next eight Saturdays, beginning on January 24, or by taking approved correspondence courses selected from a list available in the Staff Development Office.

When you look back at it, you decide fifty-seven words is too long. Here are three ways you might rewrite that sentence to make it easier to read: using transitions, internal enumeration, or bullet points.

Here is one possible rewrite, using **transitions.** Chop the long sentence into a series of shorter sentences, and add transitional words:

Regardless of their seniority, all employees who hope to be promoted will continue their education in one of two ways. *First,* they may enroll in the special courses offered by the ABC Company, scheduled to be given on the next eight Saturdays, beginning on January 24. *Second,* they may take approved correspondence courses selected from a list available in the Staff Development Office.

Here is a second possible rewrite, using **internal enumeration.** The term *internal enumeration* refers to numbers in parentheses within the sentence itself, like this: (l), (2), (3). Internal enumeration differs from a list of numbers down the side of the page like this:

1.

2.

3.

Listing numbers down the side of the page is appropriate if you want to emphasize each point; each point stands out more prominently that way. If, however, you merely want to separate ideas for your reader without emphasizing them that much, try internal enumeration. For example:

Regardless of their seniority, all employees who hope to be promoted will continue their education by either: (l) enrolling in the special courses offered by the ABC Company, scheduled to be given on the next eight Saturdays, beginning on January 24, or (2) taking approved correspondence courses selected from a list available in the Staff Development Office.

A third way to rewrite an overly long sentence is to use **bullet points** to break up the ideas. Bullet points emphasize the ideas more than internal enumeration, but they are not numbered. Therefore, bullet points do not imply a hierarchy or chronological order, as numbers might. Here is the same sentence rewritten with bullet points:

Regardless of their seniority, all employees who hope to be promoted will continue their education in one of two ways:

- by enrolling in the special courses offered by the ABC Company, scheduled to be given on the next eight Saturdays, beginning on January 24, or

- by taking approved correspondence courses selected from a list available in the Staff Development Office.

Variety and rhythm

Your choices about sentence length, however, are more subtle than merely limiting your sentences to twenty to twenty-five words in every single circumstance. If everybody did that all the time, our writing would be very boring and repetitive. A lack of **variety** in sentence length or structure can be just as deadening as strings of long sentences. Therefore, watch out for short, monotonous, identically structured sentences. Here is an example of monotonous sentence structure:

We should invest in plastics research immediately. We should build and staff three research laboratories. We should expand our involvement in scientific associations. We must not let research overshadow our practical image. That image should be preserved through advertising campaigns.

The sentence lengths in that example are: seven words, eight words, eight words, nine words, and eight words. Clearly, the writing is choppy. Here is a possible rewrite:

> We should invest in plastics research immediately by: (1) building and staffing three research laboratories and (2) expanding our involvement in scientific associations. Research, however, must not overshadow our practical image, which we will continue to reinforce in our advertising campaign.

The new sentence lengths are twenty-one words and seventeen words, well within the twenty to twenty-five rule—and rhythmically different from each other.

Here is another example of a series of short, choppy sentences, of six, six, three, and four words:

> She objected to funding the project. She argued it was too expensive. Her boss disagreed. The project was approved.

Even though the rewritten sentence is longer, at twenty words, it is less choppy and has a better rhythm:

> She objected to funding the project, arguing it was too expensive; her boss disagreed, however, and the project was funded.

Perhaps the most subtle concept of all in sentence length is the concept of **rhythm**. The following paragraph, for example, contains sentences of varied length: forty-eight, ten, and thirty-nine words. Even with the variation, however, the sentences are hard to read because they lack rhythm:

> Each person to whom this memo is written is entitled to submit, or request his or her supervisor to submit, to the Personnel Department at the address above, a request for reconsideration of the question as to whether he or she should have been considered for internal promotion. The supervisor may or may not countersign such a request. If such a request is submitted, and the Personnel Department declines to reconsider the decision, the person so requesting may submit an appeal to the Personnel Executive Committee regarding those matters on which the Personnel Department declined to comment.

This paragraph proves that varying your sentence length does not guarantee effective sentences. These sentences lack shape and rhythm. No rule can standardize sentence rhythm for you. Instead, you must rely on an intuitive guide: how the sentence *sounds*. "If prose is hard to read aloud, it will be hard to read silently. If it offers the voice no guidance, does not invite it to stress this and elide that, to rise and fall in pitch, then it is going to be hard to follow."[2] Take, for example, the first sentence of the previous paragraph:

> Each person to whom this memo is written is entitled to submit, or request his or her supervisor to submit, to the Personnel Department at the address above, a request for reconsideration of the question as to whether he or she should have been considered for internal promotion.

The same sentence might be written:

> You or your supervisor may write to the Personnel Department if you think you should have been considered for an internal promotion.

Read the new sentence aloud. It allows your voice to rise and fall naturally. It has rhythm. It sounds like English.

See Table 9.2 for a summary of techniques for establishing proper sentence length.

TABLE 9.2

Watch your sentence length.

The problems	*Possible solutions*
Too long: too long to understand / too many *and*s / overly complex	**Shorten:** add transitional words: *First, . . . second, . . .* use internal enumeration: (1). . . . (2). . . . use bullet points: ● ● ●
Lack of variety: too many sentences of similar length	**Add variety:** use varying sentence lengths
Lack of rhythm: sounds boring or singsong	**Add rhythm:** rewrite to allow voice to rise and fall, like spoken English

---

[2]R. Lanham, *Revising Business Prose* (New York: Scribner's, 1981, pp. 42–43.

Use Vigorous Verbs.

As business people are fond of pointing out to students, business is the "real world." What people do each day in business is practical and active, they say, not abstract or theoretical. Managers *decide;* workers *produce;* profits (we hope) *increase.* To express this world and its action, business writers must use action words—vigorous verbs.

All too often, alas, business writers lose the force of their action words, bogging down into lifeless, heavy prose. The verb *decide* becomes *make a decision regarding* or *it has been decided that; produce* becomes *is produced by; increase* becomes *show an increase in.*

Avoid overusing nouns.

How can you avoid these lifeless verbs? For one thing, watch out for overusing nouns at the expense of verbs. Nouns, of course, are useful and necessary; verbs, however, give language its life and movement. For example, consider the difference between two versions of the same sentence:

> The *subject* of this *report* is low-*budget* employee *activity-enhancement techniques.* (six nouns)

> This *report* explains how to increase employee *activities* without spending too much *money.* (three nouns)

Chains of nouns like those in the first example pile up in phrases such as *motorized attendance modules* (buses), *interior intrusion detection systems* (burglar alarms) and *ball activity area* (gym). Author Richard Wydick advises a "noun chain confusion avoidance technique."[3] As his tongue-in-cheek phrasing demonstrates, a long chain of nouns is apt to strangle the reader.

Along with strangulating noun chains is the problem of misusing nouns as verbs. As I am about to do incorrectly in the next sentence, do not make nouns into verbs. *Don't verbize nouns.* Incorrect business writers do so in two ways. First, they take a perfectly harmless noun, such as *gift,* and use it incorrectly as a verb, *to gift.* Here are some examples of such nonverbs:

---

[3]R. Wydick, "Plain English for Lawyers," *California Law Review,* 66:727 (1978), 752.

Avoid these nonverbs:	Use these verbs instead:
to access*	to obtain, to gain access, to get in
to author	to write
to downsize	to make smaller
to gift	to give a gift
to impact	to influence, to affect
to interface*	to discuss, to meet
to headquarter	to have headquarters at
to mandate	to command, to order, to decree
to retool	to do it over
to target	to aim toward
to total down	to enter the total
to upscale	to make better

Second, incorrect writers take another perfectly harmless noun, such as *attitude*, and use it incorrectly as a verb by adding *-ize*, as in *attitudinize*. Here are some examples of *-ize nonverbs:*

Avoid these nonverbs.

to attitudinize	to inferiorize
to circularize	to normalize
to computerize	to optimize
to conceptualize	to prioritize
to cosmetize	to productionize
to definitize	to scenarioize
to finalize	to suboptimize
to globalize	to synopsize
to incrementalize	to systematize

In other words, do not make verbs out of nouns. Similarly, do not make adjectives out of nouns, as I do in the next sentence. *Avoid being incorrect, adjectivewise.* According to Strunk and White: "There is not a noun in the language to which *-wise* cannot be added if the spirit moves one to add it. The sober writer will abstain from the use of this wild additive."[4] Just imagine, for example, what would have happened to English literature if poets had not heeded this advice: "Oh, my love is

---

*Does not refer to proper use in computing.

[4]W. Strunk and E. B. White, *The Elements of Style,* 3rd ed. (New York: Macmillan, 1979), p. 64.

like a red, red rose—colorwise." Here are some more likely business examples:

Avoid these nonadjectives.

businesswise	policywise
costwise	profitwise
moneywise	taxwise
personnelwise	timewise

So, by avoiding overusing nouns—noun chains, "verbized" nouns, and "adjectivized" nouns—you will allow your writing to become more vigorous.

Avoid overusing weak verbs.

A second step toward vigorous verbs is to avoid overusing weak verbs: *be, become, look, seem, appear,* and *sound.* Don't take this advice to mean you should never use these six verbs; obviously, sometimes you will need to do so. Instead, avoid boring your reader by overusing them. As a very general rule of thumb, writers can usually cut over 50 percent of these verbs from their first draft.

Why, then, should you cut them at all? What makes these verbs "weak"? They are weak because you can usually get rid of them to make your sentences shorter and more forceful. For example, the sentence

Plant A is successful in terms of production

uses the weak verb *is,* and is eight words long. That sentence might be edited to read:

Plant A produces well.

This sentence uses the strong verb *produces,* and reduces the word count by 50 percent to four words. As another example, the sentence opening

There appears to be a tendency on the part of our customers . . .

uses the weak verb *appears* (not to mention the weak opening *there*) and racks up a word count of twelve. A possible rewrite,

Our customers tend . . .

uses the stronger verb *tend* and reduces the word count by 75 percent to three words.

Avoid elongated verbs.

Besides avoiding the six weak verbs, prefer concise one-word verbs to elongated verb forms. For example, *analyze* is a concise one-word verb; *perform an analysis of* is an elongated verb. The verb *analyze* is short and forceful; the verb *perform* plus the noun *analysis* plus the preposition *of* is wordy. Elongated verbs (verb plus noun plus preposition) produce more verbiage through which your readers must wade. Again, elongated verbs are not always bad; sometimes you need them. But do not overuse them in place of concise verbs.

When you see elongated verbs in your writing, stop to see if you can make your sentences stronger by using a one-word verb instead. One way to spot elongated verbs is to watch for these noun endings: *-ment, -ion, -tion, -ance, -ence -ancy, -ency, -ant,* and *-ent.* For example, you might spot the *tion* in *examination,* as in *make an examination of* and substitute *examine.* Or, you might catch the *ant* in *cognizant,* as in *be cognizant of,* and shorten it to *know.* Another way to check for elongated verbs is to study the following list of the most common examples:

Avoid elongated verbs.

Write	*Avoid*
act	take action on
allow	afford the opportunity to make it possible to
analyze	perform an analysis of
assume	make an assumption about
believe	take the position that
can	be in a position to
change	effect a change in
collide	have a collision with
conclude	come to a conclusion about draw a conclusion about reach a conclusion about
correct	is corrective of
decide	make a decision about
depends	is dependent on
end	bring to the end of
examine	make an examination of

Write	Avoid
help	be of service to
	provide assistance to
increase	show an increase in
know	be aware of the fact that
	be cognizant of
order	to place an order for
pay	make a payment toward
realize	make a realization about
recommend	make a recommendation regarding
reduce	effect a reduction in
suggest	venture a suggestion about
tend	exhibit a tendency to
try	make every effort to

Avoid overusing passive verbs.

In addition to avoiding overused elongated verbs, avoid overusing passive verbs. Passive verbs are a certain usage of the verb *to be* that is especially common among business writers. Let's look first at what passive verbs are, and then at why overusing them can harm your writing.

To **define** the term *passive*, keep in mind that the word has nothing to do with the concept of past. In other words, *passive* does not mean the action you're describing occurred in the past; similarly, just because you're writing about something that occurred in the past does not mean your verb is passive.

The word *passive*, instead, is the opposite of the word *active*. When you use the active voice, the subject of the sentence acts:

The engineer invented the product.

When you use the passive voice, the subject of the sentence is *passive*, acted upon:

The product was invented by the engineer.

Some students find it helpful to remember the difference between *passive* and *active* by thinking of a scene in a short, active sentence. "Len wrecked his car." "Debbie lifted the weights." "Hector kicked the wall." In each scene, the active agent of the sentence—the person performing the action—is the subject of the sentence. The verbs are active: *wreck, lift,* and *kick.* The passive versions of these active sentences would be: "The car was wrecked by Len." "The weights were lifted by Debbie." "The wall was kicked by Hector." In each of these second examples, the passive agent of the sentence —the thing to which something gets *done*—is the subject. The action is done *by* someone.

Another way to remember the difference between *passive* and *active* is to remember an equation. The passive voice always includes two things: (l) a form of the verb *to be* and (2) an action done *by* someone or something. "The file drawer was slammed by him" is passive: it includes a form of the verb *to be (was)* and an action done *by* someone *(by him)*.

Whether you remember by imagining a scene or by using a formula, the passive voice is tricky to catch—especially if you're using it by habit, not choice. Every time you see a sentence with a form of *to be* in it, you know you have a weak verb, but you don't know it's passive; to be passive, the sentence must have an action done *by* someone or something. But just because you have a sentence without the word *by* in it doesn't mean you've avoided the passive: the word *by* may be implied and not stated. The following sentences, for example, are all passive: "The car was wrecked" (wrecked by whom?). "The weights were lifted" (lifted by whom?). "The wall was kicked" (kicked by whom?). In each case, the reader does not know who is performing the action. Even though the wording *by so-and-so* does not appear, the phrase is implied because it's unclear who is doing what.

Once you have mastered the art of recognizing the passive, you may well ask, "So what? What's wrong with using these kinds of verbs?" The answer is that habitual overuse of the passive can lead to **problems:**

1. The passive is usually more wordy. The sentence "They were not told by anyone" is passive and six words long. The sentence "Nobody told them" is active and only three words long. When you move from the passive to the active, your reader will thank you for leaving out unnecessary words.

2. The passive is often more pompous and weighty. The sentence "A fair decision was rendered difficult by my supervisor's bias" is passive and pompous (especially the phrase *rendered difficult*). The active version, "Because my supervisor was biased, she could not decide fairly" is less weighty and formal.

3. The passive is often unclear. The sentence "It is urged that special study be given to the recommendations in this report" might confuse your reader: who is urging? you alone? the group? the task force? the supervisor? a football team? The active version, "We urge you to study carefully the recommendations in this report," makes it clear that the authors of the report are urging this action.

4. The passive wastes your reader's time. I have never heard a business

person complain about having too little to do or wanting more to read. Some research shows that it takes readers significantly longer to decode and understand a sentence written in the passive than one written in the active.[5] Since you don't want to waste your reader's time, why take that chance by using the more weighty, unclear passive construction?

Many students are quick to point out that in some situations the passive voice is appropriate. You might want to use the passive, for example, if you are trying to soften a blow or appear tentative: "It is suggested that you start sharing your office with Bill." Or you might use the passive for the sake of sentence variety. And sometimes—depending on your boss, of course—a writer in a lower position than the reader should use passive verbs. Instead of accusing your boss by writing "You are wasting time at meetings," you might say "Time is being wasted at meetings." Finally, you might want to use the passive when you are trying to avoid responsibility for an action, such as "The bunsen burner was left on all night and the lab was burned down" instead of "I left on the bunsen burner all night and burned down the lab." A more likely example might be your writing "Several objections might be raised" instead of "I have several objections."

As long as you make the conscious, strategic choice to use the passive—to soften a blow, to add variety, to emphasize the recipient of an action, to avoid ordering a superior, or to avoid responsibility for an action—the verb form is certainly not grammatically incorrect. But, if you are habitually, unthinkingly using the passive—potentially slowing down your reader, adding unnecessary words, being pompous, making your meaning unclear, and coming off as a weak and indirect person—you will certainly impair your writing and your effectiveness.

The four rules for using vigorous verbs are summarized in Table 9.3.

In summary, good, clear business writing is not based only on choosing your communication strategy and editing your document and paragraphs. You must also construct and edit carefully arranged, vigorous sentences of appropriate length.

[5]See D. Felker (ed.), *Guidelines for Document Designers* (Washington, D.C.: American Institutes for Research, 1981); and L. Reder, "Literature Review on Comprehension and Retention of Prose," Technical Report No. 108, University of Illinois, Champaign-Urbana, Center for the Study of Reading, 1978.

TABLE 9.3			
Use vigorous verbs.			

		Examples	
Rule	Grammar	Write	Avoid
1. Avoid overusing nouns.	Chains of three or more nouns	gym	ball activity area
	Nonverbs invented from nouns	set priorities	prioritize
2. Avoid overusing weak verbs.	The verbs *to be, to become, to look, to appear, to sound, to seem*	produces	is produced
		tends	appears to tend
3. Avoid elongated verbs.	Verb plus noun plus preposition	act	take action on
		depends	is dependent upon
4. Avoid overusing passive verbs.	Verb *to be* plus action done *by* someone or something	they decided	it was decided that
		she won the award	the award was won by her

REVIEW QUESTIONS

To check your understanding

1. What two effects does changing the word order have on a sentence?
2. What is a main clause and how can you recognize it?
3. What goes into the subordinate part of a sentence?
4. Why is it advisable to place the verb near the subject?
5. What is a modifier and where should it go?
6. Explain a dangling modifier and its dangers.
7. What is a good rule of thumb for deciding if your sentence is overly compound?

8. Cite three ways you can simplify overly long, overly complex, or overly compound sentences.

9. What is the importance of variety and rhythm in sentence length?

10. What does it mean to "verbize" a noun, and why shouldn't you do it?

11. What three other kinds of verbs should you avoid?

12. Define the passive voice.

13. Give three reasons why the passive voice can harm your writing.

14. When can the passive voice be useful?

APPLICATION QUESTIONS

To apply your knowledge

1. Rewrite the following sentences so that they emphasize the important words. (The important words appear in parentheses.)

   a. Many employees list a full insurance program as one of their most important benefits. (a full insurance program)

   b. Signaling that the meeting was over, the director rose and left the room. (signaling that the meeting was over)

   c. An effective sentence contains not only a subject, but a vigorous verb as well. (vigorous verb)

   d. Unless unforeseen problems arise, Donald intends to attend the meeting in Philadelphia on January third. (unforeseen problems)

2. Reposition the verb nearer the subject in the following sentences.

   a. Business majors, if they are to get a job in today's competitive job market, must possess the necessary communication skills.

   b. Sue Connelly, the director of marketing for a large Midwestern manufacturer and a close friend of my former boss, has offered to help me design a policy study.

   c. The consultant, who was hired by the company to study employee relations and offer a cost/benefit analysis of hiring a staff psychologist, will submit a written report no later than next Thursday.

   d. Employees wishing to attend a seminar entitled "Where You Are Going in Your Career and How to Get There" must sign up no later than 3 P.M. today.

3. The following sentences and groups of sentences have problems

with length: they are too long, too complex, too choppy, or too monotonous. Rewrite them so that they are clear and easy to read.

a. The boss called her employee into her office. She asked him to sit down. She asked him if he would like a promotion.

b. Whenever I am called upon to reflect on my experiences at XYZ Printing, I always think about the wonderful people I have met here, and I would like to let you know how much I appreciate your help and I want you to feel free to call on me in the future.

c. Despite the strong presence that Maurice succeeded in establishing in Franklin, Harrison, and Dodge counties, his performance in the field of sales has not been spectacular of late and therefore I suggest we terminate his contract and ask him to turn in his samples and pay him his final fees.

d. The next meeting of the *ad hoc* committee will take place on Wednesday in Stinson Hall, which is across the road from the fire hall, on the second floor, in room 23G, at 9 P.M.

e. Joan made many valid points in her report to the planning board, including her critique of the company's hiring policy, her emphasis on the need for affirmative-action guidelines, and her recommendation that someone be appointed to oversee its implementation.

f. I wish to remind you that these assumptions are based on a study conducted last year by the Business Research Association, which showed that college graduates tend to prefer blue cars, as opposed to high school graduates, who usually buy red.

g. No matter how high our profits, a depressed market still faces us. Despite the measures already taken to fight it, many more remain to be tried. Unless a realistic assessment of the situation is made, financial disaster looms.

h. Among the advantages of a permanent headquarters in New York are the proximity of three major airports, a large and well-trained work force, the presence of major financial institutions, and easy communication with Europe and the rest of the country.

i. I have three recommendations to make. One is that we increase our advertising budget. Another is that we open a new store downtown. Another is that we hire local citizens to work there.

j. Satellite communications enable us to correspond instantaneously with overseas distributors, and word processors help us get our reports out quickly, and photocopiers allow us to make as many copies as we need.

4. Rewrite the following sentences, using more effective, vigorous verbs. Make additional improvements where necessary.

   a. Giving ample consideration to the problems beforehand serves to expedite the process of finding solutions for them.

   b. All sales inquiries are to be referred to Mr. Roundhead.

   c. The older plants are in need of extensive renovation; this problem should be dealt with immediately.

   d. The solution was proposed by Lisa Jenkins and will be put into implementation by her staff.

   e. Employee sick-leave requirements are in the process of being reviewed by Ms. Haverford, who is charged with the responsibility of seeing that the proposed changes are fair to all concerned.

   f. In order to market the new liquid detergent, research on potential consumer reaction to the product is needed.

   g. The following recommendations, which were developed by the Palmer Consulting Group, serve to expedite our transition to computerized bookkeeping.

   h. If we make an examination of the responses received by our sales letters, we are sure to acquire the data necessary to reach a conclusion about the correspondence between writing style and sales.

   i. The letter was drafted and submitted by my secretary, but I had it reviewed by one of the paralegals in the office.

   j. Ms. Samuelson is the one in the position to make a recommendation concerning when staff meetings should be held.

5. Decide if the following sentences are active or passive. Rewrite the passive sentences into the active voice. Where necessary, invent an appropriate subject.

   a. In 1979, Baker Software, Inc., was acquired by Williams and Williams.

   b. George was very proud of his accomplishments while he was in that division.

   c. All the profits should be reinvested immediately.

   d. It is recommended that Mr. Wilkes be relieved of his responsibilities.

  e. Government intervention was avoided through responsible, long-term corporate planning.

  f. It has been decided that the contract will not be renewed.

  g. The following recommendations will serve to expedite the bookkeeping process.

  h. The phone, in the late afternoon, was ringing incessantly.

  i. The savings intended by the current administration could be easily achieved if the welfare recording system were updated.

  j. It is argued that price supports are preferable to cash benefits.

6. Revise the following sentences, correctly placing modifying words and phrases.

  a. His salary increase nearly was $2000.

  b. She even worked on Saturdays to complete the project.

  c. Newspapers reported the company's losses in every state in the union.

  d. Amalgamated Computers devised a program for small businesses with Standard English commands.

  e. Ms. Parkinson said in the morning work will resume.

  f. The boss was upset that coffee was served to visitors in plastic cups.

  g. The new product will only cost $3.50.

  h. Pioneer Auto Repair says it is essential for its employees to clearly and succinctly inform patrons of the limits of the warranty.

  i. Having decided to fire her entire staff, all that remained was for Ms. Hardesty to call a meeting and do it.

  j. Forgetting about strong foreign competition, heavy losses surprised the company.

CASES

To practice what you learned

See cases at the end of chapter 7, pages 175-81.

10

Choosing Words

Be Brief.
Watch your prepositions. • *Watch your repetitions.*

Be Simple.
Avoid pompous words. • *Avoid unnecessary jargon.*

Be Correct.

CONSIDER these three sentences: "The new electronic substrate of managerial parameters will increasingly obsolete the traditional reward factors for key executives. For the proactive manager who can, in the evolving electronic era, access the strategic thrust of his organization and assimilate its integral goals, significant recompense awaits. The author utilizes the vertical ascendancy of an individual to elucidate the process."[1]

These sentences exhibit none of the problems we discussed in the previous chapter: their average length is eighteen words; their order is not convoluted; they do not use the kinds of weak verbs we have examined. Yet, they are still next to impossible to understand because they are full of long, fancy, and misused words. A *Wall Street Journal* article parodied these problems with word choice in an article entitled "Employers prioritize utilization of words to impact quality. Translation: business schools and firms increase emphasis on good writing courses."[2]

To avoid these kinds of problems with your writing, make sure your wording is (1) brief, (2) simple, and (3) correct.

Be Brief.

Just as a document should contain no unnecessary paragraphs, and a paragraph no unnecessary sentences, a sentence should contain no unnecessary words. In the words of Strunk and White, "Omit needless words. Vigorous writing is concise." They go on to explain that "this requires not that the writer make all his sentences short, or that he avoid all detail and treat his subjects only in outline, but that every word tell."[3]

[1]M. Buss, "Making it Electronically," *Harvard Business Review* (January–February 1982), p. 89. Reprinted by permission of the *Harvard Business Review*. Copyright © 1982 by the President and Fellows of Harvard College; all rights reserved.

[2]N. Ronalds, "Employers Prioritize Utilization of Words to Impact Quality," *Wall Street Journal*, November 6, 1979, p. 30.

[3]W. Strunk and E. B. White, *The Elements of Style*, 3rd ed. (New York: Macmillan, 1979), p. 23.

Make every word count. Apply accounting principles to your writing and make each word cost-effective. Cut, for example, *he was aware of the fact that* to *he knew*. You have saved your reader the trouble of reading five unnecessary words. Cut *circular in shape, blue in color*, and *eight in number* to *circular, blue*, and *eight*. Cut *the city of Phoenix, the fiscal year of 1990*, and *the price of seventeen dollars* to *Phoenix, fiscal 1990*, and *seventeen dollars*.

To make your writing cost-effective, watch your prepositions and watch your repetitions.

Watch your prepositions.

Prepositions are short words—such as *after, by, for*, and *to*—that link and relate another word to the rest of the sentence. Here is a list of the words most commonly used as prepositions.

Watch your prepositions.

about	concerning	over
above	despite	past
across	down	regarding
after	during	round
against	except	since
along	excepting	through
among	for	throughout
around	from	till
at	in	to
before	inside	toward
behind	into	under
below	like	underneath
beneath	near	until
besides	of	up
between	off	upon
beyond	on	with
but	onto	within
by	out	without

Prepositions, of course, are not always bad; they serve a needed function in the language. The idea behind being brief, then, is *not* to avoid using prepositions altogether, but rather to avoid compound prepositions and overused prepositions.

Compound prepositions are groups of prepositional words you can easily shorten to one word. Here is a list of compound prepositional phrases to avoid.

Avoid compound prepositions.

Write	Avoid
about	in regard to, in the matter of, with reference to, in relation to, with regard to
after	after the conclusion of, at future points in time, subsequent to
although	despite the fact that, notwithstanding the fact that
because, since	accounted for by the fact that, as a result of, due to the fact that, inasmuch as, in the event that, for the reason that, in view of the fact that, on the grounds that, owing to the fact that
before	in advance of, prior to, previous to
by, under	by means of, by virtue of, in accordance with, on the basis of
for	in favor of, for the period of, for the purpose of
if	in the event that
in	in terms of
later	at a later date
like, another	along the lines of, an additional, in addition to, in the nature of, similar to
near	in the proximity of
now, then	as of this date, at the present time, as of this writing, at this/that time, at this/that point in time
on	on the occasion of
soon	at an early date, in the very near future
to	in order to, for the purpose of, so as to, with a view toward
until	until such time as
when, during	at this/that point in time, at such time, at which time, as soon as, during the course of, during the time that, during this/that period of time, on the occasion of, until such date as
whether	as to whether, the question as to whether
with	accompanied by, in connection with

Besides avoiding just those compound prepositions, watch out for **overused prepositions** of any variety. Try circling all of the prepositions in a sample page of your own writing. If you consistently find more than four prepositions in a sentence, you need to revise to be more brief. *Of* is usually the most overused preposition.

For example, count the prepositions in this sentence:

The committee should give consideration **to** publishing further information **with** a view **toward** anticipating probable questions that may occur **at** future points **in** time.

Five prepositions is your clue that the sentence is not as brief as it could be. A possible rewrite:

Anticipating probable questions, the committee should consider publishing more information.

By cutting the preposition count from five to zero, the author cuts the word count in half.

As another example, count the prepositions in this sentence:

Central **to** our understanding **of** the problem **of** the organizational structure **in** the widget division **of** the Qualpro Company is the chain **of** command **below** the position **of** the divisional vice-president, which is not connected **with** all **of** the subordinate departments.

Here again, the prepositions mount up—ten, to be exact. As writing expert Richard Lanham points out, these overused prepositions pile up in what sounds like a boring, singsong laundry list.[4] Listen to the *sound* of that sentence:

Central
to our understanding
of the problem
of the organizational structure
in the widget division
of the Qualpro Company is the chain
of command
below the position
of the divisional vice-president, which is not connected
with all
of the subordinate departments.

Rewritten, the same sentence reads:

The organization problem **at** the Qualpro Company's widget divi-

[4]R. Lanham, *Revising Business Prose*, videocassette (New York: Scribner's, 1981).

sion centers **on** the unclear connection **between** the divisional vice-president and the subordinate departments.

The sentence is pared from eleven prepositions to three, which decreases the word count from forty-one to twenty-two.

Watch your repetitions.

Besides watching your prepositions, watch your repetitions. Many business writers use repetitious phrasing. Why say *consensus of opinion*, *midway between*, or *visible to the eye* when *consensus*, *midway*, and *visible* will do just fine? If two items are identical, you waste words by calling them *exactly identical*; if you state your opinion, you waste words by calling it your *personal opinion*. Here is a list of repetitious phrases to watch for in business writing:

Avoid repetitions.

absolutely complete	free and clear
active considerations	full and complete
actual truth	future plans
alter or change	great majority
assemble together	important essentials
attached hereto	integral part
basic fundamentals	midway between
causal factor	new changes
cease and desist	numerous and sundry
collect together	past history
complete stop	personal opinion
consensus of opinion	potential opportunity
contributing factor	reduce down
dollar amount	refer back
each and every	repeat again
enclosed herewith	return back
end result	serious crisis
entirely complete	true and correct
exactly identical	very unique
first and foremost	visible to the eye
follows after	vitally essential

Although an expression such as *very unique* is *always* repetitious, some expressions are *sometimes* repetitious. The word *character*, for example, may be fine in many situations; when you use it in the phrase *skills of a professional character*, however, it's wordy. The phrase *professional skills* says the same thing with less than half the words. Beware, then, of the following expressions that may be adding unnecessary words:

Avoid potential repetitions.

Avoid overuse of	Write	Instead of
area	communication	the area of communication
basis	fee-for-service	on a fee-for-service basis
case	often	in many cases
character	professional skills	skills of a professional character
circumstance	usually	in the majority of circumstances
context	in business	in a business context
degree	the staff's commitment	the degree of the staff's commitment
field	law	legal field
instance	sometimes	in some instances
level	supervisors should deal with this	We should deal with this on a supervisory level.
nature	uncooperative behavior	behavior of an uncooperative nature
situation	problem	problem situation
sphere	within her division	within the sphere of her division
who/which	Smith, a consumer advocate	Smith, who is a consumer advocate
	St. Louis, where the plant is located	St. Louis, which is where the plant is located

Be Simple.

Simplicity in writing differs from brevity. If your writing is concise, you have cut out unnecessary words: *whether* instead of *the question as to whether; because* instead of *due to the fact that;* and so forth. To make your writing simple, on the other hand, you do not necessarily cut words. Instead, you change them. You move from overly fancy words to simple, direct ones: *limit* instead of *parameter; place* instead of *locality; best* instead of *optimum.*

Simplicity, then, means moving away from pompous words and from unnecessary jargon.

Avoid pompous words.

Here is a longer example of pompous word choice: "Per your request of today's date, enclosed please find the figures on the Shaw account." A translation into simple language: "Here are the figures on the Shaw account you asked for this morning." Here's another: "Should additional assistance be required, please do not hesitate to contact the undersigned." Put more simply, "Call me if you need any more help."

Why do business writers, especially young business writers, use these words? Some people do so because they think that these kinds of words sound impressive and professional, that it somehow sounds more businesslike to say *per our discussion* than *we talked about,* to say *individuals* instead of *people.* They have the misconception that readers will equate big words with a big brain. Actually, these big, stilted words are the opposite of businesslike: they are inefficient because they make you waste your time composing and your readers, deciphering.

Other people write this way to imitate others in business: habits are passed from generation to generation. This explains why we see so many outdated expressions. *The aforementioned is attached hereto* may have been typical wording a hundred years ago, but it is not typical of contemporary English. The structure of the English language has simplified in the last century. Trying to write with outdated wording is about as sensible as trying to copy everything by quill and ink instead of using reprographic machines.

Finally, some people write this way because they think that's what top management wants. Bosses who insist on stodgy, pompous writing are certainly the exception. Most managers, in fact, don't want wordy, stilted language. According to the *Harvard Business Review,* most high-level executives use a straightforward, personal style. "It is simple; it is personal; it is warm without being syrupy; it is forceful, like a firm handshake. Almost everyone in business likes this style, although lower-level managers often find themselves afraid to write so forthrightly."[5] Managers don't want wordy convoluted sentences; they want short and simple ones. Most large corporations even provide training programs in writing aimed at teaching employees to write more forthrightly.

[5]J. Fielden, "What Do You Mean You Don't Like My Style?" *Harvard Business Review* (May–June, 1982), p. 131. Reprinted by permission of the *Harvard Business Review.* Copyright © 1982 by the President and Fellows of Harvard College; all rights reserved.

Whatever the causes may be, the cure for pompous writing is to ask yourself if you would ever *say* to your reader what you are writing. Can you imagine saying, for example, "Enclosed please find your order for four (4) component parts"? Instead, you would probably say something along the lines of: "Here are the four parts you ordered." (Why say "please find" when nothing is lost?) You probably can't imagine yourself saying "Reductions in the total number of units may be indicated" instead of the more simple "We might be cutting down on the units."

Let me emphasize, however, what writing conversationally does *not* mean. It does not mean you should limit your vocabulary. Instead, it does mean you should not use big words just because they are big. There is no special meaning that makes *utilization* better than *use*, or *the undersigned* better than *me*. If you need to use a technical term your audience understands, by all means do so. But avoid using big words for their own sake: write to express your meaning, not to impress your readers with your vocabulary.

Writing conversationally does not mean you should use slang, either. If you were speaking to your boss, or a colleague who is not a friend, or to a customer you do not know, you certainly would not use slang. By writing simply and conversationally, you will write as naturally, humanly, and persuasively as you speak.

Here are some examples of pompous wording—big words and stilted constructions—by business writers.

Avoid unnecessary big words.

Write	*Avoid*
about	regarding, concerning
agree	corroborate
appear	materialize
begin	commence, initiate
best	optimal, optimum
bulky	voluminous
chance to contribute	opportunity to input
change	modification
common	commonality
cost	fiscal expenditure
ended	terminated
enough	sufficient
equal	equivalent
first	initial
get	procure
go	proceed
guess	conjecture

Write	Avoid
help	be of assistance, facilitate
here/there	herein/therein
hurry	expedite
improve	ameliorate
learn, find out	ascertain
limit	parameter
me	the undersigned
meet	encounter
need	require
next	subsequent
pay	remunerate, compensate
people	individuals
place	locality
please	kindly
prevent	obviate
say	state, indicate
send	forward, transmit
shortage	insufficiency
tell, let me know	advise, acquaint
this	the subject, the aforementioned
try	endeavor
use	utilize, utilization of

Avoid stilted constructions.

Write	Avoid
about	pursuant to, in reference to
around	in the periphery of
ask us for additional copies	application should be made to this office for additional copies
as you asked	per your request/our discussion
as you requested	pursuant to your request/our discussion
as we discussed	as per your request/our discussion
	in accordance with your request
	in compliance with your request
be aware	be cognizant of
get the facts	ascertain the data
here are/here is	enclosed please find, attached hereto please find
if you need more help	should additional assistance be required
if you need more widgets	should the supply of widgets sent you prove insufficient to your requirements

Write	Avoid
On October 13 you asked me. . . .	Reference is made to your letter of October 13, in which you requested me. . . .
please note that our widget	I wish to bring to your attention the fact that our widget
question about	query relative to the status of
separately	under separate cover
stop	render inoperative
until	pending determination of
we will consider	will be given our careful consideration
We must set up new procedures for promoting people.	The establishment of new personnel-promotion procedures is a mandatory administrative priority.

Avoid unnecessary jargon.

Besides choosing fancy and stilted words, ineffective business writers choose jargon words. By *jargon,* I mean what other people have called *officialese, bureaucratese, legalese, buzz words,* and *gobbledygook*—words that garble your meaning.

PROFESSIONAL JARGON: One prevalent kind of jargon is caused by writers inappropriately using terminology associated with their field: professional jargon. Every profession has its jargon. An economist might write

> The choice of exogenous variables in relation to multi-collinearity is contingent upon the deviations of certain multiple coefficients.

instead of

> Supply determines demand.

A lawyer might write

> This policy is used in consideration of the application therefore, copy of which application is attached hereto and made part hereof, and of the payment for said insurance on the life of the above-named insured.

instead of

> Here is your life insurance policy.

A professor might think it sounds more academic to say

> Realization has grown that the curriculum or the experience of learners changes and improves only as those who are most directly involved examine their goals, improve their understanding, and increase their skill in performing the tasks necessary to reach newly defined goals. This places the focus upon teacher, lay citizen, and learner as partners in curricular improvement and as the individuals who must change, if there is to be curriculum change.

instead of

> If we are going to change the curriculum, teachers, parents, and students must all help.

Finally, here is an example of computer jargon, from a press release for the general public:

> The LSI 24/24 is a synchours 2400 bps modem with a full-dplex operation on two-wire dial-up or leased lines. Asynorous data can be accommodated by using an optional "async" adapter. The data rate is selectable from a nominal rate of 2400 bps for average quality lines, a fall-forward rate of 3200 bps for high quality lines, and a fallback rate of 1600 bps for degraded lines.

One of the biggest problems with business writing today stems from writers using jargon when writing to people outside their technical fields. For example, the word *bit* has a different meaning to computer engineers than to equestrians. The words *upstream* and *downstream* have different meanings to corporate planners than to anglers. And acronyms such as EPS, LIFO, FIFO, IRR, and ROI mean nothing to people without accounting or finance experience.

Sometimes, when you are writing to people all within your field, jargon can be appropriate. Overusing jargon, however, may be caused by what David Ewing calls *pathological professionalism*. He asks: "Why do the perpetrators of these verbal monstrosities, knowing the material must be read and understood by innocent people, proceed with such sinister dedication? They rejoice in the difficulty of their trade. They find psychic rewards in producing esoterica and abstruse word combinations. They revel in the fact that only a small group, an elite counterculture, knows what in hell they are trying to say. Hence, the term pathological professionalism."[6]

[6]D. Ewing, *Writing for Results in Business, Government, the Sciences, the Professions*, 2nd ed. (New York: John Wiley, 1979), p. 262.

FIGURE 10.1

Director of personnel, industrial, and agrarian priorities

Description of Duties and Responsibilities
(Immediate Appointment)

Without direct or intermediate supervision and with broad latitude for independent judgment and discretion, the incumbent directs, controls, and regulates the movement of interstate commerce representing a complete cross-section of the wealth of the American economy.

Based only on his personal judgment and past experience, conditioned and disciplined by patience, the incumbent integrates the variables in an evolving situation and on the basis of intellect makes a binding decision relative to the priority of flow in interstate and intrastate commerce. His decisions are irreversible, not subject to review by higher authority and excluded from judicial review.

The decisions of the incumbent are important to the national economy. His decision is final and affects the movement of agricultural and food products, forest products, small business, large business, public utilities, and government employees.

In the effective implementation of these responsibilities, the incumbent must exercise initiative, ingenuity, imagination, intelligence, industry, and discerning versatility. The incumbent must be able to deal effectively on a one-to-one basis with all types of personality and all levels of education from ditch digger to college president.

Above all, the incumbent must possess decisiveness and the ability to implement motivation on the part of others consistent with his decision. His erroneous decision could create a complex obfuscation of personnel and equipment generating an untold loss of mental equilibrium on the part of innumerable personnel in American industry and commerce who are, in turn, responsible for formulation of day-to-day policy and guidance implementation of the conveyance of transportation both interstate and intrastate.

This example was provided by Professor D. Andrews, University of Southern Californa, and is used with his permission.

In other words, professional jargon makes writers feel elite and important. Using professional jargon is the opposite of being audience-centered: jargon makes writers feel elite and important; potentially, therefore, readers feel left out, unimportant, and unable to comprehend. So save jargon for cases when it furthers communication, rather than blocks it.

EUPHEMISMS: Besides unintelligible words specific to your profession, watch out for another form of jargon: euphemisms. Euphemisms are words that substitute an agreeable or inoffensive meaning for one that may suggest something unpleasant. Euphemisms, of course—just like professional jargon—have a positive function. For example, asking a bereaved person about her or his "loved one" or "dearly departed" who "passed away" may seem a bit trite, but surely it's more considerate than inquiring after the "dead relative" or "the corpse."

But merely because euphemisms have some legitimate function in situations requiring a good deal of tact does not mean we should perpetrate them unnecessarily in our writing. We should not, for instance, use euphemisms manipulatively. *Revenue enhancement* is a manipulative way of disguising *tax increase*. *Nonselected* is a euphemism for *fired*. Here are some further examples, from some advice to real estate salespeople:

> Don't say "down payment"; say "initial investment." Don't ask for a "listing"; ask for "an authorization to sell." Don't say "second mortgage"; say "perhaps we can find additional financing." Don't use the word "lot"; call it a "homesite." Don't say "sign here"; say "write your name as you want it to appear on the deed."[7]

Another problem with euphemisms is that they make something sound more important than it really is. *Sanitation engineer,* for example, is a pompous euphemism for *garbage collector*. Figure 10.1 shows another euphemistic job description. Can you figure out what job is being described? (The answer appears later in the chapter.)

CLICHÉS: Finally, you can keep your writing simple by avoiding overuse of business clichés. Business clichés are set words and phrases that business people overuse, perhaps without thinking. Clichéd writers always *venture a suggestion,* or describe alternatives as *viable*. Marketing is always *aggressive*, and proposals inevitably seem to have a *main thrust* or a

---

[7]*Sonoma County Realtor,* quoted in *Consumer Reports,* October 1972. Copyright 1972 by Consumers Union of United States, Inc., Mount Vernon, N.Y. 10533. Reprinted by permission from *Consumer Reports,* October 1972.

TABLE 10.1
Instant cliché phrases*

Column 1	Column 2	Column 3
0. integrated	0. management	0. options
1. total	1. organizational	1. flexibility
2. systematized	2. monitored	2. capability
3. parallel	3. reciprocal	3. mobility
4. functional	4. digital	4. programming
5. responsive	5. logistical	5. concept
6. optional	6. transitional	6. time-phase
7. synchronized	7. incremental	7. projection
8. compatible	8. third-generation	8. hardware
9. balanced	9. policy	9. contingency

Think of any three numbers at random—272, for example. Then read off the corresponding cliché phrase, *systematized incremental capability.*

three-pronged approach. Increasing costs, of course, are always *skyrocketing.* Other common clichéd business phrases include: *bottom line, gainfully employed, in the last analysis, half the battle, as much as the traffic will bear, ground zero, day one,* and *back to square one.*

You will also find individual words that are so overused they have become clichés. Avoid overusing them in your writing: *alternative, concept, contingency, enhance, ensure, factor, flexibility, functional, incremental, integrated, options, organizational, projection, responsive, scenario, third-generation, time frame, time phase,* and *transitional. Newsweek* ran a feature on these kinds of words, which is reproduced in Table 10.1.

The point of the "instant cliché" chart is, of course, that careful writers should put more into their word choice than three numbers at random—or an unthinking overuse of clichés, euphemisms, and professional jargon. (By the way, the "Director of Personnel, Industrial, and Agrarian Priorities" is a flag operator for a road-construction crew.)

Be Correct.

What you write, of course, is always your own choice. Although normally you would want to be coherent, you can imagine situations in which you might want to be incoherent. Although normally you would want to be concise and straightforward, on occasion, you might choose to be long-winded and pompous. And you have the same kind of choice with correctness: you can choose to be absolutely proper, or, in some situations, you can choose not to bother. Correctness in business writing has to do with: (1) word choice, and (2) grammar, usage, punctuation, and mechanics.

WORD CHOICE: Proper word choice—that is, using words precisely as the dictionary defines them—has often been compared to good table manners. Eating with your mouth full or slurping your beverage gets the job of eating done. Similarly, even with incorrect words, you may still get the job of communicating done. However, when you choose to use bad table manners, as when you choose to ignore precise word meanings, you run the risk of offending your audience. To misuse *impact,* to confuse *affect* and *effect,* or to use a nonstandard form like *hisself* may jar your reader and undercut your business credibility in the same way drooling might.

If you have made the commitment to attempt to succeed in the business culture, you have had to agree to act, dress, and behave in certain ways. One part of that culture, if you want to succeed in business, is to communicate properly.

Even if you have made the commitment to write and speak properly, however, you will find that your choices are not as clear-cut as "Put your napkin on your lap" or "Don't drink from your finger bowl." Unfortunately (for those of us who want to learn "the rules" of language) and fortunately (for those of us who delight in the ever-changing nature of language), language and usage change over time. If you have read Chaucer's tales, Shakespeare's plays, or Jefferson's Declaration of Independence, you know that language has changed since those documents were written.

Word usage has also changed more recently. For example, in the 1920s, people started using the noun *contact* as a verb, *to contact.* For many years, traditionalists railed at the new verb, which in fact did not appear in dictionaries until years later. Now, of course, the verb is acceptable. As another example, in 1957 the Russians sent a rocket into the sky. English immediately added a new word: *sputnik.* New words must come into the language when new inventions do.

Even today, word usage is changing. Let me illustrate with the example of the word *data,* as writing expert Carter Daniel has done.[8] Most properly, business writers say "data are," not "data is," because the word

---

[8]C. Daniel and C. Smith, "An Argument for *Data* as a Collective Singular," *ABCA Bulletin,* September 1982, pp. 31–33.

data is plural (one datum, many data). So far, so good. *Data* should be plural: "data are." Consider two facts, however. (1) For many similar words, usage has changed over time. These once-plural words are now singular. We would never say the "agenda are," "trivia are," "insignia are," "macaroni are," or "spaghetti are." (2) The highest authorities—dictionary writers—are condoning the use of "data is." Fowler's famous *Modern English Usage,* which had insisted on "data are" since 1926, admitted "data is" in 1965. The *Random House Dictionary* followed suit in 1966, *Funk and Wagnall's* in 1973, and *Webster's New World* in 1978.

In short, we cannot put together a definitive dictionary of proper usage because usage changes. So what should we do? One choice is to give up on the idea of finding a proper language—because it's impossible to do so. In fact, many modern linguists would argue that since usage rules have no scientific or logical justifications, all we can do is describe some usages as *standard* and others as *nonstandard.* An opposite choice is to defend tradition. In fact, many modern language writers (such as John Simon and Edwin Newman) argue that we must prescribe correct usage and obliterate incorrect usage.

Somewhere in between these two choices is a sensible middle ground.[9] As business writers, we must uphold tradition without being too rigid; we must be open-minded without being too permissive. In appendix A, I have judged—the best I could—the correct use of words. By the time you read this book, usage will have already changed. By the time you're out in the business world, usage will have changed even more. Use these lists in the appendix, then, as a way to increase your sensitivity to the nuances of word choice—not as hard-and-fast rules. The appendix includes: (1) misused words, (2) confused pairs of words, and (3) misused nonstandard forms.

GRAMMAR: The other aspect of correctness is your grammar, usage, punctuation, and mechanics. When you hear those words: Stop. Don't think of some prim, bespeckled grammar teacher waggling a finger at you. Don't think of your parents berating you at the dinner table. Don't think of sweating over college applications.

Instead, think of yourself some years in the future, a success in the business world. What are you doing? (Whatever you think of as business success.) What are you wearing? (Whatever you think of as appropriate business garb.) How are you writing and speaking? (With correct grammar, if you are indeed to be a success.)

Grammar is not all that difficult. Try to disregard all the negative connotations you may associate with the word, and approach it as a business problem. Anyone who can master accounting and finance can

---

[9] See G. Nunberg, "The Decline of Grammar," *Atlantic Monthly,* December 1983, pp. 31–46.

certainly master grammar. Unlike mathematical formulas, however, grammar and language change over time. Therefore, appendixes 2 and 3 explain the most important and unchanging rules—and I'll point out these occasional rules that are less important or in the process of change.

Having said that, I'll leave you with these words of wisdom: don't risk spoiling all your brilliant ideas and otherwise brilliant writing by undercutting your credibility with bad grammar. Bad grammar is bad business.

We started the writing section of this book by thinking about the large issues in writing, such as your strategy and your organization. Now, we have worked our way down to the smallest issues: punctuation marks and the mechanics of abbreviation and capitalization. When you edit, you should usually check for these problems last. Just because you do so last, however, does not mean these issues are unimportant. Misused punctuation or mechanics can block communication severely; your reader can infer that you are ignorant and that your ideas are therefore wrong. It's foolish to take that risk with punctuation and mechanical errors—errors that are relatively easy to fix.[10] Appendix D provides a reference for punctuation and mechanics.

REVIEW QUESTIONS
To check your understanding

1. Why should you aim to be brief in your writing?
2. What is a preposition?
3. What kinds of prepositions should you avoid?
4. What is repetitious writing?
5. How can you overcome pompous writing?
6. What is professional jargon?
7. What is the problem with using professional jargon?
8. Why are euphemisms undesirable?
9. What is a cliché?
10. How is proper word choice like good table manners?
11. Why is proper word choice hard to define?

---

[10]Various computer programs may be available in college and in businesses to help you check your punctuation and mechanics. See M. Munter, "Using Computers in Business Communication Courses," *Journal of Business Communication*, Winter 1986, pp. 31–42.

12. What is the middle ground in proper word choice that business writers should try to keep?

APPLICATION QUESTIONS

To apply your knowledge

1. Rewrite the following sentences for more brevity and simplicity.

    a. In your memo of January 3, you requested that I prioritize the main factors.

    b. It was suggested by Mr. Pryor that we internationalize our distribution function.

    c. A managerial employee must give authorization for a secretary to send a communication on paper bearing the company letterhead prior to the time the letter is sent.

    d. Utilizing a variety of operational methods for the conducting of the seminar proved interesting in predicting efficiency, costwise.

    e. This procedural outline was designed to facilitate the expeditious transferal of selected commodities.

    f. Since most American citizens gain monetary resources through wages earned by labor, the poverty problem principally reflects the inability of a segment of the population to earn a sufficient wage through productive employment.

    g. A preplanned reduction in uncertainty factors serves to further productive creativity in the event that it promotes in the businessperson involved a degree of incentive in producing programs for advertising purposes.

    h. Parker Darker Window Shades should focalize its objectives so as to result in a minimization of salesman involvement in decisions regarding company policy.

    i. Optimization of the cost/benefit ratio of improved interfacing between departmental entities is the ideal objective for the future intracompany communications design mode.

2. Rewrite the following sentences to eliminate repetitious phrasing.

    a. The sum total of our net gains is one million dollars.

    b. Each and every employee is invited to submit his or her personal opinion in regard to the final outcome of this year's elections.

    c. Barry offered to give an exactly accurate assessment of the areas of problem within Dora's sphere of division.

    d. This product has a character of a uniquely individual nature.

    e. I look forward to meeting you soon and getting together to discuss our future plans.

3. Rewrite the following sentences to eliminate pompous words and jargon.

    a. You will find enclosed six copies of the aforementioned document per your order in your memo of yesterday's date.

    b. Supervisors are hereby advised that rest-room access implements should be available for acquisition by staff members upon verbal request.

    c. The following instructions pertain to the eventuality that fiscal expenditures overrun budgeted funds.

    d. Every effort will be made to ameliorate the situation and expedite your claim through the appropriate channels.

    e. Should you find that additional information is required pursuant to the meeting held on the date of July 15, please do not hesitate to get in touch with me to facilitate the meeting of your needs.

    f. A proactive stance by members of the marketing task force will yield significant results by impacting consumer awareness.

    g. Please affix the appropriate signatures and forward said document to the undersigned.

    h. Relative to our conversation of August 2, I am initiating procedures for establishing a permanent panel to oversee the company's future development.

    i. Skyrocketing costs and a depressed market inevitably lead to the conclusion that more drastic pricing measures are called for.

    j. Functional logistical flexibility necessitates a balanced approach to issues of employee nonwork time and its scheduling.

CASES

To practice what you learned

See cases at the end of chapter 7, pages 175–81.

SPEAKING CHECKLIST

1. Is your nonverbal communication effective?
   (See chapter 11.)
   > **Body (poise, gestures, facial expression, eye contact)**
   > *(See pages 258–63.)*
   > **Voice (inflection, rate, fillers, enunciation)**
   > *(See pages 263–65.)*
   > **Space and objects around you**
   > *(See pages 265–73.)*

2. Is your structure effective?
   (See chapter 12.)
   > **For a presentation (opening, preview, main points, closing)**
   > *(See pages 293–303.)*
   > **For other kinds of speeches**
   > *(See pages 303–10.)*

3. Are your visuals effective?
   (See chapter 13.)
   > **Composition (appropriate formality, necessary function, message title and detail, readability)**
   > *(See pages 315–29.)*
   > **Equipment**
   > *(See pages 329–36.)*
   > **Use (familiarity, integration)**
   > *(See pages 336–41.)*

4. Have you handled other speaking situations well?
   (See chapter 14.)
   > **Meetings (task and process functions)**
   > *(See pages 347–57.)*
   > **Answering questions (question-and-answer sessions, panels, media interviews)**
   > *(See pages 357–67.)*

11

Nonverbal Communication

Definition and Importance

Analyze the Elements of Nonverbal Communication.
Body • Voice • Space around you • Objects around you

Improve Your Nonverbal Skills.
Practice and arrange. • Relax and gain confidence.

GOOD speaking, like good writing, is based on your communication strategy. All of the fabulous visual aids, body language, and arrangements in the world will not do you a bit of good unless you have done an effective job of establishing your goals, analyzing your audience, and structuring your message appropriately. Once again—just as we discussed in the chapters on writing skill—remember that speaking skill is only effective if you have good strategy. So, plan your strategy (as explained in part I of this book) *before* you plan any presentation.

Although speaking and writing should both be based on good strategy, they differ in many ways as communication channels. (See chapter 2 for a discussion of these differences.) Undoubtedly, their biggest difference is that speaking includes nonverbal as well as verbal communication. Therefore, let's examine nonverbal communication, or "how you say it," first; in the next chapter, we will look at "what you say" in an oral presentation.

Definition and Importance

What, exactly, is nonverbal communication? It is any message you give other than the literal interpretation of your words—the way you move, speak, appear. Our words make up only a portion of what we communicate, and what we don't say is sometimes more important than what we do say. A noted anthropologist with the unforgettable name of Ray Birdwhistell estimates that the nonverbal element accounts for 65 percent of what gets communicated when you speak.[1] Another expert, Albert Mehra-

[1] R. Birdwhistell, *Kinesics and Context* (Philadelphia: University of Pennsylvania Press, 1970).

bian, estimates the nonverbal share at as high as 93 percent.[2] Using such precise percentages to describe something as imprecise as communication may seem a bit ridiculous, but nonetheless, most people today are aware of—and know the importance of—nonverbal communication. In fact, for a concept so important, it's hard to believe that the idea of nonverbal communication is so new: the word *nonverbal* first appeared in a book title as recently as 1956; the term *body language* was invented in 1970.

Nonverbal communication is so important because most people believe "how you say it" more than "what you say." If you say, "Yeah, that's a great idea" in a sarcastic tone of voice, the person to whom you're talking will probably believe your tone, not the meaning of your words. As another example, here is an anecdote often told about Franklin Delano Roosevelt: To fight off the boredom of standing in a long reception line, he is reported to have entertained himself with a little experiment. As each guest asked, "How are you?" he said with a warm, pleasant smile, "I just murdered my mother-in-law." No one in the line reacted to the remark; they reacted only to his nonverbal communication.

The concept has, alas, been badly used at times. For one thing, we must constantly keep in mind that effective nonverbal behavior is based on the culture and specific situation in which you are communicating. What we will be discussing in this chapter is appropriate for the American business world, and may be wildly inappropriate in other cultures. (See pages 32–35 for more information about cross-cultural differences.) Another problem plaguing the notion of nonverbal communication is the many overly simplified interpretations that sound like magic formulas, such as "Crossed arms always indicate a closed personality" or "If you walk this way, you are guaranteed to make more money." Other unfortunate research has attempted overly scientific quantifications of the unquantifiable. Merely because nonverbal communication has been ill used, however, does not mean we should dismiss it. There is also a good deal of useful research on the subject. Although nonverbal communication is no magic, perfectly quantified key to success, understanding it can enable us to increase—or at least avoid hindering—effective communication by helping us to send appropriate signals and to be more sensitive to what other people really mean.[3]

[2]A. Mehrabian, *Silent Messages* (Belmont, Calif.: Wadsworth, 1972). Birdwhistell and Mehrabian's work is not recent, but the two of them are still respected as major pioneers in the field.

[3]One way to judge your sensitivity to nonverbal signs is to take the Profile of Nonverbal Sensitivity (PONS) test. The results of this test show that females tend to be more sensitive to nonverbal cues than males, and that actors and visual artists are

Given that nonverbal communication is so important in business, let's take a closer look at its elements. Researchers use terms such as *kinesics* (body motion), *paralanguage* (vocal qualities), *proxemics* (use and perception of space), and *indicators* (appearance and environment). Since we are studying business communication, however, and know enough to avoid unnecessary jargon, we can just as easily say that nonverbal communication includes body, voice, space, and objects.

As we discuss each of these elements, I'll be giving you some very specific advice on how to improve your nonverbal delivery skills. Reading about all these techniques, you may feel somewhat overwhelmed. "Stand this way; look that way; don't move this way." The first times you practice speaking, in fact, you may feel you have so much to remember about "how you say it" that you can't possibly say anything. If you remember when you were learning to drive, you probably felt the same way: "Check this mirror; that's the brake; don't accelerate so fast." After practice, however, all the parts of driving fell together naturally. The same thing will happen to these four elements of nonverbal communication.

Analyze the Elements of Nonverbal Communication.

The four components of nonverbal communication are: (1) body, (2) voice, (3) space, and (4) surroundings.[4] Let's look at each in some detail.

Body

Among all the aspects of nonverbal communication, we are probably most familiar with the concept of what many people refer to as *body language*.

---

more sensitive than business executives or teachers. Sensitivity is not in any way correlated to race, IQ, class rank, or vocabulary level. Many business schools recognize its importance by teaching nonverbal awareness, not only in business communication courses but also in organizational behavior and career counseling courses.

[4]See M. Knapp, *Essentials of Nonverbal Communication* (New York: Holt, Rinehart & Winston, 1980) for more on the four components of nonverbal communication. Knapp does an excellent job of summarizing the major nonverbal research studies, and I am indebted to him for many of the ideas in the first half of this chapter. See also K. Cooper, *Nonverbal Communication for Business Success* (New York: AMACOM, 1979) for an easy to read source written specifically for business people.

Consciously or unconsciously, we analyze people's attitudes on the basis of their body language, drawing conclusions when they put their hands on their hips, wrinkle their noses, or turn away from us. What, specifically, are the main aspects of body language? (1) posture, (2) gestures, and (3) face and eyes.

POSTURE: Your posture—the way you stand or sit—is the first major influence on the initial impression you make. Although you may not be aware of it, your posture indicates your confidence, your openness, and your attitude. Many people who write about nonverbal communication emphasize "the center" as an important aspect of posture. The center is that point where a line between your armpits intersects another line piercing your midchest from front to back. For example, if you shuffle up to the front of the room and slump in front of your audience, you have hidden your center: you may communicate a lack of interest or lack of enthusiasm you really do not feel. Or, if you suddenly cross your arms and turn away from someone sitting in your office, you have closed your center: you might imply you are disagreeing with him or her, even if that's not what you mean.

How can you improve your posture for effective nonverbal business communication? Whether you are standing or sitting, do so in a relaxed, professional manner—that is, comfortably upright, squarely facing your audience, with your weight distributed evenly. If you are sitting, avoid an overly formal, ramrod-straight back, an overly informal slouch in your chair, an overly submissive leaning too far away, or an overly aggressive leaning too close. If you are standing, avoid an overly formal "Attention!" posture, an overly informal slouch to one side or onto the lectern, an overly submissive stance with your feet too close together, and an overly aggressive stance with your feet too wide apart (the "cowpoke straddle"). When you stand, your feet should be about as far apart as your shoulders. Figure 11.1 illustrates these postures.

GESTURES: A second aspect of body language is movement and gestures. All people unconsciously use gestures to back up what they are saying. Watch people talking—at a party, during a meeting, during a class, in the hallways. They all use their hands. For example, people might use certain gestures, called *emblems*, that have a direct verbal translation in our culture, such as "A–OK" or "Shame on you." They might also use gestures to illustrate what they are saying, such as using their hands to describe an object or a motion, or enumerating a list of main points.

Gestures not only reinforce what people say, they also reveal people's attitude. People may perceive gestures as either "warm" or "cold." In our culture, warm gestures might include: leaning toward people with an

Open
Poised, professional
Face other person

Closed
Slumped, arms crossed
Turned away

Aggressive
Chest out, chin forward
Feet too widely apart

Submissive
Bowed shoulders, eyes down
Feet too close together

FIGURE 11.1

Implications of posture

open posture and open gestures, directly facing them, smiling, touching, and gesturing expressively. Cold gestures might include: keeping your hands on your hips, slumping, avoiding eye contact, not smiling, and gesturing nervously—such as cleaning your fingernails, drumming your fingers, fiddling with objects or jewelry, or looking at your watch.

Most people naturally use good gestures when they are sitting, because they are not thinking about what to do with their hands. When you are sitting, remember to avoid nervous gestures and a stony facial expression.

When people stand in front of a group, however, it's a different story. "What should I do with my hands?" they ask. The answer is simple: use your hands naturally, the way *you* would in conversation. Speaking in front of a group is not radically different from speaking one to one. Some people gesture quite a bit; some people gesture less. The important thing is to be yourself. Don't use stylized or artificial gestures. Instead, gesture naturally, as *you* would if you weren't in front of a group. You might, for example, describe a size or shape, emphasize an important point, enumerate a list, or point to a specific item.

On the other hand, do not gesture nervously; avoid, for example, tugging at your ears, scratching your arms, or licking your lips. Once you are aware of nervous gestures—either by seeing yourself on video or receiving feedback from your instructor or classmates—you will probably find it relatively easy to get rid of them. Finally, do not use any one gesture repeatedly or stay locked in any one hand position. Figure 11.2 illustrates both effective gestures and the most common "frozen gestures": the "fig leaf" (hands clasped in front), the "parade rest" (hands clasped in back), the "pocket change jingle," and the "lectern clutch."

Along with relaxing to gesture naturally, feel free to move your whole body as well. You might move to change the mood or pace, to draw attention to your visual aids, to make a transition (by stepping to the side), or to make an important point (by leaning forward). Naturally, you should not move randomly or nervously, or continually pace or sway.

FACE AND EYES: A third aspect of body language is expressing ourselves through our face and eyes. Our face and eyes are probably the most expressive parts of our body. We can establish rapport with our facial expression: raising and lowering our eyebrows, smiling, nodding, even winking. We can also regulate the conversation flow. For example, we might open communication with a waiter by catching his eye—and we might avoid conversation with our boss by avoiding his or her eye. We indicate that we want to speak by opening our mouth, breathing in rapidly, and raising our eyebrows. When we are ready to stop talking, we will break eye contact, usually by looking down. If we want to continue

Examples of Ineffective "Frozen" Gestures

The parade rest

The fig leaf

The pocket jingle

The lectern clutch

Examples of Effective Natural Gestures

Emphasize a point

Describe a shape

Point to an item

Enumerate a list

FIGURE 11.2 Gestures

talking, we will tend to maintain eye contact, keep our head up, and increase our volume and rate of speech; if we do look away, we look up, not down. Listeners who wish to break in when we are speaking will maintain unbroken eye contact, change their position, and clear their throat.

How much eye contact is appropriate? Too much is perceived as aggressive, dominant, or uncomfortable. Too little is seen as submissive, shifty, inattentive, or unfriendly. Although I said at the outset that we cannot overquantify nonverbal communication, here are a couple of general rules of thumb. Effective speakers maintain more eye contact than ineffective ones. This does not mean you want to engage in a staring contest. In conversation, maintain eye contact about 50 to 60 percent of the time when you are speaking and 75 to 85 percent of the time when you are listening. In a group presentation, of course, you need to maintain eye contact almost 100 percent of the time.

You cannot achieve good eye contact in a group presentation if you are reading your notes word for word; your audience sees a view of the top of your head instead. Most people cannot achieve good eye contact if they try to memorize every single speech either; usually, memorizers get a glazed, vacant look in their eyes. You cannot fake eye contact by looking at the middle of the back of the room or by using the "lighthouse scan" back and forth across the room.

Instead, good eye contact means establishing human contact with actual people in your audience. You might try, for starters, looking at the friendly faces; their nodding and smiling will encourage you. Eventually, however, you should look at everyone—especially the key decision-makers in the group. Establish momentary human contact (about a second or two) with each person. In the words of speech expert Charlotte Rosen: "Next time you give a speech, see if you can recall the reactions of individuals in your audience the next day. If you can't, then chances are you weren't making significant eye contact with anyone. If you can, then you know you weren't just speaking *at* your listeners, but *to* them, and your speech was probably the better for it."[5]

Voice

Even those of us who are sensitive to the implications of body language do not always realize the importance of what the scholars call *paralanguage:* the sound of the voice. Consider, for example, the four ways you might say this sentence:

[5]C. Rosen, presentation to the Managerial Communication Association, April 12, 1985.

Where have you been?

Where *have* you been?

Where have *you* been?

Where have you *been?*

Or consider the difference between "Enough!" and "Enough?"

Voice can tell you a great deal about the speaker's emotional state. Even when the speaker's words are muffled so listeners can follow only the pitch, rate, and volume, the listeners can still ascertain the speaker's emotions.

The most important aspect of voice seems to be inflection— variations in volume, rate, and pitch that make you sound more expressive. One study showed that good inflection increases your audience's comprehension. The subjects listened to the same material, presented either with "good intonation" or with "monopitch." Multiple-choice tests revealed that the monopitch decreased comprehension by more than 10 percent.[6] Another researcher developed a persuasive speech and had it recorded by actors in two different styles: one "dispassionate," with consistent rate and pitch, and few changes in volume or inflection; the other "more emotional," with more pauses and variations in the voice. Although listeners judged the two as equally competent, the more emotional speaker ranked higher in terms of trust, dynamism, honesty, and people-orientation.[7]

What should you do to develop an effective speaking voice? One, use effective pitch. Speak expressively and enthusiastically instead of in a boring monotone. Use a warm, pleasant tone instead of a distracting tone (nasal, high, rough, whiny). Speak audibly. Be especially aware of this pitfall if you are using visual aids, if you are a woman, or if your volume tends to drop toward the ends of your sentences.

Two, speak with the correct rate and enunciation. Speak slowly enough so you can be understood, yet quickly enough to maintain energy. (Curiously, I have found that speaking too slowly is more of a problem in business presentations than speaking too fast.) Vary your rate to avoid droning. Use effective pauses: before or after a key term, separating items in a series, or indicating a major break in your thought.

Three, enunciate clearly. Clear articulation means not running your words together, as in "didja" for "did you," "wanna" for "want to," "lemme" for "let me," or "otta" for "ought to." It also means not leaving out syllables, as in "Murcan" for "American," "depenbility" for "depend-

[6]G. Glasglow, Knapp, cited in *Essentials*, p. 218.

[7]W. Pearce, Knapp, cited in *Essentials*, pp. 219–20.

ability," "Saddy" for "Saturday," or "guvmint" for "government." Finally, it means not dropping middle consonants, as in "with" for "width," "libery" for "library," or "strenth" for "strength"—or final consonants, as in "thousan" for "thousand," "jus" for "just," or "goin" for "going."

Four, avoid distracting overuse of *filler words*. Filler words are vocalized pauses, such as "uh," "um," "er," and "ya know." Everyone uses them occasionally, so don't overreact if you notice a few when you speak. If you hear a distracting, habitual use of filler words, however, remember that most people find it relatively easy to remedy this problem once they recognize it.

The Delivery Checklist at the end of this chapter summarizes techniques to improve your body and voice.

Space around you

Nonverbal communication also includes the ways you communicate through distance, or the space around you.

STANDING: As a first aspect of distance, think about what you communicate with space when you are standing. We have all felt intimate, uncomfortable, accepted, or snubbed because of the distance between us and the people with whom we were talking. Edward Hall, perhaps the most influential thinker on this subject, has identified four zones of space (shown in Figure 11.3), determined by the distance between people: (1) public space (over twelve feet), typical of standing in a lobby, (2) social space (four to twelve feet), typical of conversing with a stranger, (3) personal space (eighteen inches to four feet), typical of conversing with friends, and (4) intimate space (zero to eighteen inches), typical of comforting.[8]

An awareness of these zones provides entertainment for both elevator- and party-watchers. In elevators, people intrude into our intimate zone—normally reserved for people who have a right to be there. Watch people back up against the walls and keep their eyes fixed on the lighted numbers over the door. At parties or in other social situations, watch people stand near one another. You can almost guess how long they've known one another by whether they stand in the social or the personal zone, and you can watch people fidget or back up once someone enters their intimate zone.

In addition to guessing relationships, you can often infer people's status by noting the distances between them. If you see a group of people

[8]E. Hall, *The Silent Language* (New York: Doubleday, 1959). As we discussed in chapter 2, Hall's book is a classic.

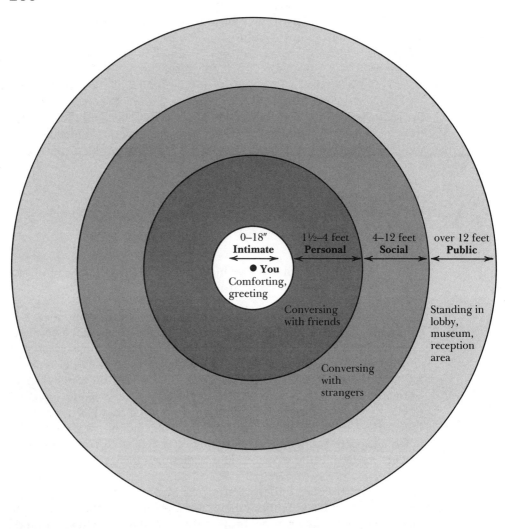

FIGURE 11.3

Distance: zones of space

talking informally—say, before a meeting or at a party—you can infer the leader, the accepted, and the rejected. You can tell if one person has significantly higher status, because the others will tend to form a circle around him or her (see Figure 11.4). In the same figure, you can also clearly differentiate accepted members of the group from nonaccepted members. Finally, watch a group of people walking: the high-status person will almost always lead the pack.

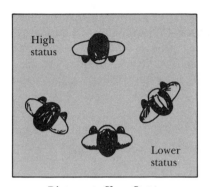

Distance to Show Status

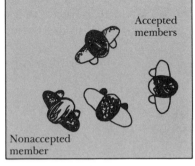

Distance to Show Acceptance

FIGURE 11.4

Distance: status and acceptance

SEATING: Status is indicated also by seating arrangements. If you find yourself spending an inordinate amount of time worrying about seating at a meeting, remember that at the Paris Peace Talks of 1968, it took eight months to reach agreement on seating arrangements. Researchers have even come up with a label for seating behavior: *small-group ecology.*

If you were the first person to arrive at a meeting, which place would you choose to sit in?

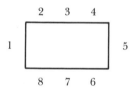

We all associate the head of the table with dominance, in both work and social relationships. Research supports this intuition. Dominant people or leaders do tend to sit at either end of the table. In one study, for example, researchers observed the deliberations of a jury consisting of strangers: the person who took a seat at the head of the table was most often selected foreman by the other jurors.[9]

The most frequent talkers tend to seat themselves at either end or the middle of the table (positions 1, 3, 5, and 7). The people seated in the middle, however, tend to be more concerned with the group process: relationships and participation. The people on the ends tend to be more

[9]See F. Strodtbeck and L. Hook, cited in Knapp, *Essentials*, p. 87.

interested in the task itself. What does all this mean? Primarily, that we seat ourselves in a position to dominate or avoid conversation.

Besides dominance, another variable in seating-arrangement research is the nature of the task itself. Sommer's research shows that the following three seating patterns tend to be conducive to different kinds of tasks.[10]

**Seating
for different tasks**

Conversation
Cooperation

Competition

Noncommunication

TOUCHING: Touching is also an important kind of nonverbal communication. Compared with people in some other cultures, Americans usually don't touch each other very much. In one study, researchers

[10]R. Sommer, cited in Knapp, *Essentials,* p. 89.

observed people seated in outdoor cafes in each of four cultures. They counted the number of touches during one hour of conversation. The results were: San Juan, Puerto Rico, 180 per hour; Paris, 110 per hour; Gainesville, Florida, 1 per hour; and London, 0 per hour.[11]

When we do touch, however, we follow patterns of where we touch. Jourard observed *where* people get touched, and came up with a list of body parts considered touchable in our culture. For both men and women, the four most acceptable places are hands, arms, top of the head, and shoulders.[12]

Another important aspect of touching in a business setting has to do with *how* we touch. Heslin breaks touching into five categories: (1) functional/professional—touching to perform a task or service, as by a dentist with a patient; (2) social/polite—touching to affirm the other person's identity as part of the species or culture, as with a handshake; (3) friendship/warmth—touching to affirm the other person's identity as a unique friend, as with a hug; (4) love/intimacy—touching to express emotional attachment or attraction, as by a full embrace or a hand on the cheek; and (5) sexual arousal—touching to affirm emotional attachment through physical intimacy (I doubt you need an example here).[13]

Touching in business communication undoubtedly has its positive side: it can communicate encouragement, support, or warmth. In one study, researchers asked the clerks at a college library to touch briefly some students' hands as they returned their library cards, and to avoid touching other students. On their way out, both sets of students were asked about their feelings toward the clerks. The students who had been touched evaluated both the clerks and the library significantly more favorably—even though most of them did not remember the touch— than did those who had not been touched.[14]

Touching, however, has its negative sides as well. For one thing, it can be interpreted as sexual. Keeping Heslin's taxonomy in mind, touching someone *functionally* (as in handing a person the mail) or *socially* (as in shaking hands) is usually unambiguous. A *friendship* touch such as a hug, though, should be reserved for special friends only. In business, never touch anyone in a way that might be interpreted as sexual harassment.

Another danger with touching is that it may be interpreted as condescending or coercive. You may, for example, intend to show encouragement by touching someone on the shoulder and saying, "Great

[11]S. Jourard, cited in Knapp, *Essentials*, p.150.

[12]Ibid.

[13]R. Heslin, cited in Knapp, *Essentials*, pp. 152−55.

[14]J. Fisher et al., cited in Knapp, *Essentials*, p. 146.

job!" The person may perceive the touch, however, as patronizing or condescending. Patting someone on the head is even more likely to be interpreted this way. You may intend to show friendliness by touching someone on the arm and saying, "Don't you agree?" But the person may perceive your action as an attempt to pressure and control. In business, avoid any touch that might be perceived as an unfair use of status or power.

Objects around you

Finally, your nonverbal communication is affected by the objects around you: how you arrange chairs, arrange your office, and dress. For large-group presentations, choose carefully among **chair** configurations, illustrated in Figure 11.5, basing your choice on the formality and the amount of participation you want to establish. For smaller-group presentations, choose a rectangular table with a person seated at the head if you have a designated discussion leader. Use a round table to encourage equality among the participants.

To analyze **office** arrangements, consider the four configurations shown in Figure 11.6. The most formal office arrangement is arrangement 1: you sit behind the desk, the visitor sits on the other side of the desk. In arrangement 2, you have several choices. You may sit as you did in arrangement 1, behind the desk; you may invite the person to sit at an angle to the side; or you may both sit side by side on the same side of the desk. For more informality and participation, choose 3. Arrangement 4 is yet more informal, resembling a living room.

You will find various combinations of these configurations in most companies. For example, a CEO's office might have enough space for all four layouts. You would be likely to see arrangement 4 in the lobby or reception area. Arrangement 3 might be available in conference rooms. Controlling the space around you, then, has a significant impact on what you communicate nonverbally.

A final variable in space and surroundings is how you **dress.** This is not a book on how to "dress for success," and you may be disappointed to know that we will not be discussing such fascinating topics as the difference between white and blue shirts, or between red and blue ties. The "dress for success" formula boils down to dressing conservatively and tastefully, preferring tailored clothes in subdued colors. The problem with the formula is that it does not take into account the differences among organizations. If you work for a fashion designer or for a boutique, naturally you should dress fashionably. If you work in a com-

Formal:
Straight lines
of chairs

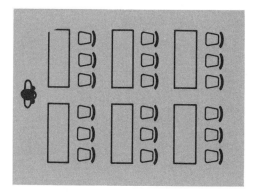 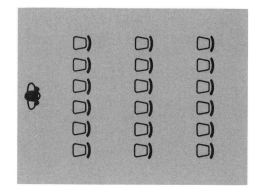

Informal:
Curved lines
of chairs

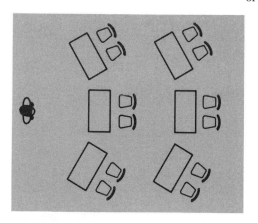 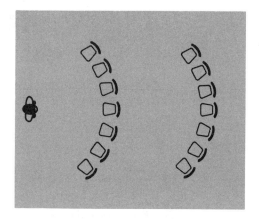

FIGURE 11.5

Chair configurations

puter company where everyone wears jeans and T-shirts, naturally you shouldn't wear the "dress for success" suit and tie.

The real formula, then, is to dress appropriately—for the audience, the occasion, and the company or organization where you work. Dress to project the image of yourself that *you* want to create. Never wear clothes that will distract from what you are saying, such as exaggerated, dangling jewelry or loud, flashy ties. Remember, as irrelevant as it may seem, what

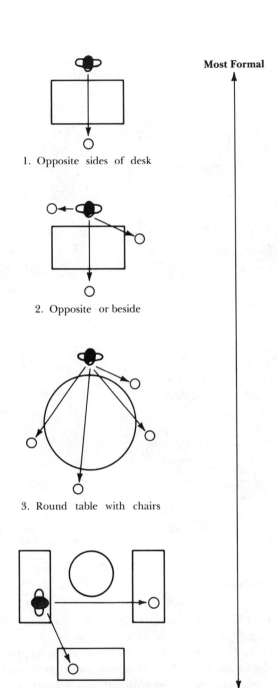

1. Opposite sides of desk

2. Opposite or beside

3. Round table with chairs

4. Round table with sofas

Most Formal

Least Formal

FIGURE 11.6

Office configurations

you wear *does* communicate something to your audience—mostly a message about whether or not you "fit" with the group.

Improve Your Nonverbal Skills.

Now that we have looked at the elements of nonverbal communication, let's examine how you can improve your nonverbal effectiveness through practice and relaxation techniques.

Practice and arrange.

Practice your presentation in advance so you can improve both your content and your delivery.

PRACTICE: Practice increases your self-confidence and poise, improves your wording so it flows naturally and spontaneously, helps you identify any flaws or gaps in what you're saying, and enables you to deal with distractions. Practice also allows you to make sure your visual aids, which we shall discuss in chapter 13, are smoothly integrated into your presentation.

To improve your content and delivery, rehearse out loud and on your feet. Knowing your content and saying it are two completely different activities. So, do not practice by sitting at your desk reading your cards over. Instead, stand up and practice aloud. Remember that you are not trying to memorize or to read, but rather to talk with your audience.

One helpful practice technique is to simulate the situation in which you will be speaking. You might, for example, practice in the place where you will actually be making the presentation. Or, you might practice in front of chairs set up as they will be when you speak. Take the time to imagine specific people in those chairs before you begin. Some speakers even practice while bouncing a ball or performing some other routine task, thereby improving their ability to withstand distractions.

While you are practicing, you can work to improve your delivery. You might speak into a mirror to improve your facial expression. Or, speak into an audio tape recorder to improve vocal expression, animation, rate, and enunciation. You might also speak in front of a friend or colleague, having him or her use the Delivery Checklist. (See pages 284–86.) Best of all, speak in front of a video tape recorder, evaluating the playback with that checklist.

When you practice, you can also time yourself to avoid the common problem of going overtime. Time yourself honestly: say the words as slowly as you would to people, not as you would quickly read them; actually take the time to change your slides or flip your charts. If you find the presentation is too long, you have the opportunity to decide in advance what you think the least important parts of your presentation are, and cut them. If you don't time yourself, you run the risk of having important parts of your presentation cut out if you get cut off for going overtime.

ARRANGEMENTS: Curb any tendency to "let the janitors take care of it" or "let the secretary take care of it." The absence of chairs or of chalk can ruin your presentation. Arrangements, therefore, are important enough for you to consider. Either make the arrangements yourself, or write explicit instructions for someone else; then make sure your instructions are carried out.

First, make sure your audience is **notified.** You need to answer four questions. One, precisely who should be invited? This question hinges on your all-important audience analysis, discussed in chapter 4. Two, how should they be notified? Speaking to people individually is more personal and flexible, and they can immediately tell you whether or not they can come. Writing to people is more formal, but usually less likely to be forgotten. A combination of both speaking and writing is appropriate for important presentations. Three, who should notify them? You? An authority figure? A group? A department? The company? Four, decide exactly what advance information you want your audience to have. People will discuss ideas more intelligently in a meeting if they have an agenda in advance. People will listen more intently to a presentation if they know the topic and why it's important.

You also need to check your **room** arrangements. Make sure the chairs are in the appropriate configuration. As suggested in Figure 11.6, use semicircles or circles for informality and group participation; use rows for more formal presentations.

Room arrangements also include other details. Make sure you have the correct number of chairs. You need enough for everyone, of course. In addition, get rid of extras before the presentation; people do not like to move once they are seated. Check also for correct lighting and adequate ventilation. Alleviate any possible distractions as much as you can. Finally, if appropriate, check for pads and pencils, name cards, refreshments, and ashtrays.

When the room has been arranged satisfactorily, check your **visuals.** Make sure all your equipment is there and working. Check all projectors and screens. Also check your film, cassette, disc, slides, or transparencies by playing or displaying one briefly. Be sure you have extra bulbs, wires, extension cords, or marking pens, if needed. For charts, check the stand's stability, the paper supply, and the pen's ink. For boards, make sure you have enough chalk or pens, and erasers. For handouts, make sure you have enough of them and know where they are.

Once you are satisfied your equipment is in working order, set it up. Sit in the farthest corner seat and see if you can read your charts. Sit in various corner seats and make sure the aids will be visible to every person in the audience. Finally, make sure your charts, slides, or handouts are arranged in the correct order.

As you can see, these kinds of arrangements involve a lot of details to remember. Use the Arrangement Checklist on page 287 to remind yourself about all the arrangements. Making arrangements may be boring, but neglecting them may be disastrous.

Relax and gain confidence.

Even after practicing and arranging presentations, most people have experienced the quivering, fidgeting, shaking, trembling, sweating, stammering, and fluttering associated with stage fright. In fact, in public opinion polls, public speaking ranks as Americans' number-one fear—ahead of both death and loneliness.

In conversation, most of us feel alert, energetic, natural, confident, and enthusiastic. We can be ourselves, not worrying about our hands or posture, not putting on a false, formal personality. When you converse, you interact naturally with your audience and concentrate on what you are trying to communicate.

Analyze, however, what happens physically when you are about to make a presentation. As when you are in any stressful situation, your body starts pumping adrenaline through your system. Tensing up or holding back the adrenaline results in the quivering, fidgeting, and shaking just described. On the other hand, if you do not tense up and just let the adrenaline flow, you can actually use that surge of energy to your advantage, and relax into being the kind of speaker you are conversationally.

"Great," you may be saying. "All I have to do is not tense up. How can I possibly do that?" The answer is that different people relax in different ways. Here, then, are a series of techniques. Use whichever ones are most useful to you.

Of course, after you have finished this business communication course, you will be well on your way toward combating stage fright. In any event, you are far less likely to be severely incapacitated by stage fright if your presentation is well organized and well rehearsed.

PHYSICAL RELAXATION: In addition to preparing well, though, you can choose from among various techniques for physical relaxation. Many people find that if they are relaxed physically, then they feel calm mentally. The most obvious physical relaxation technique is exercise. Exercise—such as calisthenics, jogging, or tennis—calms people through physical exertion.

For some people, stage fright manifests itself in certain parts of their bodies—in tensed shoulders, quivering arms, shaking knees, and so forth. Here are some exercises for **relaxing your body**.[15]

To relax your head—and get rid of a choking sensation—try these neck-rolling exercises. (1) *Side neck rolls*. With your head facing front, tip your head sideways to the right. Keeping your face front, slowly tip your head sideways to the left. Then tip back to the right. Repeat ten to twelve times. Caution: Start these neck rolls *slowly* and then increase to the speed you wish. (2) *Front/back neck rolls*. Drop your head and chin to your chest. Then raise your head and tilt it back. Always maintain support of the head when tipping back. Repeat this front-to-back motion ten to twelve times. (3) *Full neck rolls*. Combine the side and front/back neck-roll exercises so that you rotate your head all the way around. Start with a full rotation to the right, then alternate directions. Finally, smooth into a full, continuous neck roll.

To relax your shoulders, do shoulder rolls. Raise your shoulder or both shoulders as if you were shrugging. Then roll the shoulder back so that the shoulder blades roll down and then forward to complete the circle. Continue the shoulder roll down and then forward. You should end in the same position with shoulders up.

To relieve tension in the arms and hands, try these two exercises. (1) *Shake-outs*. Begin shaking the arm only at the shoulder. Gradually allow the arm to move at the elbow, and then let the hand flop at the wrist. This will loosen the entire arm. (2) *Fist clenches*. Release tension in your hands by rolling the hand into a closed fist. Start with an open hand, and close each finger one by one until you have formed a fist.

Another well-known technique for relaxing your entire body is called the *progressive relaxation technique*.[16] This technique, developed by psychologist Edmund Jacobson, involves tensing and relaxing all the muscle groups, instead of isolating certain ones only. To practice this technique, set aside about twenty minutes of undisturbed time, and find a

---

[15]P. Argenti, "Note on Oral and Physical Relaxation Skills" (unpublished paper, Amos Tuck School of Business, Dartmouth College, 1984). Professor Argenti's paper is also the source of the vocal warm-up exercises discussed later in this section. I am deeply indebted to Professor Argenti.

[16]See E. Jacobson, *You Must Relax*, 5th ed. (New York: McGraw-Hill, 1976).

comfortable, darkened place where you can lie down. Tense and relax each of the following muscle groups in turn: hands, arms, forehead, neck and throat, upper back, lower back, chest, stomach, buttocks, thighs, calves, and feet. Repeat the procedure at least twice, tensing and relaxing each group of muscles in turn. Finally, check your body to find if any areas still feel tense; repeat the tense-and-relax cycle in those areas.

These techniques may prove helpful well before your presentation, but obviously you cannot get down on the floor and start doing push-ups the moment before you start speaking. Fortunately, however, there is a technique you can use to relax your body at the last minute: *isometric exercise.* Isometric exercise involves clenching and then quickly relaxing your muscles. For example, you might press or wiggle your feet against the floor, your hand against your other hand, or your hands against the table or chair; you might clench your fists, thighs, or toes. Then, quickly relax whatever muscles you just clenched. No one can see you doing this exercise right before you start to speak.

For other people, stage fright manifests itself in their voice, in the form of cracking, quivering, and so forth. Here are some suggestions for **relaxing your voice.**

One vocal warm-up exercise is humming. Hum slowly and carefully—never try to force the voice for greater volume. Also, hum with a full range of pitches; this will open up a greater range for you to use when you start speaking.

A second voice warm-up is a breathing exercise. If you practice controlled inhalations and exhalations, your voice will have more support and control. The exhalation may be a series of short, staccato bursts of air, or one long, continuous release of air as slowly as possible. Throughout the exercise you should focus upon the basics of correct breathing: expanding around the waist when taking a breath, and using the diaphragm (and sheath muscles of the waist) to control air release and support of the voice.

In addition to vocal warm-up exercises, here are some general suggestions for keeping your voice in shape. (l) Be awake two to three hours before your speech. This provides a natural warm-up period for your voice. (2) A hot shower is an excellent way to wake up your voice, or to soothe a tired and irritated set of vocal cords. Steam is very soothing and will help your vocal cords shed any mucus or phlegm that has built up on them. (3) Avoid drinking milk or consuming dairy products before you speak. Dairy products tend to coat the vocal cords and may cause problems during your presentation. (4) If your voice is tired, any warm liquids will soothe the voice. Ideal candidates are tea or coffee. (5) Perhaps the best way to assure a good vocal performance is to get enough rest the night before any presentation.

Again, you can't sleep or hum in front of your audience at the very last minute. You can, however, relax your voice by taking a couple of deep breaths. Obviously, no one would suggest hyperventilation. Instead, try inhaling a couple of times, slowly and deeply. Then exhale slowly and completely, feeling your stomach flatten as you exhale. You can also relax your throat and voice by taking a sip of room-temperature water right before, or during, your talk.

MENTAL RELAXATION: Whereas some people prefer physical relaxation, others prefer mental relaxation. Mental relaxation is based on the assumption that if you calm yourself mentally, all the physical sensations (shaking knees, quivering voice, and so forth) will go away. In other words, for some people the physical follows the mental. Here are four techniques that you can use to relax yourself mentally before making a presentation.

First, you might try the *systematic desensitization* technique.[17] In this procedure, developed by psychiatrist Joseph Wolpe, you force yourself to relax as you imagine or act out a series of successively more anxiety-ridden situations. Complete any one of the physical-relaxation exercises described previously before you start the sessions; force yourself to remain physically relaxed during the sessions. For example, here is a series of four sessions in which you imagine each of the following: (1) preparing a presentation, (2) practicing a presentation, (3) walking to the front of the room, and (4) delivering a presentation. As another example, here is a series of four sessions that you might act out with a small group of people: (1) reading a presentation aloud, (2) standing in front of the group, (3) reading the presentation in front of the group, and (4) speaking in front of the group.

Second, there's the Dale Carnegie *think positive* argument.[18] According to Carnegie, if you regulate your actions first, then your thinking will change. Specifically, if you act as if you were brave, you will soon feel brave. Therefore, to develop courage in front of an audience, simply act as if you already have it.

Or, you might base your thinking on Eastern philosophy and *think nonjudgmentally*. Tennis expert W. Tim Gallwey applies this method to tennis players.[19] Avoid both positive and negative evaluations of your ability. Instead, describe your habits (such as "I notice a monotone"; "I see a nervous gesture"); do not evaluate those habits (don't say "I have a

---

[17]See J. Wolpe, *The Practice of Behavior Theory*, 3rd ed. (Elmsford, N.Y.: Pergamon Press, 1982).

[18]See D. Carnegie, *Public Speaking and Influencing Men* [sic] *in Business* (New York: Associated Press, 1926).

[19]See W. T. Gallwey, *The Inner Game of Tennis* (New York: Bantam, 1974).

terrible voice!" "I'm a terrible speaker!"). Then, instruct yourself by concentrating on a visual image of what you want to look like; do not use word commands (don't say "Stand up straight!"; "Speak up!"). Finally, trust your body to acquire the desired behavior in your visual image; do not continually castigate yourself for failing.

A final mental technique is based on the *rational-emotive* system developed by psychologist Albert Ellis.[20] He advises people to transcend the ABCs of emotional reactions: *A* stands for an activating event (such as "I used a nervous gesture!"), which sparks *B*, a belief system (such as "Oh no, what a total disaster!"), which causes *C*, a consequence (such as depression or anxiety). The way to transcend this response is to dispute irrational *belief systems* with rational thought. For example, here are some common *belief systems* that you might dispute: "Everybody must totally approve of everything I do," "I have to be perfect in every way," "It's a catastrophe when something isn't perfect," "I cannot influence or change my behavior," "I'll never be a decent speaker," or "If I'm not perfect, then I'm terrible."

Again, just before you begin to speak, you do not have the time to go through a long series of mental processes. Still, even at the last minute, you may attack stage fright mentally by using what behavioral psychologists call *internal dialogue,* which means, of course, talking to yourself. (l) Give yourself a pep talk: "What I am about to say is important," "I am ready," "They are just people." (2) Play down your audience's importance: imagine they are all cabbages; imagine they are all wearing nothing but their socks. (3) Repeat positive phrases: "I'm glad I'm here; I'm glad you're here"; "I know I know"; "I care about you."

RELAXATION AS YOU SPEAK: Even if you have relaxed yourself physically or mentally, something different happens in that magic moment when you are standing in front of the group, actually starting to speak. What can you do for relaxation as you speak? For one thing, try talking to the interested listeners. There are always a few kind souls out there who nod, smile, and generally react favorably. Especially at the beginning of your presentation, look at them, not at the people reading, looking out the window, or yawning. Looking at your positive listeners will increase your confidence. Pretty soon you will be looking at the people around those good listeners, and then at every person in the audience.

Also as you speak, remember that you probably look better than you think you look. This statement might sound a little too optimistic to be believed, so let me back it up with two kinds of evidence. First, having watched thousands of videotaped playbacks with students, I'm amazed at

[20]See A. Ellis, *Growth through Reason*, (N. Hollywood, Calif.: Wilshire, n.d.).

the number of them who say: "Hey, I look better than I thought I would!" Second, many trained speech instructors report that they do not see all the nervous symptoms a speaker thinks he or she is exhibiting.

Finally, concentrate on what is happening right now. Think about what you are communicating, and about your audience. Do not allow yourself to think of either regrets ("I should have used a slide projector!") or uncertainties ("I wonder how my boss will react.") Instead, concentrate completely on communicating *information* to *people*.

In conclusion, effective nonverbal communication is a very powerful tool for good speaking. To channel that power, analyze the nonverbal elements of speaking, including how you use your body, your voice, space, and the objects around you. Then, when you make an oral presentation, you can improve your delivery by using the techniques outlined in this chapter to practice and to gain confidence. Remember, how you look and sound are just as important to your success as what you say.

REVIEW QUESTIONS
To check your understanding

1. What is nonverbal communication and why is it important?
2. What four factors does nonverbal communication include?
3. Describe the ways of sitting and standing that are best suited to effective business communication.
4. Explain the difference between "warm" and "cold" gestures.
5. What does good eye contact say about your attitude toward your listeners? Your listeners' attitude toward you?
6. Define inflection. What makes it the most important aspect of voice?
7. List four ways that you can achieve an effective speaking voice.
8. What are the four "zones of space"?
9. Explain how the status of each of the following three kinds of people is revealed by seating arrangement: (1) dominant, (2) frequent talkers, and (3) those concerned with participation.
10. In what way do dress and office arrangement take part in nonverbal communication?
11. What are some aspects of your presentation that practice can improve?
12. What are three important arrangements you should make in advance?

13. How can you relax physically at the last minute, unseen by your audience?

14. What is the principle of mental relaxation?

15. Instead of thinking about yourself or your shortcomings, what should you concentrate on when you stand in front of an audience?

APPLICATION QUESTIONS
To apply your knowledge

1. What kind of seating arrangement would you use for an informal, information-sharing meeting with your co-workers? Why?

2. Choose a well-known public speaker or actor and analyze the nonverbal techniques that he or she uses to communicate effectively.

3. Present a business situation in which a formal manner seems appropriate. How could you convey a positive formality in the way you move, speak, and appear?

4. What kind of office arrangement would you adopt for conducting interviews? For negotiating contracts?

5. Think of ten "warm" gestures that can be employed before a small group. Would they all work as effectively before a large group?

6. Select a paragraph from a magazine or newspaper and practice reading it aloud with inflections that convey dispassion, emotion, sarcasm, enthusiasm.

7. What nonverbal techniques can help you put your audience at ease, and also convince them that you are relaxed as well?

8. What would you wear to make a formal presentation to your superiors? To attend a luncheon? To mingle with associates at an informal party? Analyze the image you are projecting with your dress in each situation.

9. What are the dangers involved with touching in a business setting? How can touch be used as a positive aid in the same situation?

10. Why is it important to consider *who* sends out notification of your presentation? What does it imply for your presentation?

11. How can the type of room your presentation is held in affect the audience's reaction? Give a specific illustration.

12. Assume you are one of a series of speakers, and all of you are seated on the stage in front of the audience awaiting your turn. What methods of relaxation can you practice while you wait?

13. List four or five activities that you find especially relaxing. Assess whether they would be appropriate for conquering the anxiety of a speaking situation.

14. What are some ways you can maintain a state of physical relaxation *while* you speak?

CASES
To practice what you learned

1. You have a job interview for a position with a record company that specializes in jazz and rock and roll. To fit in with what you assume will be the climate of the company, you dress in a stylish, informal fashion. Upon being shown into the interview room, however, you are dismayed to discover that your calculation was wrong: the entire staff is in pinstripes and wing tips. You feel that you are caught in an innocent but obvious mistake. What nonverbal techniques can you use to counteract your error in dress, and convey a message of sobriety more in line with your prospective employers?

2. You are new to a company and unsure of the personal relationships among the various other staff members in your office. The nature of the business demands frequent consultations and effective team-work among the staff members, but you sense that there are hidden tensions. You are anxious to stay clear of these pitfalls, but also want to impress your boss as a friendly and cooperative co-worker. During the staff meetings and a private party that take place your first week on the job, what unspoken signals can you look for that will tell you how the staff members feel about each other and interact as a group? At the same time, how can you effectively create the impression you wish?

3. Now you are the interviewer and are searching for an assistant to help you in your dealings with your clients. A large part of the job will consist of direct interaction with your clients, conveying information to them; and it will also involve keeping you attuned to their opinions and needs. You have narrowed your search to two candidates. Candidate A comes with impeccable credentials and a solid understanding of the business. During the interview he grasped the arms of his chair, tapping his foot and glancing repeatedly around the room. He seemed reluctant to leave your office. Candidate B is less experienced. During her interview she nodded frequently as you spoke to her, leaned forward as she answered your questions,

and shook your hand promptly when you signaled that the interview was over. Whom would you hire and why?

4. You are in charge of arranging an important meeting for your company. The entire twelve-member board of directors will be present. You are in charge of all the arrangements, although the company president will be running the meeting. He is especially anxious to avoid confrontations with Mr. X and Dr. Y, two board members prone to opinionated remarks and aggressive behavior. Above all, it is important that the group reach a consensus concerning the coming year's agenda. What sort of seating arrangement will best accomplish the task set to you by the president?

5. You must give a speech in front of a local civic group. The topic concerns the community's forecasted economic growth, and the audience consists largely of shopowners, industrial workers, and housewives—people for the most part without advanced economic training. You are eager to enliven this potentially dry topic, but unfortunately the hall in which you will be meeting is not equipped to accommodate a slide projector or other audio-visual aids. You must carry the ball yourself. You make a list before your speech of the twelve ways in which you can nonverbally maintain your audience's interest and impress them favorably with your clarity and goodwill. What does your list say?

6. You are delivering an important sales pitch to a group of your company's supervisors as part of a competition to come up with the best marketing strategy for the new season. You and five others in the competition are scheduled for the same day; you will be last, making your presentation at 5 P.M. Describe the techniques you will use during the day to relax in preparation for your presentation.

7. You are giving your first presentation before a small group, an association of college administrators. You fly into town the day before and would like to practice your presentation, which will take place in a seminar room at the local university. Unfortunately, you are unable to gain access to the room and so must rehearse instead in your hotel room. How would you simulate the situation you will be facing?

8. You are giving a lecture to a group of about 100. Your lecture includes slides, handouts, and a questionnaire. You arrive early with your supplies at the designated room and discover a number of chairs set up and the rest stacked against the wall. A slide projector sits on a table at the back of the room. Make a list of your activities in the hour before the group arrives.

DELIVERY CHECKLIST
for body and voice improvement

Body

Posture

Do
- stand or sit in a relaxed, professional manner—comfortably upright, squarely facing your audience, your weight evenly distributed;
- stand with your feet neither too close nor too far apart.

Don't
- stand in a formal, militaristic "Attention!" pose;
- stand in an informal slouch (keeping weight to one side or swaying from side to side);
- stand in a narrow-angle, ankles-together, "reciting schoolchild" stance;
- stand in a wide-angle "cowpoke straddle."

Hand gestures

Do
- gesture naturally, as you would in conversation;
- gesture to reinforce your content (such as describing a size or shape, emphasizing an important point, enumerating a list, or pointing to a specific item in your visual aid).

Don't
- gesture nervously, such as tugging your ear, scratching your arm, or licking your lips;
- keep your hands in any one position for too long, especially: the "fig leaf" (hands clasped in front), the "parade rest" (hands clasped in back), the "pocket change jingle," or the "podium clutch";
- use stylized, artificial, unvaried, constantly repeated gestures.

Body gestures

Do
- move to change mood or pace;
- move to draw attention to and from your visual aid;
- move to reinforce an idea (such as by stepping to the side to make a transition or leaning forward to emphasize an important point).

Don't
- move nervously;
- move continually, such as pacing or swaying constantly.

284

Eye contact

Do
- look at the entire group, rather than at just one side of the room;
- look at the key decision-makers in the group;
- look at good listeners who nod and react.

Don't
- look at a prepared script, which you read word for word, showing your audience a constant view of the top of your head;
- look at the middle of the back of the room;
- look at the bad listeners who may distract you.

Facial expression

Do
- maintain a relaxed, animated, conversational facial expression.

Don't
- maintain a stony, deadpan expression.

Voice

Pitch

Do
- speak with good inflection—expressively and enthusiastically;
- speak in a warm, pleasant tone;
- speak audibly.

Don't
- speak without good inflection—in a boring monotone;
- speak in a distracting tone (nasal, high, rough, or whiny);
- speak too quietly. Be aware of this pitfall especially if (1) you are using visual aids, (2) you are a woman, or (3) your volume tends to drop toward the ends of your sentences.

Rate

Do
- speak at the correct speed: slowly enough so you can be understood, quickly enough to maintain energy;
- vary your rate to avoid droning;
- use effective pauses, such as before or after a key term, when separating items in a series, or when indicating a major break in your thought.

Don't
- speak too slowly (which may bore your listeners) or too quickly (which may lose them);
- speak at a completely consistent speed, droning on with no variation or pauses.

Filler words

Don't   ● use distracting, habitual filler words, such as "uh," "um," "er," "ya know").

Enunciation

Do   ● articulate clearly.

Don't   ● run your words together (as in "didja" for "did you");

     ● omit syllables (as in "guvmint" for "government");

     ● drop middle consonants (as in "with" for "width") or final consonants (as in "goin" for "going").

ARRANGEMENT CHECKLIST

I. Audience notification
    A. List people to be notified.

    B. Decide how people are to be notifed (in writing, in person, by phone, combination).

    C. Decide under whose name or auspices the audience is to be notified.

    D. State information to be included in the notification (including agendas or background material if appropriate).

II. Room arrangement
    A. Sketch chair setup (formal/informal, with/without tables).

    B. Note equipment needs: pads, paper; writing instruments; name cards; ashtrays; other.

III. Visual aids arrangement
Note which of the following you will provide, and which someone else will provide.

Projections:	*For any projection:*
Film projector	
Films	
Video tape player	
cassettes/tapes/discs	
Slide projector	Screen
Carousel	Extension cords
Slides	Spare bulbs
Overhead projector	
Acetate slides	
Acetate pens	

Charts:	*For any chart:*
Flip-chart	
Paper	Stand
Cardboard chart	Pens
Desk-top chart	

Boards:	*For any board:*
Chalkboard	Chalk or pens
Plastic board	Erasing instrument

Handouts

287

12

Structuring a Presentation

Definition of a Presentation

Presentation Structure
Limit your main points. ● *Make your main ideas stand out.*
● *Use an effective opening and closing.* ● *Case example*

Other Kinds of Speech Structures
Manuscript and impromptu speeches ● *Speaker
introductions and team presentations*

NOW that we have looked at the nonverbal aspects of speaking—
"how you say it"—let's examine the verbal aspects—"what you say." First,
we'll define a presentation. Then, we'll discuss how to structure a typical
business presentation. Finally, we'll look at how to structure other kinds
of speeches.

Definition
of a Presentation

Before we examine how to structure a presentation, let's define some
terms. Imagine all the different kinds of speaking you'll be doing in
business: casual chatting, phone conversations, panel discussions, interviewing, conferences, seminars, meetings, speeches, question-and-
answer periods, presentations—and probably others. These activities easily fall into two groups: those in which you are speaking to *one* other
person and those in which you are speaking to a *group* of people. Let's put
aside the one-to-one speaking for right now (we discussed listening skills
in chapter 6 and will discuss interviews in chapter 15), and concentrate
on speaking to a group.

What, then, are the different ways you will speak to a group of
people? What, in other words, are the differences among speeches, brainstorming sessions, question-and-answer periods, lectures, discussions,
panel discussions, meetings, and presentations?

Usually, you speak to a group of people in one of **three situations**:
(1) when you are doing most of the speaking yourself, either to inform or
to persuade, (2) when you have more give-and-take with your audience, to
answer questions, or (3) when your audience is doing most of the talking,
to solve problems as a group. Certainly, most people would agree that
terms such as *speech* or *lecture* imply that the speaker is doing most of the
talking; *question-and-answer periods* or *panel discussions* involve answering
questions; and that *meetings,* or *brainstorming sessions* mean the audience is

doing most of the talking. In fact, you might think of the various kinds of group-speaking situations on a continuum, as illustrated on Figure 12.1.

We all know there are exceptions to the classifications shown in this figure. You may have sat through a "meeting" that consisted of nothing but announcements. You may have heard "lectures" that turned into free-floating question-and-answer sessions. But for our purposes, let's use the terms in Figure 12.1 to define the different kinds of business speaking situations. In chapter 14, we shall look at how to structure your speaking when you are answering questions and holding meetings. In this chapter, we shall be concerned only with speaking situations in which you are doing most of the talking.

To narrow our definition one step further, think of the various ways in which you might do such speaking: a manuscript is completely prepared in advance and written out; an impromptu speech is completely unprepared and spur-of-the-moment. In between these two extremes, we find the prepared presentation. By *prepared presentation,* then, I mean you prepare what you say, but you do not read it word for word.

This kind of presentation is extremely common in virtually all kinds of businesses. You use it to explain or persuade. For example, suppose

FIGURE 12.1

Group-speaking situations

Who does most of the speaking	You	You and your audience	Your audience
Possible purpose(s)	• To inform or explain • To persuade or sell	• To answer questions • To exchange information	• To solve problems as a group • To make decisions as a group

Examples
 	
Types of presentations
	• Speech
	• Lecture
	• Presentation
	  • Impromptu
	  • Prepared
	  • Manuscript
		• Question-and-answer session
		• Panel discussion
			• Meeting
			• Brainstorming session

Covered in this book	chapter 12	chapter 14	

you were working on the company newsletter. You have some recommendations to make about upgrading it with new printing, graphics, and colors, but the upgrading will increase your department's costs. When you appear before the budget committee, you'll give a presentation to persuade. Or, suppose you are a real-estate broker. You want to develop a certain building, but the site is not zoned for development. When you appear before the zoning board, you'll give a presentation to persuade. Or, suppose you are an agent for a health-insurance company. If you are asked to explain your company's benefits to a group of employees, you'll be giving a presentation to inform.

In each case, you'll be talking *with* a group, not *to* a group. In a business presentation, you do not read a paper, as an eminent professor does at an academic conference. Unlike the audience at the academic conference, your business audience may well be insulted by your reading to them. "If this is all written out," they may think, "why bother to take all this time hearing it? Why not just give everyone a copy of the document?" If your audience has taken the time to be with you, they deserve to be talked with. In a business presentation, you do not memorize and recite a paper either, the way an eminent actor does on stage. Most recited speeches end up sounding formal, stilted, and literary—not at all the way you would talk with someone. Leave the speeches and scripts alone for now. Later in this chapter, we'll discuss those rare circumstances when you might give a manuscript speech.

How then, do you go about preparing "what to say" in a presentation? As in any communication, you go through the same first steps: (1) establish your objective ("As a result of this presentation, my audience will _____"); (2) analyze your audience; and (3) structure your main points. Once you have your idea tree (explained in chapter 5), write an outline of what to say; you do not have to write out a presentation word for word. Since you don't want to bore your audience by reading word for word, why go to the trouble of writing it word for word? Since you won't possibly have the time to memorize every presentation you give in business, just make **notes** you can refer to. Your idea tree will be enough to jog your memory. When you are actually presenting, you will be forced to use your own words and to look at your audience. The important idea, then, is to work from a brief outline or an idea tree.

Most business presenters prefer to use five-by-seven-inch or four-by-six-inch note cards for their outlines. Regular-size paper is too large and awkward to move; using it forces you to stay at a lectern. On the other hand, three-by-five-inch cards are too small; changing cards constantly can be distracting. The larger five-by-seven or four-by-six cards, on the other hand, are not only easier to hold, they also make it possible for you to move—to your visual aid, for example—taking your notes with you.

Print your main ideas on one side of the card only. Never print complete sentences; instead, pare your thoughts down to words, phrases, and numbers. Always include at least five minutes' worth of information on each card. In other words, use about one card for a five-minute presentation, two cards for a ten-minute presentation, and so forth. The whole advantage of using cards—your ability to interact with your audience—is lost if you write out sentences on cards and read them. Color-

FIGURE 12.2

Sample note card

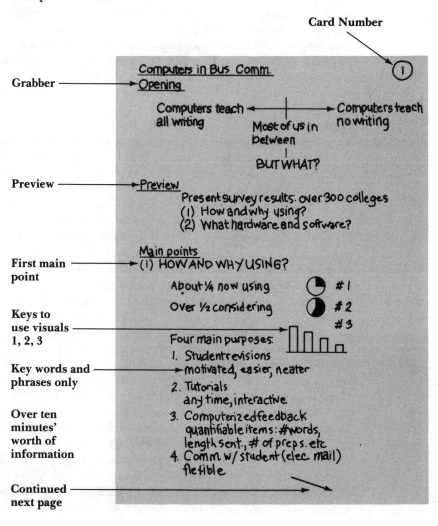

code your main points; underline them in red, for example. And color-code the appearance of your visual aids. Figure 12.2 shows a sample card.

Since presentations are not written word for word, most presenters have major problems with **timing.** When you finish writing something, obviously, you know exactly how many pages it is. When you are preparing a presentation, however, you do not know how long it will take to speak it aloud. Most people are terrified about running out of things to say. In fact, most people misjudge so badly that they end up talking at least *twice as long* as they expected to. If you don't believe me, watch how many speakers go overtime in your business communication class, or indeed in business. Or jot down notes for what you consider two minutes' worth of talking, and then time yourself as you speak from these notes in front of an audience (not as you read them over at your desk).

When you are designing a presentation, then, aim short. Your presentation will probably take longer than you anticipate; it will probably grow as you work on it; actual delivery, audience interaction, and use of visuals will make it longer than you may think; and if it's a bit short, so what? Which would you prefer if you were in the audience—a presentation that ran a bit short and gave you an unexpected prelunch break, or a presentation that ran long and cut into your lunch hour? Slightly short presentations have virtually no drawbacks. Slightly long presentations can be disastrous: you may have to rush, or even omit important points.

The other aspect of timing has to do with audience breaks. According to the research, for best audience attention the longest you should speak without a break is forty to fifty minutes. If you have to speak longer, include time for breaks. It's preferable to have several short breaks than fewer long ones. For example, if you are speaking for three hours, insert two ten-minute breaks rather than one twenty-minute break. Always try to end on a high note just before a break. And, if your presentation breaks into sections of unequal length, place the longest section first.

Presentation Structure

So, you've got your cards set and your timing thought out. What should you say? When you present information orally, you need to say it in a very different way than you do when you write. Here are three steps to go through as you compose your presentation: (l) limit your main points; (2) make your main ideas stand out; (3) use an effective opening and closing. For each of these three steps, we will use short and simple examples. After we've gone through all three, we will look at a longer, more complex case.

Limit your main points.

Once again, always remember that speaking is not the same as writing. You simply cannot present your audience with the same amount of detail as you can in writing. Speakers very often commit this error of over-whelming their audience with information. Imagine, for example, a speaker in an impeccable business suit going up to an overhead projector and slapping down an agenda slide with about twenty-five points to cover. The audience simply cannot process it all. How many points can they process? The cognitive psychologists disagree somewhat on this question: some say seven; others say four. To play it safe, however, limit the number of main points you make in a presentation to three, four, or five.

"Three to five points?" I can imagine you asking. "How can I say only three to five things in, say, an hour-long presentation?" Making three to five points does not mean stating sentences and then sitting down. What it does mean is that you group your multitudinous ideas into three to five main categories—not just for your audience's benefit, but also for your own: your audience won't remember more than that many points. (For a refresher on how to group ideas, see the section on providing a hierarchy in chapter 5.)

"All right," you may agree, "so they'll only remember three to five points. But won't I sound simplistic?" The answer to this question is a subtle one. Yes, you will sound more simplistic than you would if you told your audience every single thing you ever thought about your topic. If your communication objective is, in fact, to show off every single thought you ever had on the subject, then by all means do so. For most presentations, however, you will want to differentiate between your thought process and what you have decided to communicate. In other words, your job as a speaker is to pick out the important points. Yes, that will make it more simple for your audience to understand, but that is not the same as simplistic. Actually, limiting your points will give you a better chance of accomplishing your objective. (For more on thinking versus communicating, once again see chapter 5.)

For example, say you had a list of 500 sales figures. You could categorize them into three regions, five salespeople, or four products and thereby limit them. As another example, say you had to explain a very complicated 17-step process for running a machine. You could categorize and limit the steps to three subsets within the process: starting the machine, running the machine, and shutting down the machine. The audience will easily remember the main points, and then can use those main points to recall some or all of the smaller points. They will feel panicked if asked to remember all 500 or all 17 points at once.

Make your main ideas stand out.

Once you have limited the number of main points, make sure each stands out. One way to do this is always to include a **preview.** A preview is an agenda, an outline, an idea of where you are going with your presentation. If you think again about the contrast between listeners and readers, you will realize that your readers can skim over a document, see how long it is, and read your headings and subheadings before they start in on the rest of the document. Your listeners, on the other hand, have no idea what you will be covering unless you tell them. I mentioned that one of the most common problems in business presentations is having too many main points. An equally common problem is lack of a preview. Always state a preview explicitly before you begin discussing your main points.

One speaking expert uses a file folder analogy to explain previews.[1] Your preview gives your audience the chance to make "file folders" in their minds, each labeled with a main point. Then, as you discuss each point, they put the information into the correct folder. With no folders ready, they spend their time during the presentation wondering where to put the bits of information, instead of listening. At the end, they have a pile of scraps of paper that make no sense to them.

In the most formal situations, a preview might sound like this: "In the next twenty minutes, I will discuss sales in each of three regions: the Southeast, the Far West, and the Midwest." On less formal occasions, your preview might be: "I'd like to go over the sales figures in three regions." In any situation, the point of the preview is to give your audience a skeleton, a very general outline, of what you will be discussing.

In addition to starting with a preview, you can also make your main points stand out by providing very **explicit transitions.** In chapter 8, we defined transitions in writing—words and phrases such as *first, second,* and *on the other hand* that signal where you are headed. To define transitions in speaking, we might continue with the file-folder analogy. Transitions tell your listeners, "Now take out the next file folder."

Again, however, remember to contrast speaking with writing: in writing, you can use those short transitions such as *first, second,* or *on the other hand.* But have you ever been listening to someone speak and heard something like this? "Bla bla bla; *second,* bla bla bla." "Second?" you ask yourself. You don't remember what the "first" was. You don't remember what this point is second in a list of. Instead of short transitions, then, use

[1] L. Rahmun, Oregon State University, Corvallis.

more explicit transitions when you speak. Here are some examples of explicit transitions: "the second recommendation is . . ." instead of "second"; or "another benefit of this system is . . ." instead of "in addition."

Finally, to make your main points stand out, use **internal summaries.** This is a simple concept; summarize between your major points or subpoints. For example, say: "Now that I have explained the major benefits of this new process, I'd like to discuss how the process actually works." This internal summary tells your audience you have finished the benefits section and are moving on to the process section.

Many students complain that they feel awkward about repeating themselves so often when they make presentations. First they preview their main points, then they give very explicit transitions and summaries. They feel as if they are following the old adage "Tell 'em what you're going to tell 'em; tell 'em; tell 'em what you told 'em." I can only counter this argument by reverting once again to the idea of being audience-centered. Yes, you may feel awkward repeating yourself, but more important, your audience will not feel awkward. Your audience simply will not remember your main points unless you make it easy for them to do so by providing them with a preview, explicit transitions, and internal summaries.

Use an effective opening and closing.

The final differences between writing and speaking have to do with openings and closings. When you speak, you neither start nor finish as quickly as you do when you write. What sounds natural in writing sounds abrupt in speaking.

OPENING: An effective presentation opening consists of what many speech experts call a *grabber*. The word *grabber* is meant to imply that you must "grab" your audience's attention before you start in on your main points. Think about your listeners, sitting out there in the audience. They are all thinking about other things: the phone messages they have to answer back in their offices, the reports they're in the midst of writing, perhaps even their golf game that afternoon. You—as a speaker—must get their attention. If you simply start into your first point, they won't hear it.

When most people think of a *grabber,* the first idea that comes to mind is to tell a joke. You do not, however, have to be humorous or entertaining to gain interest. **Using humor** in business communication is tricky. Naturally, you should use humor only if it fits your own style and personality. If you can't or don't want to tell jokes, don't. Furthermore, if humor is not appropriate for your audience, your topic, or the specific occasion, don't use it. When you do choose in certain situations to pep up your communication with humor, keep in mind these four rules.

First, humor in a business setting should never be offensive to any member of your audience. Biting, scathing satire is funny from certain comedians, but not from business people. Therefore, avoid racial, ethnic, and bawdy jokes; avoid shocking references to sex, disease, and death. To avoid offending your audience, you should try to know as much about them as possible. You could test out jokes on colleagues or on potential listeners before you say them in public. If you don't get the reaction you want, be willing to change or toss the jokes. For example, consider the classic one-liner, "Apart from that, Mrs. Lincoln, how did you enjoy the play?" In some situations this may be funny—since your audience is over a hundred years removed from the assassination. But you wouldn't want to have said, "Apart from that, Mrs. Kennedy, how did you enjoy your trip to Dallas?" in November of 1963, or "Apart from that, Arnold, how did you enjoy your trip to the hospital?" after a colleague's mother just died. Be sensitive to the possible reactions of everyone to whom you are speaking.

Besides not offending or discrediting anyone in your audience, don't put yourself down. Neither one person or group nor you yourself should be the target of your humor. Many humor experts disagree with me on this point, and certainly self-deprecation can be charming in many social situations. In business, however, especially when you are young, unknown, or unpracticed, belittling yourself may encourage your audience to look for faults, may bore them with the details of your anxieties, or may lead them to believe you lack confidence or competence. (Pomposity, of course, is just as harmful an approach.)

Rule number three is to use humor in small doses. You are not being paid to be a stand-up comic; you don't want to be the company clown; you want to avoid telling too many jokes. As one expert says, if you tell "one gag after another, your audience may be rolling on the floor with laughter, but they will not be getting the message; they will be waiting for the next punch line. Use humor in business the way you use spices in a meal—sparingly, to accent the basic flavor."[2]

[2]L. Meuse, *Making Business and Technical Presentations* (Boston: CBI Publishers, 1980), pp. 150–51.

The fourth rule is that your humor should be related to the topic or the occasion. A completely out-of-context joke may be appropriate at a dinner party, but not in business communication. Don't, for example, start a presentation with a series of unrelated jokes, and then say "Well, now that the jokes are over, let me get on with my presentation." Your audience is likely to feel disjointed. Introduce your humor unexpectedly, not blatantly. Never preface a joke by saying "that reminds me of a joke" or "I heard a good joke the other day." This almost challenges your audience, as if you were saying "You better laugh now."

In summary, if you feel comfortable opening a presentation on a humorous note, fine. But don't feel you have to. You can grab your audience's interest in one of two effective ways: by referring to the unusual or referring to the familiar.

Referring to the unusual gains audience attention by telling people something they did not know, to arouse their curiosity. Such openings include: rhetorical questions (that is, a question you do not intend your audience to answer), a promise of what your presentation will deliver, a vivid image, a startling example or story, or an important statistic. As an example of a rhetorical question, you might ask: "So what new telephone system should we install?" As an example of an important statistic, you might open with: "There are more telephones in America than there are bathtubs."

Referring to the familiar gains audience attention by tying into something your listeners already know; you appeal to your understanding of them rather than to their curiosity. Such openings include references to your audience, the occasion, the relationship between you and your audience, the relationship between the audience and the topic, the relationship between you and your topic, or someone or something familiar to the audience. As examples: "It's great to be back at the Detroit office again"; "I know you all want to hear about our new bonus plan"; "Audrey has asked me to bring you up to date on the Blaydon account."

Remember that your opening should be brief. Imagine how confused your audience will feel if you go on for over a minute or two with a long story or loads of introductory material.

CLOSING: The final step in structuring an oral presentation is to use an effective closing. As the Audience Memory Curve illustrates, your audience is most likely to remember your first and last words. (See chapter 5 for more information on the implications of the Audience Memory Curve.)

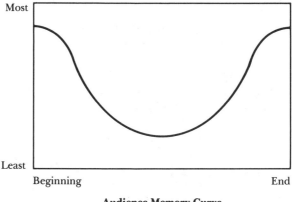

Audience Memory Curve

If you ever doubt that your audience listens at the end of a presentation, try saying "So, in conclusion . . ." or "To summarize, then . . ." and watch the nonverbal signs from your audience. They perk up and listen. What happens so often in business presentations, however, is that speakers waste this valuable time. You've probably heard speakers wind up by saying something as useless as "Well, I guess that's about all I have to say" or "I guess that's about it." Avoid this syndrome!

Instead, use a strong transitional phrase, such as "In conclusion," or "To summarize," to introduce your closing remarks. Then, for formal presentations, close with a restatement of your main points. (Again, you may feel you are being repetitive, but this kind of reinforcement is extremely effective if you are explaining or instructing.) As other options, you could close with a reference to your opening: the rhetorical question, the promise, the image, story, or statistic you used to "grab" your audience's attention. Finally, you might choose the classic sales-presentation ending: close with the "what next?" step. What precisely do you want your audience to do? Be sure to refer again to the benefits they will accrue from taking that "what next" action.

Case example

So, those are the three steps you go through to structure a presentation. Sounds easy? Unfortunately, it's often not. Let's take a look at a more complex example.

You work in the Personnel Department at Solartrom Company. The benefits have just changed: employees may now choose medical plan A or plan B. Your boss has asked you to go to a Marketing Department meeting to explain the new benefits. He says, "I know this information isn't very clearly presented. But since you had that terrific business communication course in college, I know you'll be able to whip it into shape to explain it clearly." Here's the information your boss hands you:

Medical Plan for Solartrom Employees

As of July 1, employees will be affected by changes in our insurance program. There are now two medical plans as well as the dental plan from which to select the coverage most suitable to your needs. The plans and their costs are as follows:

	Deductible	Co-Insurance	Monthly Cost
Plan A:	$100/person $200/family	10% of next $2000/person 10% of next $2000/person	1 Person $ 71.53 2 Persons $138.27 Family $185.31
Plan B:	$250/person $500/family	20% of next $1250/person 20% of next $2500/family	1 Person $ 62.58 2 Persons $120.11 Family $161.11
Dental:	none	No co-insurance	1 Person $ 10.42 2 Persons $ 27.89 Family $ 27.89

These premium rates are subject to increase yearly. The company will contribute $73 per month toward the selected insurance coverage (for part-time employees, a prorated amount based on the percentage of full-time effort according to our records).

You check with your boss to make sure you understand the terms. The *deductible* is the amount the employee pays before receiving any insurance payment. *Co-insurance* refers to the percentages paid by the employee and by the company. (For example, *10% of next $2000* means the employee pays 10 percent of $2000 after paying the deductible; the insurance company pays the other 90 percent of that $2000.) After the co-insurance limit runs out, the insurance company pays 100 percent.

Step 1: Limit your main points.

The main points in the document your boss handed you are all mixed up. The employees are supposed to choose between plan A and plan B; they automatically get the dental plan. Therefore, the dental plan should not be presented "in line" with plans A and B as if it were a third option. The monthly costs listed in the last column are confusing: the monthly cost is really the medical plan (A or B) plus the dental plan minus the amount the company contributes.

Put yourself in the employee's shoes: What would you want to know? The employee must choose plan A or plan B. Naturally, she or he would want to know: How do the plans differ in terms of cost? How do the plans differ in terms of benefits? Your two main points, then, are *costs* and *benefits:*

Costs		*Medical*	*Dental*	*Company contribution*	*Total/ month*	*Total/ year*
Plan A	1 person	71.53 +	10.42 −	73.00 =	8.95	$107.40
	2 persons	138.27 +	27.89 −	73.00 =	93.16	$1117.92
	3 or more	185.31 +	27.89 −	73.00 =	140.20	$1682.40
Plan B	1 person	62.58 +	10.42 −	73.00 =	0	0
	2 persons	120.11 +	27.89 −	73.00 =	75.00	$900.00
	3 or more	161.11 +	27.89 −	73.00 =	116.00	$1392.00

Benefits		*Deductible Employee Pays First*	*Co-insurance Employee Pays*	*Total possible paid by employee/year*	*Covered by insurance company*
Plan A	1 person	$100	10% of next $2000	$300	over $2000/ person
	2 or more	$200	10% of next $2000	$300/person	person
Plan B	1 person	$250	20% of next $1250	$500	over $1250/ person
	2 or more	$500	20% of next $2500	$500/family	over $2500/ family

Step 2: State your main points clearly.

To state your main points clearly, you include a preview, explicit transitions, and internal summaries. For example:

Preview: "To help you make the choice between plan A and plan B, in the next few minutes I'll explain the differences between the two plans: first, in terms of how much each plan will cost you, and second, in terms of what kinds of benefits you will receive from each plan."

Explicit transitions: After you have explained the costs of plans A and B, say: "Now that we've gone over the costs of the two plans, let's take a look at the different benefits offered by each plan."

Internal summary: As you are making that explicit transition between *costs* and *benefits,* say: "Now that we've gone over the costs of the two plans—and we've seen that plan A is more expensive—let's take a look at the difference in benefits offered by each plan."

Step 3: Use an effective opening and closing.

An effective opening grabs your audience's attention by referring to the unusual or to the familiar. Here is an example of each:

1. Openings referring to the unusual (something your audience does not know):

   Rhetorical question: "By the end of this week, each of you will have to select medical plan A or B. How can you make this decision?"

   A promise: "At the end of this ten-minute presentation, you should have a good idea of the differences between plan A and plan B so you can decide which one to choose."

   Vivid image: "Are you a single person who rarely goes to the drugstore—much less to the doctor? Or are you a part of a large family that seems to be constantly in and out of the doctor's office? We have designed two medical plans to deal with these different kinds of needs."

   Important statistic: "Think about your decision to select plan A or plan B. If you're single, there's about a $100-a-year difference in the plan costs. If you have a family, we're looking at a $300-a-year difference."

2. Openings referring to the familiar (something your audience does know):

   The audience: "As all of you in the Marketing Department know, different customers have different needs. That's precisely why the Personnel Department has come up with two medical plans: to meet your differing needs."

The occasion: "Today I'm happy to join those of you who work on the third floor—so I can explain the new plan those of us who work on the first floor have cooked up."

The relationship between the audience and the subject: "Medical benefits are extremely important to all of us. Each of us has a choice to make about two medical plans, and I'd like to explain the ramifications of each."

Someone or something familiar to the audience: "I'm glad Bob asked me to join you this morning to explain . . ." or "I know you've all been hard at work explaining the differences between instrument X and instrument Y to our customers. This afternoon, I'd like to explain the differences between our company's medical plans A and B."

Closings:

Summary: "So, you can see plan A costs more initially, but has a lower deductible. Plan B costs less initially, but has a higher deductible."

Refer to opening: "I hope that with this information, you'll be able to make your decision" (reference to unusual); "After your sales presentations, our customers know the difference between instrument X and instrument Y. By now, I hope *you* understand the differences between medical plan A and plan B." (reference to familiar)

"What next?" step: "Now that I have outlined the costs and benefits of these plans, I would like you to take this pamphlet summarizing my talk, think about the right plan for you, and inform the Personnel Department by July 1 of your decision."

Other Kinds of Speech Structures

The bulk of this chapter has been concerned with what we have defined in Figure 12.1 as *prepared presentations*— speaking that is prepared, but not read word for word—because that is the kind of speaking most people do most often in business.

You may, however, also find that at certain times in your business career you are called on to speak from a manuscript, to speak off the cuff, to introduce someone, or to deliver a team presentation. This section discusses "what to say" in these other kinds of situations.

Manuscript and impromptu speeches

Manuscript and impromptu speeches are exact opposites. You read a manuscript word for word; you deliver an impromptu off the cuff. Let's look at how to structure each of them.

MANUSCRIPT SPEECH: The most formal kind of business speaking is a manuscript speech.[3] Since you read a manuscript speech word for word, you have the least direct interaction with your audience of any form of speaking. Such speeches are relatively infrequent in most businesses: presentations and meetings are usually more common. There are, however, some situations in which you might need to give a manuscript speech. For instance, you might want to make sure you have exact, precise wording—speaking on a sensitive legal matter, for example, or giving testimony. Or you might need to check the exact wording with other people—with a lawyer, perhaps, or a CPA. Finally, you may need to write out a speech for someone else to deliver. As a speechwriter, you act very much like a consultant does: you confer with the speaker in advance, write the speech, then modify it based on his or her reactions.

When you sit down to write a manuscript speech, naturally, you go through the usual process: establish the objective, analyze the audience, structure the message. However, instead of writing notes in outline form on cards—as you would for a presentation—you write sentences and paragraphs on paper. The main problem people have in writing manuscript speeches is with **wording;** they use *written style* instead of *spoken style*. A speech in written style looks fine on paper, but sounds stilted, formal, or pompous.

You must constantly ask yourself: Is there anything written here that no one would say? Does it sound stilted? Is it hard to pronounce? For example, you might write on a page "If you were asked to do so," but you would say in a speech "If someone asked you to do that." You might write on a page "ensure participation," but you would *say* in a speech "make sure everyone participates." As speech consultant Ralph Proodian says: "Words like 'participation,' 'obstinacy,' and even 'evaluate' are not as good in speech as 'work,' 'stubbornness,' and 'consider.' Stick to normal words used in daily conversation. Unless, of course, you swear a lot."[4] You must

---

[3] I am indebted to two sources for ideas on manuscript speeches: A. Thrash, A. Shelby, and J. Tarver, *Speaking Up Successfully* (New York: Holt, Rinehart & Winston, 1984), chap. 14; and A. Jay, *Effective Presentation* (London: British Institute of Management Foundation, 1979), chap. 5.

[4] R. Proodian, "How to Make your Next Speech One to Remember," *Wall Street Journal*, October 8, 1984, p. 30.

also consider ease of pronunciation. You can easily write "increased trusts," "intends to pretend," or "this year's winner's gear"—but you cannot easily say them.

In addition to different wording, you use slightly different **sentences** in speeches. For one thing, avoid phrases separating subject and verb. Your reader can easily follow this sentence: "Caroline Henderson, who is currently the president of ABC Company, will be the first speaker on the panel." You make it much easier for a listener, however, if you do not separate the subject from the verb: "President Caroline Henderson will be the first speaker on the panel." As another example, you might write for a reader: "XYZ, which is a real-estate company, increased its profits this year." You should speech-write for a listener: "XYZ Real-Estate Company showed increased profits this year." Also, use different sentence lengths. Although your sentence lengths—as in regular writing—should vary, in speech writing they must break down into shorter units, and you may use sentence fragments.

Finally, remember that in speech writing, **rhythm** is much more important than in regular writing. Consider, for example, how the impact of Patrick Henry's famous quotation "Give me liberty or give me death" is based on rhythm. Contrast his version with the unrhythmic "Give me liberty or death." Similarly, John Kennedy's rhythmic "Ask not what your country can do for you; ask what you can do for your country" is more effective than the unrhythmic "Don't ask what your country can do for you, but what you can do for it." As a final example, here is an excerpt from one of Winston Churchill's speeches, as he actually wrote it on the page to emphasize pauses and rhythm:

> We cannot yet see how deliverance will come
> or when it will come.
>
> But nothing is more certain
> than that every trace of Hitler's footsteps,
>
> every stain of his infected
> and corroding fingers,
>
> will be sponged and purged
> and, if need be, blasted
> from the surface of the earth.[5]

Keeping these considerations in mind, write the first draft. Or, better, write notes (as you would for a presentation), then record yourself speaking from those notes. You will automatically use spoken style,

[5]Quoted in W. Manchester, *The Last Lion: Winston Spencer Churchill; Visions of Glory 1874–1932* (Boston: Little, Brown, 1983), p. 33.

thereby avoiding the pitfalls we just discussed. The transcript of what you just recorded becomes the draft of the speech. Once you have a draft, edit it (see chapter 8 through 10 for editing techniques), and then read it aloud or have the person for whom you're writing the speech read it aloud. After making any changes necessary, you are ready to type the manuscript in its final form.

A speech manuscript looks different from a regular page of writing, as you can see in Figure 12.3. For one thing, it should be typed in large

FIGURE 12.3

Sample page of manuscript

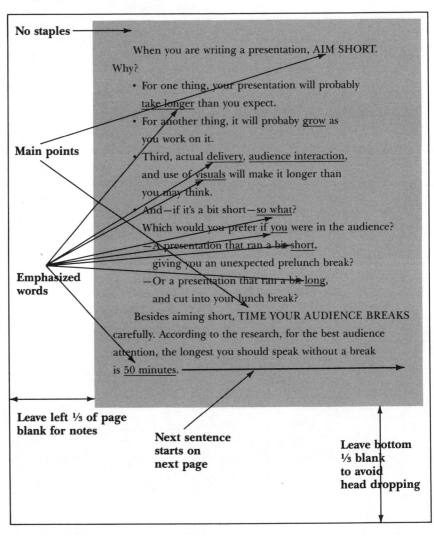

print. Some typewriters have *orator* or *presenter* typefaces; some computers will print out extra bold or extra large letters. The margins also look strange: leave about one third of the page blank on the left side for notes; leave about one third of the page blank at the bottom so the speech reader's head will not drop down too low. Since it is awkward to read a sentence that starts on one page and finishes on the next, never break a sentence between two pages in a speech manuscript. In fact, many speech experts suggest never breaking even a paragraph between two pages. Never staple the pages of a speech; the speaker should be able to slide the page to one side. Finally, many speakers like to underline key words for vocal emphasis. What all these conventions of speech manuscripts add up to is a lot of paper. A ten-minute speech may be written on twenty pieces of paper.

IMPROMPTU SPEAKING: Impromptu speaking is talking on the spur of the moment, without advance preparation. Your boss may suddenly say, "Bring us up to date on a certain project," or a customer may ask you to explain a certain service. Usually, of course, you will not be asked to make impromptu remarks unless you have some knowledge in the area.

Here are some suggestions to help you in impromptu speaking situations: (1) Anticipate. Try to avoid truly impromptu situations. Guess at the probability of your being called on during discussions, meetings, or interviews. Guess at the topics you might be asked to discuss. (2) Keep it short. Say what you have to say and then stop. Do not ramble on, feeling you must deliver a lengthy lecture. (3) Organize as well as you can. If you have a few seconds, jot down your main points. Stick to them; avoid tangents. (4) Relate to experience. You will speak more easily and confidently if you try to relate the topic to your specific experiences, and to topics you know best.

Speaker introductions and team presentations

A final set of situations in which you may be speaking in business are those in which you are not the only one "on stage." This section provides some suggestions for how to introduce a speaker, and how to deliver a team presentation.

INTRODUCTIONS: When you are asked to make an introduction for someone who is about to speak, your job is to make the audience want to listen. You want to interest them in the topic and increase their respect for the speaker.

An introduction usually starts with a greeting or welcome to the audience. Often this initial greeting includes the name of the sponsoring organization, the nature of the gathering, or your name and function (if they do not know you). After you have greeted and welcomed your audience, identify the subject by indicating its importance and arousing their curiosity.

The longest part of the introduction should be devoted to creating a favorable impression of the speaker. You can use information about the speakers from their résumés—or, better yet, from interviewing them. Don't bore your audience by reading every detail on the speaker's résumé, however. Instead, select from the details: omit information the audience already knows; choose the speaker's most distinctive qualification or experiences—those most relevant to this audience and to this occasion. Finally, at the end of your introduction, present the speaker by name.

How long should an introduction be? Certainly no longer than five minutes. Generally, the less the speaker is known to your audience, the longer the introduction needs to be. If, for example, you were introducing the president of your company to a group of employees, you might just say "It's my pleasure to introduce our president, William Joyce." If, on the other hand, you were introducing someone the audience did not know, you'd want to include more details. Here's an example:

> Good afternoon and welcome—especially to the new members—to the Middletown monthly meeting. I'm Betsey Neslin, your vice-president. (Greet audience; include name of organization, nature of gathering, your name and function.) As we all know, the state legislature has recently appropriated funds for a new highway that will pass directly through Middletown. This highway will have a major impact on all of our businesses. (Identify subject, arouse curiosity, indicate importance.) This afternoon, we are happy to have Sarah Allen with us to explain the details of this highway. For the past two years, Ms. Allen has served as the legislative assistant to our state representative, Chris Brokaw. She was involved in writing up the highway bill, and in lobbying for its passage. Ms. Allen received her bachelor's and master's degrees in engineering from Middlestate University. She has also written several articles for the *Middlestate Journal* on the influence of highway construction on surrounding businesses. (Choose important details about speaker's background.) I am glad to present Ms. Sarah Allen. (Introduce speaker by name.)

As we discussed in chapter 11, your nonverbal communication is just as important as, if not more important than, what you say. Remember to maintain effective eye contact and facial expression with the person you are introducing. If you speak favorably, but look unfavorable or indifferent, your audience may well ignore your words.

TEAM PRESENTATIONS: Team presentations are just like any other presentation in terms of structure, visuals, and so forth. The only difference is that instead of one person delivering the entire presentation, a series of people deliver it. Team presentations are fairly common in business—both because you may want your audience to get to know the entire group, and because you may want your whole team to receive recognition.

The major problem with team presentations occurs when each presenter prepares his or her own parts—and the parts never coalesce into a whole. A team presentation is *not* a panel discussion. It is, instead, a coherent, organized, presentation that is to be spoken by various people instead of one person. Therefore, team presentations should be organized as a whole.

An important part of that coherence is the need for very clear transitions between the speakers. For example, one team member might give the introduction and preview—including what each subsequent team member will discuss. As each new team member starts, she or he should provide transition between the parts, such as "Now that Mr. Bower has discussed our proposal, I'd like to show you the financial results we can expect if we decide to go ahead with this proposal." Often, team presentations end with the same team member who opened the session returning to deliver the closing.

Finally, the visual aids in a team presentation should look consistent. Use the same color coding—for example, blue for all main headings throughout. Use the same typeface and type size. In many team presentations, one member is assigned to handle the visual aids—changing the overhead transparencies, for instance. This method can work very smoothly; however, you risk having that one team member look like an assistant or subordinate. Another method is to have each member take a turn handling the visuals (right after she or he finishes speaking, perhaps). This method demands more rehearsal if it is to work smoothly.

To put together a team presentation that is coherent in its organization, its transitions between speakers, and its visual aids, the team must meet as a group to structure the presentation, to discuss visual aids, and to divide up speaking responsibilities. The group should also rehearse together. Normally, group presentations involve at least two rehearsals. In a "dry run" rehearsal, run through what you will say, how you will provide transitions, and what visual aids you will use. Later, a full dress rehearsal will allow you to perfect your delivery and flow.

Two final words of warning about team presentations. One, remember that every member of the team is always "on stage" to the audience. From the moment you walk into the room, the audience is watching all of you. Keep this in mind especially as you are listening to one another speak. Act interested in one another's speeches. Don't yawn, slouch, or whisper to one another unnecessarily. Two, if there is to be a question-and-answer period after the presentation, either assign one person as moderator to decide who will handle each question, or assign each person to answer automatically all questions in his or her clearly defined area of expertise.

As you can see from this chapter, speaking involves "what you say" in addition to "how you say it"—the nonverbal elements we discussed in the previous chapter. Usually, structuring a presentation means limiting your topic to three to five main points; making your main points stand out by using a preview (or agenda), explicit transitions, and internal summaries; and using an effective opening and closing.

REVIEW QUESTIONS

To check your understanding

1. What are the three main types of group speaking situations?
2. How is a presentation different from a speech?
3. Describe three steps you should go through when you prepare what to say in a presentation.
4. What are the two main rules to remember about timing a presentation?
5. Name two reasons why it is important to limit your main points.
6. How many main points should you plan on making in a presentation?
7. What are the three ways you can make your main points stand out?
8. Explain the function of a *grabber*.
9. List ways other than humor that a grabber can be effective.
10. Why should you usually avoid manuscript speeches?
11. What are four ingredients of an effective speaker introduction?
12. What are the three ingredients of a successful team presentation?

APPLICATION QUESTIONS
To apply your knowledge

1. Prepare a five-minute presentation on your reasons for studying business communication. Formulate an idea tree and an outline of your main points. Write your main ideas on a note card, color-coding the main points.

2. Assume that you are giving a two-hour presentation based on this chapter, with your main points and subpoints those listed on the first page of the chapter. Where would you position your breaks?

3. Give an example of a grabber that you have heard used recently. Why was it or was it not effective?

4. Among the following three methods of imparting information—presentation, manuscript speech, impromptu speech—which would you likely use in each of the following situations: sales meeting, interview, legal testimony, banquet toast?

5. Describe an impromptu speaking situation that you have experienced. What was the major challenge of handling it? Was your response effective?

6. Give examples of transitions that might be used in a team presentation. How are these similar to the explicit transitions included in a presentation that you make alone?

7. Describe a situation in which humor would be inappropriate in a grabber. Substitute a grabber you would use instead.

8. Clip an article from the business pages of the newspaper and determine its main points. Formulate a closing for the article.

9. Rewrite this paragraph in language more appropriate for a manuscript speech:

   The economic prognosis for the coming year is one that favors amplified spending on the part of consumers and, for our company, a resulting potential for unlimited gains and accelerated growth. I therefore exhort company field representatives to try their utmost to encourage the public to purchase our products and thus contribute to their own welfare as well as ours.

10. Assume that you are the featured speaker at a meeting of the alumni association of your college or university. Prepare an introduction for

yourself, stressing those aspects of your background that you think will appeal to your audience.

CASES
To practice what you learned

1. You have been sent by your company to represent its interests in England. The company is eager to be perceived as a concern devoted to the well-being of local residents, and you have accordingly been advised to take an active part in the community's business association. The group's members are interested in learning more about America, and have asked you to explain to them that mysterious but fascinating American pastime, baseball. You know the game's rules are hopelessly complicated. How would you go about structuring your presentation? What grabber would you use for an audience that knows nothing of the game?

2. You have been asked by your boss to give a presentation to the division's "top brass" during a formal luncheon. Your topic will be your department's activities during the past year. At the conclusion of your presentation you are also asked to introduce the next speaker—the new vice-president, who will outline the agenda for the coming year. How would you formulate an effective closing that also serves as an introduction?

3. You are attending a banquet in honor of local business leaders. Between the main course and dessert, the host of the evening falls ill and must leave abruptly. His assistant asks you if you would be willing to officiate as master of ceremonies during the awards portion of the evening. You graciously agree, and with only fifteen minutes to spare, excuse yourself in order to prepare notes for the ten-minute speech you must deliver. How do you approach this situation and what kind of preparation do you make?

4. You are part of a committee that is planning an important company brochure. Other members of the committee include representatives of the finance, marketing, public relations, and graphics departments; you represent the planning department. Everyone agrees that a new, more youthful design is needed for the brochure, but the problem is convincing the executives, who are attached to the old design, which has been in use since the founding of the company. How would you go about planning a team presentation that would persuade the executives to adopt your recommendation?

5. You have been invited to speak at a conference. By an unlucky draw, you are scheduled to make your presentation at the end of the last day, wrapping up a full afternoon of speeches and meetings. You have been allotted an hour and a half, but intend to speak only an hour, in order to let your audience leave in plenty of time for the final night's festivities. What other methods do you use to get your audience's attention and keep it?

13

Visual Aids

Compose Your Visual Aid Content.
Appropriate formality • Necessary function • Clear message title and supporting detail • Easy readability

Choose Your Visual Aid Equipment.
Animated projection • Still projections • Nonprojection visuals

Use Your Visuals Effectively.
General techniques for all visuals • Specific techniques for certain kinds of visuals

$\mathbf{P}$REPARING an effective presentation involves more than structure and delivery. Another important consideration is what kind of visuals to use. People in your audience have a limited attention span. Even if they are interested in your subject and listening quite intently, they are still liable to use another part of their consciousness to think about other matters. If they are bored, that tendency to think about other things increases, perhaps to the point where they are not listening at all. Therefore, no matter how skilled you may be at presenting information, your audience has the brain capacity to think about other things, to daydream; you just cannot keep up with their brains' processing potential.

What can you do to keep them concentrating on your ideas? Give them something visual to look at, to back up what you're saying. Visual aids increase your audience's comprehension and retention. Seeing something in addition to hearing it is much more effective than either just seeing it or just hearing it. Visuals add interest, variety, and impact, and remain in the memory longer than words.

In most business and professional settings, visual aids of some kind are appropriate. In some situations, however, the group you are addressing may ask you not to use aids, or may request that you use only certain kinds of aids. Naturally, audience considerations should always govern your aid selection.

Once you have met your audience's needs, follow these three steps: (1) compose your content, (2) choose your equipment, and (3) use your visuals effectively.

Compose Your Visual Aid Content.

Unfortunately, many people giving business presentations get involved with fancy technology or colored graphics that don't communicate anything useful. The best way to compose visual aids is to think about what you're trying to communicate—before you think about the artwork, the computer graphics, or the medium you might use to say it. The content of your visual aids should have appropriate formality, a necessary function, a clear message title and supporting detail, and easy readability. Let's look at each of these four criteria.

Appropriate formality

Your first question should always be: "How formal do I want to be on this specific occasion?" A **formal** tone results from visual aids created entirely in advance, before the presentation starts. If the occasion is formal, you may use slides, overhead transparencies, or flip charts; the important variable is your having prepared them in advance. Formal aids may be produced by professional artists or by computers, and often in many colors. They assure you of a great deal of control over your presentation's time and content. At the same time, you give up the chance to include your audience's comments. (See chapter 3 for a review of the various styles of communication.)

A **semiformal** tone comes from creating your aids partially in advance and partially during the presentation. For example, you might prepare part of a chart, and then, for more dramatic effect, write certain numbers as you speak. Or you might have blanks that you will fill with audience responses. A semiformal tone allows you to maintain some control with some flexibility and spontaneity.

Finally, if you want to establish a more **informal** tone, create your visuals during the presentation itself. You might, for example, choose to write on a blackboard, a flip chart, or even an overhead transparency during the talk. Informal aids are the most flexible and spontaneous; they involve your audience the most—but naturally you exert far less control over their content and as you write you may waste valuable time.

This kind of analysis sounds simple, but you will often see severe problems with visual aids in business because presenters neglect these considerations. For example, they bring professionally prepared slides into a brainstorming session and seem surprised when people don't participate. Or they scribble hastily on a blackboard and seem surprised when people assume they haven't prepared in advance.

Necessary function

After you've thought about how formal you want to be, decide what function you want your visuals to provide. Again, this advice may sound simple and obvious, but unnecessary visuals—that is, visuals serving no function—clog many business presentations. You may have seen, for example, ineffective presenters slapping up slides at the rate of about one every fifteen seconds, or laboriously reading slides that echo practically word for word what they are saying. What a waste of the audience's time. Unnecessary aids are like unnecessary words in writing. Get rid of them.

How can you decide if an aid is necessary or not? (1) Word charts should show your agenda or emphasize your main ideas, and (2) graphs should demonstrate relationships visually.

WORD CHARTS: Word charts consist—obviously—of words rather than figures. One kind of word chart is an *agenda* chart, or a list of your three to five main points. If you use an agenda chart, always show it at the beginning of the presentation (during your preview)—whether it's on a flip chart, a slide, the board, or even a handout. You may also elect to leave the agenda chart showing throughout your presentation and point to it each time you move to a new section. A *main idea* or *recommendations* chart lists your main conclusions. Display it at the beginning of a presentation if your listeners are likely to agree with you, and at the end if they are not likely to agree. Other than for your agenda and main ideas, use word charts sparingly—only when you think your audience would get lost without one.

Avoid overusing word charts in your presentations. One of the worst possible kind of so-called visual aids is a word-for-word script of your presentation displayed at the same time you say something. Figure 13.1 shows an example of a typical ineffective, *word script* aid. What's wrong with it? For one thing, word scripts insult your audience's intelligence, by almost forcing them to read practically word for word what you're saying. They also often cause the problem of allowing the audience to read ahead. Finally, they allow your audience to read one idea at the same time they are listening to another.

GRAPHS: Besides using word charts (sparingly, usually for agendas and main conclusions only), use graphs to show ideas visually. Graphs are true visual aids because they are actually visual, using design elements rather than just words. The Audience Memory Curve illustrated in the previous chapter is an example of a graph. It demonstrates visually how your audience remembers more at the beginning and the end of a presentation.

How do you decide if a graph is necessary? Use graphs as illustrations: maps, assembly lines, pictures, or diagrams. If you are illustrating quantitative information, here are six main uses of various kinds of graphs: (l) to show parts of one item, use a pie chart; (2) to show

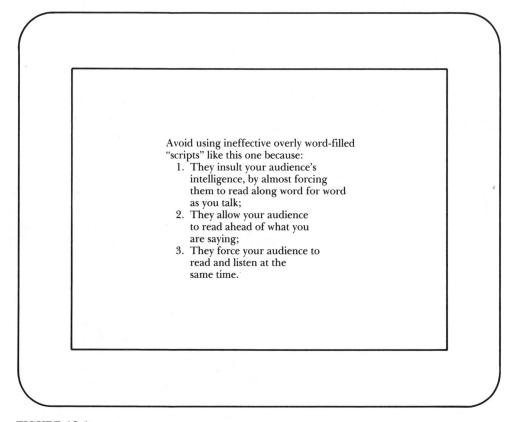

Avoid using ineffective overly word-filled
"scripts" like this one because:
1. They insult your audience's
   intelligence, by almost forcing
   them to read along word for word
   as you talk;
2. They allow your audience
   to read ahead of what you
   are saying;
3. They force your audience to
   read and listen at the
   same time.

FIGURE 13.1

Ineffective word script

rank or contrast, use a bar chart; (3) to show variation over time, use a
column or line chart; (4) to show parts of more than one item, use a
divided bar or column; (5) to show sequence, use a flow chart; (6) to show
correlation between items, use a scatter or paired-bar chart. That list
sounds somewhat confusing, doesn't it? Look at Table 13.1 for an illustration of how seeing concepts displayed visually makes them easier to
comprehend.[1]

[1]Two excellent books for more information on designing charts and graphs are: J.
White, *Using Charts and Graphs* (New York: R.R. Bowker, 1984); and G. Zelazny, *Say It
with Charts* (Homewood, Ill.: Dow Jones–Irwin, 1985). The term *message title* is
Zelazny's.

TABLE 13.1

Six main uses for a graph

If you want to show	Graph to use	Tips
1. Parts of one item (contributions, percentages, shares, proportions)	Pie **Entire Item** broken into components	Arrange with most important component at twelve o'clock; if components are equally important, arrange from smallest to largest. Usually, limit to no more than five components.
2. Parts of more than one item (contributions, percentages, shares, proportions)	Divided bar  **Series of Items** broken into components	Use divided bars to show breakdown of items, because columns imply a time sequence.
	Divided column 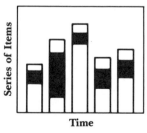	Use columns to show time sequence.

TABLE 13.1 (Continued)

If you want to show	Graph to use	Tips
3. Rank or contrast comparison (more/less, variation, difference between)	Bar	Arrange in order to suit your needs: alphabetical, low to high, high to low. Use bar chart, because column chart implies a time sequence.
4. Variation over time or frequency distribution (increases/decreases, changes, trends, concentrations)	Column Line	Use column chart to emphasize extreme variability or level of magnitude. Limit to smaller number of time periods or plottings, with discrete class intervals. Use line chart to emphasize movement of change. Use for large number of time periods. Usually, limit to no more than three lines.
5. Sequence (process, organization, line of command, time stages)	Flow	

TABLE 13.1 *(Continued)*

If you want to show	*Graph to use*	*Tips*

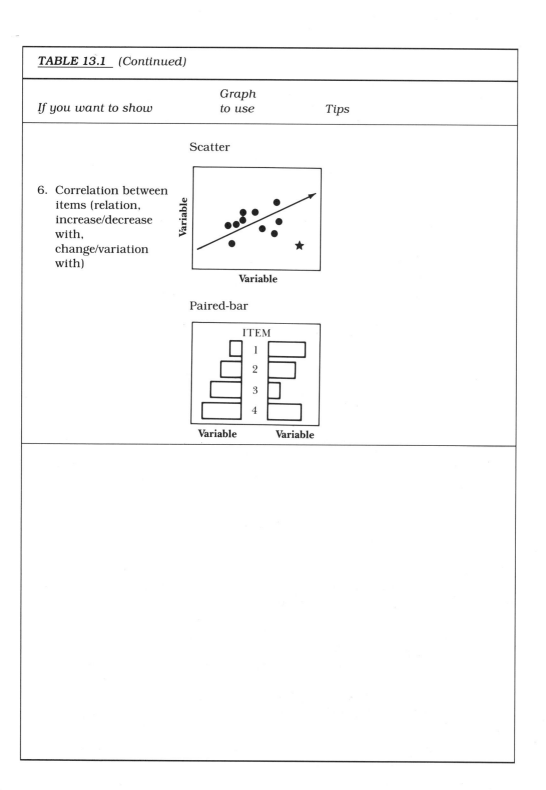

Scatter

6. Correlation between items (relation, increase/decrease with, change/variation with)

Paired-bar

321

Clear message title and supporting detail

Effective visual aids also include both a message title and supporting detail. Consider this ineffective chart; it includes only specific detail and draws no main message:

Market share in 1983
was 21%.

Or consider this ineffective chart; it merely states a message title without any supporting detail:

Market share has
decreased.

Effective visual aids, on the other hand, include both the main message title and the details. Treat a visual aid as if it were a paragraph: the message title is like a topic sentence, such as "Market share has decreased over 4 years." The specific details are like supporting sentences, such as "1984 21%, 1985 18%, 1986 16%, 1987 7%." (See chapter 8 for a review of the concept of topic sentences.) These data are displayed visually in Figure 13.2.

Figure 13.3 (page 324) is another example of an effective visual that includes both the message title (that there were more products overstocked in April than in any other of the six months), and specific detail (for any given month, specifically what product or products were overstocked).

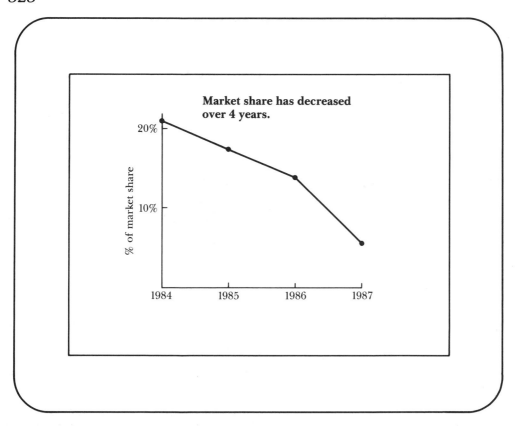

FIGURE 13.2

Effective chart: includes clear message title and supporting detail

Easy readability

If your visual, like a paragraph, includes both a main message and supporting detail, you don't need to go overboard with design elements. Your audience should think: "What an interesting idea," or "What interesting data!" not "What spiffy graphics!"

UNCLUTTERED DESIGN: First of all, keep your chart as a whole uncluttered. Don't overdesign. Or in the words of graphic expert Edward Tufte, "Get rid of 'chartjunk.' "[2] Chartjunk is any decoration that does not add to your meaning.

[2]See E. Tufte, *The Visual Display of Quantitative Information* (Cheshire, Conn.: Graphics Press, 1983), chap. 5. Chapters 4–6 of this book are excellent.

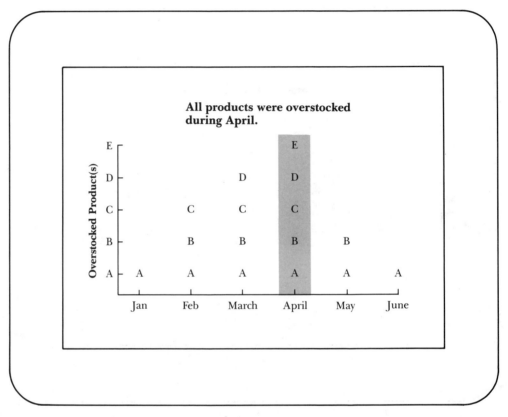

FIGURE 13.3

Effective chart: includes message title and supporting detail

Figure 13.4 illustrates a typical ineffective chartjunk-infested chart. The most obvious kind of chartjunk is gratuitous (totally unnecessary) design elements—such as shading. Another typical chartjunk problem is the use of ornamental cross-hatching. Increased use of computer graphics and dry-transfer rub-on design sheets have led to an increased amount of cross-hatching shimmering through visual aids. The shimmering effect of cross-hatching interacts with the viewer's eye to produce an optical illusion of vibration and movement. Some graphic design uses this effect beautifully, but shimmering "op art" belongs in museums, not in your business presentations. Instead of cross-hatching, use various colors, or various shades of gray. A third problem shown in Figure 13.4, and one

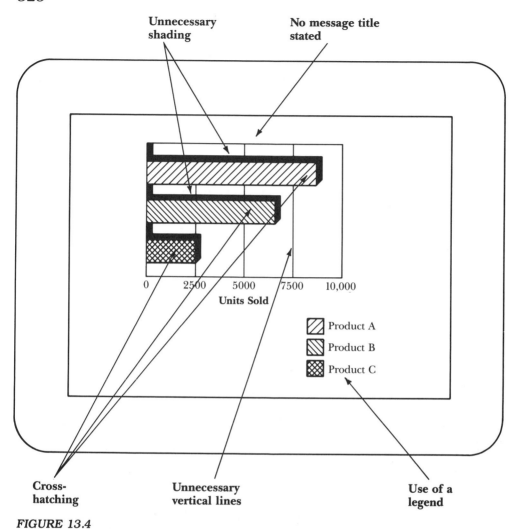

FIGURE 13.4

Ineffective chart: lots of "chartjunk," no message title

associated with cross-hatching, is the need to encode information with a key or legend, which forces the viewer to look back and forth. Instead of encoding information with various kinds of cross-hatching, label the specific area right on the visual itself in such a way that no legend is required. Choose computer graphics programs that allow you to avoid cross-hatching and legends.

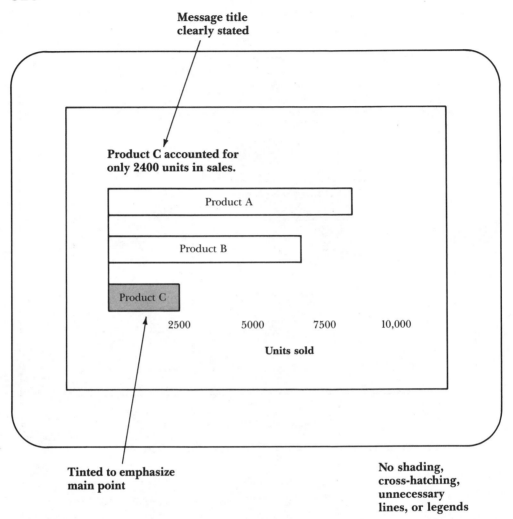

Message title clearly stated

Product C accounted for only 2400 units in sales.

Product A

Product B

Product C

2500   5000   7500   10,000

Units sold

Tinted to emphasize main point

No shading, cross-hatching, unnecessary lines, or legends

FIGURE 13.5

Effective chart: no "chartjunk." clear message title

In addition to avoiding gratuitous design elements, ornamental cross-hatching, and elaborate coding systems, you can make your visuals uncluttered by deleting anything unnecessary. Just as you edit words in your writing, edit ink in your graphics. For example, Figure 13.5 shows how you can edit the same bar chart down to the essentials.

Getting rid of chartjunk is, of course, just the first step toward making your chart as a whole easy to comprehend. Charts should never be overloaded. As a general rule, include no more than ten lines on a chart. Charts should be easy to grasp: avoid overly complex diagrams. Finally, if you use colors, do so carefully. Use a consistent color code (such as blue for your main headings throughout). Dark colors (blue, black, red, or green) are easier for the audience to see than washed-out colors (yellow or orange). Save your darkest and most contrasting color for your most important idea. Since 5 to 10 percent of the population is color-blind, choose your colors so these people can understand the graphic. Most color-deficient people can distinguish blue; most of them cannot distinguish between red and green.

CLEAR WORDS AND LETTERS: Once your chart as a whole is easy to read, make sure your **words** are equally easy to read. Pare down your words to key words and phrases only. Never give complete sentences. Never, never give complete paragraphs. A visual aid is not the same as a script. Any word important enough to put on a visual is important enough to spell out; avoid mysterious abbreviations that might confuse the audience.

Finally, make sure your visual is easy to read by using effective **lettering.** Your letters must be large enough so your audience can see them. This statement sounds embarrassingly obvious, yet overly small lettering is one of the most common problems in visual aids. We cannot establish exact rules of thumb for letter size, because letter size varies with audience size and with projection distance. In general, seat yourself in the back row of your audience to check letter size. You may be surprised how large you need to write on a flip chart or board. You may be surprised to see how unreadable typed overhead transparencies are even if you use a large print typewriter. Usually, the letters on the transparencies themselves should be at least eighteen-point type for small groups, at least twenty-four- or thirty-six-point type for large groups. Figure 13.6 illustrates these sizes.

Lettering should also be clear and precise. Clear, large lettering by hand is preferable to clotted or small lettering produced by machine. Research in ophthalmology reveals that the more letters are differentiated from one another, the easier they are to read.[3] Therefore, choose a serif typeface and avoid using all capital letters, as illustrated in Figure 13.7.

[3]See R. Rehe, *Typography: How to Make It Most Legible* (Carmel, Ind.: Design Research International, 1974), for a review of this research on typography.

This is twelve-point type. It is too small for overheads.

This is eighteen-point type. It is the minimum size to use in overheads for small groups.

This is thirty-six-point type. Use this size for overheads for large groups.

FIGURE 13.6

Lettering: Type size measured in points

As you can see from this figure, sans-serif type is harder to read because the lack of serifs gives the reader's eye less to "wrap around." Capitals are harder to read because their equal height, volume, and width also give the reader's eye less to wrap around. Obviously, then, sans-serif capitals are the hardest letters of all to read; serif lowercase letters are the easiest to read.

Many people think sans-serif type looks more "modern." Remember, however, it is harder to read, so use it sparingly.

Serif type is easier to read than sans-serif type because the letters are easier to differentiate.

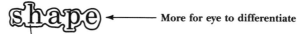 ← More for eye to differentiate

This is serif type; these marks are called *serifs*.

This is sans-serif type (*sans* means "without"); it has no serif marks.

Lowercase letters are easier to read than capital letters, again because they are easier to differentiate.

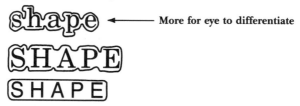 ← More for eye to differentiate

FIGURE 13.7

Lettering: serif versus sans serif
lowercase versus capitals

Choose Your Visual Aid Equipment.

Different kinds of equipment are appropriate on different occasions. For example, in a brainstorming session, you would probably choose a chalkboard or a flip chart; professionally produced 35-mm slides would defeat the purpose of that kind of occasion. On the other hand, if you were giving a final report, you might choose slides. Again we find that your communication objective, style, audience, and content—not to mention what equipment is available—should dictate what equipment you choose. Make your choice based on your strategy, not on the technological "bells and whistles."

Keeping that caveat in mind, then, let's examine the three types of equipment available to you.[4] These three types of equipment—animated projection, still projections, and nonprojection visuals—are summarized in Table 13.2, pages 332–33.

Animated projection

The first type of equipment, animated projection, includes film and video. Animated projection is useful to show motion, such as an assembly-line procedure, a skill demonstration, or research test results at high speed.

FILM: Until the 1980s, film was the major kind of animated projection. Film equipment includes a projector and, of course, the film itself. Film comes in two different formats. The word *format* refers to the film's width. The two most common formats are 16-mm and super 8. Your film projector must be compatible with your film; that is, 16-mm plays only on a 16-mm projector, super 8 only on a super 8 projector.

Sixteen-mm film is by far the more common, because it is more readily available and superior in quality, especially on a large screen. You might choose super 8 format, however, if you need to present a film to a small number of people at various locations. Super 8 equipment is more compact, travels more easily, and has good quality when projected on a small screen.

VIDEO: The second type of animated projection is the videocassette or videodisc. Videos are used for the same purposes as films: to show motion. Their biggest advantage over film is that you can easily stop and start them. You can interrupt, backspace, or *freeze* a frame to inject comments, ask questions, or answer questions. Other advantages of video include instant development and reusable tape.

Depending on your needs, you may choose one of three video systems: a monitor playback, a large-screen playback, or a recording system. (1) A television monitor system includes: a television monitor plus either a videocassette recorder (VCR), which, like an audio tape recorder, both plays back and records, or a videocassette player (VCP), which only plays back. With a monitor system, your audience watches your cassette on the television monitor or monitors. Use these systems if you need some portability, because they may be moved from room to room on carts. (2) A

---

[4]See M. Kenny, *Presenting Yourself* (New York: John Wiley, 1982), for more on visual aid equipment. This book borders on being an advertisement for Kodak, so beware of the author's bias.

large-screen system includes: a video projector and a VCR or VCP. Your audience watches the video on a screen, as they would watch a movie. Although these projection systems can be portable, usually you use them with expert adjustment and some warm-up time. Usually, they are permanently installed. (3) Finally, a video-recording system includes: a TV monitor, a VCR, a camera and tripod, a microphone, and possibly lights. Some of these units, called camcorders, are light and portable: a battery-operated VCR and camera sit on the camera operator's shoulders. Other recording systems are nonmovable, set up permanently in recording studios.

Videocassettes come in various formats. These include: 2-inch or 1-inch *television quality,* $\frac{3}{4}$-inch *professional quality,* and $\frac{1}{2}$-inch *home quality.* To further complicate matters, there are two separate $\frac{1}{2}$-inch formats— Beta and VHS. Furthermore, a $\frac{1}{4}$-inch format may be the wave of the future.

Generally, the larger the tape's width, the better its quality and the more expensive it is to produce. Usually, 2- and 1-inch formats are used only by television studios. Most businesses use $\frac{3}{4}$-inch, $\frac{1}{2}$-inch Beta, or $\frac{1}{2}$-inch VHS. Use $\frac{3}{4}$-inch for higher quality and better editing. You'll probably find, however, that $\frac{1}{2}$-inch offers sufficient quality for most situations.

The main thing to keep in mind when using video for visual aids is format compatibility. Make sure that the playback unit (VCR or VCP) is the same format as the tape you have. A tape of any particular width can be played only on a machine designed for that width. For example, a $\frac{1}{2}$-inch Beta tape will only run on a $\frac{1}{2}$-inch Beta machine. If your tape format differs, either order a different playback unit (VCR or VCP), or have your tape transferred to a different format.

Still projections

If you don't need to show motion, you can choose from three kinds of still projections—slides, filmstrips, and overhead transparencies. These projections range from the very formal and prepared to the very informal and spontaneous.

SLIDES: Slides are most useful when you don't have to write on your visual, or when you are giving a multimedia presentation (that is, when you're using many projectors on many screens). One advantage of using slides is that you can select and arrange the sequence yourself, unlike animated projection, which requires special equipment and training. You can also easily change the sequence later to suit a different

TABLE 13.2
Visual aid equipment

Equipment	Main advantage(s)	Main disadvantage(s)	Speaker flexibility	Audience involvement	Lighting
Animated projection					
Film	Animated	Dark room; little audience involvement; you cannot freeze-frame	None	None	Dark
Video	Animated; you can interrupt, backspace, or freeze-frame	Formats of all parts of equipment must be compatible (all $\frac{3}{4}$-inch, all $\frac{1}{2}$-inch VHS, etc.)	None	Limited, but possible	Dark

Still projections

Slide	Flexible sequence; projector at back of room	More expensive than overhead slides	Some	Limited, usually none	Dark
Overhead	Flexible sequence; versatile (informal to formal); you can write and face audience	Slightly awkward to manipulate; projector clumsy, may block view	Some	Possible	Dim

Nonprojection visuals

Charts	Room brighter; less likely to break down	Clumsy to transport	A lot	Possible	Bright
Boards	Room brighter; may be more spontaneous	Back to audience when you write	A lot	Possible	Bright

audience. A final advantage is that the projector sits in the back of the room, not blocking anyone's view.

The main disadvantage of slides is the need for a darkened room, which decreases your interaction with your audience. Some new slide projectors, however, work in lighter rooms. Slides are also generally—but not always—more time-consuming and expensive to produce than overhead transparencies.

The most popular size for slides is the 135 slide, usually called the 35-mm slide. Other sizes include the "super slide," for extremely large images, and the less expensive, lesser-quality 126 slide, for small images. Slide projectors include a carousel on top in which you load the slides. They may also include a zoom lens, which allows you to vary your projected image without having to move your projector. This feature is important if you make presentations in rooms of various sizes. Another possible feature is the remote-control unit (either with or without wires), which you use to advance, reverse, and focus the slides. A remote control is essential if you're speaking without an assistant. During your presentation, you should be standing next to the screen, not by the projector. A host of other features are available for more extravagant slide presentations.

OVERHEADS: Overhead transparencies (sometimes called *acetates* or *foils*) are much more popular in business presentations. The equipment consists of the transparencies and the projector. The transparencies are usually eight-by-ten-inch acetate sheets, often mounted in a plastic or paperboard frame. If you are only going to write on them as you speak, you might use a continuous roll of acetate instead of individual transparencies. To write on the acetate, you also need grease pencils or an acetate marker; regular marking pens won't work. The projectors come in two varieties. The common overhead projector uses the acetate sheets. The less common opaque projector is much bigger, and projects solid paper, such as books, magazines, or brochures. Since the opaque projector is so bulky, use it sparingly.

The main advantage of overheads is their versatility. You can use them informally, writing directly onto the acetate sheet as you face your audience. You can use them semiformally, highlighting or adding information on a partially prepared transparency. Or you can prepare more formal transparencies from computer-generated type, from dry-transfer type, or from other printed type run through either a special copying machine or a special transparency machine. Overhead transparencies are also easy to use. During your presentation, you place the transparency on the illuminated glass surface of the projector, positioned so that you can read it (not upside down or backwards). You can also use overlay transparencies of additional material, or use a cover-up mask to disclose information progressively.

Overheads also have their drawbacks. They are more awkward to change than slides; you must quickly change them yourself or have an assistant do so, whereas you can change two slides instantaneously. Another drawback is the size of the transparencies. At eight by ten inches, they are many times larger than a two-by-two-inch slide, so they take up more storage space. The main disadvantage is the projector itself. Unlike other projectors, the overhead projector sits up front—possibly blocking someone's view. For formal presentations, if you don't have to write as you speak, consider slides instead of overheads—especially if you have access to a machine that doesn't require a darkened room.

Nonprojection visuals

Other visual aids do not involve projection: charts, boards, and handouts.

CHARTS: Various kinds of charts include: flip charts, cardboard charts, and desk-top charts. Chart equipment is far less complex than projection equipment since no electricity or wires are involved. A flip chart comprises a pad or series of pieces of paper, a stand, and markers. The flip-chart paper may be flipped over the stand, or ripped off and attached to the wall. A cardboard chart stands alone because it is printed on sturdy cardboard. It may be any size you wish. You need, however, a board chalk ledge or some other way to stand it up. A desk-top chart is like a miniature flip chart. This kind of chart is appropriate only when you are presenting to a very small number of people.

The main advantage of all these charts over all projections is the lighting: you can keep the room well illuminated and keep eye contact with your audience—whether you're showing formal charts prepared in advance, or informal charts prepared during the presentation. Another advantage of charts is their lack of technology. They have no electrical parts that might break down. The disadvantage of charts is their size. They are quite clumsy to transport.

If you are using flip charts, here are a few tips to keep in mind. Remember that most paper is so thin your audience can see through it. Therefore, leave a blank piece beneath each page you have written on. You may also need to leave blank sheets if you have times during your presentation you don't want any chart showing.

BOARDS: Boards, like charts, have the advantage of being used in bright light; they often elicit the most audience interaction; and they are often the most spontaneous and flexible of any kind of equipment. Their main disadvantage is that your back is usually turned toward your audience as you write. (You face the audience when you write on an overhead-projector transparency.)

Boards come in two varieties. Chalkboards are the familiar green or black boards you see in classrooms. The chalk is usually yellow or white, although some presenters use colored chalks effectively. On blackboards, yellow chalk shows up better than white. Plastic boards are more common in business than in schools. They are made of white plastic, with specially made colored markers. They have all the advantages of a chalkboard, without the disadvantage of possibly getting chalk dust all over your three-piece suit (or, indeed, even your two-piece suit). Regardless of the kind of board you use, always find out before you begin how large it is, and how to erase it (the plastic boards take special erasers).

HANDOUTS: Handouts are the final kind of visual aid. Handouts have one enormous advantage over the other kinds of visual aids: they provide copy your audience members can take away with them. They have a huge disadvantage as well: you cannot control your audience's reading ahead of you. To overcome that disadvantage, use handouts only in these four ways. First, give summary handouts only at the end of the presentation, or your audience will read ahead. Second, use handouts for the very detailed data your audience must see, but which are too complex to put on a slide or chart. Give these complex-data handouts only when you get to the point in your presentation when you are discussing them. Third, avoid passing around a single copy of a handout, so that people are seeing it at different times. Finally, some presenters use handouts to encourage people to take notes. Since you'll obviously give note-taking handouts at the beginning of the presentation, be sure they are vague and general enough so people won't be reading them. An agenda or outline—with plenty of blank space around each item—serves as an effective note-taking handout.

Use Your Visuals Effectively.

All the work you put in on composing and selecting your visual aids will be wasted unless you use them effectively during the presentation. You don't want to spoil the effect of your aids—not to mention your entire presentation—by a ragged performance along the lines of: "How do you turn this thing on?" or "Whoops! Just a minute while I get this set up" or "Sorry about that; I guess the slide is upside down." Practicing with your visuals means that (l) with *all* visuals, you become familiar with your equipment and integrate what you say with what you show, and (2) with *some* visuals, you use special techniques.

General techniques
for all visuals

"Become familiar with your equipment." That advice sounds so obvious, and yet many speakers have had their entire credibility and confidence undercut because a chart fell over or a projector wouldn't turn on. To practice with your equipment, then, actually flip the pages, turn on the projector, press the buttons. Make sure you know how to position the slides, insert the cassette, or write large enough. Practice with any given piece of equipment long enough so you can use it casually.

Once you know your equipment, **practice integrating** every visual smoothly into your presentation. It's hard to believe how often a presenter puts up a visual aid—and continues talking with only the faintest reference to it, leaving the audience to wonder about the visual instead of listening to the speaker. Never show a visual aid without explaining it and showing how it ties to what you are saying. Obviously, you should "walk through" each new visual with your audience as soon as you present it. For example, to "walk through" the chart shown in Figure 13.8, say: "As you can see, this chart is organized with the months across the horizontal axis and the prices along the vertical axis. As this line shows, prices have been increasing steadily over the past eight months."

Another aspect of integrating your visuals is called *metering out* information when, and only when, you want your audience to see it. Always assume the people in your audience will read whatever is in front of them, regardless of what you are saying. They can't help it; they can read faster than you can talk. So don't show them anything until you want them to see it. As examples: don't pass out a long handout at the beginning of your presentation and expect your audience not to read ahead; don't put up a slide with your conclusion visible until you want your audience to see it. With formal aids, you can use a mask (such as a piece of cardboard) to cover up information until you're ready to present it, or use a series of overlays to add information when you want to. With informal aids, write information only as you discuss it. With handouts, be particularly cautious: avoid giving out detailed handouts (perhaps all handouts except agendas) until the end of your presentation.

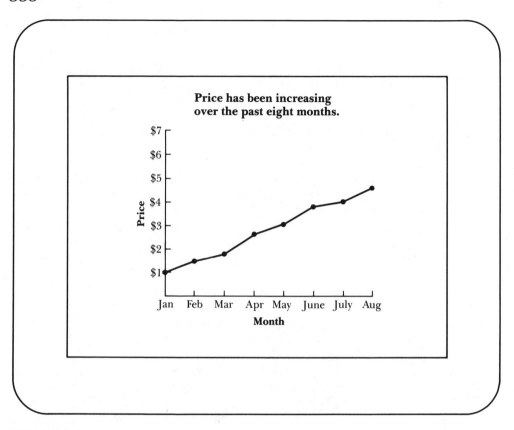

FIGURE 13.8

Effective integration: "walk through" your visual aid

Smooth integration also involves getting rid of visuals after you're through discussing them. You can easily turn off slides and erase boards. Flip charts are a bit more problematic. Decide in advance what you're going to do: detach pages to post on the wall, or flip to blank sheets in between charts. Avoid ripping off sheets and scattering them on the floor, which can look sloppy and unprofessional.

Finally, smooth integration means paying special attention to two potential delivery problems. First, speak a bit more loudly than usual, because speakers tend unknowingly to decrease their volume when they use visuals. Also, you may need to speak more loudly to compensate for the sound made by your equipment. Second, keep up your eye contact. Speakers also tend to get so engrossed with their machinery or charts that they forget to look at their audience.

Specific techniques for certain kinds of visuals

So far, we have been discussing techniques for all visuals: becoming familiar with them by practicing in advance and integrating them smoothly into your presentation by explaining them, metering them out, getting rid of them when you're no longer discussing them, and watching for potential delivery problems. You have some additional techniques to keep in mind, however, if you have chosen aids that involve writing as you speak (such as an overhead, flip chart, or board), pointing, or projecting.

Writing during the presentation. For one thing, try to avoid writing for longer than several seconds at a time. If you have to write for longer than that, either stop talking momentarily or talk twice as loud as usual when your back is to the audience. Avoid giving your audience the impression you are "confiding in the blackboard."[5] Another technique allows you to write faster during the presentation: before you speak, draw straight lines, circles, other figures, or even numbers in very faint pencil or chalk (so faint, that is, that your audience can't see them); then trace over the faint lines during the presentation.

Projecting. Each time a new projection (overhead transparency or slide) comes on the screen, check very quickly to make sure it is positioned on the screen correctly; centered, focused, and right side up. After you've checked it, turn back and talk to your audience, not to the screen. I repeat: do not talk to the screen.

Here are some added tips for overhead projections. Remember, they are right side up when you can read them while standing behind the projector. Get your first transparency in focus and position before the presentation starts. Then, simply leave it in place on the projector so that all you have to do is turn the projector on when you want to show your first visual. Finally, unless you have to write on the projector or cannot reach the screen, stand next to the screen—not the projector—and point to the screen instead of the projector. Standing next to the screen generally affords you better eye contact and enables you to avoid mumbling toward the machine, projecting on screen your quivering finger, or balancing an awkward pointer.

Pointing. Pointing is a very effective way to work with your visual. You can point to the exact place you want your audience's eyes to focus. Again, remember to keep facing your audience as you point. As Figure 13.9 shows, when pointing to a board or chart, always point with your

[5]A. Jay, *Effective Presentation* (London: British Institute of Management, Professional Publishing Ltd., 1979), p. 46. A short witty source.

When you point like this, with your "inside arm" (the one closer to the board or chart,) you can face your audience.

When you point like this, with your "outside arm" (the one farther from the board or chart), you put your shoulder or back to your audience.

FIGURE 13.9

Always point with your "inside" hand and arm

"inside" or "upstage" hand and arm—that is, the one closer to your equipment; never point with your "outside" hand and arm, because to do so you must wrap your arm around your body and put your back to the audience.

In general, do not use a pointer unless absolutely necessary—that is, when you cannot reach what you're pointing to—because pointers often cause a fidgeting problem. In the words of the speech expert Anthony Jay: "Suppress all impulses to use it as a swagger stick, conductor's baton, backscratcher, or toothpick."[6] If you do use a pointer, don't let it wander

[6]Ibid.

vaguely. Point at what you want, leave it there momentarily, then take it away.

As you can see, you have a lot to gain from using visual aids: increased impact, comprehension, and retention. To use them successfully, however, you must compose and choose them thoughtfully, and use them effectively.

REVIEW QUESTIONS

To check your understanding

1. List three reasons why you should consider using visual aids.
2. What are the three steps for choosing and using visual aids?
3. Explain the three degrees of visual aid formality.
4. How can you tell if your visual is really necessary?
5. What should word charts usually be used for?
6. What is "chartjunk"? List at least three elements of chartjunk.
7. What is the main advantage of film and videocassettes over other forms of projection?
8. What are two advantages of using 35-mm slides? Of using overhead transparencies?
9. What are four ways you can avoid having your audience read ahead of you when you use handouts?
10. What are four ways to integrate visuals into your presentation?

APPLICATION QUESTIONS

To apply your knowledge

1. Think of three presentation situations that call for different levels of formality in your visual aids. What is the basis on which your assessments are made?
2. Determine which graph form you would use to represent the following data:

a. Production levels

January	65,000
February	72,000
March	89,500
April	52,000
May	55,000
June	67,000

b. Percentage of total market

Northeast	35%
South	20%
Midwest	25%
Southwest	10%
West	10%

c. Percentage of consumers purchasing product in population groups of varying size

Hispanics	90% of 400,000 people
Asians	14% of 800,000 people
Blacks	59% of 1,200,000 people
Anglos	30% of 8,900,000 people

d. Relation of product price to volume of sales

Product A	10,000 sold at $10 each
Product B	5000 sold at $6 each
Product C	18,000 sold at $4 each
Product D	12,000 sold at $1 each

3. What is ineffective about the following visual aids?

a.

There are five steps in the manufacturing process:
1. The raw materials are selected
2. The raw materials are refined
3. The refined materials are shipped to processing plants
4. The product is processed
5. The final product is packaged

b.

What is the importance of employee satisfaction?

c.

Breakdown of employee age groups:

d.

The ratio of sugar to fruit in Pucker's jam is 50:50.

e.

Breakdown of employee age groups:

30–40-year olds
3%

20–30-year olds
30%

16–20-year olds
2%

60–65-year olds
20%

50–60-year olds
25%

4. For the amateur technician, why might video be preferable to film? Why is video better suited to the conditions of today's business world?

5. In general, what level of formality would you associate with animated projection? With slides? With overhead transparencies? Why?

6. How would you handle the distribution of handouts to a large group? A small group? Why is it important to consider distribution in integrating your visual aids?

CASES

To practice what you learned

1. You are a whiz at presentations and have been chosen to present your company's new product, a computer designed especially for children, to three different groups: an in-house sales group, potential retailers of the product, and classrooms of children at the local elementary school. The computer features a child-sized keyboard, simplified software, and graphics options with educational applications. Do the three groups call for the same level of formality? Describe the type of visual aids you would use to make your presentation interesting and informative to each group.

2. You have to prepare a presentation for new employees at your corporation—an orientation talk in which you inform them of company policy, and at the same time project a positive, upbeat image of the experiences they are likely to enjoy. The groups are usually no larger than twenty. Among the information you must impart are health-insurance benefits, the number of days off allowed each year, and the company structure—dry enough topics, but ones you feel can be made lively with the right visual aids. You have at your disposal a slide projector and an overhead projector. Which would you use? What type of images, words, charts, or graphs would you include? Explain how your choices would help you achieve an informative and emotionally stimulating presentation.

3. The presentation you have prepared about the new manufacturing equipment adopted by your company relies on video footage to illustrate its operation. The footage includes shots of workers involved in operating the machinery at each stage of production. At one of your company's branch offices, where you have flown to make your presentation, you are told that the video projector is broken. Your videocassette is useless, and you must somehow use the available overhead projector if you are to have any visual aids at all. How would you translate your video images into word charts and graphs you can use on the overhead projector? What would the focus of your revised visual aids be?

4. Your presentation concerns the business trip you made to another state to meet with company branch managers. It is an informal, in-house presentation that focuses on facts and figures. You have already determined that it would be best to use the chalkboard at the front of the room to present your data. But you feel that slides of the branch office and its personnel might relieve the tedium and add a

human dimension. What is the feasibility of using two media in a single presentation? Describe how you might integrate the two.

5. A friend has asked you to give a critique of her use of visual aids in a presentation. Her talk is about improving customer relations, and she has chosen to use cardboard charts. Graphically, they are quite sophisticated: each is in at least four colors (predominantly orange), with borders and headlines keyed to the various levels of her talk's organization (that is, her main points and supporting points). She has them on an easel at the front of the room (which seats about 250) and is careful not to stand in front of them when she talks. Each chart measures about two feet by one foot and has at least one dozen words. During a twenty-minute presentation she uses about thirty charts. What criticism do you offer?

14

Holding Meetings and Answering Questions

Holding Meetings
Participating in meetings • Chairing meetings

Answering Questions
Question-and-answer sessions •
Panel discussions • Media interviews

$\mathbf{A}$S we discussed in chapter 12, you speak to a group in business in various situations: when you are doing most of the speaking, to inform or persuade (what we called a *presentation*), when your audience is doing most of the speaking (a *meeting*), and when you have some give-and-take with your audience (*answering questions*). So far, we have been concerned primarily with presentation skills—that is, skills to help you when you are doing most of the talking. In this chapter, we'll look at the other sets of skills: (1) how to confer with your audience in meetings, and (2) how to answer questions in question-and-answer sessions, panel discussions, and media interviews.

Holding Meetings

Meetings are an extremely common form of business communication. They range from large and formal to small and informal; they include regular staff meetings, project-team meetings, special or ongoing committee meetings—any time a group of people meets to solve a problem or accomplish a task. Remember, we are defining a meeting as a chance primarily to confer with, that is, work with, your audience—as opposed to speeches or presentations, where you primarily speak to your audience.

How do you decide whether you want to impart information or to hold a meeting? In general, you should make a presentation when: (1) you have enough information and don't need any more; (2) you have the power, authority, and credibility to implement your ideas or decisions; (3) you are explaining an established policy or procedure; or (4) you are pressed for time. On the other hand, call a meeting when: (1) you need more information from other people; (2) you lack the power, authority, and credibility to implement your ideas and decisions yourself and need your audience to "buy in"; and (3) you want to increase your audience's sense of morale or participation in the decision-making process.

In reality, of course, some companies might call informational presentations "meetings." But the point is this: if you want to inform or persuade, use the skills we discussed in chapter 12; if, on the other hand, you want to confer and work with your audience, use these *meeting* skills.

If you are going to a meeting (either as the chair or as a participant), naturally you should go through the usual steps in the communication strategy. When you analyze your audience before a meeting, however, you consider not only the personalities of the people who will be attending—but also the personality of the group itself. In other words, ask yourself how the *group* functions in meetings.[1] Here are some questions you might ask: (1) What kind of atmosphere or relationships do you sense? Are people close or distant, friendly or unfriendly? (2) How much do the people participate in meetings? Equally? Some more than others? (3) How are disagreements handled in their meetings? Resolved? Brushed aside? Handled by dictate? (4) How much are feelings shared? Openly and directly? Not expressed? (5) What are the group *norms*—or unstated rules—for meetings? Do they start on time? Are the people prepared? Are they polite? By analyzing the group in advance, you can alter your style as necessary for that particular set of people.

Here are some more specific techniques to use as a participant or as a chair in a meeting. These techniques are summarized in Figure 14.1.

FIGURE 14.1

Communicating effectively in meetings

As a participant:
> Explain your ideas.
> Relate to other participants' ideas.
> Help facilitate the group process.

As a chair:
> Perform task functions
>> Prepare an agenda.
>> Decide on discussion procedure.
>> Decide on a decision-making procedure.
>
> Perform process functions
>> Encourage support, diversity, and listening.
>> Avoid one person dominating.
>> Avoid hostile conflict.

[1]A. Cohen et al., *Effective Behavior in Organizations* (Homewood, Ill.: Irwin, 1976), chapters 3–6.

Participating in meetings

As a participant in a meeting, remember that you are just that: a participant. The purpose of a meeting is to work as a group, not to force your predetermined ideas on everyone else there. Specifically, as a participant in a meeting, you have three jobs: to explain your ideas, to react to other people's ideas, and to help the chair keep the process going.

First, when you **explain** your own ideas in a meeting, you usually do so in a quicker and less formal manner than you would in a presentation. For one thing, your structure is different in a meeting: you don't need a "grabber" because people are involved already and know the importance of the subject; usually, you make no more than one or two main points, because you want to give the others the best chance to react; and you don't need a formal closing. Also, your delivery is less formal: usually you won't stand up, and you will have more eye contact and pause more often to increase your interaction with your audience. In fact—unless you have been asked to give a formal report or to present detailed information—you usually won't talk for more than about five minutes at a time.

Not only do you speak for less time and less formally, you should speak only when appropriate. Stick to the agenda and don't bring up extraneous ideas. Also, don't bring up ideas at the wrong time during the meeting. You may find it helpful to keep in mind what one expert calls the four phases of a meeting: (1) "orientation" to the problem or issues at hand, (2) "conflict" over various possibilities or solutions, (3) "emergence" of the group's solution, and (4) "reinforcement" or implementation plan for the solution.[2] Therefore, for example, don't start questioning the solution all over again after the group has already agreed to implement it.

Second, as a meeting participant you should not only explain your own ideas, but also **relate** to the other participants' ideas. In fact, most of your time at a meeting should be devoted to interacting with others, not to presenting your own views. Use the listening skills discussed in chapter 6 to make sure you understand. Once you've understood, if you agree, you might supply supporting material such as examples, statistics, or applications of the idea. If you disagree, state your disagreements carefully. You can avoid humiliating people and putting them on the defensive by disagreeing with their idea—not with them as people. Say, for example, "That project may be very time-consuming" instead of "George's suggested project will take too long!" Say "The wording of that sentence is

---

[2]B. Fisher, quoted in E. Skopec, *Business and Professional Speaking* (Englewood Cliffs, N.J.: Prentice-Hall, 1983), p. 229. I am indebted to this book, and to A. Thrash, A. Shelby, and J. Tarver, *Speaking Up Successfully* (New York: Holt, Rinehart & Winston, 1984), for many ideas on meetings.

unclear" instead of "Martha's sentence is unclear." Disagree by saying "I'm not comfortable with" or "I'm worried about" instead of "I disagree with."

Third, a participant should help the chairperson **facilitate** the group's process. Of course, that doesn't mean you should start running the meeting. Instead, you might help the chairperson stay on the agenda. You could say, for example, "It seems to me we've covered this topic fairly well now. If the rest of you agree, perhaps we can wrap this item up with a decision now." Or "It looks as if we need more information before we can resolve this item. May I suggest we table this discussion until our next meeting?" You can also assist with the process by encouraging people to participate, not disrupt. For example, you might ask, "James, what was your group's experience with the Consolidated Microchip Computer?"

Chairing meetings

Chairing a meeting involves two very different kinds of skills. One set of skills has to do with the *task*—that is, the goal at hand. The other set of skills is usually referred to as running the *process*—that is, getting people to participate. Experts in meeting management disagree on whether it is possible for one person to fulfill both the task and the process functions. The traditional view is that it can be done, but many contemporary experts suggest separation of the roles. They feel that one person—usually called a *facilitator* instead of a chairperson or leader—should run the process, and should be concerned only with keeping things running smoothly. Let's take a look at the task and the process responsibilities; then, you can decide for yourself the situations where you can handle both and the situations where you should handle one only.

TASK FUNCTIONS: The task functions for the leader to take care of include: deciding what tasks you are going to try to accomplish, deciding how you are going to discuss issues, and deciding how you are going to reach a decision.

To decide what tasks will be covered, the chair must prepare an **agenda**. An agenda is not like a shopping list—everything you can think of off the top of your head. Instead, the agenda is a written plan for what you want to accomplish at the meeting. Here are some considerations to keep in mind as you prepare the agenda.

First, think about timing. Almost all the experts agree that meetings should not run over two hours. For example, as Anthony Jay states in the *Harvard Business Review*: "Very few business meetings achieve anything of value after two hours, and an hour and a half is enough time to allocate for most purposes."[3] Therefore, include both the scheduled finishing time as well as the starting time. Besides delineating the time for the meeting, remember the Audience Memory Curve (see chapters 5 and 12): put important ideas first on the agenda (when people are most more likely to be lively and creative) or last (if their interest in that item will hold them through the meeting)—not "buried" in the middle. To avoid spending too much time on trivial items, budget tentative times for each item on the agenda. If your meetings tend to drag on, start them one hour before lunch or one hour before the end of the work day.

Second, think about the content of agenda items. Include only those items that are consistent with the task or tasks you are trying to accomplish. If you solicit and include agenda items from the other people in advance, you will not only increase their sense of participation, but will also avoid having them enter the meeting with *hidden agendas*. Differentiate the goals for the various agenda items: "for your information" for announcements or short reports given during the meeting, "for discussion" for items you want to talk about without reaching a decision, and "for a decision" for items you want to resolve. Word agenda items "for a decision" as neutrally as you can—not as an argument for the solution you prefer. Finally, avoid listing "any other business" at the end: this is an invitation to waste time.

Third, consider how the agenda might be used in advance. If—after all—the primary purpose of a meeting is to solicit other people's ideas, you'll get much better responses if they can think about the ideas before the meeting. As a general rule, distribute agendas two or three days in advance. Then, participants will have enough time to prepare, but (we hope!) will be less likely to lose or forget about the agenda than if they receive it too far in advance. If you include names of people in charge of certain sections, other participants can volunteer information to those people before the meeting. If you include references to source materials or reports, participants can read them before the meeting, and perhaps bring them along.

Besides coming up with an agenda of tasks, the chair decides how the group will **discuss** each issue he or she wants the group to reach a decision about.

One discussion procedure is called the *reflective thinking model* or the *problem solving model*.[4] In this process, the group: (1) defines the problem

---

[3]A. Jay, "How to Run a Meeting," *Harvard Business Review* (March–April 1976), p. 50. Reprinted by permission of the *Harvard Business Review*. Copyright © 1976 by the President and Fellows of Harvard College; all rights reserved.

[4]J. Dewey, *How We Think* (Boston: Heath, 1910). An old classic that has had enormous impact on scholarship in thinking and communicating.

specifically; (2) analyzes the problem—looks at information, policies, the organizational schemes, the data; (3) determines standards or criteria by which it will measure any solution; (4) lists possible solutions; (5) selects the best solution; and (6) decides how to implement the solution.

Another procedure is called the *nominal group model*.[5] This is an unusual, but increasingly popular, way of making sure everyone at the meeting participates. In this procedure, each participant lists his or her ideas *independently*, not talking with other group members. Then, as a group, the participants compile a separate list, recording one item from each person's list until all are included. They then revise this group list, rewording, combining, and avoiding duplicates. Next, again independently, each person orders the master list. Finally, as a group, they collate these orderings.

A third decision-making process is called *brainstorming*. The most important key to success in a brainstorming session is to divide the session into two distinct stages. During stage one, you simply record ideas—not evaluating, reacting to, or deciding on any of them. Everyone blurts out any and every association that comes to mind. No one is allowed to criticize or evaluate the ideas. It is very important to record every single idea as it is stated. Usually, this recording is done on flip charts or the blackboard. During stage two, the group reviews the list of ideas, grouping related ideas and striking irrelevant ones. From this more organized list, the group can work on reaching a decision.

This brings us to the final set of task decisions: how you will resolve or **decide** the issues you have discussed. After the discussion is over, how will you decide what to do?

One option is a decision made by one person—either the chairperson or the person "in charge." With this option, the purpose of the group is to serve as an advisory board. The participants must be informed in advance about who will be making the final decision so they won't expect to be voting, but merely advising.

A second—and probably the most familiar—option is decision by majority rule. According to parliamentary procedure, a decision or resolution is offered in the form of a motion, such as "I move that we purchase the Consolidated Microchip Copying Machine." Another person must *second* the motion. Participants cannot ignore a motion: they may debate it, amend it, or vote on it. To debate the motion, participants are limited to discussing ideas relevant to the motion only. To amend the motion, a participant could say, for example: "I move to amend the motion by adding the words 'provided the total cost does not exceed $3000.' " (If the

[5]Cited in Skopec, *Business and Professional Speaking*, p. 140.

amendment is seconded, the amendment is voted on before the original motion.)

In addition to these kinds of content motions, parliamentary procedure includes various procedural motions. For example, you can make a motion to curtail debate, to set a motion aside, or to clarify a procedure. Each procedure is slightly different: some require a second, some do not; some are debatable; some are amendable; for some, you say "move *to*," for others "move *a*"; some need a majority to pass, others two thirds. Table 14.1 summarizes the various parliamentary motions.

Both one-person decision and majority rule are especially useful when the decision is not all that important or when there are severe time pressures. The problem with these ways of making group decisions is that some people may feel left out, ignored, or defeated. The third and fourth options for decision-making—consensus and unanimity—may be more appropriate when a decision is very important or when you need everyone's support to implement it.

The third option—one that is becoming increasingly popular in business meetings—is decision by consensus. Consensus develops when the group reaches a decision that may not be everybody's first choice, but that each person is willing to agree to and implement. Consensus usually involves hearing all points of view and incorporating these viewpoints into the solution. Also, consensus is usually not reached by vote, but rather by agreement. For example, the chairperson might ask all participants: "Do you feel comfortable with this solution?" Or, if one person seems to be the lone holdout for a position, "Well, Dave, we understand your argument clearly, but the rest of us don't want that solution. Can you live with this one instead?"

The final option—unanimity—is very rarely used in business meetings. Unanimity means that the decision is the first choice of everyone present—unlike the compromise implied by consensus. Unanimity, therefore, gives each participant veto power and may drag on the decision-making. It is appropriate only in extremely important decisions or when everyone shares a faith and commitment in the possibility of unanimity working.[6]

After the group reaches a decision, the chair should see to it that the group defines how the decision will be implemented. The group should list very specifically what has to be done, who will do it, and when it is to be done. If the "when" step is too far in the future, you may want to set up interim dates for progress reports.

---

[6]See, for example, M. Sheeran, *Beyond Majority Rule* (Philadelphia: Philadelphia Yearly Meeting, 1981).

TABLE 14.1

Parliamentary procedure

If you want to:	You can:	Requires a second?	Debatable?	Amendable?	Vote
Content motions					
Suggest an action	"Move to do X"	Yes	Yes	Yes	Majority
Amend the motion (= first-degree amendment)	"Move to amend the motion by substituting or adding Y"	Yes	Yes	Yes	Majority*
Amend the amendment (= second-degree amendment)	"Move to substitute Z for Y"	Yes	Yes	No	Majority**
Procedural motions					
Curtail debate	"Move to limit debate to X minutes"	Yes	Yes (only on amount of time)	Yes	Two-thirds
	"Move to call for the question" (ask for a vote now)	Yes	No	No	Two-thirds
	"Move to adjourn"	Yes	No	No	Majority
Put a motion aside	"Move to table" (put aside until recalled, maybe forever)	Yes	No	No	Majority
	"Move to postpone definitely" (put aside for a specific time) or "Postpone definitely"	Yes	Yes (on how long to postpone)	Yes	Majority

		Requires			
If you want to:	*You can:*	*a second?*	*Debatable?*	*Amendable?*	*Vote*
	"Move to refer to committee"	Yes	Yes (on merit of referral)	Yes	Majority
	"Move to withdraw" (only if *you* made original motion)	No	No	No	No
Clarify procedure	"Move a point of order" (question if correct procedure is being followed)	No	No	No	No
	"Move a point of parliamentary inquiry" (ask for correct procedure)	No	No	No	No
Ask a question or	"Move a point of information"	No	No	No	No
Make a personal observation	"Move a point of personal privilege" (make an observation not germane to motion)	No	No	No	No
Revote on a motion already passed or defeated	"Move to reconsider" (applies only to motions voted on in *same* meeting)	Yes	Yes	No	Majority

(Continued)

<table>
<tr><td colspan="6">

TABLE 14.1 *(Continued)*

</td></tr>
</table>

If you want to:	*You can:*	*Requires a second?*	*Debatable?*	*Amendable?*	*Vote*
	"Move to rescind" (applies only to motions voted on in earlier meetings)	Yes	Yes	Yes	Majority

*Vote taken on first-degree amendment before vote taken on motion.
**Vote taken on second-degree amendment before vote taken on first-degree amendment.

To repeat, the three task functions are preparing the agenda, deciding how you are going to discuss issues, and deciding how you are going to reach a decision. These task functions are concerned with reaching decisions on accomplishing your goal.

PROCESS FUNCTIONS: The process functions, on the other hand, are concerned only with making sure everyone participates. Fulfilling the following three process functions should help you meet that goal.

To do a good job at facilitating the group process, **encourage support**, diversity, and listening. Remember that supporting others' right to speak does not necessarily mean you agree with them. Instead, it means you respect them, accept them, and allow them to express their opinions. Responses that might show your support include: "That idea shows a lot of thought. What do the rest of you think?" or "Let's consider what Kathy has just recommended." Responses that do not show your support for someone's right to speak, on the other hand, include: "I disagree" or "That's wrong, because. . . "

Also, keep in mind that a good facilitator encourages diversity of opinions. A group can make better decisions if it has a wider range of options. You'll never discover that range if everyone agrees with one another all the time. Some experts even claim that groups make better decisions when there is more diversity.

Along with encouraging support and diversity, you can encourage participation by using the listening skills we discussed in chapter 6. For example, ask open-ended questions, questions that cannot be answered yes or no. You would be more likely to increase participation if you asked: "What do you think of this idea?" than "Do you like this idea?"

A second process function is to **avoid dominance** by any one person—you or someone else. To control yourself, avoid interrupting; don't talk for more than a couple of minutes; keep asking the other people to contribute; ask someone else to present background information; and hold your opinions until the end. To control others—especially those with high status or authority who tend to talk too much and interrupt more often—avoid a direct confrontation in front of the group. Instead, try talking to the person outside the meeting. If that doesn't work, try non-verbal signs—such as attention and visible signs of approval to other people trying to get a word in. As a next step, try a tactful but firm interruption, such as "Excuse me, Elenora, but we need to keep our remarks brief so everyone has the chance to talk" or "That's a good point, Nick. I'd like to hear what the others here think of it." Another technique is to place the disrupter at your side, rather than across from you, and call on him or her minimally. Finally, you might try giving the disrupter a job to do—keeping the minutes, chairing a subcommittee. Often, these people are looking for some kind of status or recognition. You can channel their energy for the good of the group.

The final process function is to **avoid hostile conflict** among group members. Conflict of ideas is healthy in groups; conflict of personalities is not. If this latter kind of conflict arises, you should summarize or para-phrase the different viewpoints, emphasizing the places where people agree. Also, be sure to keep the discussion centered on ideas, not on attacking people. Instead of asking other participants to choose sides, try to work toward a solution that allows all sides to win and maintain their pride.

Answering Questions

Various situations in which you must answer specific audience questions are also common in business. In this section, we will look at some tech-niques for doing so. First, we will consider a very common situation, the question-and-answer period often included in business presentations. Then, we will turn to two other question-and-answer situations: panel discussions and media interviews.

Question-and-answer sessions

Sometimes speeches or presentations include some give-and-take between speakers and their audiences by means of question-and-answer periods. Some people are more comfortable with a question-and-answer format than a straight presentation format. If you are, and if you have the freedom to structure the talk as you like, integrate as much question-and-answer as possible—keeping in mind the risks of tangential discussion. Other people are more comfortable with less audience questioning. If you are, you might choose to limit question-and-answer periods. You will not, however, be able to avoid them entirely. Many times the format will be set for you; many times you will get asked questions even if you don't want them. So, whatever format you feel most comfortable with, consider these three issues: (1) when to take questions, (2) how to take questions, and (3) how to deal with difficult questions.

WHEN: You should definitely control the issue of when to take questions. Do not let your audience overrun your presentation with too many questions; on the other hand, do not make them hold back unnecessarily if they do not understand a key point. Make your stance clear from the start. Say, for example, "Please feel free to ask questions as they come up," or "Please hold all your questions until the end of the presentation," or "Feel free to interrupt with questions of understanding or clarification, but, since we only have an hour together, please hold questions of debate or discussion until the end."

Unless, of course, your format is already set for you (you might be told, for instance, "We always have a fifteen-minute question-and-answer period following each presentation"), consider these advantages and disadvantages when you decide whether to take questions during or after your presentation.

If you take questions **during** the presentation, the questions will be more meaningful to the questioner, the feedback will be more immediate to you, and your audience may listen more actively. On the other hand, questions during the presentation can upset your schedule, waste time, and introduce information prematurely. To alleviate these problems: (1) allow extra time for questions, (2) control digressions, and (3) make it clear you will discuss an issue later rather than introduce it prematurely.

If, on the other hand, you take questions **after** the presentation, you will control the schedule and the flow of information, although you risk losing people's attention and even comprehension if they cannot interrupt with their questions. Since audiences tend to remember the most from the beginning and the end of a presentation, however, having

"Q-and-A" last places undue emphasis on the question period. To alleviate this problem, save time for a two- to three-minute summary after the question period.

HOW: Once you've established when to take questions, prepare yourself for how to take questions. Before questions even come up, you can prepare yourself by controlling your attitude. Avoid a defensive attitude. Instead, think of it as a compliment that your listeners are interested enough to ask for clarification, amplification, or justification. Put yourself in their shoes. They probably see themselves as reasonable or curious, not as hostile or villainous. You can also prepare by anticipating possible questions. Try to guess what the questions will be. Bring along extra information—for example, an extra slide with additional data—just in case they ask for it. Another way to anticipate questions is to ask a colleague to play devil's advocate during your rehearsal.

During the session itself, keep everyone involved by calling on people from locations throughout the audience. Once someone asks a question, be sure you understand it before you answer. Paraphrase complicated questions to make sure you're on the right track. If the group is large, paraphrase or repeat all questions to be sure everyone in the audience hears them. Then, decide how to answer, always keeping your communication objective in mind. Try to divert the question back to your main ideas. Even if you know a lot of information for your answer, limit yourself to that which advances your objective.

Based on your communication objective, then, answer the question. What if someone asks a question you don't understand? Say "I'm sorry. I don't understand the question," not "Your question isn't clear." What if someone asks a question you had planned to cover later in your talk? Make it clear you will get to that point later instead of divulging information prematurely. What if someone asks a question to which you cannot think of an answer? In those cases, try one of these five methods to buy time: (1) Repeat by saying: "You're wondering how to deal with this situation." (2) Turn around: "How would *you* deal with this situation?" (3) Turn outward: "How would the rest of you deal with this situation?" (4) Reflect: "Good question. Let's think about that for a few moments" or (5) Write: If you are using a suitable visual aid, write down the main point of the question as you think. What about a question to which you are positive you just don't know the answer? Simply admit you don't know, rather than trying to bluff. Better yet, tell the questioner exactly how and when he or she can get the answers.

When you answer questions, avoid getting into a one-to-one conversation with a single member of the audience. Therefore, unless someone looks extremely confused, avoid asking for approval of your answer, such as "Does that answer your question?" Remember to maintain eye contact with the entire audience, not just the person who asked the question. Also avoid ending your answer by looking right at the questioner: he or she may feel invited to ask another question.

DIFFICULT QUESTIONERS: Although most people will be genuinely interested in understanding or reacting to your presentation, you may occasionally encounter difficult questioners—people trying to show off, gain control, and so forth. In these difficult situations, you want to appear friendly and professional. If you lose your temper or become sarcastic, you risk losing credibility with the rest of the audience as they watch the exchange—as well as with the person asking the irritating questions. Here are some types to watch for and some possible strategies for answering them.

The first step in answering difficult questions is to compliment the questioner. For example, say "Good question. Let's explore that in more detail after the presentation is over" or "That's an interesting point. I wish we had more time to discuss it."

The second step is to divert the question. Here are five types of distressing questioners, and ways to divert their questions back onto your track. (1) Show-offs who want to talk: control their answer time or invite them to talk after the presentation. (2) Hotshots who ask loaded questions: ask how they would answer the question. (3) Gossips who ask personal questions: make the irrelevance clear; don't answer, or answer in general, impersonal terms. (4) Windbags who ask long, rambling questions: paraphrase to shorten the question, then answer, or invite them to talk after the presentation. (5) Controllers who ask questions that focus on their own interests only: direct your answer back to your communication objective.

In addition to difficult questioners with hidden agendas, beware of unfair questions. One of the most common unfair questions is known as the *loaded preface*—a damaging preamble to the question. For example, "The widget business is under suspicion in many quarters for price fixing and bribery. Ms. Biz, can you tell us what it's like to be one of the few women in this industry?" The question here deals with women in the industry, not price fixing and bribery. Ms. Biz should not let that loaded preface stand unchallenged; her failure to refute it would imply consent. She should either disagree with the preface or acknowledge that some people may feel that way, then answer the question.

Another example of an unfair question is known as the *either/or* question. Here, the questioner poses two unacceptable alternatives: "Mr.

Biz, you are one of the few minority employees at Widget, Inc. Is this due to discrimination or to poor recruiting?" Mr. Biz should refuse to choose either of the two alternatives if they are both unacceptable.

Two other unfair questions involve unfair speculation. The *what if* question asks a question based on something that hasn't happened yet. For example, "I know it hasn't been announced officially yet, but what will you do if the benefits package is changed?" The *irrelevant* question asks you about material totally unrelated to the subject you are discussing. For example, following a presentation on several legal matters influencing your business, you are asked about your views on legalizing marijuana. If asked either type of question, refuse to answer, making the irrelevance clear.

Another unfair question involves a *false relationship*—assumption that because an event precedes an outcome, it necessarily caused it. For example, "Mail delivery has been slower since you were hired here. Would you care to comment on this?" Beware of such false relationships and don't let them go unchallenged.

A final example of an unfair question to be aware of is the *popular prejudice*. Here the questioner appeals to a popular idea, rather than addressing the topic at hand. For example, "Don't you think it's un-American for Congress to bail out Widget, Inc.?" Try to define or challenge expressions such as *un-American* and *bail out* before moving on to your answer.

Remember that although you may occasionally run into unfair questions, most question-and-answer sessions are friendly exchanges. If you analyze when and how to take questions and remain graceful when answering them, the sessions should be mutually beneficial and satisfying experiences.

Panel discussions

Sometimes, the business situation calls for a series of speakers to answer questions in a panel discussion. For example, if a subject is too complex for one person to handle, a panel may be convened so a group of specialists can speak. Or perhaps the audience needs to be introduced or exposed to various people or viewpoints at the same session.

Panel discussions, however, differ from team presentations. Their purposes are different. In a team presentation, the group presents an agreed-upon view; in a panel discussion, the purpose is to present differing views. Also, in team presentations, usually speakers stand as they speak; in panel discussions, usually speakers sit the whole time. More important, in team presentations, the team members work together to create and coordinate the presentation, and simply divide up who says what. In panel discussions, on the other hand, each speaker prepares separately. The other speakers hear one another for the first time at the session itself.

Technically, a *panel discussion* consists of questions and answers only, and a *symposium* consists of a series of prepared speeches, followed by questions and answers. You'll probably find, however, that people in business use the two terms interchangeably. It doesn't really matter, after all, what the session is called as long as you make sure you understand in advance what it will consist of.

If you are asked to **sit** on a panel, first find out if you are expected to give a short speech or to answer questions only. When you know what you're supposed to do, follow the guidelines discussed in chapter 12 on speeches or in the preceding pages on question and answer sessions.

If you are asked to **chair** a panel, you will have a different set of responsibilities. Before the session, the chair must see to it that the participants agree on: the purpose of the panel, the roles each participant will take, and the length of the session. As the chair, you should make clear to each participant what to cover, when to speak, how long to speak, and when it is appropriate or inappropriate to comment on other participants' ideas.

Your second obligation as chair is to introduce the panel members. As we discussed in the section on speaker introductions in chapter 12, you should welcome the audience and identify the subject and its importance. To introduce each panel member, you might introduce each person right before he or she speaks. Or, you might introduce everyone on the panel at once, at the beginning of the discussion.

During the session, the chair must monitor time and manage questions. If each participant is making a speech for a set period of time, the chair should signal the speaker at the "one minute to go" mark and at the "stop" mark. If a speaker goes more than a minute or two overtime, the chair should interrupt as gracefully as possible along the lines of: "Sorry to have to cut in, John, but we have to get on to the next speaker now." If the participants are answering questions from the floor, the chair must make sure that one speaker does not dominate. To do so, you might call on panelists to answer in different orders (not always the same person first), direct certain questions to certain panelists, or see to it that other panelists get a chance to answer the same question if they wish to.

Finally, at the end of the panel discussion, the chair should summarize the discussion and thank the panel members.

Media interviews

A final example of a business situation where you answer questions is dealing with the press. If you wonder why media interviews should be covered in a chapter on speaking with a group, remember that media interviews are not aimed at just one person (the reporter); they are also aimed at the reporter's listeners or readers.

Fifty years ago, a business person was unlikely to have to deal with the media. Today, however, business is news. The public is interested in topics such as the environment, consumerism, and the economy. Therefore, dealing with the press is a communication skill many business people must consider—not simply a matter to leave to the public relations office. Media interview skills include: anticipating questions, planning responses, analyzing your two audiences, stating points emphatically, and using good nonverbal communication.[7]

ANTICIPATE QUESTIONS: The first step in preparing for a media interview is to anticipate questions. To do so, first discover whatever you can from the reporter about what you will be discussing. If you are called on the phone, you can ask what the interviewer will cover and whether you might call back later. If you are speaking on a talk show, you might ask what areas you will be discussing. Do not expect reporters to give you a list of questions written out in advance. Usually, however, they are willing to let you know the general topics of discussion.

Perhaps even more important than eliciting clues from reporters or their staff is to brainstorm possible questions. If you were the reporter, what would you ask? If you read that newspaper or journal or listened to that program, what would you be interested in hearing about? Anticipate questions. Ask colleagues and potential audience members to anticipate questions.

As a part of your brainstorming, be sure to prepare for attacks. Imagine the worst. List all possible problem questions.

PLAN YOUR RESPONSE: After you have analyzed what you are likely to be asked, analyze the interview from the opposite point of view: plan your response. Think about the main messages you hope to get across and about the details that will support your main points. Give the

---

[7]Much of the information on media interviews is based on M. Munter, "How to Conduct a Successful Media Interview," *California Management Review*, 25 (Summer 1983), 143–150. See also J. Hilton and M. Knoblauch, *On Television! A Survival Guide for Media Interviews* (New York: AMACOM, 1980).

reporter some news. Think of ideas that will interest, benefit, or appeal to your audience. Plan what you want to say.

Structure your main ideas into effective answers for ready use. This means short, crisp statements. If you are being quoted in an article or on a film clip, the reporter will need short statements, usually no longer than eighty-five words. If you are on a talk show, you will want to repeat your short statements throughout.

In addition to structuring some snappy statements that advocate your main ideas, research some facts that will make your interview interesting. Two useful methods for adding interest are statistics and anecdotes.

Use three rules of thumb to make your statistics effective. First, they should be easy to grasp: "The latest Gallup poll shows that 78 percent of Americans agree with me on this issue." Second, they should relate to your audience's interest: "This system will save the consumer forty-two dollars a year." Third, they should show broad trends: "Five years ago, we spent $7000 on safety controls; this year, we are spending $525,000 on those controls." Make sure your statistics are not too complex (note that figures a reader can study may be too complicated for a listener to follow), and do not use more than two statistics per sentence. Say "60 percent are for the bill, 10 percent against," not "60 percent are for the bill, including 75 percent of the city dwellers and 33 percent of the women, and 10 percent oppose it if services are cut more than 50 percent."

In addition to appropriate statistics, come up with some anecdotes (stories). In your business courses, you may have been trained to trust only the statistically significant; readers or listeners, on the other hand, may be persuaded by the individual or specific.

ANALYZE TWO AUDIENCES: One of the problems associated with media interviews is that you are dealing with two audiences: the reporter and his or her listeners or readers. You must analyze two audiences.

Many business people assume the reporter will be hostile. This stereotype of Evil Media is just as unfair as the oft-bemoaned stereotype of the Evil Business. Instead of concentrating on negative prejudgments of the media, try to enter the interview with a sound attitude.

Consider, first, reporters in general. Most of them are serious, hardworking professionals, just like you. Their job is to find newsworthy stories that will interest their audience. They are under time pressures (meeting deadlines), commercial pressures (increasing advertising revenues), and competitive pressures (scooping their rivals). They must compress what you say to fit space or airtime. They want to come up with something arousing and engaging.

Consider also the individual reporters. What do they know about you? What do you represent to them? How do they perceive your expertise? What do you know about their age, training, and background? What are their opinions and interests? What are they likely to agree with? To disagree with? Are they expert business reporters, or general reporters for whom you may have to simplify and define terms?

Next, consider your second audience: the readers or listeners. Who are they? Middle America watching a general talk show or specialists reading a technical journal? What do they know about you, your topic, and your relationship to your topic? Once you have established their level of expertise, be sure to talk in terms they will understand. Unless you are dealing with colleagues or specialists, avoid business jargon or any terms your audience might not understand. Instead of saying, "The BOD recommended product resegmentation to improve the ROI," you might say, "The board of directors recommended we sell different products in order to increase our profits."

Finally, as in any communication, tie your remarks to your readers' or listeners' benefits. Why should they read or listen to what you have to say? If possible, tie your message to their needs. Solve problems your audience might be facing.

One of the most prevalent problems business people have with the media is their inability to get across what they want to say. They simply react to the reporter's questions. In the words of Chester Burger, "They fail to make the points they wanted to make, and then they blame the reporter. Usually, it is their own fault. They have been playing what is called the 'ping-pong game.' The reporter asks a question; they answer it. He asks another; they answer it. Back and forth the ball bounces but the executive does not know how to squeeze in what he regards as *his* important points."[8]

STATE YOUR MAIN POINTS: To overcome this problem, state your main points emphatically. In media interviews, you have good reason for a direct approach: the ends of your statements may very well be cut, either by the writer or by the film editor. Think of your statement as an inverted funnel: put your major point at the top, and your amplification further down because chances are it won't be used.

You must be concise. News—especially on television—is a headline medium. In a presentation, you may have thirty to sixty minutes to present your point in twenty to thirty seconds. Practice stating your main points with a timer. Make your points emphatic by providing the film or

[8]C. Burger, "How to Meet the Press," *Harvard Business Review*, 53 (July–August 1975), 65. Reprinted by permission of the *Harvard Business Review*. Copyright © 1975 by the President and Fellows of Harvard College; all rights reserved.

print editors with clear transitions, or *flags*, such as "The most important point is. . ."

In some instances, you may feel it is inappropriate to answer a question. Unless you are a highly skilled politico, never, never answer "off the record." Some reporters won't respect their promises; others may include the quote without your name; at the very least, the information will be planted in the reporter's mind. Therefore, if you do not wish to answer, try "I'd rather not answer that question" instead of the brusque "No comment." Better yet, if possible, explain why you would rather not answer.

In other cases, you may not be able to respond because you don't know the answer. In these instances, never hazard a guess. Never lie. Instead, tell the reporter where to get the answer, or, better yet, offer to get the answer yourself.

USE GOOD NONVERBAL COMMUNICATION: Using good nonverbal communication is, of course, an important aspect of media interviews. Remember that when you are on television, your audience is likely to remember how you appear longer than they remember what you say. If you are talking on the radio or by phone, your voice can be equally important. Even in media situations where you will hear or read your quotes only through the reporter, how you look and sound can have an important impact on him or her.

In terms of **body** language, naturally you want to avoid looking either insecure or arrogant. The following rules for effective body language may seem obvious, yet I have seen hundreds of videotapes in which participants in media-interview role plays are making mistakes. The first rule is to avoid any kind of body language that looks defensive. Typical problems include: clenched fists, hunched shoulders, tightened facial expression, hands in front of (or anywhere near) the face, and lack of eye contact. Rule two is to avoid any overly aggressive body language, such as gloating, arrogant glances, or an unsympathetic facial expression. Instead, use relaxed body language: sit comfortably and professionally (crossing your legs is fine); use the same kind of relaxed gestures you would use naturally in conversation; relax your facial expression.

If you are appearing on television, you have two other aspects of body language to keep in mind. First of all, establish effective eye contact. Obviously, do not read your notes word for word. Eye contact is one of your biggest advantages on television, so use it to its fullest. In general, look at the reporter or other panelists; occasionally—for heightened emotional impact and emphasis—look directly into the camera (imagining a person there) with the red light on. Second, always assume you are on camera. Do not, for example, smirk or mop your brow when someone else is talking. You may be recorded for a reaction shot. Finally, avoid nodding unless you agree with the point.

To use your **voice** effectively: use expressive inflection; keep your volume appropriate (avoid yelling, which makes you look too aggressive, and dropping off in volume, which makes you look unsure); maintain the appropriate rate (avoid speeding up if you get nervous or angry); avoid filler words; and enunciate clearly.

If you are using a microphone, you must keep in mind four other voice techniques. First, remember to speak conversationally, as though you were addressing a small group of people. Second, speak into the microphone, keeping your distance (which can vary from two to twenty inches) constant. Control your breathing: avoid gasping or wheezing into the microphone. Finally, avoid unwanted sounds, such as rattling your paper, drumming your fingers, scraping your chair, or jingling coins.

When you are appearing on television, **dress** unobtrusively. In general, dress in solid colors—gray, blue, beige. Avoid tweeds, stripes, and patterns that appear to jump around on the screen. Avoid white, which may glare, and black, which absorbs light. Other than a watch or wedding ring, avoid jewelry, especially if it is jangling or distracting. Men should be sure to wear long socks, darker than their suits. Women should be sure to wear something they feel comfortable sitting in.

Perhaps the most important ingredient in how you look and sound is your **attitude**. Never gloat over a successful answer; you may be skewered on the next question. Don't look aggressive. Don't use sarcasm. You want to look professional and competent; you do not want to look arrogant and unsympathetic.

Effective media relations are an increasingly important set of business communication skills. Think about these skills now, so when the time comes to use them, you will feel confident and in control.

As you can see, the skills involved in holding meetings and answering questions are very different from those you use in presentations. As a business communicator, you will be able to handle all of these kinds of speaking situations.

REVIEW QUESTIONS

To check your understanding

1. Describe the difference between a presentation and a meeting.
2. As a meeting participant, what are your three most important duties?
3. What are the three task functions of chairing a meeting?

4. List three points to consider while preparing an agenda.

5. What are the advantages of taking questions during the presentation? After the presentation?

6. What are five ways of dealing with questions you cannot answer immediately?

7. Explain the two steps in responding to difficult questions.

8. Explain how to deal with unfair questions.

9. What is the main difference between a panel discussion and a team presentation?

10. What should a panel chair do before the session? At the beginning of the session? During the session? At the end of the session?

11. What two audiences must you bear in mind in a media interview?

12. Why is nonverbal communication important in a media interview?

APPLICATION QUESTIONS

To apply your knowledge

1. You have made a presentation and have begun a question-and-answer session. But the people in your audience seem reluctant to speak up. How would you go about encouraging them to ask you questions?

2. How would you respond to a well-meant question that obviously has missed the point of your entire presentation?

3. List three possible contexts for a panel discussion, and explain why a panel discussion is preferable to a team presentation in these situations.

4. During a panel discussion, members of the audience persist in addressing unfair questions to one of the panelists. How would you respond as that panelist? As the panel chair?

5. In preparing for a radio interview, what are the most important nonverbal aspects of communication that you should pay attention to?

6. You have been invited to be interviewed on a television talk show with which you are unfamiliar. How would you go about assessing the audience of the show so that you can prepare effectively?

7. Think up three other methods besides statistics and anecdotes that you can use to make an interview interesting.

8. You are participating in a meeting that is poorly run: the agenda is being ignored and the discussion is making no progress. What would you, as a participant, do to help get the meeting back on course?

9. Give examples of meetings in which you can act as both leader and facilitator, and meetings in which these responsibilities would best be divided between two persons. On what criteria are your decisions based?

10. You are chairing a meeting with a very full agenda and a limited time in which to accomplish it. What techniques would you use to make sure that you get through the entire agenda in the allotted time?

11. During a business meeting you are unable to reach a necessary consensus because of hostile disagreements among various participants, which have led to an exchange of insults. What steps would you, the facilitator, take to deal with this situation in order to lead the group to a consensus?

CASES
To practice what you learned

1. Your company has recently taken the controversial step of acquiring a large computer, which will be used to systematize the enormous amount of data upon which your company's business is based. You have been assigned the task of explaining the computer's capabilities to the department heads. You have an enormous body of highly technical information to present in a limited time. In planning your presentation, you face two main concerns—the necessity that your audience understand your material completely, so that the computer can be effectively utilized; and the possibility that some members of the audience might use your presentation as an opportunity to express dissatisfaction with computerization. What strategy should you adopt regarding questions from the audience? Consider such factors as stipulating the timing of questions, limiting questions, and responding to hostile questions.

2. You have been asked to speak before a community group about your company's purchase of a large tract of land on the edge of town. Your company intends to use the land for an industrial park, but local environmentalists object. During the question-and-answer period, one or two members of the audience sympathetic to the environmentalists heckle you—drowning out your responses, shouting

slogans, yelling rhetorical questions. How would you deal with this extreme case of hostile questioning?

3. You are being interviewed on television about your company's hiring policies. You have reiterated your main idea—that your company follows affirmative-action guidelines—but you still have doubts that you have gotten your message across clearly and concisely. A reporter asks you an irrelevant question about your company's profit margin in the last quarter. How can you divert this question in such a way that your main point is emphatically restated?

4. You have seven people working for you and are considering restructuring the group somewhat. You have drafted a new organizational chart and now would like to introduce the changes to your subordinates. Would a meeting or presentation be more effective? Defend your choice with a specific reference to the function of each of these types of communication.

15

Job-Search
Communication

by Paul A. Argenti

Plan Your Career.

Write Your Résumé and Cover Letter.
Résumés • Cover letters

Learn to Interview and Follow Up.
Interviews • Follow-ups

FOR most business students, one of the most important communication tasks is preparing your résumé. This document will represent you in offices you've never seen, and—if poorly written—in offices you'll never see. The résumé is just one aspect of a complete communication package that everyone must put together before he or she enters the business world. This package should also include a healthy amount of career planning and self-assessment before you even start thinking about a résumé. In addition, after you've written a résumé you need to think about writing cover letters, preparing yourself for interviews, and planning strategies for following up interviews with letters and telephone calls.

This job-search communication package ends up looking very much like a sales pitch for yourself. In this chapter, we will look at what goes into creating that sales pitch: (1) career planning, (2) résumé and cover-letter writing, and (3) interviewing and following up interviews. The whole purpose of this book and this course is to improve your communication strategies and skills in business. Let's now look at the communication strategies and skills you need to get into business.

Plan Your Career.

Before you can sell a product, you need to know what that product is all about. In addition, most people in sales and marketing will tell you that the best salespeople are those who really believe in the product they are selling. This is true for salespeople at high-technology companies such as IBM and for those who sell products door to door for companies such as Avon.

What does all this have to do with finding a job? Much like the people working for IBM and Avon, you need to first know everything you can discover about the product—in this case, yourself—and then you need to convince yourself that the product is worth selling. Sounds fairly easy, doesn't it? But one of the biggest problems students have with their job search is that of understanding and believing in themselves enough to convince a potential employer that they are truly worthwhile applicants. This is particularly true for those students who are looking for their first job. Just like new products entering the marketplace for the first time, these people must convince the world that they can do as well as or better than those who came before them.

How then do you begin assessing what you have to offer and then putting together a convincing sales pitch? Most experts will tell you that the first thing you need to do is to **set realistic objectives** for yourself. You clearly don't expect to be managing a major corporation or earning hundreds of thousands of dollars on your first job. Similarly, you probably hope that you won't be fixing stamps onto envelopes for $100 a week. But you may still have your sights set too high or too low if you haven't established realistic objectives.

To begin setting objectives, you may want to ask yourself a series of questions to clarify your thinking. These may be questions about your own strengths and weaknesses, questions about your goals, or a realistic appraisal of your abilities. Let's look at some issues you will want to consider during this phase of the self-assessment process:

1. *Major strengths and weaknesses:* What subjects have you done particularly well or poorly in at school? Do not limit yourself to the academic environment, however. Ask yourself to define your own strengths and weaknesses as a human being. For example, maybe you are very good with numbers, but not very effective working with groups of people.

2. *Goals:* What are your goals for the short and long term? What kinds of things do you think of when you picture yourself as successful?

3. *Major achievements:* What have you done at school, at work, or in your leisure time that you feel proud of? List every example you can think of.

4. *Lifestyle:* Are you looking for an eight-hour a day, forty-hour-a-week job? Or do you hope to immerse yourself in a total commitment that may involve lots of travel, weekend work, and many other business obligations? Ask yourself what trade-offs you are really willing to make for your career or personal life.

5. *Needs:* Is your most important need to make money to pay back college loans? Or do you wish to remain close to family and friends, no matter what the cost?

As you begin to think about the answers to these questions, you will find yourself branching off into other areas as well, such as: the kinds of people you'd like to work with; the industries, products, and services that appeal to you; the ideal location for you; the abilities you have that would be useful in various industries, and so on.

Take some time off from the hustle and bustle of everyday life to think through questions like these very carefully. What you will end up with is a realistic appraisal of your own abilities and goals. The next task you need to accomplish is to **narrow down the field** of companies or organizations that you would like to work for, given your own abilities and career goals.

For many students this is not such a difficult task. For example, if you have already declared yourself an accounting major, you will probably be looking for jobs that will use the skills you're already acquiring. For others, the task of narrowing down the field is more difficult because they may have a broader range of interests or be less excited about the subject they are majoring in. Much like the child in the candy store or the new patron in a Chinese restaurant, these students need to line up their own abilities against an array of choices. Let's look at the functional areas of business and their activities as a first step in narrowing the field.

1. *Finance:* Students interested in finance go to work for investment banks, commercial banks, savings and loans corporations, and brokerage houses. You may find yourself, for example, in a two-year program at one of the investment banks, learning all about the business, or you may start as a teller at the local bank.

2. *Accounting:* Students interested in accounting go to work for public accounting firms or work as controllers or financial planners in companies. Activities in these jobs can range from reviewing financial records or balance sheets to monitoring business plans.

3. *Marketing and sales:* In marketing, students go to work for companies that sell consumer products, industrial products, high-technology products, or services (such as banking). Students may also work for advertising, marketing-research, and retail firms. In these fields, you could find yourself doing everything from selling a product to working on an advertising campaign.

4. *Human relations/personnel:* Just about every organization you can think of from the smallest to the biggest has a personnel function. Students interested in this field may end up working in employee relations, training, or benefits administration.

5. *Operations management:* Students interested in operations or line management work for manufacturing, production, or distribution.

You may work on anything from quality control to the coordination of integrated production systems.

6. *Communication:* Those who choose careers in communication work for public relations firms, corporate communications departments, and advertising agencies. In this field you may find yourself writing press releases, analyzing corporate images, or working on the company newsletter.

7. *Management information systems:* Students with specialized interests in MIS work for data-processing, time-sharing, and accounting firms. However, virtually all firms have MIS departments. In this field, you may work in the planning and design of computer-based systems or you may apply quantitative models to business decisions.

These are just some of the fields that are based on the functional areas of the business school curriculum. Certainly, you can expand this list to include consulting, strategic planning, general management, and engineering. Whatever your list looks like, the important thing is to begin matching the attributes you gleaned from your own assessment of your abilities against the attributes one needs for a career in a particular field. For example, if Karen majored in accounting and is interested primarily in numbers, she may not want to pursue a career in personnel administration because that field requires people-management skills more than number-crunching skills.

Once you have narrowed the field, you are ready to **begin looking for specific information** on individual companies. Most business libraries at colleges and universities have a wealth of information and are good places to begin. Just as a few examples, *Disclosure* publishes copies of 10-Ks, annual reports, and proxy statements for NYSE and AMEX companies. *F&S Index of Corporations* indexes all articles written about each company each year. *Standard and Poor's Stock Reports* cover financial data and recent company developments. See the subsection in appendix E entitled "For information about a company" for a comprehensive listing of possible sources for your job search.

As a last step in looking for specific information about companies, students will often set up informational interviews with employees at corporations. You should be sure at the outset, however, to specify that you are looking only for information—not a job. The best sources of information of this kind tend to be friends, family, and alumni from your school. Many people refer to this practice as *networking.* That is, what you are really doing is increasing the number of contacts within specific industries. This can often lead to referrals, references, and, once in a while, even a job.

Be sure to follow these guidelines when setting up informational interviews:

1. *Prepare questions in advance.* Although you are looking in part for a kind of education, be sure that you have clarified in your own mind what specific questions fit in with your career goals. Try to develop questions that will truly assess what people do on the job. You may, in fact, want to research the company before your visit to build up a reservoir of questions.

2. *Set up the interview; record information.* Look upon this activity as a research project rather than a job interview. Do not walk into a company without first calling or writing for an appointment. Just as you would for a research project, maintain information on each interview for your later reference.

3. *Handle the interview effectively.* Be courteous. Realize that the person is doing you a favor. Bring a copy of your résumé, ask questions, and get the names of other people to contact in the field. Try to limit the person's time to ten or fifteen minutes. Finally, be sure to thank the person at the end of the meeting and later in writing.

Once you have completed a self-assessment by setting your objectives, narrowing down the field, and looking for specific information, you will find it much easier to sell the product you are putting on the marketplace—yourself. The reason most people have difficulty selling themselves in both résumés and interviews is that they haven't assessed their own abilities, set realistic objectives, or researched the various industries and companies. If you follow the advice in this chapter, you will feel more confident and ready to make a sales pitch for yourself. It's as simple as that.

Write Your Résumé and Cover Letter.

Your résumé and cover letter are the first pitches you make into the real world of business. How do you write them to describe your abilities to potential employers?

Résumés

Later in life, you may be cautioned that a résumé is not a complete life history. In other words, be brief. Many college students, however, have the opposite fear: "How can I possibly fill up one page describing what little I've accomplished so far?" At both stages in your career development, the most important thing to remember is that you should describe only what is most relevant for getting a job. As we discussed in chapter 4, on audience analysis, you must realize that the person reading your résumé, like the person receiving a report or letter, is probably busy and therefore interested only in the task at hand—filling the position with the best candidate.

Thus, your job in creating this aspect of the sales pitch for yourself is to provoke the potential employer's interest. You do this by writing a document that is concise, logically organized, easy to read, and, at the same time, interesting. Take a look at Figure 15.1—the first two pages of a ten-page résumé that was actually sent in to a firm in New England. This resume may well be described as interesting: the use of sketches, a thumbprint, and anecdotal information immediately grabs the reader's attention. Your résumé, however, should not be merely a tool for entertainment. Robert Huntington, by not organizing logically, writing more information than necessary, and taking far too long to get to the point, has not thought enough about his audience.

In contrast, let's look at another example, in Figure 15.2. In less than one page, Averell Harriman summed up his career quite concisely. Unfortunately, few of us have the amazing qualifications of Mr. Harriman. Somewhere in between these two models you will probably find your own model for a correct résumé. No matter what you've done or where you've been, however, you should follow Mr. Harriman's example and keep the résumé to one page.

The only subject areas you generally include in a résumé are: (1) a career objective, (2) an education section, (3) a work-experience section, and (4) personal information. Let's look at each of these areas in more detail. The **career objective** is not necessary, although it is often included in résumés. If you do not have a very specific career objective such as "a sales position in a consumer products firm," you should probably not include an objective. Often, students try to cover all bases with an objective and thus end up accomplishing nothing. For example, the following objective tells the reader little about your interests: "a challenging position in business." Needless to say, those who have clarified their goals and worked on self-assessment as suggested earlier in this chapter

FIGURE 15.1

Ineffective sample résumé

RÉSUMÉ

Name:	Robert Huntington
Nationality:	United States of America
Birthdate:	25 February 1968
Birthplace:	San Francisco, California
Height:	198.5 cm (6 ft. 5 in.)
Weight:	94 kg (207 lb)

WANTED FOR: Hard work and satisfying results

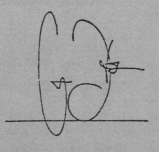 

Signature   Thumb Print

Family background:

Rob grew up on an 80 acre farm in Clovis, Calif, among valedictorians, star athletes, exchange students, junior philharmonic musicians, student body officers, and other upper middle class overachievers.

Father: Jack Donald H.: Thoracic and Cardiovascular Surgeon
Mother: Margaret Carpenter H.: Professor of Nursing Science,
                  CSUF
Siblings: Kim Marie H.: Resident of Internal Medicine, UCSF
          Kirk Robert H.: High School Teacher and Coach
          Margaret Ann H.: Swedish Folk Musician and Student
                  Veterinary Medicine, UCB

Schooling:

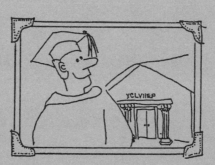

K−8:   Jefferson Elementary School, Clovis, Calif. Basketball,
         4-H Club, Student body Pres.
8−12:   Clovis High School. Sophomore Class Pres. Swim Team
         Most Valuable Player, American Field Service, Extracurricular Photography and Raku Pottery. Straight A's. Often expelled for truancy and dress code violations.
College: California State College, Fullerton. Art Major. Regents
         Scholar. Leave of Absence 1 year. 1 year Conservation of
         Natural Resources Major.

FIGURE 15.2

Averell Harriman

1. B.A. Yale 1913
2. V.P. Union Pacific Railroad 1915–1917
3. Chairman Union Pacific Railroad 1932–1942
4. Partner Brown Brothers Harriman Company 1931
5. Chairman Executive Committee, Illinois Central Railroad Co. 1931–42; Director 1915–46
6. Administrative Office NRA 1934–35
7. Member Business Advisory Council, Department of Commerce 1935
8. Chairman Advisory Council, Department of Commerce 1937–39
9. Ambassador to USSR 1943–45
10. Ambassador to United Kingdom 1946
11. Secretary of Commerce 1946–48
12. U.S. Representative in Europe for Economic Cooperation Act 1948–50
13. American Representative to NATO to study Western Defense Plans 1951
14. Director Mutual Security Agency 1951–53
15. Governor of New York 1955–58
16. Assistant Secretary of State for Eastern Affairs 1961–63
17. Under Secretary of State for Political Affairs 1963–68
18. Personal Representative of President for Vietnam Peace Negotiations 1968–69
19. Author: *Peace with Russia?* 1959
20. Author: *America and Russia in a Changing World* 1971
21. Currently Ambassador at Large (1961–)

Presented by A. Harriman to the Columbia Executive Program, Harriman, NY, August, 1982.

may very well be ready to put down a specific career objective. You shouldn't feel obliged to do so, however; personnel specialists cannot agree on the merits of including a career or job objective in a résumé.

Some simple rules follow for those who do have very specific career goals: (1) Keep the statement short—a maximum of one sentence. (2) Be sure the objective is very specific rather than general. (3) Remember to focus on near-term objectives rather than long-term goals.

The **education** section should include the name of your college and its location, the degree you expect to receive and the date you will receive it, your major, coursework related to the career you have chosen, any honors, and carefully selected extracurricular activities. Here is an example of an education section from business student Michael Davis's résumé:

Education

1988–	UNIVERSITY OF DENVER DENVER, COLORADO
	Candidate for the Bachelor of Science degree in Business Administration, May 1992. Emphasis in sales management and marketing. Dean's List, three terms. Vice-president, marketing club. Co-chair, business career day committee.

Notice that the category heading and dates of attendance appear to the left while the information about the school appears on the right. The name of the school and location appear in capital letters, the degrees and dates are not abbreviated, and extracurricular activities include titles, if any.

Many students wonder whether to include high school on their résumé. Generally, the answer is no because most of the high school experience is so common and typically unrelated to the job search. There are some exceptions, however. If you attended a school that is well known nationally or is known to the employer, you might want to include this information; it may provide an opportunity for conversation in an interview or it may be a mark of distinction for you. The same is true for those who've attended special preparatory high schools like the Boston Latin School or Bronx Science in the East. In the long run, you need to think about how much this information really adds to your sales pitch. Ask yourself whether you could easily do without the information. Nine times out of ten, the answer will be yes.

The **work experience** section should include for each job: employer's name, location of company, dates of employment, your title, your responsibilities, your major accomplishments, and any significant skills you developed on the job. You should include all relevant experience, whether full-time or part-time, paid or unpaid.

As with other aspects of the résumé, every job description should be geared to your primary career objective. That is, be sure to pick out the most important points for each past job that relate to the position you seek. This does not mean that you leave out unrelated experience, but you shouldn't pad the résumé with details of your experience as a canoe coach at summer camp if you're looking for a position in sales.

Search diligently for experience to put on the résumé. If you have had little or no experience, for example, put down volunteer work, jobs you held in school, or even work related to club activities. Employers look for patterns of experience rather than just specific amounts of experience. Once you have identified the various experiences you want to include, you are ready to begin asking yourself key questions for each job:

1. *What did I really do?*
   Many times the job description doesn't describe your accomplishments. You often need to go beyond the title to truly understand the nature of your job. For example, you may have worked officially as a stock boy or stock girl, but in reality you were heavily involved in maintaining inventory.

2. *Did I improve the position I was hired for? If so, how?*
   Employers need to know how you grew in the job. This is a way of showing innovation and accomplishment.

3. *What specific skills did I use?*
   As in answering question 1, be sure to think about all of the skills you used—particularly emphasizing those most relevant to the job you would like to have.

4. *Did I save my employer money or come up with a novel idea?*
   Again, as potential employers try to weave together a pattern of experience, they look for unusual and innovative examples.

5. *What were my specific responsibilities?*
   Avoid the pat "responsibilities included" approach and stick with action verbs like these:

accomplished	defined	identified
achieved	delivered	implemented
arranged	demonstrated	improved
assisted	determined	influenced
broadened	developed	installed
built	discovered	managed
calculated	distributed	minimized
clarified	earned	modified
combined	edited	monitored
completed	estimated	motivated
conceived	evaluated	operated
concluded	examined	ordered
condensed	exceeded	organized
coordinated	formed	overcame
corrected	generated	participated
created	handled	performed

planned	revised	studied
prepared	saved	suggested
presented	scheduled	summarized
processed	served	supported
programmed	set up	tested
proposed	showed	trimmed
realized	simplified	undertook
recommended	sold	used
reported	solved	widened
researched	strengthened	wrote

Let's look at another example from Michael Davis's résumé:

<u>Experience</u>

Summer JOHNSON'S DRUG STORE
1989   ALLENTOWN, PENNSYLVANIA
        Managed the consumer products counter for this two million dollar drug and department store. Sold over one-half of all store sales for three month period. Improved sales by 28%. Influenced buying decisions. Recommended new hires.

Part-time SALTERS BOOKSTORE
1987-   DENVER, COLORADO
           Ordered books for college-oriented bookstore. Simplified ordering process. Conceived new books rack at check-out counter.

Notice that the experience appears in reverse chronological order. Also, the position at the bookstore comes *second* even though Michael still works there part time. The start date, then, determines placement on the résumé. Finally, notice that Michael didn't dwell on the ordering process at Salters except to discuss the simplification of orders; instead, he adds an important piece of information about his new-book rack—an example of innovation.

Like the job objective, the **personal information** section is not absolutely necessary, but most people do include it. Often a conversation starter, personal information can also augment the various skills and experiences you've listed in the education and work experience sections. Again, remember this is a sales pitch, not a laundry list.

With that in mind, try above all to use good judgment and to be a bit creative as well. The list below should offer some guidelines as you try to develop a personal section:

1. Include all business-related hobbies or achievements, such as Junior Achievement.

2. Do not repeat information that already appears on the résumé. For example, don't put down skiing as an interest if you have already stated that you are on the ski team in college.

3. Be specific. Instead of writing "enjoy cooking, movies, and literature," write "enjoy Italian cooking, foreign films, and science fiction."

4. Be sure to include any fluency in foreign languages or computer languages. Notice the emphasis on fluency rather than minor understanding.

Let's take a final look at Michael Davis's résumé—including now a job objective and a personal section—in Figure 15.3. Michael is now ready to send his sales pitch out into the marketplace. His goal now is to write a cover letter to go along with the résumé.

Cover letters

The primary goal of a cover letter is to motivate the person who receives it to read your résumé and then ask you for an interview. You also may want to elaborate on examples from the résumé, mention any personal contacts, or show an interest in a particular aspect of the company you are writing to. Figure 15.4 shows a model you can use for most situations. Be sure to avoid writing form letters, however. Each letter should be unique.

Figure 15.5 shows a sample cover letter for Michael Davis.

Keep some general guidelines in mind whenever you compose a cover letter. First, letters to people to whom you have been referred (during the networking stage, for example) are much more potent than those sent out to someone with whom you have no connection at all. Likewise, letters sent to a specific person are better than those sent blindly to a title such as "Personnel Director." Second, type each letter individually, trying not to fall into a form-letter pattern. Cover letters may open the door to a world of experience, so you need to remain crisp and original for each one you write. Finally, be sure to follow up on each letter. If you write that you will call on a certain date, be sure to do so. The job-search process involves good organization as well as communication skills. Keep clear, easy-to-identify files for easy reference.

The cover letter and résumé may open the door for you, but what do you say when you walk in, at the actual sale of the "product"? How can you prepare for this important interaction, and how do you follow up? That's the subject of discussion for the final section of this chapter.

FIGURE 15.3

Sample résumé

Michael Phelps Davis
218 Low Road
Denver, Colorado
(303)351−6113

Objective   A sales position in a consumer products firm.

Education

1988−   UNIVERSITY OF DENVER
DENVER, COLORADO

Candidate for the Bachelor of Science degree in
Business Administration, May 1992. Emphasis in
sales management and marketing. Dean's List,
three terms. Vice-president, marketing club.
Co-chair, business career day committee.

Experience

Summer   JOHNSON'S DRUG STORE
1989   ALLENTOWN, PENNSYLVANIA
Managed the consumer products counter for this
two million dollar drug and department store.
Sold over one-half of all store sales for three
month period. Improved sales by 28%. Influenced
buying decisions. Recommended new hires.

Part-time   SALTERS BOOKSTORE
1987−   DENVER, COLORADO
Ordered books for college-oriented bookstore.
Simplified ordering process. Conceived new books
rack at check-out counter.

Personal   Fluent in Spanish. Extensive experience with the
IBM personal computer. Enjoy tennis, American
literature, and the commodities market.

FIGURE 15.4

Model for a cover letter

Full Address
with Zip Code
Date

Name
Title
Company or Agency Name
Full Address with Zip Code

Dear _____:

    Arouse the employer's interest by mentioning briefly something you are preparing for or have done that relates to the job you're applying for. Tell where you heard of the opening or why you have selected this employer for an inquiry. Also mention any personal contacts here.

    Describe your interest in the position, in the field of work, or in the organization. If you have work experience, be sure to mention pertinent data or accomplishments to show that you have specific qualifications in this field or for this particular type of work.

    Refer the employer to your résumé. Expand on anything in it that relates to the job or employer. Indicate that you are willing to provide additional data.

    The closing paragraph should suggest your eagerness to arrange an interview. Mention that you will call to set up an interview by a specific date.

Very truly yours,

Jane Smith

[signature]

full name, typed

Enclosure [your résumé]

FIGURE 15.5

Sample cover letter

218 Low Road
Denver, Colorado (zip)
February 8, 1992

Ms. Linda Bell
Personnel Director
Best Products Corporation
Chicago, Illinois (zip)

Dear Ms. Bell:

I am writing to inquire about a sales position at Best Products. As the enclosed résumé indicates, I will be graduating with a business degree from the University of Denver this spring. Last week, the president of Best Products spoke to our marketing club and gave me your name. My experience in a large drug and department store allowed me to use some of the skills I have developed as a sales management and marketing major in college. The improvement I was able to achieve in that short time gave me the confidence to pursue a position with a larger firm such as yours.

My interest in sales and marketing also helped me to develop a "new books" rack at the local bookstore this past fall. By placing the rack next to the check-out counter, we were able to stimulate interest in untested products.

I will be visiting Chicago during our spring break, March 12–19, and would appreciate the opportunity to meet with you in person. I will call you in two weeks so that you can suggest a convenient time for us to meet.

Very truly yours,

Michael P. Davis

[signature]

Michael P. Davis

Enclosure

Learn to Interview and Follow Up.

The last step in the job search includes the interview and its follow-up.

Interviews

In many ways, job interviews are very much like blind dates. You get all dressed up and excited to meet someone for the first time in the hope that you will be starting a lasting relationship. There the similarity ends, however. In reality, interviews represent the culmination of all your self-assessment, planning, research, and résumé writing. During the brief time you will spend (usually thirty to forty-five minutes for initial interviews), you will have to pull together all the threads you have been weaving for your sales pitch.

On the other side of the desk sits someone who has never met you in person. That person is looking for certain skills and impressions to fill a position for what may be many years. What can you do to prepare yourself for this most important presentation? Remember that you need to prepare yourself both physically and mentally for this task.

In many ways the **physical preparation** is the easier of the two. The most important thing to remember is that you should dress appropriately for an interview. You wouldn't wear a T-shirt to a formal, nor would you wear a tuxedo to a basketball game. Similarly, you shouldn't wear casual clothes to an interview with a major corporation, nor should you wear a three-piece suit to an interview for a position at a check-out counter.

You need to realize, however, that first impressions are critical. Many recruiters say they can make a decision just by looking at someone. Thus, your goal should be to look neat, appropriate, and well groomed. Pay attention to details like clean shoes and snagless hosiery. Everything counts as you try to create an impression of a responsible, capable potential employee.

Of course, even the best-dressed people can fail in interviews because they have not given themselves sufficient **mental preparation.** Presumably, you will have done your homework for each organization you visit, but you need also to think about specific questions the interviewer may ask and above all what the audience is looking for.

The following list contains several questions that are normally asked in interviews:

1. Tell me about yourself.
2. What are your strengths and weaknesses?
3. Why should our company hire you?
4. What are your long-term goals?
5. Why did you select your college major?
6. Why did you decide to go to that college?
7. What interests you about this position?
8. Do you like working alone or in groups?
9. What was your greatest accomplishment? Disappointment?
10. How would your best friend describe you? Your worst enemy?
11. Do your grades adequately reflect your ability?
12. Why do you want to work in this industry?
13. What have you done to prepare for work in this industry?
14. How do you measure success?
15. What else can you tell me about yourself that relates to this job?
16. What book have you read lately?
17. Would you accept a position with this company if I offered it to you right now?
18. Why is a manhole cover round?
19. What will you do if we do not hire you?
20. What if . . . ?

Notice that these kinds of questions reflect several different kinds of interviewing styles. For example, the "Tell me about yourself" question is an example of an open-ended nondirective interview style. If asked such questions, you will have great flexibility in defining the bounds of the interview. Questions like "Why is a manhole cover round?"(answer: so it won't fall through the hole) and "What if . . . ?" represent problem-solving, interactive, and situational styles. The interviewer is really testing your analytical ability.

Many of the questions may also prove stressful. For example, describing weaknesses and disappointments, talking about grades, and even solving problems can create stress. This may be what the interviewer intends to do, or merely a way of analyzing your thinking. In either case, you need to prepare.

The best way to prepare answers to these twenty questions, and any others you can generate, is to think about how you would answer each one. Do not sit down and write out specific answers and memorize them.

You should have a general idea of how you will react rather than a series of pat answers. Remember also that your answers should always relate specifically to the job you seek.

Some of the most stressful questions may in reality be illegal. For example, employers cannot ask questions about race, color, religion, sex, national origin, marital status, pregnancy, number of children, provision for child care, or age. What do you do, however, if you are asked an illegal question—for instance, "Are you married?" The problem is that even though the question is illegal, you still have to deal with it at that moment. Essentially, you have to decide what boundaries you wish to set for yourself. Are you willing to give up the job for a matter of principle? Some people would say yes, others no. Maybe the interviewer doesn't even know that the question is illegal.

No matter what, you do have recourse following the interview, whether the interviewer was malicious or not. First, you should alert the placement director on campus and ask him or her whom you should discuss the matter with further. Second, you should decide how you want to deal with the interviewer. Maybe you can actually help avoid problems if he or she didn't know better.

With all the preparation behind you—both physical and mental— you are now ready to walk into **the interview.** Most interviews, you will find, tend to follow a fairly predictable series of five phases.

First is the "getting to know you" phase. Interviewers may refer to the personal section of your résumé, discuss the weather, or simply make small talk. Relax. Be yourself. Do not try to be someone you are not just to please the interviewer. Remember, though, that everything you say contributes to the interviewer's impression of you.

The second phase may be an offshoot of the first. That is, the recruiter may wish to share his or her background with you, or give you a short introduction to the firm. Usually, the first two phases last a maximum of five minutes.

The third phase, and the most important, is the questioning phase. Sometimes the recruiter will move chronologically through your résumé or focus in on specific information that relates to the job. A good interviewer will ask lots of open-ended questions. Use this opportunity to show yourself in the best light. Emphasize attributes that demonstrate your ability to perform well on the job. This third phase takes up most of an interview and can last from fifteen to twenty minutes.

Phase four is the reverse of phase three. Here you get to ask questions of the interviewer. You should prepare these in advance during your research on each company. Do not ask questions to create an impression of how intelligent you are. Rather, you should be asking for answers to questions you are truly curious about. Similarly, do not ask questions that you could have easily found the answer to, such as "What were the company's sales last quarter?" That information will be in any annual report. Ask instead "What is a day on the job like at Best Products?" This phase usually runs for five to ten minutes.

The fifth and last phase is the closing. If you feel that something was unclear, this is the time to clarify. If some qualifications never came out, now is the time to emphasize those strengths. More important, you need to close the interview with the same kind of small talk you began with. Be on your guard to pick up any signs that things went particularly well or poorly. You should not, however, be too blunt. For example, do not ask "So, do I have the job?" If employers want you, they will let you know.

Follow-ups

After the interview is over, you need to continue working on wrapping up the sales pitch that began during the self-assessment process. The first thing you must do is write notes to yourself about people you met, impressions you have, and what follow-up is necessary. Record keeping is very important, especially if you are interviewing with many different companies.

Generally, you will also want to follow up with a thank-you letter to the person or people with whom you spoke. This courtesy keeps you on the interviewer's mind and may serve as an opportunity to elaborate on some aspect of the interview. If you are particularly interested in the firm, more than others you've spoken to, let them know this as well. In the reverse case, when you know you are no longer interested in the company, say so. Someone else may want the job and may be waiting for you to bow out.

After you have thanked the interviewer, you have essentially completed the sales pitch. This is often the most difficult time for someone seeking employment. You need to be patient and wait for a response. Students always ask "How long should I wait?" First, you should try to find out at the interview when you are likely to hear from the company, either about an interview with other people or an actual offer. You do not have to be so courteous as to wait in agony for weeks when a simple question would clarify the time frame.

If you do not hear within the allotted time, you should wait a few extra days before calling the company. Do not press for a decision, however. Let the normal business patterns rule the process, or you may find yourself losing an opportunity.

When you do hear positively from a company, be sure to ask for confirmation in writing. Students often are horrified to find that offers made on the phone dwindle to nothing later on. Even after you have a firm offer, do not feel obliged to respond immediately. Think through how the job fits in with your self-assessment, goals, and the other positions you've applied for. As soon as you have decided, call the firm and let them know. Finally, write to other firms you spoke with and let them know you've accepted an offer.

The job search can be an invigorating communication experience. From self-assessment to résumé to interview to job offer, you will find communication challenges that enlighten you, and frighten you, but in the end you will have learned a great deal about yourself and your ability to communicate.

REVIEW QUESTIONS
To check your understanding

1. What two similarities exist between selling a product and finding a job?
2. List at least three issues to consider when setting realistic job objectives.
3. What functional area would be most likely to train you for a job in banking? In a controller's office? In data processing?
4. What is another term for *informational interviewing?*
5. What are the four subject areas in a résumé?
6. Should a career-objective statement focus on near-term or long-range goals?
7. What should you write on your résumé if you have not yet completed your bachelor's degree?
8. How should you prepare to answer interview questions?
9. What do you do during phase four of a job interview?
10. What two actions should you take after the job interview?

APPLICATION QUESTIONS
To apply your knowledge

1. Consider the five self-assessment issues listed in this chapter (major strengths and weaknesses, goals, major achievements, lifestyle, and needs). Answer the questions given in that list.

2. Choose a field of interest to you. From that field, choose one company. Xerox and turn in at least three pages of information about that company. (See the subsection of appendix 5 entitled "For information about a company" for sources of information.)

3. Prepare three questions you would ask if you had an informational interview at the company you chose in question 2.

4. Write a career objective for yourself that meets the three criteria outlined in this chapter.

5. Write an education section for yourself, following the suggestions in this chapter.

6. Write a description of one job or other work experience you have had. Use the action verbs listed in this chapter.

7. Write a cover letter to Mr. James Morrison, Director of Personnel at the company you examined in question 2. Mr. Morrison is an alumnus of your college.

8. *Getting to know you role play:* Break into groups of three. Have one student role-play the interviewer, one student role-play the interviewee, and one student give feedback on the interviewee's nonverbal manner (handshake, sitting posture, eye contact, etc.) and verbal first impression. Take turns so each student takes each role.

9. *Job questions role play:* Break into groups of three. Have one student role-play an interviewer (asking any of the twenty questions listed in this chapter, or any others), one student role-play the interviewee, and the third student give feedback on both nonverbal and verbal impressions. Take turns so each student takes each role.

10. Write a follow-up letter for the interview you just role-played.

A

Correct Words

Misused Words

Confused Pairs of Words

Misused Nonstandard Words

Misused Words

Word	Does not mean	Does mean
aggravate	to annoy or irritate NOT Her gum chewing aggravated me.	to make worse His shouting aggravated the already tense situation.
anticipate	simple expectation NOT I anticipated I would enjoy this class.	to look forward to as certain I anticipated the class would end before noon.
anxious	eager NOT He is anxiously awaiting his fiancée's visit (unless he is worried about it).	worried He is anxious about speaking in public.
calculate	decide, suppose NOT We calculate he will be late.	determine with mathematical precision The engineers calculated the stress level.
crucial	important NOT Her presence at the meeting is crucial.	resulting in a decision Her tie-breaking vote was crucial.
enormity	immensity NOT Visitors are surprised at the enormity of our New England division.	monstrousness, wickedness The jurors were surprised at the enormity of the crime.

Word	Does not mean	Does mean
enthuse	to be enthusiastic NOT She is enthused about the new idea.	to make enthusiastic Her proposal enthused the committee.
entity	agency, collective group NOT The corporate entity is housed on the seventeenth floor.	independent, separate existence The corporate entity differs from its professed politics.
factor	aspect NOT Stress is a factor of everyday life.	a cause or contributing agent Inflation is a factor of high prices.
fortuitous	lucky, fortunate NOT Fortuitously, she found a fifty-dollar bill on the street.	occurring by chance (good or bad) Fortuitously, she slipped on the ice.
hopefully	I hope NOT Hopefully, the stock prices will rise.	with hope Hopefully, the groom walked up the aisle.
impact	to affect (verb) NOT This pricing structure impacted sales.	crush together (verb) His wisdom teeth were impacted. effect (noun) The impact of my previous statement should be clear enough.
individual	person NOT All the individuals in this office attended.	single person as opposed to a group Despite the peer pressure, she voted as an individual.
interface	confer, discuss NOT Let's interface with the publicity department on that.	connect by means of an interface The computer interfaces with the machine.

Word	Does not mean	Does mean
legitimate	truthful, real, appropriate NOT That's a legitimate concern.	legal, lawful You have a legitimate claim on the estate.
literally	figuratively, in a manner of speaking NOT He literally exploded when he heard the news (unless he was, indeed, blown to bits).	exactly, to the letter He counted literally every paper clip he used.
majority	most (applied to items, not people) NOT On the majority of work days, I drive to my job.	51 percent to 99 percent (applies only to people) Although the boss opposed the idea, the majority of the group supported it.
mandate	to command, to order, to require (verb) NOT Company policies mandate your participation.	to establish a colony (verb) The British mandated India. a command or the wishes of constituents (noun) The landslide vote gave her a mandate to change her politics.
marginal	small NOT I have only a marginal interest in working for that firm.	borderline I earned a marginal B in that course.
momentarily	in a moment NOT I'm expecting her to be in momentarily (unless she's leaving soon!).	for a moment She's just in her office momentarily; she's due in a conference soon.
parameter	limit, extent, cause	a quantity that describes a statistical population (mathematical term)

Word	Does not mean	Does mean
	NOT We have to stay within the parameters of our budget.	The parameters of this investment model are alpha and omega.
philosophy	slogan or isolated belief NOT "Let's eat lunch" philosophy.	entire system of serious thought Hegelian philosophy
presently	now NOT He's busy presently.	quite soon He will be available presently.
reason	cause by an unreasoning being or thing NOT the reason the bridge collapsed is. . .	decision by a reasoning being The reason I decided to go is. . .
reticent	reluctant NOT She was reticent to take on the new responsibilities.	tending to be quiet A reticent committee chairperson, he never dominated the group's decisions.
scenario	prediction, outcome NOT Here is the best case/worst case scenario.	outline of play or movie The actress approved the film scenario.
similar	same, identical NOT Each chair in the auditorium was similar.	having resemblance (but possible differences) The two companies were similar in several ways.
tangible	sound, clear, real NOT tangible claims, tangible solutions	touchable His visual aids included tangible evidence—a rusted drainpipe.
type	kind of NOT that type job, that type interview, that type computer	kind that type of job, that type of interview, that type of computer
via	by means of	by way of (geographically)

Word	Does not mean	Does mean
	NOT She bought her ticket via credit card.	She flew to Ithaca via Pittsburgh.
viable	practical, workable, possible	capable of staying alive
	NOT Meeting for dinner tonight would be a viable plan; we have three viable options for the staff party.	Without medication, the diabetic would not be viable; without a loan, the bankrupt company would not be viable.
vis-à-vis	regarding or concerning	confronted with or in comparison with
	NOT I am writing vis-à-vis the Forman account.	The Forman account is quite small vis-à-vis the Yates account.
while	although, and, but	at the time that
	NOT While the account was small, it was still important.	While he was in New York, he visited the head office.

Confused Pairs of Words

accept/except   accept: approve or receive
                 We accepted the recommendations.
                 except: exclude, make exception of, apart from
                 Everyone left except the members of the subcommittee.

adapt/adopt   adapt: to change
                 They adapted the proposal to meet their division's needs.
                 adopt: to take possession
                 They adopted the proposal, because they agreed with every idea in it.

advice/advise   advice: counsel (noun; rhymes with *nice*)
                 I suggest you take your supervisor's advice.
                 advise: to counsel (verb; rhymes with *size*)
                 Your supervisor advises you to be on time.

affect/effect	affect: to influence (*Affect* is always used as a verb.) His speaking voice affected our ability to hear his presentation. effect: result (*Effect* is usually used as a noun.) The effect of the decision was to increase job security. effect: to bring about (*Effect* is occasionally used as a verb.) The new sales campaign effected a change in the profits.
allude/elude	allude: to mention indirectly She alluded to the research study. elude: escape She eluded the pushy salesperson.
allusion/illusion	allusion: an indirect reference Her allusion to Japanese management style illustrated her point. illusion: false idea or unreal image Her idea that the group cooperated completely was an illusion.
already/all ready	already: by the time specified or before The workshop was already full by the time we tried to sign up. all ready: completely prepared The group was all ready for the big presentation.
altogether/ all together	altogether: thoroughly That rule is altogether ridiculous. all together: in a group They waited all together in the conference room.
among/between	among: refers to three or more objects or people She chose among the top four candidates. between: refers to two objects or people She chose between the top two candidates.
amount/number little/few less/fewer	amount, little, less: followed by singular nouns amount of time, little space, less doubt number, few, fewer: followed by plural nouns number of people, few reasons, fewer notebooks
anyone/any one everyone/every one someone/some one	anyone, everyone, someone: any, every, or some person (not specific) Anyone can run the copying machine. Everyone is invited to the picnic. Someone will be there to let you in. any one, every one, some one: refers to a specific person or object

	Any one of those executives can run the copying machine.
	Every one of them came to the picnic.
	Some one of my staff members will let you in.
as/like	as: use before phrases and clauses
	as in the past, as a cigarette should
	like: use before nouns and pronouns
	like Susan, like us
assure/ ensure/ insure	assure: to give assurance
	I assure you I will be there.
	NOT The board tried to assure continued profitability.
	ensure, insure: to safeguard, make certain
	The board tried to ensure continued profitability.
	We tried to insure the security of employees working at night.
awhile/ a while	awhile: an adverb
	After the meeting, we relaxed awhile.
	a while: a noun (usually used as an object of a preposition)
	After the meeting, we relaxed for a while.
beside/besides	beside: at the side of
	He sat beside the vice-president.
	besides: in addition to
	Besides being a good cook, he's also a good sales rep.
between/among	*See* among/between
can/may	can: refers to ability
	The secretary can (is able to) type 120 words per minute.
	may: refers to permission
	The secretary may (has permission to) leave early today.
compare to/ compare with	compare to: point out resemblances
	A business presentation might be compared to a stage presentation: both involve effective delivery.
	compare with: point out differences
	Teleconferencing was less expensive, compared with the cost of flying everyone in for a group meeting.
complementary/ complimentary	complementary: completing, fitting together
	We worked together well because we had complementary talents.

complimentary: expressing praise, giving free
She wrote a complimentary note, praising their performance.
They offered complimentary samples of the new product.

comprise/
constitute

comprise: include
The whole comprises the parts.
Our corporation comprises three subsidiaries.
constitute: compose, be composed of
The parts compose/constitute the whole.
Our corporation is composed/constituted of three subsidiaries.

conscious/
conscience

conscious: aware
We were conscious of the noise in that room.
conscience: sense of right and wrong
After he embezzled the funds, his conscience started bothering him.

continual/
continuous

continual: at intervals
Customers interrupted the receptionist continually.
continuous: without interruption
The air conditioner buzzed continuously.

council/counsel

council: governing body
The student council met yesterday.
counsel: lawyer or advice (noun); advise (verb)
My counsel counseled me.

differ from/
differ with

differ from: to stand apart from
The blond differed from the redhead.
differ with: to disagree
One juror differed with the other.

disinterested/
uninterested

disinterested: impartial
The judge made a disinterested decision.
uninterested: not interested in
The public was uninterested in the judge's decision.

e.g./i.e.

e.g.: for example
We sell many consumer products, e.g., toothbrushes, soap, and hair spray.
i.e.: that is
We decided—i.e., our boss decided—to attend the session.

effect/affect

See affect/effect

elicit/illicit

elicit: bring out or evoke (verb)

We hope to elicit a response from over 50 percent of those surveyed.
illicit: illegal or improper (adjective)
Larceny involves an illicit use of funds.

elude/allude	*See* allude/elude
emigrate/ immigrate	emigrate from: to go out of one country and settle in another Many farm workers emigrated from Mexico. immigrate to: to come into a country Many Scandinavians immigrated to Minnesota.
eminent/imminent	eminent: distinguished The engineer is eminent in her profession. imminent: about to happen, threatening A snowstorm seemed imminent.
enhance/ escalate/ increase	enhance: to increase in quality (not in quantity) The brochure enhanced our understanding of the new tax laws. NOT The new product line enhanced our profits. escalate: to increase by carefully planned steps By hiring two extra people each year, the company escalated the number of employees on the payroll. NOT The bad publicity escalated our fears. increase: to go up by unplanned steps or in quantity The new product line increased our profits. The bad publicity increased our fears.
ensure/ insure/ assure	*See* assure/ensure/insure
et al./etc.	et al.: and other people The book was by Maloney, Hansen, et al. (*Et* is not followed by a period.) etc.: and other things We packed the books, furniture, etc. (Don't use *etc.* for padding. Make sure that (1) other things you could name actually exist, and (2) naming them is not important. Never precede *etc.* with *and*.)
ever so often/ every so often	ever so often: very often When I was at work, I thought of vacation ever so often. every so often: occasionally When I was on vacation, I thought of my job every so often.

everyone/every one	*See* anyone/any one
except/accept	*See* accept/except

explicit/implicit	explicit: expressed directly
	  Her message was explicit: "Sit down and be quiet!"
	implicit: expressed indirectly
	  He communicated his disapproval implicitly by raising his eyebrows and shrugging his shoulders.

farther/further	farther: refers to distance
	  Reno is farther west than Los Angeles.
	further: refers to time or quantity
	  We shall pursue this subject further.

few/little	*See* amount/number
fewer/less	*See* amount/number

good/well	good: an adjective
	  She did a good job.
	  NOT She did good.
	well: an adverb
	  She did well.

i.e./e.g.	*See* e.g./i.e.
illicit/elicit	*See* elicit/illicit
illusion/allusion	*See* allusion/illusion
immigrate/emigrate	*See* emigrate/immigrate
imminent/eminent	*See* eminent/imminent
implicit/explicit	*See* explicit/implicit

imply/infer	imply: to suggest
	  His scowl implied that he disagreed.
	  NOT His scowl inferred that he disagreed.
	infer: to deduce
	  I inferred from his scowl that he disagreed.
	  I inferred that the stockbroker thought we ought to sell the bonds now.

incidence/
incident/
instance
	incidence: rate or frequency of occurrence
	  The incidence of violent crime increased.
	incident: single occurrence
	  The incident set off a riot.
	instance: example
	  For instance, burglary decreased 6 percent last year.

insure/assure	*See* assure/ensure/insure

its/it's	its: possessive pronoun meaning "belonging to it" A company is responsible to its stockholders. it's: contraction of *it is* It's our responsibility. It's time to go home. (Never use *it's* unless you can substitute the words *it is*.)
later/latter	later: refers to time He turned in his report later than the others did. latter: refers to the second one of two She wrote a long report and an executive summary; her boss read only the latter.
lay/lie	lay: usually means to set down He lays the memo on his desk. Today, he lays it down; yesterday, he laid it down; he has laid it down; he is laying it down. NOT Lay down if you feel faint. In the present tense, *lay* always means to "set down." lie: to repose I will lie down if I feel faint. Today, he lies on the sofa; yesterday he lay on the sofa; he has lain on the sofa; he is lying on the sofa.
lend/loan	lend: to give (verb) Lend me your calculator. Today, she lends it; yesterday, she lent it; she has lent it; she is lending it. loan: the object lent (noun) The bank loan totaled $10,000. NOT The bank loaned us $10,000.
less/fewer	*See* amount/number
like/as	*See* as/like
little/few	*See* amount/number
lose/loose	lose: a verb to lose the election, will lose the election loose: usually an adjective a loose knot, a loose connection
may/can	*See* can/may
mean/ median	mean: the average; result of adding a series of numbers and dividing the sum by the number of elements added

median: the midpoint; the point at which there are an equal number of elements above and below

moral/morale

moral: right or ethical (usually an adjective)
a moral person, a moral decision
morale: mood or spirit (always a noun)
team morale, high morale

number/amount

See amount/number

oral/verbal

oral: by mouth
He gave an oral presentation.
Should we make an oral or a written presentation?
NOT Should we make a verbal or a written presentation?
verbal: in words
Both writing and speaking are verbal.

percent/percentage

percent: unit
They financed the deal at 11 percent.
percentage: proportion represented
What percentage of the population still smokes?
NOT What percent of the population still smokes?

precede/proceed

precede: to go ahead of
My boss preceded me as we walked into the corridor.
proceed: to go forward with
I recommend we proceed with the project.

principal/
principle

principal: main, most important
The principal problem with this idea is. . .
principle: law, truth
Although I agree in principle, . . .

raise/rise

raise: to lift, to bring up, to increase (a transitive verb—takes an object)
The storekeeper raised her prices.
Today, she raises prices; yesterday, she raised prices; she has raised prices; she is raising prices.
NOT She rose the prices.
rise: to get up, to extend upward, to ascend (an intransitive verb—does not take an object)
The stock price rose suddenly.
Today, the price rises; yesterday, the price rose; the price has risen; the price is rising.

respectively/
respectfully

respectively: in the order given
I considered majoring in premed, prelaw, and business, respectively.

	respectfully: courteously Since I changed my major so often, my parents stopped listening to my career plans respectfully.
set/sit	set: to put down He set the memo on the desk. Today he set it down; yesterday he set it down; he has set it down; he is setting it down. sit: to be seated or situated Sit down and make yourself at home. Today, she sits on the sofa; yesterday, she sat on the sofa; she has sat on the sofa; she is sitting on the sofa.
someone/ some one	*See* anyone/any one
stationary/ stationery	stationary: in a fixed position The personal computer was stationary on the desk. stationery: writing paper The printer typed out the final version on corporate stationery.
that/which	that: use before essential information Pick up the file that is on my desk. ("That is on my desk" is essential information for showing which file.) which: use before nonessential information The file, which is on my desk, is unorganized. ("Which is on my desk" is not essential information.)
their/ there/ they're	their: possessive pronoun meaning "belonging to them" their office, their solution there: a sentence element that precedes the verb and the subject There is no reason for this kind of response. they're: contraction of *they are* They're late because they got caught in traffic. (Never use *they're* unless you can substitute the words *they are* in the sentence.)
uninterested/ disinterested	*See* disinterested/uninterested
verbal/oral	*See* oral/verbal
well/good	*See* good/well

which/that	*See* that/which

who's/whose	who's: contraction of *who is*
	   Who's in charge here?
	whose: possessive pronoun meaning "belonging to whom"
	   Whose terminal is this?
	   (Never use *whose* if you can substitute
	   who is in the sentence.)

your/you're	your: possessive pronoun meaning "belonging to you"
	   Don't forget your briefcase.
	   (Never use *your* if you can substitute
	   you are.)
	you're: contraction of *you are*
	   If you're not here, we cannot make the decision.

Frequently confused singulars and plurals

Singular	*Plural*
agendum	agenda*
alumna (female)	alumnae (female only)
alumnus (male)	alumni (male or female and male)
analysis	analyses
basis	bases
criterion	criteria
datum	data*
diagnosis	diagnoses
medium	media*
parenthesis	parentheses
phenomenon	phenomena
stratum	strata
synopsis	synopses
thesis	theses

*Usually acceptable to use a singular verb for the properly plural forms *agenda, data,* and *media.*

Misused Nonstandard Words

Nonstandard/ *informal/slang*	*Standard*
a half a	half a, a half
ain't	isn't

Nonstandard/ informal/slang	Standard
A.M., P.M. (in the A.M., in the P.M.)	morning, afternoon (in the morning, in the afternoon)
anyways, anywheres	anyway, anywhere
as (I don't know as)	whether (I don't know whether)
awful (awful nice)	very (very nice)
be sure and	be sure to
being as, being that	since, because
broke (My pencil was broke.)	broken (My pencil was broken.)
bunch of (bunch of people)	many (many people)
bust, busted (busted the chair)	break, broke (broke the chair)
but what (no doubt but what)	that (no doubt that)
could of	could have
done (She has done gone.)	already (She has already gone.)
done (Who done it?)	did (Who did it?)
don't (He don't want to.)	doesn't (He doesn't want to.)
enthused (We are enthused about working here.)	enthusiastic (We are enthusiastic about working here.)
fixing to	about to, getting ready to
folks	parents
guy(s)	person (people)
had of, had have (I wish I had of gone.)	had (I wish I had gone.)
had ought, hadn't ought	ought, ought not
hisself	himself
how come (They know how come it happened.)	why (They know why it happened.)
kind of a	kind of
learn (That'll learn her!)	teach (That'll teach her!)
leave (Leave me go!)	let (Let me go!)
let's us	let's, let us
me and (Me and Sue went home.)	and I (Sue and I went home.) (See pages 435-37 for more information on *I* and *me*, pronoun case.)
mighty (mighty large)	very (very large)
most (most everyone)	almost (almost everyone)
neither (In double negatives: I don't like typing neither.)	either (I don't like typing either.)

Nonstandard/ informal/slang	Standard
no-account, no-count, no-good	worthless
nohow	not at all, anyway
no such a (no such a place)	no such (no such place)
not *plus* no/none/nothing (double negatives: We did not want no ink/ none/nothing.)	not *plus* any/anything (single negatives: We did not want any ink/ any/anything *or* We wanted no ink/ none/nothing.)
nowheres	nowhere
of (could of gone)	have (could have gone)
plenty (plenty fine)	quite (quite fine)
rarely ever	rarely, hardly ever
real (real excited)	extremely, very (very excited)
reason . . . because (The reason he was fired was because he never came to work.)	reason . . . that (The reason he was fired was that he never came to work.)
reckon	guess, think, suppose
right (a right clear report)	very (a very clear report)
seldom ever	seldom
some (was some presentation, was hurting some)	extraordinary (was an extraordinary presentation); a little, somewhat (was hurting somewhat)
somewheres	somewhere
sort of a	sort of
superior than	better than, superior to
suppose to	supposed to
sure (sure was correct)	certainly (certainly was correct)
theirself, theirselves	themselves
them (them telephones)	those *or* these (those *or* these telephones)
this here, that there, these here, them there	this, that, these, those
try and	try to
use to (use to be fun)	used to (used to be fun)
used to could	used to be able
wait on (We were waiting on the results.)	wait for (We were waiting for the results.)

Nonstandard/ informal/slang	Standard
want for (I want for you to help.)	want (I want you to help.)
want in, out, down, up, off, through	want to get in, out, down, up, off, through
want(s) that (She wants that she can attend.)	want(s) (She wants to attend.)
ways (It's a long ways to the top.)	way (It's a long way to the top.)
what (The person what wrote that was brilliant.)	who (The person who wrote that was brilliant.)
where (I saw where profits are up.)	that (I saw that profits are up.)
where . . . at (Where is it at?)	where (Where is it?)
where . . . to (Where is he going to?)	where (Where is he going?)
would of	would have
youse	you
you was (You was at the meeting.)	You were (You were at the meeting.)

APPLICATION QUESTIONS

To apply your knowledge

1. For each of the following sentences, determine whether the underlined word is used correctly or misused. If not, form a sentence illustrating its correct use.

   a. Mark was literally in stitches when I told him about the incident.

   b. His contribution to the meeting was marginal.

   c. There are tangible benefits in this three-tiered marketing approach.

   d. The package will hopefully arrive no later than next Monday.

   e. A viable alternative would be to share the cost of the equipment.

2. Choose the correct word from the pairs of words given in parentheses.

   a. The discovery of gold (affected/effected) an unexpected development in the country's economy.

   b. She gave no (fewer/less) than ten reasons for last month's increase in sales.

    c. (As/Like) Jeffrey said at the staff meeting, (anyone/any one) person from each department may attend.

    d. The reservation was intended to (ensure/insure) participation.

    e. The (preceding/proceeding) day Susan asked for (its/it's) address.

3. Correct the nonstandard words in the following sentences.

    a. When she found out it was broke, Sue wanted to know how come we hadn't let the telecopier be.

    b. Most all the employees are entitled to some kind of vacation.

    c. It ain't neither a no-count nor useless idea; I reckon it's a right good one.

    d. Some guy asked Mr. Bartlet if he was fixing to try and get a raise.

    e. The accounts were seldom ever checked, because the division was waiting on a new budget manager.

B

Grammatical Definitions

Grammatical Functions of Words
Grammatical Functions of Sentence Parts

Grammatical Functions
of Words

NOUNS: words that indicate people, places, or things

my boss, Los Angeles, the basketball hoop
(nouns)

CONCRETE NOUNS: nouns that stand for something you can see or touch

John, desk, firecracker
(concrete nouns)

ABSTRACT NOUNS: nouns that stand for something you cannot see or touch

friendship, pride, procedure
(abstract nouns)

PROPER NOUNS: nouns that stand for a specific person or place

Ms. Rahmun, Delaware, Pawley Pavilion, the Middle East
(proper nouns)

PRONOUNS: words used in place of nouns (see pages 433-39 for more information on pronouns.)

she, their, myself
(pronouns)

PRONOUN ANTECEDENT: the specific noun for which a pronoun stands

Colin *was late. He usually is.*
(Colin is the antecedent of the pronoun He.*)*

The **executive** *broke her pencil.*
(Executive is the antecedent of the pronoun her.*)*

414

PRONOUN CASE: the function of a pronoun in a sentence: as the subject, object, possessive, or reflexive/intensive

> **I** *am tap-dancing.*
> *(subjective case)*

> *You are tap-dancing with* **me.**
> *(objective case)*

> *I am tap-dancing with* **my** *cane.*
> *(possessive case)*

> *I am tap-dancing by* **myself.**
> *(reflexive/intensive case)*

PRONOUN NUMBER: the number of people or things referred to by a pronoun: either singular for pronouns referring to a single person or thing, or plural for pronouns referring to more than one person or thing

> *The executive broke* **her** *pencil.*
> *(singular pronoun)*

> *The executives broke* **their** *pencils.*
> *(plural pronoun)*

INTERROGATIVE PRONOUNS: pronouns used to ask a question: *who, whom, whose, which, what*

> **Who** *is attending?* **Which** *form is correct?*
> *(interrogative pronouns)*

RELATIVE PRONOUNS: pronouns used to subordinate: *who, whom, whose, which, that, what, whoever, whomever, whichever, whatever*

> *The person* **who** *is attending. . .*

> *She is attending,* **whatever** *the reasons may be.*
> *(relative pronouns)*

VERBS: words that show action or a state of being (see pages 427-33 for more information on verbs.)

> *She* **kicks.** *I* **think;** *therefore, I* **am.**
> *(verbs)*

VERB MOOD: the writer's attitude: stating a fact or asking a question; requesting or commanding; desiring or supposing

> *The copy machine* **breaks** *daily. Is the copy machine* **broken** *again?*
> *(indicative mood: states a fact or asks a question)*

Please **fix** *that machine.* **Copy** *those reports on the other machine.*

> *(imperative mood: states a request or command)*

I wish the machine **were** *working. If I* **were** *in charge, I would buy a new machine.*

(subjunctive mood: indicates doubt, supposition, desire, wishfulness)

VERB NUMBER: the number of people or things affected by the verb: either singular for verbs affecting a single person or thing, or plural for verbs affecting more than one person or thing

> *The copy machine* **breaks** *daily.*
> > *(singular verb)*
>
> *All the copy machines* **break** *daily.*
> > *(plural verb)*

VERB PERSON: the person affected by the verb: first person, second person, or third person

> **I** *choke;* **we** *choke.*
> *(first person: involves the speaker or writer)*
>
> **You** *choke; all of* **you** *choke.*
> *(second person: involves "you")*
>
> **He/she/it** *chokes;* **they** *choke.*
> *(third person: involves someone else)*

AUXILIARY VERBS: "helping" verbs, added to the main verb

> **could have** *gone,* **did** *go,* **should** *go*
> > *(auxiliary verbs)*
>
> *could have* **gone,** *did* **go,** *should* **go**
> > *(main verbs)*

ADJECTIVES: words that modify or qualify nouns or pronouns (See pages 440–41 for more information on adjectives.)

> *That was a* **dull** *meeting.*
> *(adjective modifying a noun)*
>
> *He was* **dull**.
> *(adjective modifying a pronoun)*

ADVERBS: words that modify or qualify verbs, adjectives, or other adverbs (See pages 441-42 for more information on adverbs.)

> *The sales rep calls here* **daily**.
> *(adverb modifying the verb calls)*

The sales rep is **never** *shy.*
(adverb modifying the adjective shy)

The sales rep **nearly** *always leaves a card.*
(adverb modifying another adverb, always)

PREPOSITIONS: words that link and relate their object to the rest of the sentence

into *the street,* **through** *the airport,* **by** *the sea*
(prepositions)

OBJECT OF A PREPOSITION: the word that is linked or related by the preposition

into the **street,** *through the* **airport,** *by the* **sea**
(objects of prepositions)

CONJUNCTIONS: connectors of words and sentence elements (See pages 424−25 for more information on conjunctions.)

George **and** *Martha   slow* **but** *deadly*
(conjunctions)

COORDINATING CONJUNCTIONS AND CORRELATIVES: connectors of sentence elements of equal grammatical rank

She moved to Cleveland **and** *he stayed in Pittsburgh.*
(coordinating conjunction)

Neither *she* **nor** *he was willing to compromise.*
(correlative conjunction)

SUBORDINATING CONJUNCTIONS: connectors of sentence elements of less grammatical rank (See pages 210−12 for more information on subordinators.)

We fell **because** *we were skiing too fast.*
(subordinating conjunction)

Grammatical Functions of Sentence Parts

SUBJECT: a noun or pronoun that governs the main verb

My boss *tossed the badly written memo into the wastebasket.*
(subject)

VERB: an element that conveys what the subject of the sentence is or does

> *My boss* **tossed** *the badly written memo into the wastebasket.*
> *(verb)*

DIRECT OBJECT: a noun or prounoun that receives the action conveyed by the verb

> *My boss tossed the* **badly written memo** *into the wastebasket.*
> *(direct object)*

INDIRECT OBJECT: a noun or pronoun identifying the party receiving the action; always equivalent to a prepositional phrase beginning with *to* or *for*

> *My boss gave* **me** *the badly written memo.*
> *(indirect object)*

COMPLEMENT: a noun or adjective that follows a linking verb (usually *be, seem,* or *appear*) and specifies something about the subject of the sentence

> *My boss seems* **upset** *about the badly written memo.*
> *(complement)*

CLAUSE: a group of related words that contains a subject and a verb

> **My boss tossed the badly written memo into the wastebasket.**
> *(independent clause: can stand alone as a sentence)*

PHRASE: a group of related words missing either a subject or a verb

> **After tossing the badly written memo into the wastebasket, . . .**
> *(verb phrase: does not include a subject)*
>
> **my angry, frustrated boss**
> *(noun phrase: does not include a verb)*

COORDINATE: equally important

> **My boss tossed the badly written memo into the wastebasket; he shouted, "Write more clearly!"**
> *(coordinate structure: implies both parts of the sentence— on either side of the semicolon—are equal in importance)*

SUBORDINATE: less important

> **Shouting "Write more clearly!",** *my boss tossed the badly written memo into the wastebasket.*
> *(subordinate structure: implies the first part of the sentence is less important)*

C

Grammar and Usage

Correct Sentences
Incomplete sentences: fragments • Double sentences • Parallelism

Correct Verbs
Verb agreement • Verb tense • Verb mood and voice • Split infinitives

Correct Pronouns
Pronoun agreement • Pronoun case • Interrogative and relative pronouns

Correct Adjectives and Adverbs
Adjectives • Adverbs

How to write real good
Correct sentences
1. About sentence fragments. 2. Don't write double sentences, they are hard to read. 3. Bad parallelism is hard to understand, incomprehension, and confusing.
Correct verbs
4. Verbs has to agree with their subjects. 5. Verb tenses were the same when they will appear in the same time frame. 6. Verb mood be consistent. 7. Try to not insert many oversplit infinitives.
Correct pronouns
8. Pronouns should agree with his antecedent. 9. Me and you know we should use correct pronoun case. 10. When using relative pronouns, figure out to who you are speaking.
Correct adjectives and adverbs
11. Use those confusingly adjectives correctly; use those confusing adverbs correct.

*For more information about each problem illustrated on this table, refer to the parallel section of this appendix.

Correct Sentences

Do not carelessly write parts of sentences or double sentences as if they were complete sentences. Incomplete sentences are called *fragments*— because they are only a fragment of a sentence. Double sentences are usually called *fused sentences* (or sometimes *run-on sentences* or *comma splices*) —because they are two sentences incorrectly stuck together.

Incomplete sentences: fragments

A fragment is not a sentence. It is part of a sentence punctuated as if it were a sentence.

To avoid misusing fragments, first check to make sure your sentence has both a subject and a verb. Here are two examples:

> Rows of chairs in front of the podium.
> Seventeen new Brooks Brothers suits.

These examples are both fragments because they lack verbs. The action or state of being for the chairs and the suits is missing. On the other hand, take these two examples:

> Returning to the office after lunch.
> And to meet the new supervisor.

These examples are fragments because they lack a subject. The person who is returning or meeting is missing.

When you see these kinds of fragments standing alone, you can spot them easily. Sometimes, however, in the context of other sentences, they aren't so obvious. For example:

> Consolidated Microchips is hiring engineers.
> Engineers with backgrounds in computer science.

The second sentence here is a fragment: it lacks a verb. Engineers do what? As another example:

> He was trying to follow the word-processing instructions. Which were hard to understand.

The second sentence is a fragment: it lacks a subject. What were hard to understand?

Spot the fragments in these sentences:

> She brought a slide projector. The one from the Audiovisual Department.

"The one from the Audiovisual Department" is a fragment because it has no verb.

> He was offered a job at Consolidated Microchips.
> And was given a starting salary larger than his father's.

"And was given a starting salary larger than his father's" is a fragment because it has no subject.

Checking for subject and verb, then, is the first step in detecting a fragment. But you have a second check as well. Say you had written this:

> After the new management had doubled the workers' production.

You check for subject (*management*) and verb (*had doubled*)—but this is still a fragment. Why? Perhaps you can hear intuitively that the sentence doesn't really end; as a reader, you are still waiting to hear the rest. The grammatical reason, however, is that the word *after* subordinates the subject and verb (as we discussed on pages 211–12). Subordinated subjects and verbs cannot stand alone as sentences. Two more examples:

> My boss believes that we should work sixty hours a week.
> And that we should never take vacations.

The second sentence here is a fragment, because of the subordinator *that*.

> We are surprised when the computer is working.
> And when the printer is working as well.

Again, the second sentence here is a fragment, because of the subordinator *when*.

In summary, to avoid carelessly writing fragments, check each sentence for a complete (unsubordinated) subject and verb.

You may, however, very occasionally use fragments for emphasis, parallelism, and conversational tone. For instance, the last two sentences in the following example use fragments consciously (not carelessly) for emphasis.

> **Use sparingly for emphasis:** Practice your speech thoroughly. Rehearse out loud. On your feet. With your visual aids.

Double sentences

A double sentence is two sentences stuck together incorrectly as if they were one sentence. Some people call double sentences *fused sentences* because they are fused together incorrectly. Some call them *run-on sentences* because they are run together incorrectly. Finally, some people call a certain type of double sentence a *comma splice* because it contains two sentences spliced together incorrectly with a comma. Regardless of what you call double sentences, they are incorrect and may confuse your reader.

Let's look at two correct sentences as an example:

Correct: The recruiter was impressed by her well-written résumé. He also noted that she appeared poised and articulate during her interview.

Now, let's look at how those two correct sentences might have been incorrectly written. First, they might have been incorrectly joined with a comma:

Incorrect: The recruiter was impressed by her well-written résumé, he also noted that she appeared poised and articulate during her interview.

Second, they might have been incorrectly joined with a dash:

Incorrect: The recruiter was impressed by her well-written résumé—he also noted that she appeared poised and articulate during her interview.

One of the most common double-sentence errors involves the use of transitional words or phrases. Transitions, as we discussed in chapter 8, are like bridges or glue between your ideas. They include such words as: *finally, however, therefore, for example,* and *and on the other hand.* (See page 199 for a complete list of transitions.) Students often write fused sentences like this one, with two complete sentences—"She color-coded. . . . " and "She used. . . .—joined incorrectly with a comma and the transition *for example:*

Incorrect: She color-coded her visual aid, for example, she used red to mark decreases in sales.

As another example, here are two complete sentences—"He delivered. . . . " and ."He did not speak. . . ."—joined incorrectly with a comma and the transition *however:*

Incorrect: He delivered a well-organized presentation, however, he did not speak loudly enough.

Watch out especially for fused sentences involving a comma plus a transition.

To de-fuse fused sentences into correct grammatical units, you have four choices. First, you can separate every main clause with a period, like this:

> **Correct:** The recruiter was impressed by her well-written résumé. He also noted that she appeared poised and articulate during her interview.

Setting off every sentence with a period implies to your reader that every sentence is equally important.

Second, you can separate sentences with a semicolon, like this:

> **Correct:** The recruiter was impressed by her well-written résumé; he also noted that she appeared poised and articulate during her interview.

In one sense, the semicolon is equal in strength to a period; they both separate sentences correctly. In another sense, however, the semicolon is different because it ties the two sentences together—more closely than they are tied to other sentences in the paragraph. For example, take a look back through this paragraph. The second sentence, starting "In one sense," consists of two sentences joined by a semicolon. Because they are joined by the semicolon, those two ideas tie together more closely than they do to the other sentences in the paragraph.

Third, you can add a coordinating conjunction, like this:

> **Correct:** The recruiter was impressed by her well-written résumé and he also noted that she appeared poised and articulate during her interview.

Coordinating conjunctions are strong connectors, strong enough to connect sentences. They are relatively easy to remember because only seven exist: *and, but, or, for, nor, so,* and *yet*. Instead of definitely separating ideas, as you do with periods, you are relating ideas if you use coordinating conjunctions: *and* relates ideas of equal importance, *but* implies a contrast is coming up, and so forth.

As a fourth choice, you can use a subordinator. Subordinators make one part of your sentence subordinate—or less important—than the other part. Typical subordinators include *although, since,* and *while*. See page 212 for a complete list. Instead of separating ideas of equal importance, as you would with a period or semicolon, when you use a subordinator you are emphasizing one part of your sentence. For example, here the writer subordinates the résumé and emphasizes the interview:

Correct: Because she had such a well-written résumé, the recruiter was not surprised that she was poised and articulate during her interview.

In the next example, the writer subordinates—or makes less important—the interview.

Correct: Although he was impressed with her interviewing skills, the interviewer commented on her well-written résumé.

Parallelism

The last thing to keep in mind to construct correct sentences is parallelism. *Parallelism* means expressing ideas of equal importance in grammatical structure of equal importance. For example, to describe three job duties, write: "*editing, proofreading,* and *designing* layout." Do NOT write: "*editing, proofreading,* and *the design* of layout." What's the difference? In the second example, the third item is not grammatically parallel to the other two items. In this case, all three items should be *-ing*-ending verbs. In other cases, items might be all nouns, all verbs, all infinitives, whatever—as long as all equally important ideas use the same form.

Why does parallelism matter? The reason, once again, is your reader: readers can understand and follow your thoughts much faster if you use effective parallelism. The following examples illustrate different kinds of parallelism, and—I hope—how parallel forms are easier to read than unparallel forms.

1. Parallel adjectives

   Correct: He was *sensitive* and *helpful.*
   Incorrect: He was *sensitive* and *a big help.*

   Correct: Your *original, clever* idea will make your boss happy.
   Incorrect: Your idea is *original, clever,* and *will make* your boss happy.

2. Parallel nouns

   Correct: The new manager is *a genius, a leader,* and *a hard worker.*
   Incorrect: The new manager is *a genius, a leader,* and *works hard.*

3. *Parallel verbs*

   Correct: If the staff members are well motivated, they will *arrive* at work on time, *correct* their own mistakes, and *use* less sick leave.

Incorrect: If the staff members are well motivated, they will *arrive* at work on time, *correct* their own mistakes, and *fewer sick days will be used.*

4. Parallel clauses

Correct: Some business professors *teach by lecturing*; others *teach by using* the case method.

Incorrect: Some business professors *teach by lecturing*, unlike *the alternative use* of the case method.

5. Parallel bullet points

Correct: The president announced we plan to
- *trim* the overseas staff,
- *cut* the domestic-marketing budget, and
- *improve* quality control.

Incorrect: The president announced we plan to
- *trim* the overseas staff,
- *cut* the domestic-marketing budget, and
- *quality control* will be improved.

6. Parallel internal enumeration

Correct: To use the word processor, (1) *insert* the program disk in drive A, (2) *insert* the file disk in drive B, and (3) *turn* on the computer in all three places.

Incorrect: To use the word processor, (1) *insert* the program disk in drive A, (2) *the file disk* goes in drive B, and (3) *don't forget to* turn on the computer in all three places.

7. Parallel coordinating conjunctions (such as *and* or *but*) or correlative conjunctions (such as *either-or*). (See page 424 for more information on conjunctions.)

Correct: Neither *expanding* the sales staff nor *increasing* the number of advertisements can save this product.

Incorrect: Neither *expanding* the sales staff nor *more advertisements* can save this product.

8. Parallel comparisons (*more than, less than, equal to*)

Correct: On the phone, first *identifying* yourself is more effective than *starting* right off with your sales pitch.

> **Incorrect:** On the phone, first *identifying* yourself is more effective than the get-right-down-to-the-sales-pitch *approach*.

9. Parallel repeated words

> **Correct:** He always hands in *his* payroll sheets, *his* data cards, and *his* time reports on the first of the month.

or

> **Correct:** He always hands in his *payroll sheets, data cards,* and *time reports* on the first of the month.

> **Incorrect:** He always hands in *his* payroll sheets, *data cards,* and *his* time report on the first of the month.

Correct Verbs

Verbs show action (such as *kick*) or a state of being (such as *is*). To use verbs correctly, watch for (1) verb agreement, (2) verb tense, (3) verb mood and voice, and (4) split infinitives.

Verb agreement

A subject and a verb should agree in number. *Number* means the number of people or things affected by the verb. There are only two such numbers. *Singular* applies to verbs affecting a single person or thing (a singular noun, or the pronouns *I, you, he, she, it*). *Plural* applies to verbs affecting more than one person or thing (a plural noun or the pronouns *we*, all of *you, they*). *Agreement* means that if the subject is singular, the verb should be singular; if the subject is plural, the verb should be plural.

For example:

> **Correct:** The building *explodes*.

In this sentence, the subject is singular (one building) and the verb is singular (it explodes). Make the subject plural, though, and you must make the verb plural also:

> **Correct:** The buildings *explode*.

Now, the subject is plural (more than one building) and the verb is plural (they explode). Obviously, the following sentences show incorrect agreement:

> **Incorrect:** The building *explode.*
> **Incorrect:** The buildings *explodes.*

In those examples, verb agreement appears to be simple. In more complex cases, however, use these eight rules to determine proper agreement.

1. Determine the verb by the subject—not by modifiers or parenthetical information that comes in between the subject and verb.

   The vice-president, as well as the staff members, *is* (NOT *are*) responsible for the project. (because vice-president, not staff members, is the subject)

   Every one of you *is* (NOT *are*) on the list. (because *every one*, not *you*, is the subject)

   The *risks* of a takeover *seem* great.
   The *risk* of a takeover *seems* great.
   (because *risks* or *risk* is the subject, not *takeover*)

   The report, as well as the oral presentation, *is* excellent.
   (because *report* is the subject; *as well as the oral presentation* is parenthetical information)

2. Use a plural verb for subjects joined by *and*—usually.

   The market and the drugstore *are* having sales.

   In rare cases, when subjects joined by *and* are considered a single unit, use the singular verb:

   Research and Development *is* often slighted.
   The founder and president *is* Emily Rubin.

3. In the case of two subjects joined by *or* or *nor, either-or,* or *neither-nor,* use the subject nearer the verb to determine the verb.

   George *or* Ringo *answers* the phone at the studio. (because *Ringo* is singular and nearer the verb)

   Neither George *nor* the other men *answer* the phone at the pool. (because *men* is plural and nearer the verb)

   Either the art department *or* the editorial department *has* the copy. (because *editorial department* is singular and nearer the verb)

4. Use a singular verb for subjects such as *each, either, another, anyone, someone, something, one, everyone, no one,* and *nothing.*

   Each of us *is.* . .
   Another one of the members *has.* . .
   Either of them *decides.* . .

5. Use a singular verb for plural nouns with a singular meaning.

   The *news is* good.
   Physics is a tough course.

6. Use a singular verb for plural subjects considered a singular unit.

   Thirty dollars is not enough.
   Fifteen minutes is far too long.

7. Use a singular verb for collective nouns, such as *group, family,* and *committee.*

   The group *reserves* the right. . .
   The family *discusses* politics. . .
   The committee *is* meeting. . .

8. Use a singular verb for articles, firm names, and slogans.

   "Defending the Barracudas" *is* interesting reading.
   Baker, Guerrero, and Kropp *is* a respected law firm.
   "The Eyes of Texas Are upon You" *is* my favorite song.

Verb tense

Verb tense indicates time. "He *acts* businesslike" indicates the action is taking place in the present. "He *acted* businesslike" indicates the action took place in the past. Like the verb *acted,* many verbs form the past tense with the suffix *-d.* Irregular verbs, however, don't use the suffix *-d.* Examples of the past tense of such verbs are *saw* and *went.*

English has six tenses. Two use single-word verbs. The other four use *helping* or *auxiliary* verbs (such as *will* or *can, had* or *have, do* or *did,* and *were* or *has been*).

Simple Tenses
present: act (acts)

past: acted

future: will (shall) act

Compound Tenses

Present: have (has) acted

Past: had acted

Future: will (shall) have acted

Use verb tenses logically, both throughout each document and within each sentence. In business writing, background information is likely to be in the past tense (such as, "the report you *requested*"; "the company *lost* money in 1980"); analysis and description in the present tense; and recommendations in the future. Do not shift tenses except when you are referring to actions in distinctly different time frames.

More specifically, watch out for these three tense problems:

1. Avoid unnecessary shifts in tense when you do not shift the time frame. For example, do not say; "If you *want* to insert a comma, use this button. If you *wanted* to insert a semicolon, use that button." Here, the writer shifts tenses unnecessarily between sentences. Do not say; "The messenger *delivers* the letters, but *left* before I had a chance to see him." Here, the writer shifts tenses unnecessarily within a sentence.

2. Shift tenses within a sentence only when the sentence includes two time frames—for example, "My friend *reminded* (past tense because the action happened in the past) us that she *is* (NOT *was*, because the action is still true in the present) working for a bank." Here is another correct tense shift: "Mr. Pincher *knows* (present because the action is true now) he *will leave* (future tense because the action is still in the future) the firm eventually."

3. Use the present tense to report an author's statements or ideas even if the article was written in the past. This convention is based on the assumption that the author still speaks to us in a continuing present. Use the present tense for either direct (with quotation marks) or indirect (without quotation marks) quotations:

In *Capitalism and Freedom*, Milton Friedman *argues* (present tense) for a laissez-faire economy.

In *The New Industrial State*, Galbraith *declares* (present tense): "Technology and associated requirements in capital and time lead. . . directly to the regulation of demand by the state."

Verb mood and voice

Mood refers to the writer's state of mind. There are only three moods in English: (1) indicative, (2) imperative, and (3) subjunctive.

Use the indicative mood to make a statement or ask a question.

> He usually *flies* in the corporate jet. (a statement)
> Does he usually *fly* in the corporate jet? (a question)

Use the imperative mood for commands and requests.

> *Fly* in the corporate jet tomorrow. (a command)

Just because you use the imperative mood does not mean you are being bossy. The imperative mood is very useful in business for explaining instructions, because it enables you to avoid having to keep repeating "You should do. . . ." For example:

> To use the video equipment, *turn* on the camera, *zoom* in on the subject's nose, *focus* on the nose, and *zoom* back out to the desired setting. (imperative for instructions)

Use the subjunctive mood to indicate conditions contrary to fact or to indicate a desire. The subjunctive mood is rarely used in English. If you want to be perfectly correct, use it in the three instances that follow. If you want to achieve the minimum literacy, at least remember to use it in the first instance—"wishful expressions" such as these:

> If I *were* (not *was*) president, I'd fire Melinda. (because being president is a wish, not a fact)

> My assistant acts as if she *were* (not *was*) my boss. (because being your boss is her wish, not a fact)

For these conditions of wishfulness—"I wish I *were*," "if I *were*," or "he acts as if he *were*"—always use the verb *to be*: use *be* for all subjects in the present tense; use *were* for all subjects in the past tense.

Also, technically you should use the subjunctive mood in *that* clauses involving recommendation:

> The group voted *that* the report *be* (not *was*) approved.
> I recommend *that* he *see* (NOT *sees*) a doctor immediately.

In these *that* clauses, use *be* or *were* as you did for conditions of wishfulness: drop the *s* in the third person of other verbs—*that* he *see*

(NOT *that* he *sees*), *that* she *run* (NOT *that* she *runs*), *that* he *quit* (NOT *that* he *quits*).

Finally, use the subjunctive in three idiomatic expressions: "If need *be*," "*Suffice* it to say," and "*Come* what may."

Voice is a matter of the subject of the sentence *acting* or *being acted upon*. Therefore, there are only two voices: *active voice* and *passive voice*. In the active voice, the subject of the sentence acts:

She locked the safe.

In the passive voice, the subject of the sentence is acted upon (in other words, the subject of the sentence is passive):

The *safe is locked* by her.

Grammatically, both voices are correct. Stylistically, however, they differ significantly. See chapter 9 (pages 226–29) for a discussion of these differences.

Split infinitives

An *infinitive* is the most general form of a verb: *to play, to work,* and *to complain* are infinitives. As students who have studied foreign languages will recall, in other languages the infinitive is one word: in Spanish, *estar* means "to be"; in French, *être* means "to be"; in German, *sein* means "to be." In other languages, speakers simply cannot split infinitives, because the infinitive is one word. In English, however, we *can* split infinitives, by separating the *to* from the rest of the verb. The question is, *should* we do so?

The most formal answer to the question is this: in most cases, do not split infinitives. For example, technically this phrase from a well-known old television show is incorrect:

Split infinitive: *To* boldly *go* where no man has gone before. . . .

Most usage experts agree, however, that it is better to split an infinitive than to sound awkward or unclear. For example, this split infinitive is acceptable:

Acceptable split infinitive: The lawyer attempted *to* clearly *state* that her remarks were off the record.

To say *attempted clearly to state* sounds awkward; to say *attempted to state clearly* leads to possible misinterpretation. Therefore, let sense and meaning take precedence over an absolute abolishment of split infinitives.

Keep in mind, however, that split infinitives remain technically incorrect, and may grate on many readers' nerves. So, don't go on an infinitive-splitting spree. Do not split them unnecessarily. And never split them with more than one word.

Correct: He was determined *to study* the problem carefully and analytically.

Incorrect: He was determined *to* carefully and analytically *study* the problem.

Correct Pronouns

Pronouns are words used in place of nouns. Obviously, you would not say, "Sue took Sue's books," but rather "Sue took *her* books." The pronoun *her*, therefore, is used in place of the noun *Sue*.

Remember that a pronoun stands for a *noun*, not for a phrase, clause, sentence, or paragraph. Therefore, do not use pronouns to stand for an entire idea, as in "If you do *that*, . . ." (What is "that"? Unless it refers back to a specific *noun*—not a general idea—you cannot use the pronoun *that*.) Instead, be more specific, as in "If you follow *these steps*, . . ." As another example, do not say "We want to hold a reception to honor the new president. *This* was approved." ("This" what? There is no *noun* to refer back to.) So instead, say, "We want to hold a reception to honor the new president. *This idea* was approved."

To use pronouns correctly, watch out for (1) pronoun agreement, (2) pronoun case, and (3) correct use of interrogative and relative pronouns.

Pronoun agreement

A pronoun and its antecedent (the word the pronoun refers to) should agree in number. There are only two "numbers" for pronouns. (1) *Singular* pronouns are those that refer to *one* person or thing: *I/me/my/mine; you/your/yours; he/him/his; she/her/hers; it/its*. (2) *Plural* pronouns are those that refer to *more than one* person or thing: *we/us/our/ours; you/your/yours; they/*

them/their/theirs. Agreement means that if the antecedent is singular, the pronoun should be singular; if the antecedent is plural, the pronoun should be plural.

For example, in this sentence,

Correct: The *cat* takes *its* time strolling across the street.

both the pronoun (*its*) and the antecedent (*cat*) are singular; therefore, they agree. In the sentence,

Correct: The *cats* take *their* time strolling across the street.

both the pronoun (*their*) and the antecedent (*cats*) are plural; therefore, they agree.

Use these five rules to avoid problems with pronoun agreement.

1. Determine the pronoun by the antecedent—not by modifiers or parenthetical information that comes between the antecedent and the pronoun. (See page 414 for a definition of *antecedent*.)

   The *manager*, not the staff members, is responsible for making *her* appointments. (because *manager* is the antecedent; *not the staff members* is merely parenthetical information)

2. Use the plural pronoun for antecedents joined by *and*.

   The secretary and the treasurer stole *their* chairs.

3. Use the noun nearer the verb to determine the pronoun for antecedents joined by *or* or *nor*. For example, say;

   Neither Cameron *nor* Seth finished *his* memo. (because *Seth*, the nearest antecedent, is singular)

   Either the supervisor *or* her staff members have made *their* (NOT *her*) group's proposal. (because *staff members*, the nearest antecedent, is plural)

4. Use a singular pronoun to refer to antecedents such as *person, woman, man, kind, each, either, neither, another, anyone, somebody, one, everybody, no one*. For example:

   Neither company had *its* (NOT *their*) books audited.

   Each of the committee members agrees to complete *his* (NOT *their*) assignment before the next meeting.

To avoid possible sexist connotations implicit in the masculine singular pronouns, see chapter 2.

5. Use a singular pronoun to refer to *collective nouns*—nouns representing a unit—such as *group, team,* or *pack.* For example:

The *group* is preparing *its* (NOT *their*) statement.

The *pack* of wolves attacked *its* (NOT *their*) prey. (The antecedent is *pack,* not *wolves,* because *wolves* describes what kind of pack.)

Pronoun case

The term *case* refers to how the pronoun is used in a sentence: as a subject (subjective case), an object (objective case), a possessive, or an intensive/reflexive. For example, consider the feminine singular pronouns: *she* serves as the subject of a sentence; *her* serves as the object of the sentence; *her* or *hers* shows possession; *herself* is the intensive/reflexive.

Let's look at some rules to keep in mind for each of these four cases.

Use the **subjective** case (*I, you, he/she/it, we, they*) when the pronoun is in the subject.

Linda and *I* (NOT *me*) went to Boston. (*I* is the subject.)

Watch out for two possible problems in the subjective case. First, beware of double (called *compound*) subjects:

She and *I* (NOT *her* and *me*) pole-vaulted. (*I* is in the compound subject.)

We (NOT *us*) track-team members pole-vaulted. (Both *we* and *members* are in the compound subject.)

He and *I* (NOT *Him* and *me*) finished the job. (*He* is in the compound subject.)

We (NOT *us*) accountants work on the third floor. (Both *we* and *accountants* are in the compound subject.)

Second, watch out for subject complements.

That may be *she* (NOT *her*). (*She* is the subject complement.)

It was *she* (NOT *her*) who paid the bill. (*She* is the subject complement.)

Use the **objective** case pronouns (*me, you, him/her/them*) when the pronoun is in the direct object, the indirect object, or the object of a preposition.

> The police officer stopped Alex and *me* (NOT *I*). (*Me* is in the object of the sentence.)
>
> The police officer wrote *me* a ticket. (*Me* is the indirect object of the sentence.)
>
> The police officer promised to send the ticket to *me*. (*Me* is the object of the preposition *to*.)

Remember especially always to use the objective case after prepositions (words such as *over, after,* and *to*). (See page 236 for a list of prepositions.)

> Just between you and *me* (NOT *I*), the police officer's ticket was a ticket to a fund-raising event. (*Me* is the object of the preposition *between*.)

Never use the subjective *you and I* unless you can substitute the subjective *we*. You would not say "just between we," so don't say "just between you and I."

Don't be afraid to use the objective case. Many students have been corrected so often for using the objective case when they should not, as in

> **Incorrect:** *Him* and *me* are leaving the scene of the ticket.
> (should be *he* and *I*)

that they don't use the objective case when they *should*. *Her and I* and *him and me*, in other words, are sometimes correct—when they are used as objects, in

> The police officer finally left *him* and *me* (NOT *he* and *I*).

Use **possessive** pronouns (*my/mine, your/yours, his/her/hers/its, our/ours, their/theirs*) to show ownership:

> *Their* office collapsed.
> *Theirs* is a more shaky building than *ours*.

Using the possessive pronouns is fairly easy. One possible problem with possessives involves apostrophes. (See pages 453–54 for apostrophe rules.) Another possible problem involves gerunds. *Gerunds* are *-ing*-ending verbs that serve as nouns:

> *Golfing* is my favorite sport.
> She enjoyed *telling* jokes.

Use possessive pronouns with gerunds:

> We were surprised at *his* (NOT *him*) resigning.
> No one had anticipated *their* (NOT *them*) departing.

Use the **intensive/reflexive** pronouns for emphasis: *myself, yourself, himself/herself, ourselves, yourselves, themselves.*

> I *myself* signed that purchase order. (*Myself* emphasizes *I.*)
> He signed that order *himself.* (*Himself* emphasizes *he.*)

The biggest problem with these forms is misuse and overuse of *myself.* Patrick Henry didn't feel obliged to say, "But as for myself, give myself liberty or give myself death." So, don't use *myself* any time you can substitute *I* or *me.*

> Leslie and *I* (NOT *myself*) designed the market survey.
> He gave the report to Spence and *me* (NOT *myself*).

Another problem is the misuse of *himself* and *themselves.* Never say "hisself" or "theirselves"; these pronouns do not exist as words.

Interrogative and relative pronouns

Interrogative pronouns are used in questions: *which, what, who, whom,* and *whose.*

> *Who* is attending?
> *Which* folder is missing?

Relative pronouns are used to introduce subordinate clauses: *there, who, whom, whose, that, which, what, whoever, whichever,* and *whatever.*

> The person *who* is attending. . .
> The folder, *which* is black, has been missing for a month.

As you can see, the five interrogative pronouns also serve as relative pronouns, so we shall consider them as a group.

One common pitfall with these kinds of pronouns arises from the differences between people and things. Use *who* or *whom* to refer to people; *which* to refer to things or animals; *that* to refer to things, animals, or people.

She is the one *who* (NOT *which*) went to the mall.
The cabinet, *which* is in my office, is overflowing.
The person *who* (NOT *which*) is in my office is sitting on the radiator.

Another rule is to place relative pronouns as close as possible to their antecedents.

The *people who* were on the list attended the meeting (NOT
The *people* attended the meeting *who* were on the list.)
The *cabinet, which* is in my office, is overflowing. (NOT
The *cabinet* is overflowing *which* is in my office.)

The final problem with interrogative and relative pronouns is the extremely tricky business of *who* versus *whom*. If you want to be formal and correct, follow the next four rules. However, in many business situations, informal usage allows *who* rather than *whom* in all cases except following a preposition. In other words, if you want to be a stickler—or, indeed, if it's important to your readers that you be absolutely correct—wade your way through all four rules. If you have the time and inclination to memorize only one of these rules, make it the third one.

1. Use *who* or *whoever* as the subject of a sentence.

   Who works here?
   Those *who* work here. . .

2. Use *whom* or *whomever* as the object of a sentence.

   Whom do you recommend? (*You* is the subject, *recommend* the verb, *whom* the object.)

   Marilyn knew *whom* to call. (*Marilyn* is the subject, *knew* the verb, *whom* the object.)

3. Use *whom* or *whomever* as the object of a preposition.

   For *whom* are they working? (*Whom* is the object of the preposition *for*.)

   To *whom* am I speaking? (*Whom* is the object of the preposition *to*.)

4. Now comes the hard part: use *who* or *whoever* as the subject of a subordinate clause; use *whom* or *whomever* as the object of a subordinate clause.

I forgot *who* approved this project. (*Who* is the subject of the clause *who approved*.)

He kowtows to *whoever* is in power. (*Whoever* is the subject of the clause *whoever is*.)

Margie told Marilyn *whom* to call. (*Whom* is the object of the clause *Marilyn to call whom*.)

To choose between *who* and *whom* in a subordinate clause, restate the clause as a statement.

He is the kind of salesperson *who?/whom?* they will promote.
Restate: They will promote *him*.
> *Him* is the objective case, so choose *whom*, also the objective case.

He is the kind of salesperson *who?/whom?* can be promoted.
Restate: *He* can be promoted.
> *He* is the subjective case, so choose *who*, also the subjective case.

Who?/whom? did you invite?
Restate: You did invite *them*.
> *Them* is the objective case, so choose *whom*, also the objective case.

Correct Adjectives and Adverbs

Adjectives and adverbs are called *modifiers*, because they change, qualify, or restrict the meaning of other words. Adjectives modify nouns or pronouns. Adverbs modify verbs, adjectives, and other adverbs. Here are some examples of adjectives and adverbs: "the *rapid* change" (adjective, modifying the noun *change*); "changed *rapidly*" (adverb, modifying the verb *changed*); "an *unusually* large organization" (adverb, modifying the adjective *large*).

There is, alas, no easy formula for telling the difference between adjectives and adverbs. Frequently, adverbs add the suffix *-ly* to the adjective form, as in *quick/quickly, harsh/harshly, pleasant/pleasantly*. Some adjectives, however, also end with the suffix *-ly*, such as *friendly*. Finally, some words function as both adjectives and adverbs—for example, *far, fast, little*, and *well*.

Adjectives

To avoid adjective errors, use adjectives to modify nouns or pronouns. Take the sentence

She sent the report to her clients.

If you want to modify the noun *report* (that is, tell what *kind* of report it is), use an adjective, such as *long:*

She sent the *long* report to her clients.

One major adjective error involves the use of complements. A *complement* is a noun or adjective that follows a linking verb (usually *be, seem*, or *appear*) and specifies something about the subject of the sentence, as in

My boss seems *upset*.

The complement *upset* follows the linking verb *seems* and specifies something about the subject, *boss*. In sentences with complements, the linking verb acts as if it were a big equal sign between the subject and the complement: "my boss = upset."

The error occurs when you use an adverb where a complement is called for. Here are two examples of the correct use of an adjective as a complement:

The coffee seems *different* (NOT *differently*) this morning.
(The adjective *different* follows the subject and the linking verb *seems*.)

The bank robber looked *suspicious* (NOT *suspiciously*) to me.
(The adjective *suspicious* follows the subject and the linking verb *looked*.)

Here are two more sentences, which illustrate the difference between a complement adjective modifying a noun and an adverb modifying a verb:

The secretary looked *cold* to me. (The adjective *cold* modifies the subject *secretary*.)

The secretary looked *coldly* at me. (The adverb *coldly* modifies the verb *looked*.)

The second major adjective error involves comparatives and superlatives. A *comparative* compares two things: *faster* is the comparative of *fast*; *higher* is the comparative of *high*. A *superlative* is an even stronger comparison, used for three or more things: *fastest* is the superlative of *fast* and *faster*; *highest* is the superlative of *high* and *higher*. In general, most short adjectives form the comparative by adding *-er* and the superlative by adding *-est* (*smart, smarter, smartest*). Longer adjectives form the comparative by adding the word *more* or *less* (*more exhausted*, NOT *exhausteder*) and the superlative by adding the word *most* or *least* (*most ridiculous*, NOT *ridiculousest*).

Adverbs

To avoid adverb errors, make sure you use adverbs to modify verbs, other adverbs, or adjectives. For example, consider this sentence:

My hasty colleague left the room.

If you want to modify the verb *left*, to tell *how* the colleague left, you'd use an adverb, such as *quickly:*

My hasty colleague left the room *quickly*.

If you want to modify the adverb *quickly* (to tell *how* quickly), you'd use an adverb—for example, *very:*

My hasty colleague left the room *very* quickly.

If you want to modify the adjective *hasty* (to tell *how* hasty the colleague is), use an adverb, such as *somewhat:*

My *somewhat* hasty colleague left the room very quickly.

The most frequent adverb error involves the adverb *well*. Don't replace it with *good*, as in

Incorrect: He played *good*.

Good in that sentence modifies a verb, *played,* so you must use an adverb instead:

Correct: He played *well.*

APPLICATION QUESTIONS

To apply your knowledge

Correct sentences

1. Complete sentences: Revise the following to make them complete sentences (that is, not fragments or double sentences).

   a. Remember to dim the lights for the slide show. During the rehearsal as well as the actual presentation.

   b. Although she is out of town for the week, Ms. Pancratz keeps in touch with the office by phone.

   c. The economic downturn was devastating, all the firms in the area suffered.

   d. Rehiring seasonal workers is good policy, as you will see, several successful bookstores in town do it.

   e. Those products are not in stock, however, we can easily order them for you.

   f. He kept pressing me for a meeting, finally I agreed.

   g. The idea was sound, however, its realization left something to be desired.

   h. The supervisor who called me into his office.

   i. He didn't call, therefore I assumed he wasn't coming.

   j. Watch out for grammatical mistakes, for example, the split infinitive.

   k. Hope to see you soon.

   l. I asked to see the books. When I realized something was wrong.

   m. He has studied accounting, thus he is prepared to go on the job market.

   n. Sean was lucky to get that job. Having never had any experience in sales.

   o. I wanted to be cooperative, I volunteered all the information I could.

2. Parallelism: Rewrite the following sentences using parallel structure.

   a. Minorities have had difficulty enrolling in certain schools and to be admitted to prestigious professions.

   b. The number of business students who studied for their degree and were holding part-time jobs is surprisingly high.

   c. For a successful public relations campaign, the corporation needs good media coverage as well as getting community support.

   d. A lot of employees want both a high salary and to have good working conditions.

   e. Last year, the company restructured the domestic managerial organization, increasing the marketing budget, and to have monthly staff gripe sessions.

   f. Not only are more married women working, but the single woman is also pursuing the management career.

   g. He objected to the time of the meeting, the selection of the room, and the manner in which the press was notified.

Correct verbs

1. Agreement: Select the correct verb for correct verb agreement.

   a. Ms. Baker and Mr. Thompson (is, are) due to arrive this afternoon.

   b. Either Marketing or R&D (is, are) going to have (its, their) budget cut.

   c. Selling stocks and bonds for private individuals (is, are) interesting work.

   d. Each one of us (have, has) to take a polygraph test.

   e. The advantages of the new antitrust bill (is, are) difficult to understand.

   f. Thompson, as well as all the members of his staff, (were, was) fired.

   g. The problem with these memos (is, are) glaring.

   h. Shoplifting prosecutions, which (create, creates) significant costs to the company, (improve, improves) the morale of security personnel.

   i. The prize (was, were) fifty phonograph records.

   j. The timing of the price increases (was, were) poorly planned.

2. Tense: Revise the following passage so that verb tenses are used consistently. Eliminate unnecessary shifts in tense.

When Wesco had first opened for business in 1969, Lawrence Hammill would have been the only black employee. At the time, Wesco had employed sixty-four workers. Over the next four years, Hammill rises to become assistant director of public relations. It was then that he begins to be using his position in the company and his good reputation to lobby for increased minority hiring. Progress was slow at first, but in 1985 Hammill had been named to devise a program that was insuring that minority hiring will have increased as Wesco expands. The goal was to have had 20 percent minority workers by 1987. Hammill achieves this goal eighteen months early, in January 1986.

3. Split infinitives: Rewrite to correct split infinitives.

a. He promised to quickly come the next time I called.

b. Howard was in a good position to effectively sell his idea.

c. My advice to her was to eventually consider moving on to another company.

d. With preparation, Shelly was able to confidently and effortlessly answer his arguments.

e. In another year, the company should be able to almost recoup all of its losses.

Correct pronouns

1. Agreement: Fix the problems with pronoun agreement in the following sentences.

a. The staff should be advised that their proposal was unanimously accepted.

b. Neither Joan nor the other woman has any opinion on this matter.

c. The company's lower-level management was quick to voice their opposition to the pay cut.

d. The supervisor, in conjunction with her staff, have developed a proposal for improving employee morale.

e. Standard Aluminum says they will.

f. Every person should be able to see their personnel file if they desire.

g. A committee of experts stated ~~their~~ *its* opinion that the investment was ill advised.

2. Case: Choose the correct pronoun case.

   a. For (who, whom) did the committee vote?

   b. The company president is younger than (me, I).

   c. The applicant (who, whom) I interviewed last week is the most promising.

   d. Between you and (I, me), it's too late to make money in precious gems.

   e. (We, Us) secretaries like the new boss, (who, whom) we respect and (who, whom) we believe respects us.

   f. I couldn't stand (his, him) complaining about other employees.

   g. Mr. Parker expected Jenny Wilcox and (me, I) to finish the report.

   h. Just between you and (me, I), the books are a mess.

   i. Jennifer and (he, him) were invited to take part in the seminar.

   j. Last May, Mr. Griffith gave a bonus to Jim and (I, me) and commended us on our work.

   k. Lance was always much more punctual than (she, her).

   l. Please sign the form and return it to Leslie or (I, me, myself).

3. Interrogative and relative pronouns: Fix the problems with the interrogative and relative pronouns in the following sentences.

   a. Who do you suggest that I call?

   b. Will the person which borrowed my phone book please return it?

   c. That man visited my office who you gave my name to.

   d. My boss told me to hire whoever I wanted.

   e. The invited speaker was Kevin, whom everyone knows is quite talented.

   f. Who is the woman who Stacy recommended for that position?

   g. The model was finally discontinued which never recorded a profit.

D

Punctuation and Mechanics

Punctuation
Period • Semicolon • Colon • Comma • Dash •
Parentheses • Brackets • Quotation marks • Apostrophe •
Ellipsis • Slash • Question mark • Exclamation point

Mechanics
Abbreviations • Capitalization

Punctuation

· Period

Use the period after most sentences (declaratives and mild imperatives), after indirect questions, and after most abbreviations. Do not use a period after shortened forms; do not end a sentence with two periods.

Declarative sentences

Usually, declarative sentences (that is, sentences that declare something) end with a period, just as this one does.

Mild imperative sentences

Use the period to end mild imperative sentences (that is, *commands*). The previous sentence is a mild imperative.

Indirect questions

He asked if he should use a period at the end of this sentence. Since the previous sentence is not a direct question (but rather a report about a question), it ends correctly with a period.

Abbreviations

Use periods in abbreviations: Mrs. Henderson, an M.D., called to R.S.V.P. the 7:30 P.M. party. (You may omit periods after well-known abbreviations, such as MD or MBA.)

NOT two periods at the end of a sentence

When an abbreviation ends a sentence, don't add a second period.

NOT after shortened form

Do not use periods after shortened forms. Therefore, write "The *premed* student went to *psych lab* after her *gym* class" with no periods after the shortened words.

; Semicolon

Use the semicolon as a period between two closely related main clauses, and as a "supercomma" to separate a series of items that themselves contain commas. Use the semicolon only between closely related elements of equal importance.

Between a main clause and a related main clause

A semicolon indicates a close connection between two main clauses of equal importance such as these; if you use a semicolon, do not join these clauses with a coordinator (*and, but, or, nor, for*). The semicolon in the previous sentence separated the two related main clauses.

Between a main clause and a transition preceding a related main clause

A semicolon indicates a close connection between two main clauses of equal importance; however, don't forget to use a semicolon to separate two such clauses even if you use a transitional word between them (such as the word *however* here).

NOT between a main clause and a subordinate element

This is a main clause; although this isn't. (Therefore, the previous semicolon is incorrect.) Since this isn't a main clause; the preceding semicolon is also incorrect.

NOT usually between items in a list

Usually do not use a semicolon to separate items in a list. Use commas instead.

Between items in a list containing internal commas

Use a semicolon as a "supercomma" in a series that is complex, like this one, containing internal commas; you need, in order to show where the stronger breaks are, to use stronger punctuation; and you want to avoid confusing your readers, who might get lost with only commas to guide them.

: Colon

Use the colon as an "introducer" to what follows, and as a mark of separation.

To introduce a list, series, quote, or statement

Use a colon to introduce the following: a list, a series, a quotation, or a statement.

Between two main clauses when the second amplifies the first

Often, writers use colons in this way: they separate two main clauses when the second amplifies or explains the first.

**After salutation
Between title and subtitle
Between biblical chapter and verse
Between hour and minute**

The colon acts as a separator between each of the following four pairs: a salutation and the rest of the letter, a title and the subtitle, a biblical chapter and the verse, the hour and the minute.

, Comma

Use a comma whenever you would have a light, natural pause, or whenever necessary to prevent misunderstanding. Here are six specific uses of the comma:

Between a main clause joined to another main clause by *and, but, or, nor, for*

A main clause has a main subject and verb, but you need a comma before the conjunction (*and, but, or, nor, for*) and the second main clause in a compound sentence. That's why there is a comma in the preceding sentence before the word *but*.

Between an introductory element and the main clause

If you find you have a fairly long introductory element in your sentence, use a comma before your main clause. In addition, use a comma after an introductory transition (such as *for example, in the second place,* or *however*).

To separate items in a series

Use a comma to separate parallel series of words, phrases, and subordinate clauses.

To set off nonessential information

Incidental information in the middle of your sentence, like this, should be set off in commas. Midsentence transitions, moreover, are also enclosed in commas (as was the word *moreover* in this sentence).

Between day of week and month, date and year, city and state

Bloomsbury, Iowa, was founded on Friday, March 13, 1889.

NOT between subject and verb
NOT between state and zip code

"The telephone, rang" is not a correctly punctuated sentence. "Ann Arbor, Michigan, 48106−3123" is not correctly punctuated either.

— Dash

Use the dash where you would use a comma, but when you want a stronger—more emphatic—break. Do not use a dash in place of a period or semicolon.

To set off emphatic nonessential information

Incidental information in the middle of your sentence—like this—should be set off in dashes if you want to emphasize it. Type a dash—with no spaces before or after the surrounding word—as two hyphens.

To set off an emphatic summary

Use a dash to emphasize interruptions, breaks in thought, emphatic nonessential information—all of which might be summarized like this at the end of the sentence.

NOT as a period
NOT as a semicolon

Do not use a dash to end a sentence—For example, the preceding and following two dashes are incorrect—

( ) Parentheses

Unlike dashes—which emphasize the importance of what they surround—parentheses minimize the importance (of what they surround). Use parentheses to set off unemphatic nonessential information, to introduce an abbreviation, or to enclose enumerating letters or numbers.

To set off unemphatic nonessential information

Use parentheses for interruptions or less important ideas (when you wish the punctuation to be less emphatic than a dash).

To explain a term's abbreviation

Parentheses are useful when you are introducing a little-known abbreviation for a long, complex term you are going to use repeatedly: "the Certified Domestic Imports Plan (CDIP)." Afterwards, you can use just CDIP.

To enclose numerals or letters

Parentheses enclose enumerators within a sentence, such as (1) letters and (2) numerals.

Punctuating around the parentheses

(If an entire sentence is within the parentheses, like this sentence, place the period inside, too.) If (on the other hand) just parts of the sentence are within the parentheses, as in this sentence, place the period or comma outside the parentheses (not inside).

[ ] *Brackets*

Use brackets to set off your comments within quoted material and to replace parentheses within parentheses.

To insert within a quotation

The author states: "Use brackets [such as these] if you insert material within my quotation."

To replace parentheses within parentheses

(If you want to read a good book on writing, read *The Elements of Style* [by Strunk and White].)

" " *Quotation marks*

Use quotation marks for direct quotations, dialogue, minor titles, and words used specially. Use single quotation marks for a quotation within a quotation.

Around direct quotations

"Use quotation marks to enclose a direct quotation," she admonished. "If, however, you have a long quotation—more than ten lines—set if off by single spacing and indenting, without quotation marks."

Around dialogue

"Use quotation marks to enclose what a person says in conversation."
"Start a new paragraph for each change of speaker."

Around minor titles

Use quotation marks to set off minor titles: those of short stories, essays, short poems, songs, articles from periodicals. Also, use them for subdivisions of a book.

Around words in a special sense

Use quotation marks to enclose words used in a special sense or words referred to as words. For example: Every time she said the word "irregardless," the audience cringed.

NOT around common nicknames, humor, or trite or well-known expressions

If you want to see some incorrect quotation marks, look at this sentence: "Muffy" thought she was "cute" when she "lost her lunch."

Single quotation marks for quotations within quotations

"Use single quotation marks when you have a quotation within a quotation, 'like this.' "
Use single quotation marks when you have a minor title within a quotation, as in referring to 'The Star-Spangled Banner' in this sentence."

Punctuating around quotation marks

"Always," he said, "place the period and comma within the quotation marks."
"Always place the colon and semicolon outside the quotation marks"; you see how easy that was?
Place the dash, question mark, and exclamation point within the quotation marks when they apply only to the quoted matter; place them outside when they apply to the whole sentence. For example: On Tuesday he said, "This idea stinks!" (exclamation point refers to quoted matter only). When he called on Thursday and said "I've changed my mind; the idea is okay," I was shocked! (exclamation point refers to whole sentence).

' *Apostrophe*

Use the apostrophe to show a noun's or a pronoun's ownership, omissions or contractions, and abbreviations.

To show possession

To form the possessive, you almost always simply add *'s:* Smith's account (one Smith), women's rights, one's own, boss's office.

In one case only, you form the possessive by adding the apostrophe *only*—that is, for plural nouns ending with an *s* or *z* sound: the Smiths' account (more than one Smith), four dollars' worth.

For groups of words in a compound, add the *'s* to the last word only: my mother-in-law's idea, the chair of the board's suggestion, Leland Stanford, Jr.'s University.

To show individual versus joint possession

To show individual ownership, use *'s* for *each* name: George's and Melinda's bicycles, the secretary's and the president's offices, Smith's and Green's accounts. To show joint ownership, use the *'s* for the *last* name only: George and Melinda's bicycle, Ms. Alpha and Mr. Beta's office, Smith and Green's account.

To show omissions in contractions

Apostrophes mark the letters or numbers left out in contractions: they are = they're; did not = didn't; fiscal 1994 = fiscal '94.

To show the plural of letters and abbreviations

Always use *'s* to form the plural of lowercase letters and abbreviations followed by periods: b's, p.s.'s. Both *'s* and *s* are permissible to form the plural of capital letters and abbreviations not followed by periods: B's or Bs; MBA's or MBAs.

NOT with pronouns:
his, hers, its, ours, yours, their, whose

Don't say: "It is our's," or "It is yours'." Instead say, "It is ours," or "It is yours."

Its versus *it's*
Whose versus *who's*

It's (*contraction* of *it is*) hard to remember that its filing system (*pronoun* meaning "belonging to it") is out of date.

She is an accountant whose results (*pronoun* meaning "the results of whom") are reliable; she is an accountant who's (*contraction* of *who is*) reliable.

... *Ellipsis*

Use an ellipsis (three spaced periods) to show an omission within a quoted passage or to mark a pause.

To show an omission within a quotation

The author states: "If you leave out any of my words, such as. . . , you must mark the omission with an ellipsis."

"If you leave out words that directly follow a period, you must type the period as well (for a total of four). . . .as you see here."

To show a reflective pause

Use ellipses extremely sparingly, if ever, in business writing to trail off or pause. . .

/ *Slash*

Use the slash to show that either of two or more terms is applicable or to show the end of a line of quoted poetry.

Between equally applicable terms

Use the slash to show this term/that term are equally applicable. In typing a slash between terms, leave no space on either this side/that side.

Between lines of poetry

When you're quoting from poetry, / Slash the end of each line, as you see. / When using the slashes like these, / Space before them and after them, please.

? *Question mark*

Use the question mark after direct questions.

After direct questions

Do you know why I used a question mark in this sentence? (Answer: because I am asking you, the reader, a direct question.)

NOT after indirect questions

He asked if you knew why I did not use a question mark here. (Answer: because I am reporting a question, not asking it directly.)

Punctuating question marks in quotations

"Do you understand this question-mark business?" he asked. He then added: "Did you notice that no comma or period follows the question mark within quotations?"

$\boxed{!}$ *Exclamation point*

Use extremely sparingly in business writing to show strong emotion.

After an emotional statement

Listen! Don't overuse exclamation points!

After an emotional quotation

She said: "Don't use a comma or a period after an exclamation point!"

Mechanics

Mechanics refers to the use of abbreviations and capitalization.

Abbreviations

It is not businesslike to abbre. inappropriately (as I did, of course, just then). Ineffective business writers abbreviate too much. Never abbreviate, for example, city names (L.A.), months (Jan.), days of the week (Mon.), the word "Christmas" (Xmas), or school subjects (econ.).

Besides watching out for abbreviation-mania in general, follow these more specific guidelines:

Do abbreviate		*Do not abbreviate*	
Specific titles	Dr. Foster St. Catherine	Unspecific titles:	the young doctor the saint's life
Agencies your audience knows	FDIC FBI	Agencies your audience may not know	LAC ASB
Expressions your audience knows	f.o.b. A.M.	Expressions your audience may not know	LIFO P.E. ratio
Company names as they appear on company letterhead	Touche, Ross & Company Andrews, Inc.	Company names if company itself does not do so	Stockwell and Binney Ward, Limited
Number in designating something	Room No. 15 Policy No. 550706782	*Number* when you are not designating something	A number (not no. or #) of employees are. . .
Compass points in addresses	Ms. Lindsay Rahmun 1257 N. Fillmore Corvallis, OR 94306-7163	Compass points not in addresses	turn north in the north
street and similar words used in addresses	Mr. Cameron Wyatt 122 Washington Ave. Los Angeles, CA 91711-5032	*Street* and similar words not used in addresses	down the avenue in the boulevard
States used in addresses	Mr. Seth Munter 223 Kendall Place Provo, UT 50425−2508	States not used in addresses	Utah Missouri
Common Latin expressions	cf. (compare) e.g. (for example) et al. (and others) etc. (and so forth) i.e. (that is) vs. or v. (versus)		

Capitalization

Do capitalize *specific proper names*		*Do not capitalize* *nonspecific common nouns* *which may be preceded by* *a, an, or every*
Names	Scruggy Loretta	dog woman

Do capitalize *specific proper names*		*Do not capitalize* *nonspecific common nouns* *which may be preceded by* *a, an,* or *every*
Names of family members	Mother Dad	my mother my dad
Places	Middletown Main Street	a main street a town
Parts of place names	Kansas City College Grand Canyon Mississippi River Microchip Company	went to college through many canyons floated downstream several companies
Organizations/institutions	United Nations Skidmore	the nations the colleges
Titles	Governor Brown W. F. Brown, Editor Ph.D.	Brown, the governor Brown, the editor doctoral program
Calendar designations	Monday August Easter	any day every month the holiday
Historical events/ documents	Civil War Constitution	the war any constitution
Holy books/deities	*Koran* Yahweh	the chapters many gods
Geographic areas	Used as place names: Far East I was born in the South.	Used as compass points: east of Tulsa birds fly south
Seasons	Winter term	during the winter

Do capitalize *first words of. . .*		*Do not capitalize*
Sentences	First letter of first word of all sentences.	
Quotations	First letter of first word of all direct quotations.	First letter of first word in indirect quotations.
	The report states: "All employees shall fill out this form."	The report states that all employees shall fill out this form.

Do capitalize specific proper names		*Do not capitalize nonspecific common nouns which may be preceded by a, an, or every*
Following colon	When formal statement or question follows.	When list or amplification sentence follows.
	This is what you should do: Always turn off your engine before you park your car.	This is what you should bring: a knife, a fork, and a spoon.
	We all wondered: Will he call on us today?	Often, writers use colons in this way: they divide clauses when the second amplifies the first.
Titles of books, plays, papers	The first word of all titles.	Non-first-word short prepositions (such as *in, with, to*), articles (*a, an, the*), and conjunctions (such as *and*).
	All words in titles except short prepositions, articles, and conjunctions.	
Salutations/ closings in letters	First word and names Dear Mr. Soandso: My dear Suchandsuch:	Words other than the first Cordially yours, Very sincerely yours,

Do capitalize		*Do not capitalize*
Pronouns	I	Any other pronouns
Peoples/ languages	English French	Other subjects: math, science
Words derived from names	Shakespearean San Franciscan Republican	—
Religions/ adherents	Buddhism Muslims	—
Abbreviations of capitalized words	D.C. (District of Columbia) CBS (Columbia Broadcasting System)	—

PUNCTUATION PRETEST

1. Insert the correct punctuation in the following sentences.

    a. In addition Mary said we shall need more group participation

    b. He did not have any money but he did have several credit cards

    c. There is no point in returning in fact it is better if we stay

    d. The day that it rained Tuesday I was supposed to fly to New York

    e. His instructions were to go right open the door and enter the first office on the left

    f. My desk was covered with books and papers in short a complete mess

    g. My suggestion is that you call the office the numbers in the phonebook and ask if you have any messages

    h. Thats not an either or situation there is only one way to look at it

    i. Lucy asked if we were intending to use the room later than nine o'clock

    j. The committee included three PhDs two MBAs a doctor and a member of the Society for Advanced Economics SAE

    k. Whether he is there or not the meeting will take place as planned

    l. What do you mean she said of course I gave you the key

    m. Is there any reason that you will not be able to attend

    n. His Aunt Stella who lives in Missouri is putting him up for the night

    o. More retail outlets are selling Carters products

2. Correct the punctuation, if necessary, in the following sentences.

    a. The visitors' bags were loaded on the plane.

    b. (We were advised that dinner would not be available.)

    c. "Are you coming?," she asked.

    d. Kenny provided us with the necessary data (eg the number of entry variables).

    e. Its no use: there are no more cars to be had.

    f. His purpose was threefold—1) to inform us, 2) to advise us, 3) to guide us.

    g. Always be sure to turn out the light upon leaving (located on the south (left) wall).

    h. If there are no directions—simply do what you think best!

    i. Usually, motorists will yield the right of way before threatening others'.

     j. "When it rains, it pours," is a famous advertising slogan.

     k. Upon graduating from college Alex went on to get his M.A.

     l. Bloomington Indiana is the location of the worlds largest widget factory.

     m. House pets—dogs, cats, etc.—are the most common substitute for a family.

     n. Lately it has come to my attention, that you smoke, said my boss.

     o. Among his effects were a will (dated Jan. 29) and a bankbook marked "First Savings and Loan".

PUNCTUATION POSTTEST

1. Insert the correct punctuation in the following sentences.

     a. The office contains two chairs which are broken a desk which is quite large but has no drawers and several bookcases

     b. Saras publications are as follows Choices in Business New York and Is There a Future in Savings and Loans Chicago

     c. Of course it doesnt work its unplugged

     d. Phoenix Arizona will be the site of next months conference topic to be announced

     e. Mister Bailey wrote It is important that we restructure our division He then forwarded the memo to Ms Wick

     f. When you see him she advised ask him for his opinion on the matter

     g. Emily Johnsons son was in the class of 79 as was Tom Brittlemeyers

     h. I wanted to go however by the time I thought of it it was too late

     i. Stay away he shouted Thats a live wire

     j. Please remember that there are two *ss* in Weissmans name

     k. He quoted these lines from Stevenss Sunday Morning casual flocks of pigeons make Ambiguous undulations as they sink

     l. Professor Smiths lecture was entitled What Price Success The Case for Ethical Practice

     m. I think its about time something was done dont you

     n. He proposed two alternatives 1 a new title 2 a raise

      o. Sally hadnt expected the third visitor the one from Wyoming

2. Correct the punctuation, if necessary, in the following sentences.

      a. "This is you're book, isn't it"? he asked.

      b. The instructor covered the following points; investments; tax shelters; and IRA's.

      c. There is—she said—no reason for this mistake.

      d. His most famous publication is "The Nature of Work" [New York].

      e. Ms. Delaneys credentials are excellent: in fact, the best I've ever seen.

      f. She asked me if I had any questions?

      g. I saw no reason to verify his statement; he seemed honest.

      h. Bruce has worked in various cities (New York, Washington, Pittsburgh, and has contacts in each).

      i. The plant is in Seattle, Washington and it will soon be expanded.

      j. She said "its ready;" then we both sat down to lunch.

      k. He would like to join us, however, he wasnt invited.

      l. In addition we should notify the stockholder's of our decision.

      m. There was no marketing strategy—But nevertheless sales were high.

      n. Barney is a member of an alumni organization (the Bay City Boosters (BCB).

      o. He said that we should [1] reorganize and [2] reassess our goals.

APPLICATION QUESTIONS
To apply your knowledge

Capitalization: The following sentences have no capital letters. Capitalize where necessary.

1. when the board of franklin savings and loan convened, ms. terry anderson moved that the meeting be open to the public.

2. "it's the american people's right to know," she argued.

3. in the fifties, several major league baseball franchises made money by relocating in the west.

4. the title of georgina massinger's new book is *the ins and outs of investment banking*; her earlier book was called *how to make money in the stock market: a guide for the complete idiot.*

5. she could have gone to san diego state university, but she didn't want to live in california.

6. instead, she went to the local college in fairbanks, alaska.

7. bill dixon is pennsylvania's only democratic senator.

8. priarton manufacturing has plants in chicago, detroit, and southern italy.

Research
and
Documentation

Business Research Sources

Business Documentation

Business Research Sources

1. For general information:
Titles and general topics

Ayer Directory: Includes current information on consumer, business, technical, professional, and farm magazines as well as newspapers published in the U.S. and Canada.

Books in Print: Lists all books currently in print by author, title, and subject. Related publications include *BIP Supplement* and *Forthcoming Books.*

Business and Economics Books and Serials in Print: Lists all books and serials currently in print for economics, industry, finance, management, and other business-related topics.

Ulrich's International Periodical Directory: Index to periodicals currently published throughout the world, listed by title and subject.

2. For specific information:
Indexes of articles by specific topic

American Statistics Index: Index to all statistical publications of the U.S. government.

Business Index: Index to articles in 750 business-related periodicals, including the *WSJ* and the *NYT* business section. (Currently available on microfilm only.)

Business Periodicals Index: Index to articles in over 300 magazines dealing with business, economics, industry, and trade; articles are listed by subject. (Available online or in print form.)

F & S Index of Corporations and Industries: Index to all articles written about each company each year. Includes 750 financial publications, business-oriented newspapers, trade magazines, and special reports. Contains corporate and new-product information, technological developments, and social and political factors affecting business.

Indexed by (1) industry, by SIC number in green pages, and (2) corporations listed alphabetically.

New York Times Index: Index to abstracts of, and annotations for, *NYT* articles. Index available online or in print; full text of *NYT* also available through *NEXIS*, an information-retrieval service.

Wall Street Journal Index: Index to abstracts of, and annotations for, *WSJ* articles. Index available online or in print; the printed index includes *Barron's* indexing. Full text of the *WSJ* also available through the *Dow Jones News/Retrieval*, an online search service.

Online Search Services:

> *BRS* and *Dialog:* These two information-retrieval services make available hundreds of data bases on many subjects. Two files in particular—ABI/Inform and Management Contents—emphasize business information. Various other bibliographic and numeric data bases are also available. Many of these data bases are available in less expensive "after hour" search services, such as BRS Afterdark and Dialog's Knowledge Index. These are available through separate subscription.

> *Compuserve:* The data base of this information-retrieval service contains information on international, national, regional, and local news, weather, sports, and commentaries; recent stock quotes or historical performance of over 40,000 stocks, bonds, and options; energy, metals, financial instruments, and agricultural commodities; and movie, restaurant, and book reviews. This service is also available in a less expensive "after hour" format.

> *Dow Jones News/Retrieval:* This service includes twenty-five data bases, among them the full text of the *WSJ* as well as company research reports, historical and current stock quotes, and other economic and financial news.

> *NEXIS:* This system includes the full text of many important financial magazines, newsletters, and newspapers, including the *NYT*.

3. For information about a company

Business Index: See subsection 2 for explanation.

Business Periodicals Index: See subsection 2 for explanation.

CIRR (Corporate and Industry Research Reports): Information on NYSE, AMEX, and OTC companies, and important industries. (Available on microfiche.)

Disclosure: Copies of 10-K's, annual reports, and proxy statements for NYSE and AMEX companies. (Available in print or online through Disclosure files in a number of retrieval services.)

F & S Index of Corporations and Industries: See subsection 2 for explanation.

Million Dollar Directory: Information on over 115,000 publicly and privately held companies in the U.S. with assets greater than $500,000. (Three-volume set.)

Moody's Bank and Finance Manual, Industrial Manual, OTC Industrial Manual, and *Public Utility Manual:* Comprehensive information on publicly held companies published annually.

New York Times Index: See subsection 2 for explanation.

Standard and Poor's Corporation Records: Information on publicly held NYSE, AMEX, and larger unlisted and regional exchange companies.

Standard and Poor's Stock Reports: Reports on NYSE, AMEX, and OTC companies, including financial data and recent company developments.

Value Line Investment Survey: Information on over 1700 publicly held companies, including financial information and investment opinions.

Wall Street Journal Index: See subsection 2 for explanation.

Ward's Directory of the Largest U.S. Corporations: Includes hard-to-find data on thousands of private and public companies. (Three-volume set.)

Online Search Services: NEXIS, Dow Jones News/Retrieval, BRS, and *Dialog* all contain files with company information. Dow Jones Spreadsheet Link allows one to download stock-price information on other financial data from data bases into a Lotus 1-2-3 spreadsheet.

See subsection 7 for information about foreign companies.

4. For information about a product or industry

Business Index: See subsection 2 for explanation.

Business Periodicals Index: See subsection 2 for explanation.

CIRR: See subsection 3 for explanation.

Current Industrial Reports: Includes Bureau of the Census reports on various industrial sectors and manufacturing groups.

F & S Index of Corporations and Industries: See subsection 2 for explanation.

Standard and Poor's Industry Surveys: Includes analysis of all major domestic industries. Listed by subject and industry group with basic analysis and current updates.

Thomas Register: Divided into sections dealing with products and services, company profiles, and catalogs.

U.S. Industrial Outlook: Contains industry reviews and forecasts, including selected service industries.

Wall Street Journal Index: See subsection 2 for explanation.

Wall Street Transcript: Includes various security firms' opinions on individual companies as well as industry outlooks.

5. For financial information

Corporate Finance Bluebook: Information on corporate financial-services personnel and outside financial-services firms serving various corporations.

Corporate Finance Sourcebook: Information on private, commercial, and other lenders providing financial services for various corporations.

Moody's Bank and Finance Manual, Industrial Manual, OTC Industrial Manual, Public Utility Manual, and *Municipal Government Manual:* See subsection 3 for explanation.

Standard and Poor's Corporation Records and *Stock Reports:* See subsection 3 for explanation.

Standard and Poor's Industry Surveys: See subsection 4 for explanation.

Venture Capital Journal: News and analysis on business-development investing.

6. For economic information

Economic Indicators: Statistical information on output, income, spending, employment, production, federal finance, and inflation, and some international statistics.

Survey of Current Business: Includes current business statistics and articles on economic issues.

7. For international business information

Business International Corporation: Weekly reports on international business developments organized by geographic divisions.

Dunn and Bradstreet International: Directory of 50,000 principle businesses in 133 countries.

F & S Europe: Index of company, product, and industry information from financial publications, magazines, newspapers, and special reports.

F & S International: Index of company, product, and industry information from financial publications, magazines, newspapers, and special reports.

International Directory of Corporate Affiliations: Directory of top foreign investors in U.S. as well as 11,000 foreign holdings of U.S. companies.

Moody's International Manual: Includes 5000 major international corporations and their capital structure, lines of business, key historical-performance statistics, and management structure as well as country-specific economic statistics.

8. For information on well-known business people

Reference Book of Corporate Management: Directory of officers and directors of 12,000 U.S. companies.

Standard and Poor's Register of Corporations, Directors, and Executives: Volume 1 organized by company, volume 2 by the officer's name; volume 3 is an index.

Wall Street Journal Index: See subsection 2 for explanation.

Who's Who in America: Biographical information on prominent Americans.

Who's Who in Finance and Industry: Biographical information on prominent people in the business field.

9. For defining business terms

Ammer, *Dictionary of Business and Economics:* Short articles defining terms in business management and economics.

Greenwald, *Encyclopedia of Economics:* Authoritative articles on business and economic concepts. Includes bibliographies with each term.

Heyel, *Encyclopedia of Management:* Articles on general business concepts.

McGraw-Hill Dictionary of Modern Economics: Short explanations of over 1000 terms, listed alphabetically.

10. For information on any other business topic

Daniells, *Business Information Sources:* Comprehensive listing of business- and economic-information sources.

Wasserman, *Encyclopedia of Business Information Sources:* Detailed list of primary subjects of interest to managers. Includes listing of books, periodicals, organizations, directories, handbooks, data bases, and other sources on each topic.

Business Documentation

When you conduct research, obviously, you gain ideas from other sources. You usually document these sources in two ways: (1) in your bibliography, listing all of your sources alphabetically; and (2) in a series of specific notes throughout the document itself.

BIBLIOGRAPHIES: A bibliography is relatively easy to write. You automatically include all of your sources in alphabetical order—thus giving your reader an alphabetical listing.

As you type each entry, begin the first line at the margin and indent any subsequent lines five spaces. Bibliographic entries consist of three units—each separated by a period:

1. *Author's name.* Place author's last name first so you can alphabetize the list.
2. *Book title.* Underline (or italicize) the title. Always include the subtitle. Capitalize the first and last words in the title and all other words except: articles (such as *a, an, the*), short conjunctions (such as *and*), and short prepositions (such as *of*).
3. *Publication information.* Place of publication, colon, publisher, comma, latest copyright date, period.

For example:

Book, Paul A. Book Title. New York: Well-Known Publishing Company, 1985.

If you use more than one work by the same author, list each work separately, but do not repeat the author's name. Instead, insert ten hyphens (or a straight line) followed by a period. Alphabetize each source by the same author by title. For example:

Book, Paul A. Book Title. New York: Well-Known Publishing Company, 1985.

———. Yet Another Book by This Guy. Chicago: Midwestern Publishing Company, 1986.

Here are some more detailed examples of bibliographic entries.

Sample bibliographic entries

Books:

One author

Book, Paul A. Book Title: Always Include the Subtitle. New York: Publishing Company, Inc., 1987.

Two authors

Author, Peter J., and Paul A. Book. Another Book Title. Dallas: Cowboy Press, 1986.

Three authors

Writer, Mary S., Peter J. Author, and Paul A. Book. Yet Another Book Title. Chicago: Lakefront Publisher, 1988.

More than three authors

Book, Paul A., et al. Note That "Et" Is Not Followed by a Period. Lexington, VA: Mason-Dixon Publishers, 1984.

Corporate author

Hightechdigimaxcompudata Company. No Doubt Some Kind of PR Piece. Cupertino, Calif.: Mellow Press, 1986.

Edition after the first

Book, Paul A. Hard to Believe This Guy Wrote Another Book. 3rd ed. New York: Popular Paperbacks, 1986.

Editors

Editor, Susan, ed. How to Publish Without Writing Anything Yourself. Boston: Stuffy Press, 1985.

Article in an anthology

Article, George. "My T.A. Wrote This for Me." In How to Publish Without Writing Anything Yourself. Ed. Susan Editor. Boston: Stuffy Press, 1985.

Magazines and newspapers: For signed articles, alphabetize under author's name. For unsigned articles, alphabetize under title.

Signed/unsigned article

Byline, Deborah. "My Name Is on This Article." Periodicalmania, April 1986, pp. 35–38.

"My Name Is Not on This Article." Periodicalmania, April 1986, pp. 39–42.

Monthly magazine

Journalist, Kenneth T. "The Meaning of the Universe." Scientific Digest, March 1981, pp. 62–63.

Weekly magazine or newspaper

Article, Rebecca. "The Future of All Nations." Newstime, 28 September 1986, pp. 50–51.

Daily newspaper

Cubreporter, Daniel. "New Meat Grinder at the Grocery Store." Localrag Newspaper, 28 March 1980, Sec. A., p. 11, cols. 3–4.

Other print sources:

Dissertation or thesis

PhDStudent, Caroline. "A Brilliant Contribution to Knowledge." PhD Thesis, Technical University, 1988.

Research paper

Researcher, John Q. "Another Brilliant Contribution to Knowledge." Research Paper No. 000, Nontechnical University, 1989.

Unpublished paper

Unpublished, David. "A No-Doubt Worthy Paper." Unpublished, Well-Known College, December 1990.

Nonprint sources:

Motion picture

Outer Space and Cute Little Monsters. Paramount-Fox, 1986.

Television or radio

Commentator, Scott. Main Street Week in Review. PBS, 24 May 1986.

Newsperson, Laura. All the News That's Fit to Say. KZZZ, Kansas City, 17 September 1984.

Lecture

Lecturer, Annette. "All the Research You Ever Wanted to Hear About." Brilliant Research Lecture Series, Prestigious University, 14 October 1983.

Interview

Interviewee, Tiffany. Personal Interview. 29 February 1987.

FOOTNOTES: A second way you document your sources is in a series of footnotes. Technically, these notes are called *endnotes* when you place them in one list at the end of the text, and *footnotes* if you place them at the bottom, or foot, of each page. We'll use *footnotes* as the general term.

Footnotes are a bit more tricky than bibliographies. In a bibliography, you automatically list all your sources. With footnotes, however, you must decide when to use them as well as how to use them.

When should you use footnotes? The answer, once again, goes back to your reader. For example, if you're stating a simple fact and the reliability of your source isn't an issue, you would not footnote. However, if you're stating a startling new fact or a fact that may lead your reader to wonder about its source, you should footnote. Here, then, are the three rules of thumb on when to footnote: (1) to give your readers a source so they can judge how reliable the information is, (2) to give them a place to look to check your facts or to find more information on the subject, or (3) to give credit to another source.

Therefore, use footnotes for direct quotations, paraphrases of ideas, and any idea that is not common knowledge. Failure to footnote under these conditions is called *plagiarism*—and it is as dishonest as telling a lie.

Once you've decided when to use a footnote, the second question is: How should you write footnotes? Two different systems of footnoting are equally acceptable in the business world: (1) the bibliography-reference system, and (2) the raised-numeral system. Base your choice, in part, on finding out which system your company or your reader prefers. In addition, keep in mind that the bibliography method is faster, but you can't add footnoted comments; the raised-numeral system takes more time and effort, but you can add footnoted comments. Regardless of the method you choose, be sure to be consistent. Don't confuse your reader by changing systems.

(1) **The bibliography-reference system** is becoming increasingly popular in business. This system directs your reader to look at certain entries in the bibliography and avoids the whole issue of typing footnotes

separately. This system is therefore more efficient; however, it is less flexible, because you cannot add comments, as you can with traditional raised-numeral footnotes.

In this system, the citation occurs in the text itself. One such method is to cite by author, date, and page number, like this: (Byline, 1986, p. 51). *Byline, 1986* keys your reader to the article by Rebecca Byline in your bibliography. Another method is by citation number and page number, like this: [12, p. 122]. The number 12 keys your reader to entry 12 in your bibliography. The author-and-date method is usually preferred, because it lets your reader know the source and date without having to refer back to the bibliography.

(2) **The raised-numeral system** is the traditional method. It takes more space and effort, but it is more flexible because you can add comments in your footnotes. Number your notes consecutively throughout the document—not starting over on each page—and place them at the foot of each page or the end of the document, whichever your reader prefers.

Place your raised numeral (raised half a line) throughout the text like this.[1] That [1] signals the reader to see note 1 in your foot- or endnotes. These numerals should come immediately after the part of the sentence to which they refer, even if that is midsentence, like this,[2] and they should come *after* all punctuation except the dash, like this.[3]

If you use the raised-numeral method, you'll need to know how your footnotes differ from bibliographic entries. In two ways, such notes are opposite of the form bibliographic entries: (1) author's or editor's first name comes first (since there is no need to alphabetize); and (2) the first line is indented five spaces with subsequent lines beginning at the margin. In addition, follow these rules in punctuating foot- or endnotes:

1. Type numerals slightly above the line, followed by a space.
2. Use commas between main items (but not before parentheses).
3. For books, enclose the publication data in parentheses. For journals, enclose the date in parentheses—except when the day of the month is given.
4. End each note with a period.

For example:

Bibliographic entry:

Book, Paul A. <u>Book Title</u>. New York: Well-Known Publishing Company, 1985.

Note entry:

[1]Paul A. Book, <u>Book Title</u> (New York: Well-Known Publishing Company, 1985), p. 6.

Here are more specific samples for first-reference notes—that is, notes as you would type them the first time you refer to a particular source.

Sample first-reference notes (footnotes or endnotes)

Books

[1]Paul A. Book, <u>Book Title</u> (New York: Publishing Company, Inc., 1987), p. 3. (Subtitle need not be included in footnote.)

[2]Peter J. Author and Paul A. Book, <u>Another Book Title</u> (Dallas: Cowboy Press, 1986), p. 355.

[3]Mary S. Writer, Peter J. Author, and Paul A. Book, <u>Yet Another Book Title</u> (Chicago: Lakefront Publisher, 1988), p. 35.

[4]Paul A. Book et al., <u>Note That "Et" Is Not Followed by a Period</u> (Lexington, Va. Mason-Dixon Publishers, 1984), p. 864.

[5]Hightechdigimaxcompudata Company, <u>No Doubt Some Kind of PR Piece</u> (Cupertino, Calif: Mellow Press, 1986), p. 3.

[6]Paul A. Book, <u>Hard to Believe This Guy Wrote Another Book</u>, 3rd ed. (New York: Popular Paperbacks, 1986), p. 63.

[7]Susan Editor, ed., <u>How to Publish Without Writing Anything Yourself</u> (Boston: Stuffy Press, 1985), p. 1.

[8]George Article, "My T.A. Wrote This for Me" in <u>How to Publish Without Writing Anything Yourself</u>, ed. Susan Editor (Boston: Stuffy Press, 1985), pp. 34–35.

Magazines and newspapers

[9]Deborah Byline,"My Name Is on This Article," <u>Periodicalmania</u>, (April 1986), p. 36.

[10]My Name Is Not on This Article," <u>Periodicalmania</u>, April 1986, p. 40.

[11]Kenneth T. Journalist, "The Meaning of the Universe," <u>Scientific Digest</u> (March 1981), p. 62.

[12]Rebecca Article, "The Future of All Nations," <u>Newstime</u>, September 28, 1986, p. 51.

[13]Daniel Cubreporter, "New Meat Grinder at the Grocery Store," Localrag Newspaper, 28 March 1980, Sec. A, p. 11, col. 3.

Other print sources

[14]Caroline PhDStudent, "A Brilliant Contribution to Knowledge," PhD Thesis, Technical University, 1988, p. 962.

[15]John Q. Researcher, "Another Brilliant Contribution to Knowledge," Research Paper No. 000, Nontechnical University, 1989.

[16]David Unpublished, "A No-Doubt Worthy Paper," unpublished, Well-Known College, December 1990.

Nonprint sources

[17]Outer Space and Cute Little Monsters, Paramount-Fox, 1986.

[18]Scott Commentator, Main Street Week in Review, PBS, 24 May 1986.

[19]Laura Newsperson, All the News That's Fit to Say, KZZZ, Kansas City, 17 September 1984.

[20]Annette Lecturer, "All the Research You Ever Wanted to Hear About," Brilliant Lecture Series, Prestigious University, 14 October 1983.

[21]Personal interview with Tiffany Interviewee, 29 February 1987.

Sample second–reference notes

If you refer to a source again, you need not type out the whole reference. Use the following shortened versions:

[22]Book, p. 22.
[23]Author and Book, pp. 687–688.
[24]"Who Would Admit to Writing This?" p. 3.

If you refer to two or more works by the same author, include titles (in shortened form if the title is long) in your second reference:

[25]Book, Book Title, p. 30.
[26]Book, Hard to Believe, p. 456.

Index

effects on communication channel
choice, 44
importance of, in social
environment theory, 7–8
See also International
communication

D

Dangling modifiers, 214–16
Daniel, C., and C. Smith, 249–50
Dash, 450
Decisions, making in meetings,
352–56
Deduction, in logic, 96–97
Defensiveness, avoiding:
through audience analysis and
motivation, 71–86
in feedback, 136
in media interviews, 366
in meetings, 357
in question-and-answer sessions,
359
Deficiency needs, 77–79
Delivery, for speaking:
analyzing elements of, 256–73
checklist for, 284–86
improving, 273–80
in listening skills, 117–18
in media interviews, 366–67
in meetings, 349
in question-and-answer sessions,
360–61
in speaker introductions, 308–9
in team presentations, 309–10
with visual aids, 338–40
Dewey, J., 351
Diagrams. *See* Idea charts
Dictation, techniques for using,
147–49
Direct approach, 108, 158–59
Direct object, 418
Dissonance theory (balance needs),
79–81
Distance. *See* Space around you
Distractions, avoiding:
for listening, 117
in presentations, 273
Documentation, methods for,
469–75
Document design:

for highlighting, 196–97
for letter formats, 155–56
in visual aids, 323–29
Document writing:
appropriate length for, 201
connection for, 198–201
definition of, 183
design of, 193–97
formats for, 152–73
organization and highlighting for,
190–97
unity and emphasis for, 183–87
Dominance, avoiding:
in meetings, 357
in panel discussions, 362
in question-and-answer sessions,
358–60
Downward communication, effects
of, 40–42
Drafting process:
for speeches, 305–6
for writing, 146–50, 151
Dress:
for job interviews, 388
for media interviews, 367
for presentations, 270–72
Drucker, P., 4, 9

E

Economics, research sources for, 467
Edge, A., and R. Greenwood, 2
Editing:
avoiding writer's block during,
150–52
business formats for, 152–73
checklist for, 142
for documents, 183–203
for grammar, 414–18, 419–42
for paragraphs, 183–203
for punctuation and mechanics,
447–58
for sentences, 210–29
techniques and process for,
148–50, 151
for visual aids, 325–26
for words, 235–51, 395–411
Electronic communication:
effect on gathering information, 29
effect on opportunities to
communicate, 3